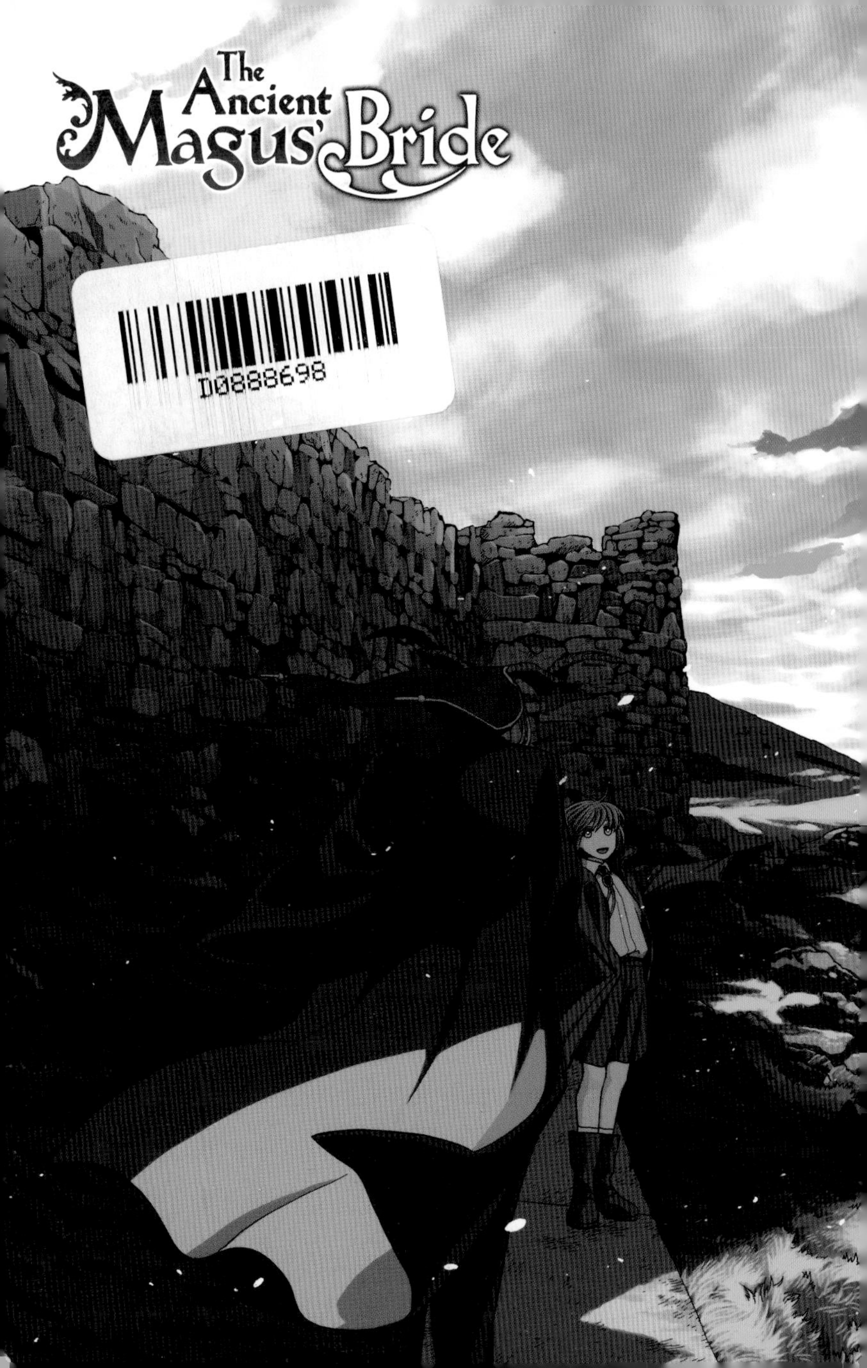
The Ancient Magus' Bride

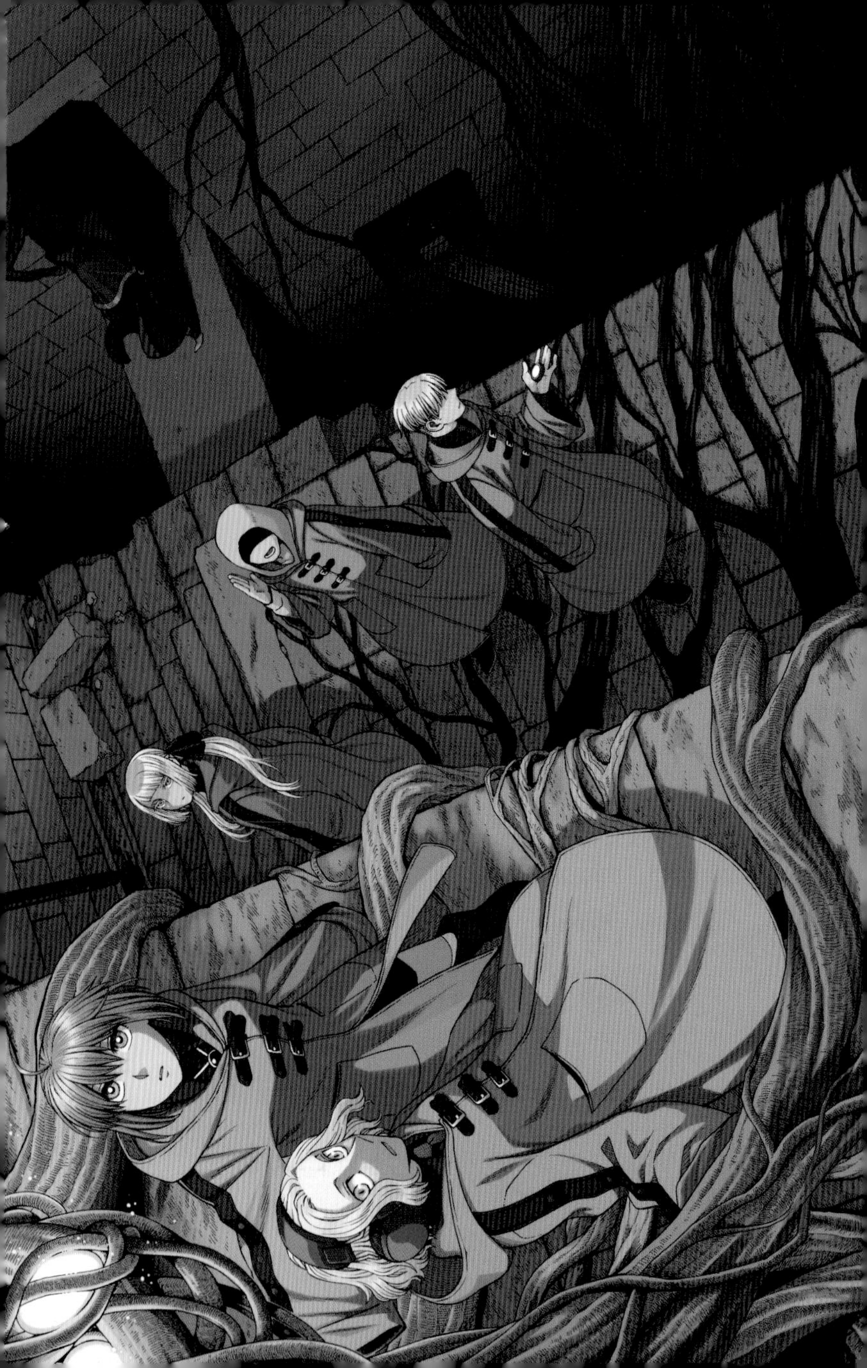

The Ancient Magus' Bride: College Arc

❖ Classmates ❖

LUCY WEBSTER

The young survivor of the Webster Tragedy. She's always made sure to keep her classmates at a distance, but since Chise became her roommate at the College, she's started to change.

PHILOMELA SARGANT

Granddaughter of the current head of the Sargant family. As retainers of House Rickenbacker, one of the Seven Shields, the Sargants specialize in espionage. Philomela is quiet and withdrawn and spends much of her time with Veronica Rickenbacker, her liege lady.

RÍAN SCRIMGEOUR

Heir to House Scrimgeour, the Guardians of the Seven Shields. A serious boy with great respect for the rules, he's the most levelheaded student in his class. He's Torrey's apprentice and seems to share his master's curiosity about mages.

ZOE IVEY

Son of a gorgon mother and an alchemist father (a researcher of demi-human languages). As a human/demi-human hybrid, he's always relied on noise-blocking earmuffs to keep his hair from shifting into snakes, but he's recently started practicing keeping his snakes under control without his earmuffs.

VERONICA RICKENBACKER

Daughter of House Rickenbacker, the Healers of the Seven Shields. She's gentle and polite, and rarely seen without a smile. She's friendly with her entire class, but spends most of her time with Philomela and the Atwood twins.

ISAAC FOWLER

An aspiring alchemist, he's good-natured and knowledgeable. Explaining things to others often falls to him. He's close enough to Rian to joke around with him. For some reason, he tends to keep his hood pulled far enough forward to hide his eyes...

ROY TRUMAN

Upset that his favorite fish-and-chips place closed down.

SOFIA HEALEY

Mildly afraid of animals, but she's working to get over it.

BEATRICE BYRNE

Enjoys hanging out with Sofia on weekends and holidays.

VIOLET ST. GEORGE

Son of House St. George, the Monster Hunters of the Seven Shields. He likes cute clothes.

JASMINE ST. GEORGE

Daughter of House St. George, the Monster Hunters of the Seven Shields.

MARTIN CHANDLER

Gets chilled so easily that he's already acquired a hot-water bottle for the season.

APRIL ATWOOD

Currently concerned about how hard it is for her to fall asleep without her brother nearby.

MAY ATWOOD

Currently concerned by how much less athletic he is than his sister.

KEVIN FORBES

He hates having other people touch his hair so much that he hasn't yet gone to the College's barber.

THE COLLEGE

The College was founded to educate both the heirs of established alchemist families and newcomers with alchemical talent, passing knowledge of the alchemy disciplines down from one generation to the next. Founded by the seven families known as the "Seven Shields," it maintains strict neutrality in order to provide a safe learning environment for all of its students.

THE SEVEN SHIELDS

Seven powerful alchemist families joined forces to establish the College. Each family specializes in a different alchemical discipline, and each boasts a large number of retainers and apprentices. These families are House Roseingrave, the Beast Tamers; House St. George, the Monster Hunters; House Rickenbacker, the Healers; House Forsyth, the Diviners; House Hohenheim, the Chemists; House Nightingale, the Bards; and House Grimmo, the Guardians.

LAZARUS McGOVERN

Currently experimenting with fusing alchemy techniques and cooking.

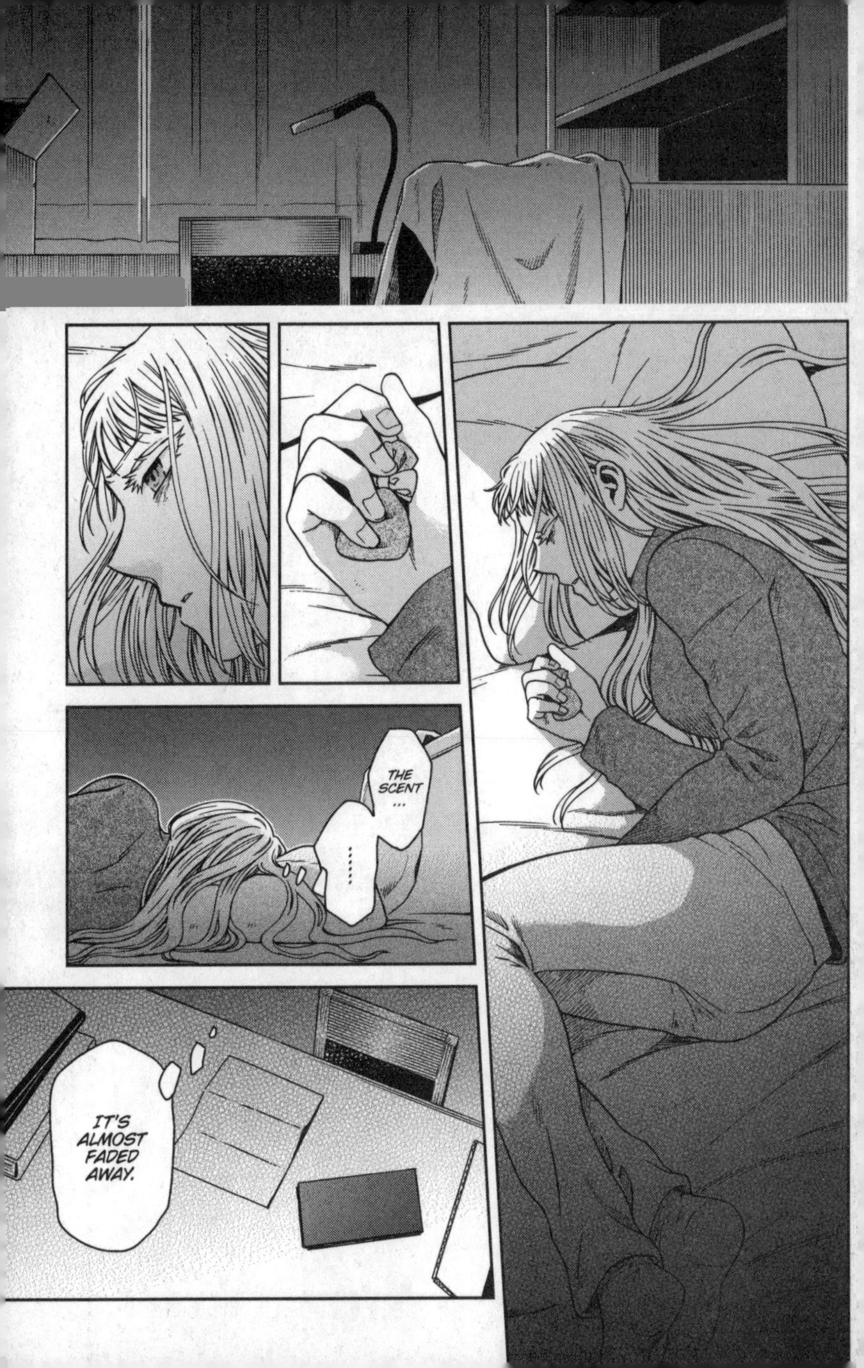
THE SCENT ...
......
IT'S ALMOST FADED AWAY.

Chapter 66:
A small leak will sink a great ship. I

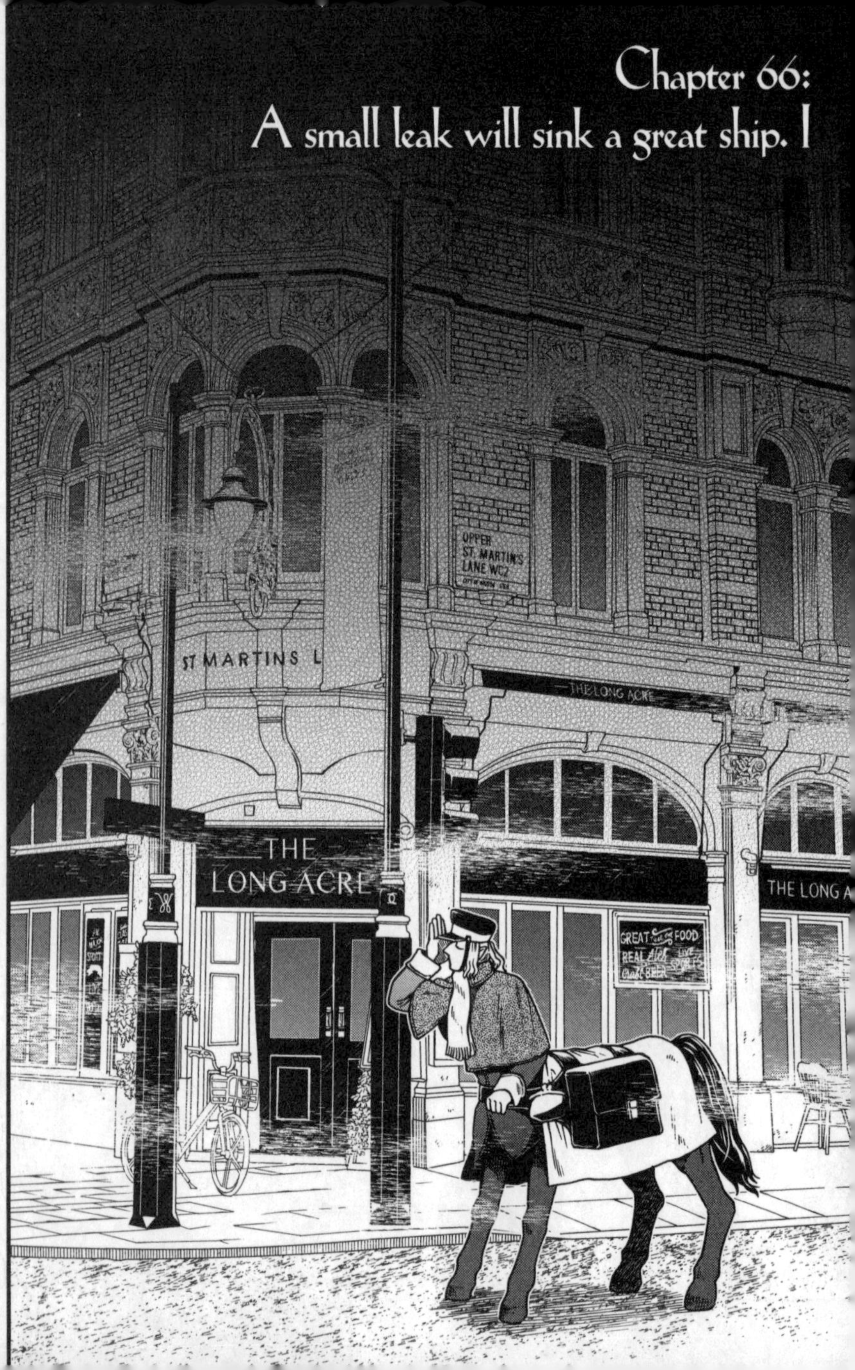
UPPER
ST. MARTIN'S
LANE WC2
ST MARTINS L
THE LONG ACRE
THE
LONG ACRE
THE LONG A
GREAT FOOD
REAL ALE
Craft BEER
LIVE SPORTS

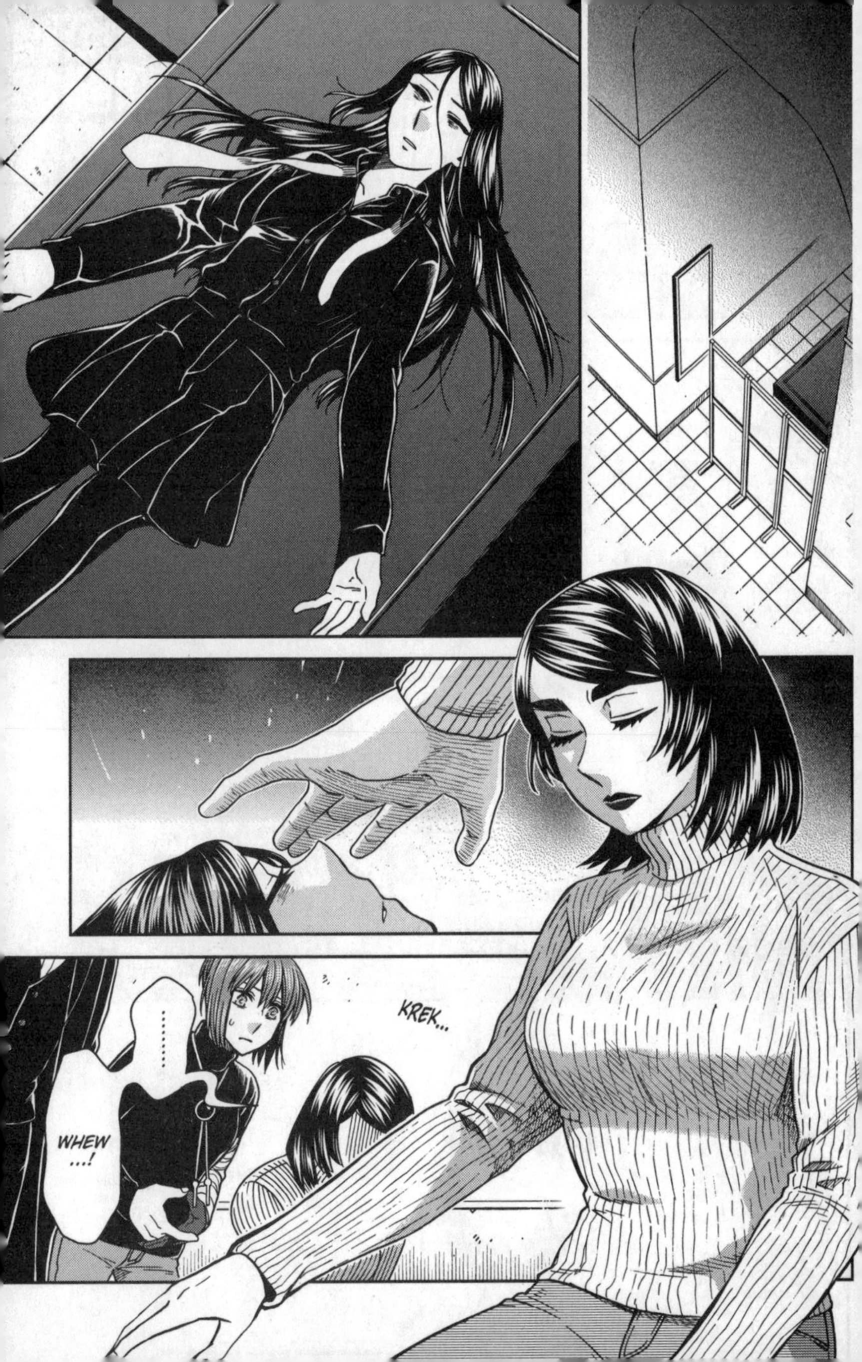
KREK...
......
WHEW ...!

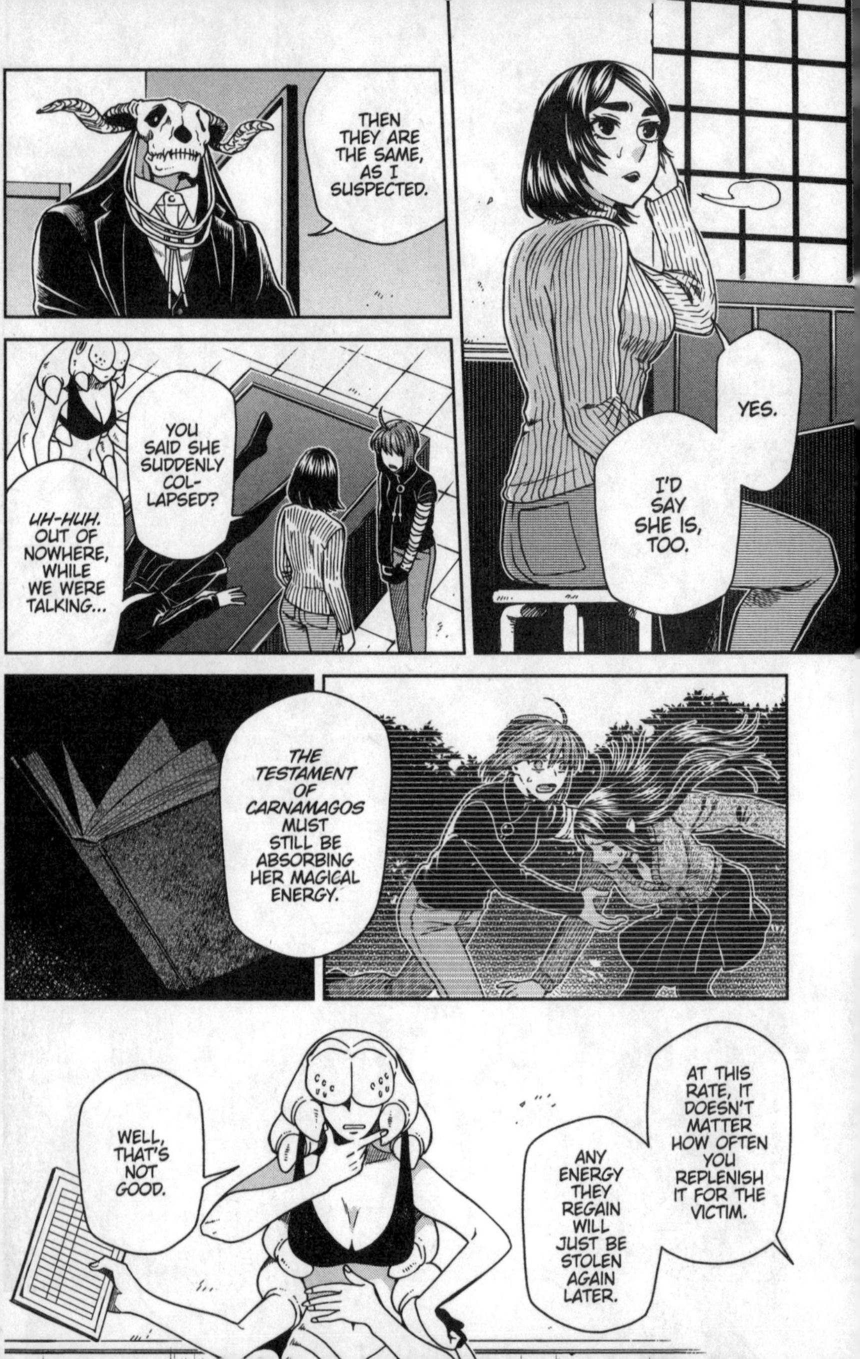
YES.
I'D SAY SHE IS, TOO.
THEN THEY ARE THE SAME, AS I SUSPECTED.
YOU SAID SHE SUDDENLY COL-LAPSED?
UH-HUH. OUT OF NOWHERE, WHILE WE WERE TALKING...
THE TESTAMENT OF CARNAMAGOS MUST STILL BE ABSORBING HER MAGICAL ENERGY.
AT THIS RATE, IT DOESN'T MATTER HOW OFTEN YOU REPLENISH IT FOR THE VICTIM.
ANY ENERGY THEY REGAIN WILL JUST BE STOLEN AGAIN LATER.
WELL, THAT'S NOT GOOD.

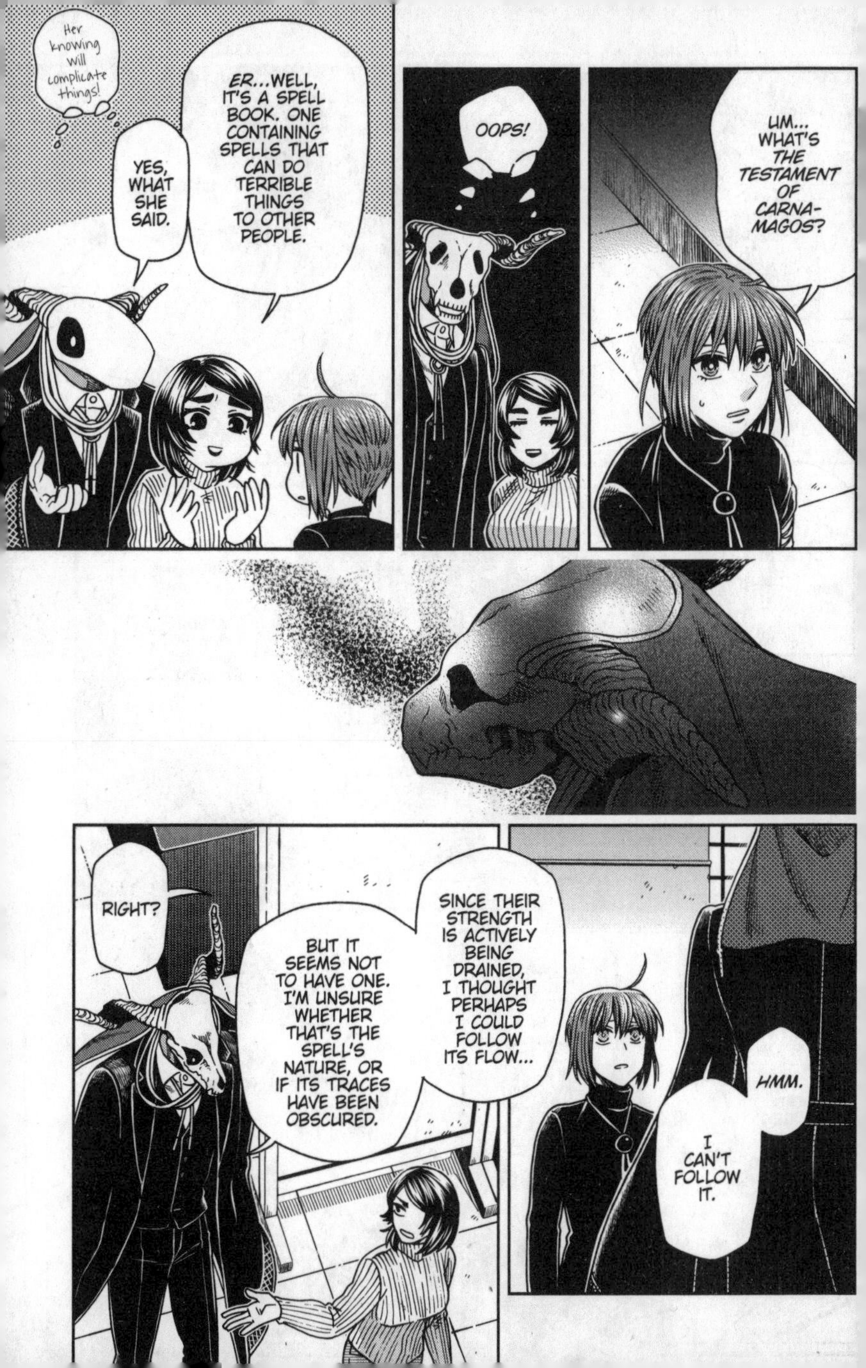
UM... WHAT'S THE TESTAMENT OF CARNA-MAGOS?
OOPS!
ER...WELL, IT'S A SPELL BOOK. ONE CONTAINING SPELLS THAT CAN DO TERRIBLE THINGS TO OTHER PEOPLE.
Her knowing will complicate things!
YES, WHAT SHE SAID.
HMM.
I CAN'T FOLLOW IT.
SINCE THEIR STRENGTH IS ACTIVELY BEING DRAINED, I THOUGHT PERHAPS I COULD FOLLOW ITS FLOW...
BUT IT SEEMS NOT TO HAVE ONE. I'M UNSURE WHETHER THAT'S THE SPELL'S NATURE, OR IF ITS TRACES HAVE BEEN OBSCURED.
RIGHT?

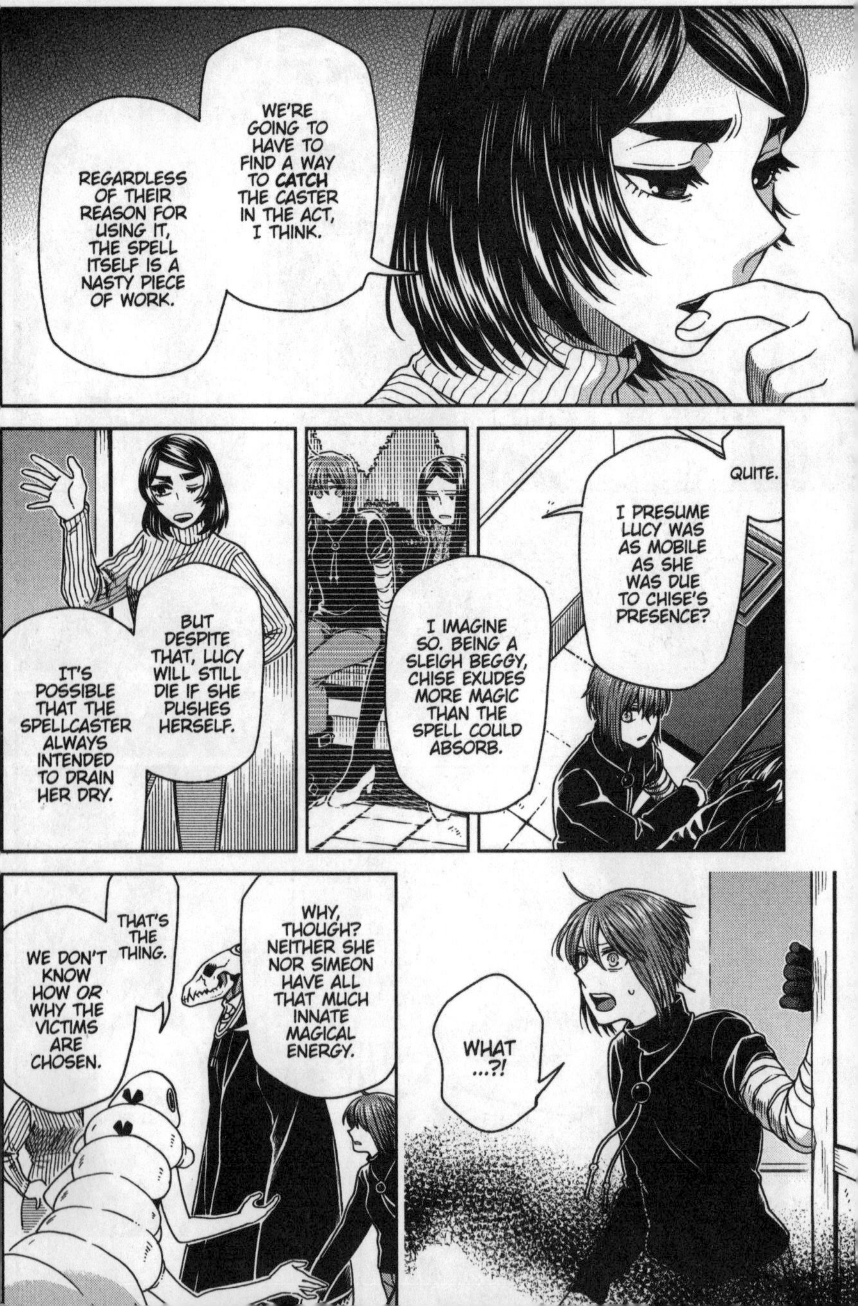
WE'RE GOING TO HAVE TO FIND A WAY TO CATCH THE CASTER IN THE ACT, I THINK.
REGARDLESS OF THEIR REASON FOR USING IT, THE SPELL ITSELF IS A NASTY PIECE OF WORK.
QUITE.
I PRESUME LUCY WAS AS MOBILE AS SHE WAS DUE TO CHISE'S PRESENCE?
I IMAGINE SO. BEING A SLEIGH BEGGY, CHISE EXUDES MORE MAGIC THAN THE SPELL COULD ABSORB.
BUT DESPITE THAT, LUCY WILL STILL DIE IF SHE PUSHES HERSELF.
IT'S POSSIBLE THAT THE SPELLCASTER ALWAYS INTENDED TO DRAIN HER DRY.
WHAT ...?!
WHY, THOUGH? NEITHER SHE NOR SIMEON HAVE ALL THAT MUCH INNATE MAGICAL ENERGY.
THAT'S THE THING.
WE DON'T KNOW HOW OR WHY THE VICTIMS ARE CHOSEN.

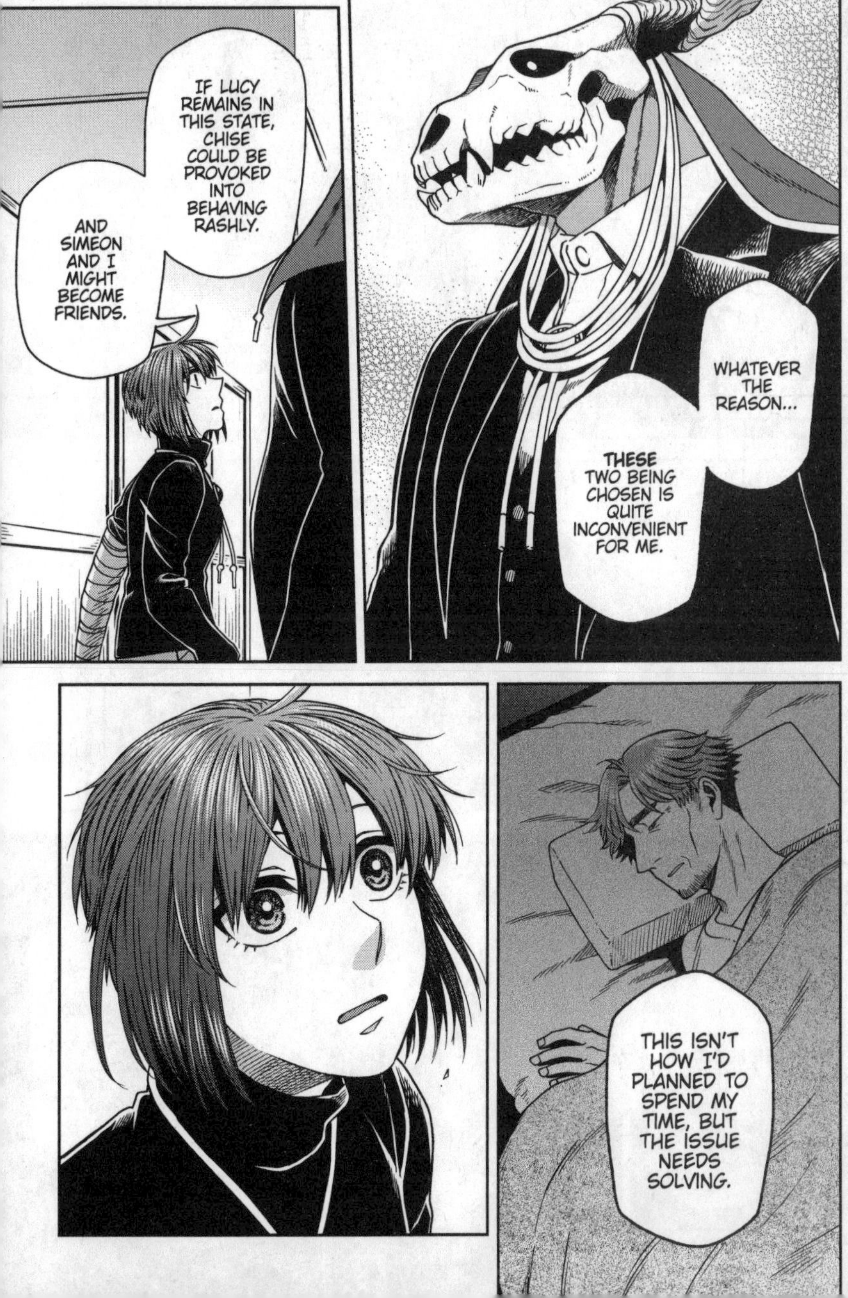
WHATEVER THE REASON...
THESE TWO BEING CHOSEN IS QUITE INCONVENIENT FOR ME.
IF LUCY REMAINS IN THIS STATE, CHISE COULD BE PROVOKED INTO BEHAVING RASHLY.
AND SIMEON AND I MIGHT BECOME FRIENDS.
THIS ISN'T HOW I'D PLANNED TO SPEND MY TIME, BUT THE ISSUE NEEDS SOLVING.

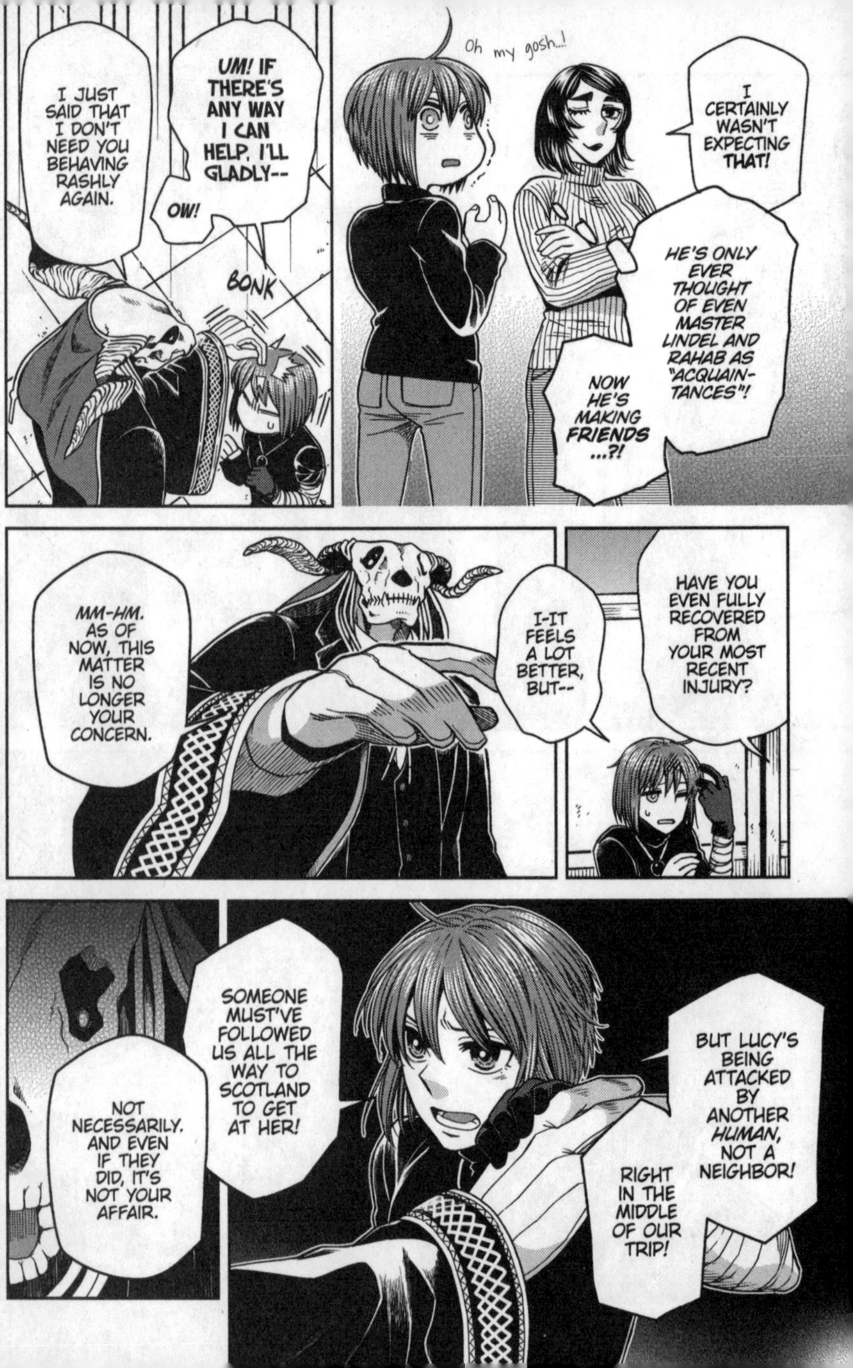
I CERTAINLY WASN'T EXPECTING THAT!
Oh my gosh...!
HE'S ONLY EVER THOUGHT OF EVEN MASTER LINDEL AND RAHAB AS "ACQUAINTANCES"!
NOW HE'S MAKING FRIENDS ...?!
UM! IF THERE'S ANY WAY I CAN HELP, I'LL GLADLY--
BONK
OW!
I JUST SAID THAT I DON'T NEED YOU BEHAVING RASHLY AGAIN.
HAVE YOU EVEN FULLY RECOVERED FROM YOUR MOST RECENT INJURY?
I-IT FEELS A LOT BETTER, BUT--
MM-HM. AS OF NOW, THIS MATTER IS NO LONGER YOUR CONCERN.
BUT LUCY'S BEING ATTACKED BY ANOTHER HUMAN, NOT A NEIGHBOR!
RIGHT IN THE MIDDLE OF OUR TRIP!
SOMEONE MUST'VE FOLLOWED US ALL THE WAY TO SCOTLAND TO GET AT HER!
NOT NECESSARILY. AND EVEN IF THEY DID, IT'S NOT YOUR AFFAIR.

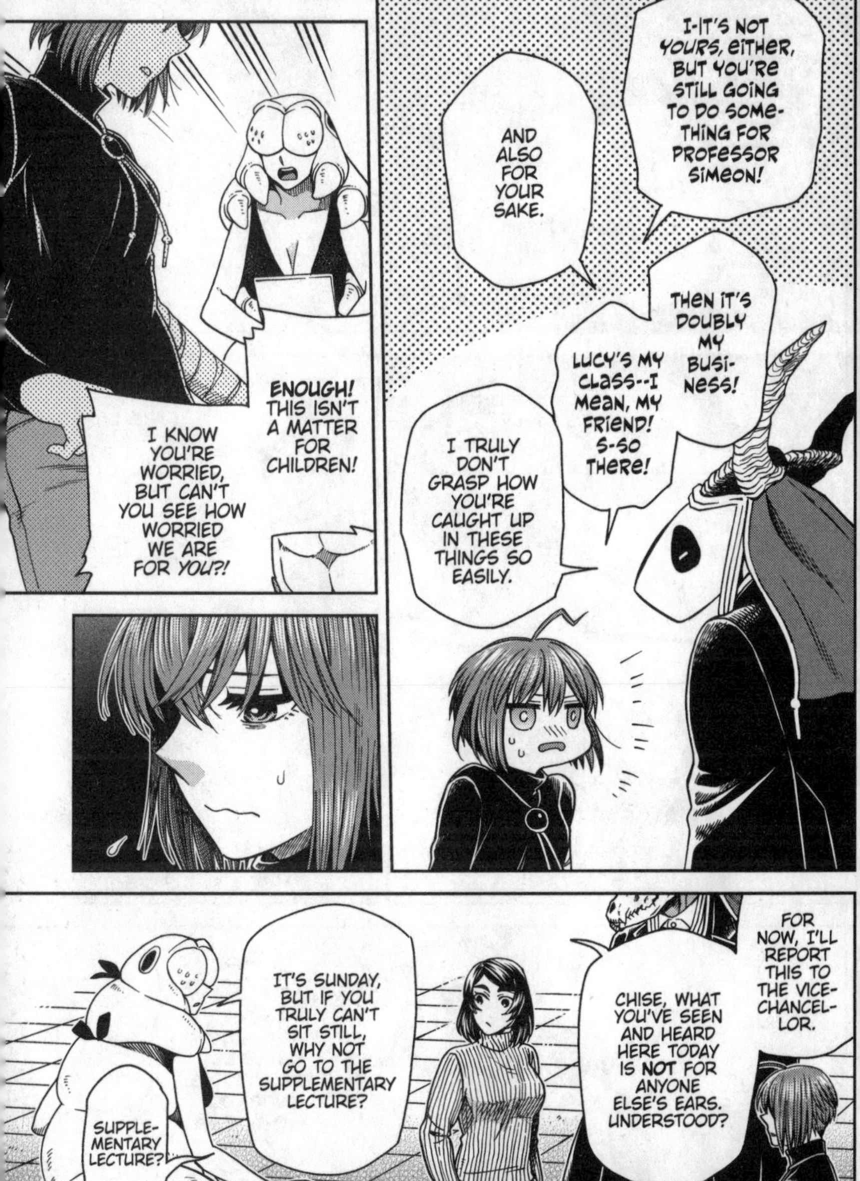
I-IT'S NOT *YOURS*, EITHER, BUT YOU'RE STILL GOING TO DO SOMETHING FOR PROFESSOR SIMEON!
AND ALSO FOR YOUR SAKE.
THEN IT'S DOUBLY MY BUSINESS!
LUCY'S MY CLASS--I MEAN, MY FRIEND! S-SO THERE!
I TRULY DON'T GRASP HOW YOU'RE CAUGHT UP IN THESE THINGS SO EASILY.
ENOUGH! THIS ISN'T A MATTER FOR CHILDREN!
I KNOW YOU'RE WORRIED, BUT CAN'T YOU SEE HOW WORRIED WE ARE FOR *YOU*?!
FOR NOW, I'LL REPORT THIS TO THE VICE-CHANCELLOR.
CHISE, WHAT YOU'VE SEEN AND HEARD HERE TODAY IS **NOT** FOR ANYONE ELSE'S EARS. UNDERSTOOD?
IT'S SUNDAY, BUT IF YOU TRULY CAN'T SIT STILL, WHY NOT GO TO THE SUPPLEMENTARY LECTURE?
SUPPLEMENTARY LECTURE?

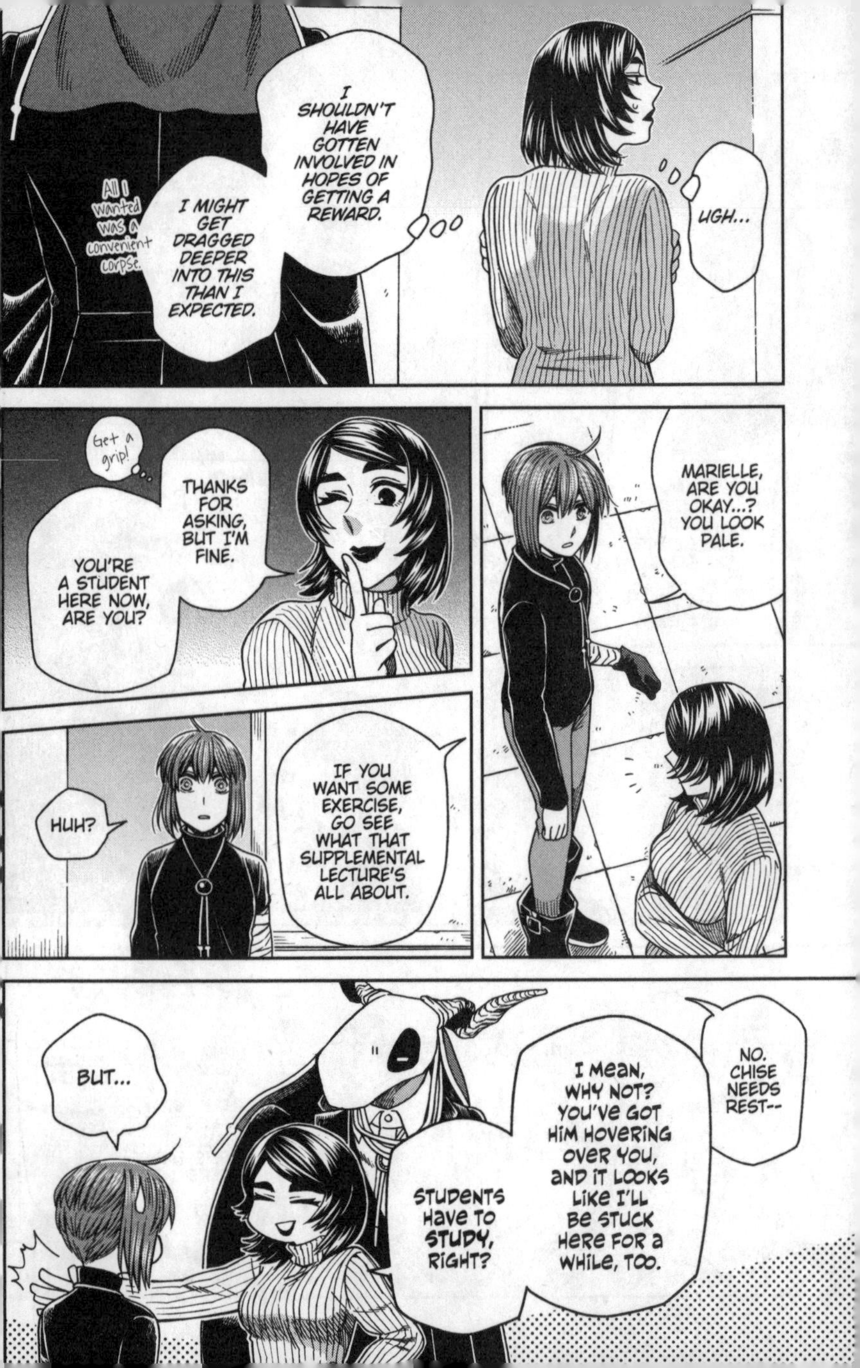
UGH...
I SHOULDN'T HAVE GOTTEN INVOLVED IN HOPES OF GETTING A REWARD.
I MIGHT GET DRAGGED DEEPER INTO THIS THAN I EXPECTED.
All I wanted was a convenient corpse.
MARIELLE, ARE YOU OKAY...? YOU LOOK PALE.
THANKS FOR ASKING, BUT I'M FINE.
Get a grip!
YOU'RE A STUDENT HERE NOW, ARE YOU?
IF YOU WANT SOME EXERCISE, GO SEE WHAT THAT SUPPLEMENTAL LECTURE'S ALL ABOUT.
HUH?
NO. CHISE NEEDS REST--
I MEAN, WHY NOT? YOU'VE GOT HIM HOVERING OVER YOU, AND IT LOOKS LIKE I'LL BE STUCK HERE FOR A WHILE, TOO.
STUDENTS HAVE TO STUDY, RIGHT?
BUT...

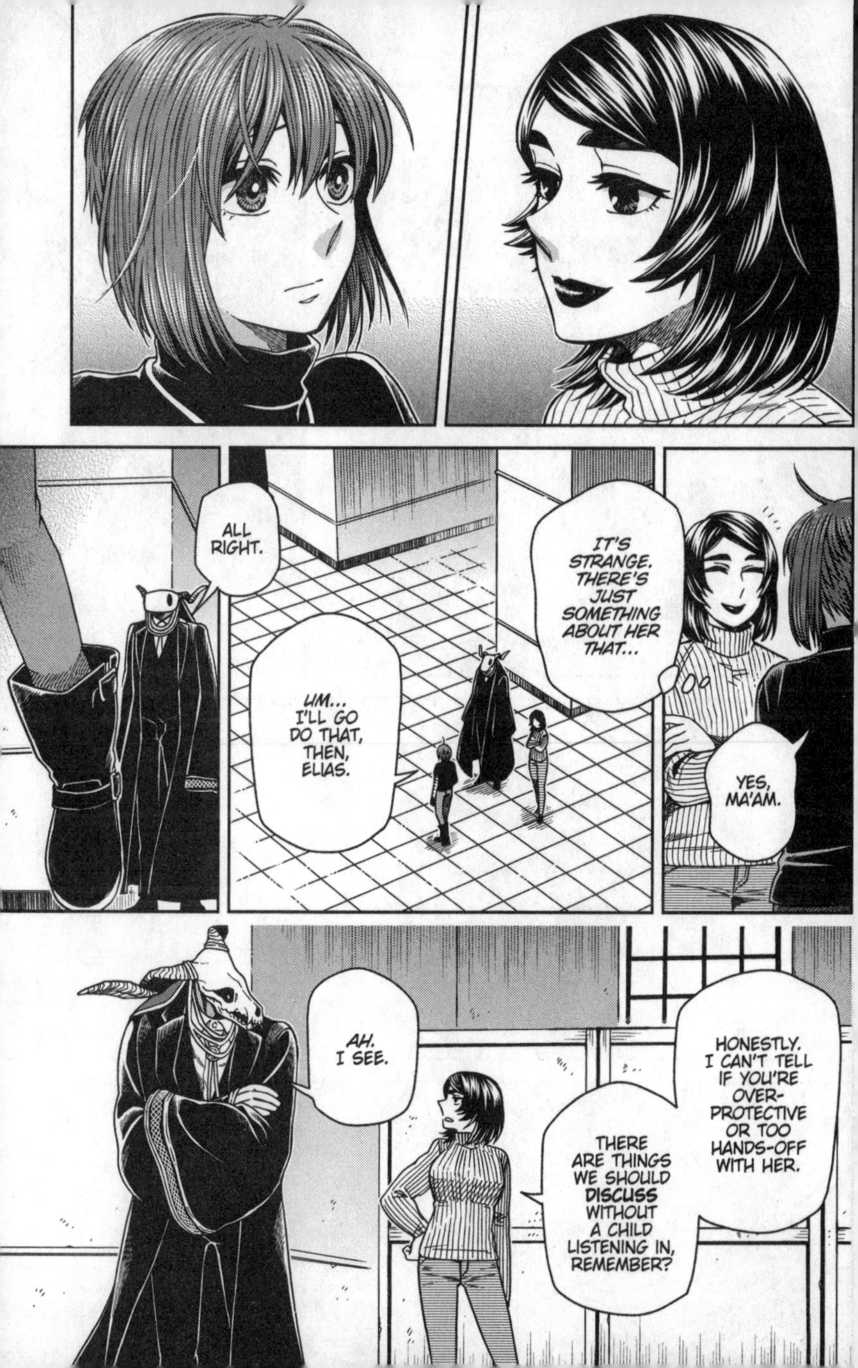
IT'S STRANGE. THERE'S JUST SOMETHING ABOUT HER THAT...
YES, MA'AM.
UM... I'LL GO DO THAT, THEN, ELIAS.
ALL RIGHT.
HONESTLY. I CAN'T TELL IF YOU'RE OVER-PROTECTIVE OR TOO HANDS-OFF WITH HER.
THERE ARE THINGS WE SHOULD **DISCUSS** WITHOUT A CHILD LISTENING IN, REMEMBER?
AH. I SEE.

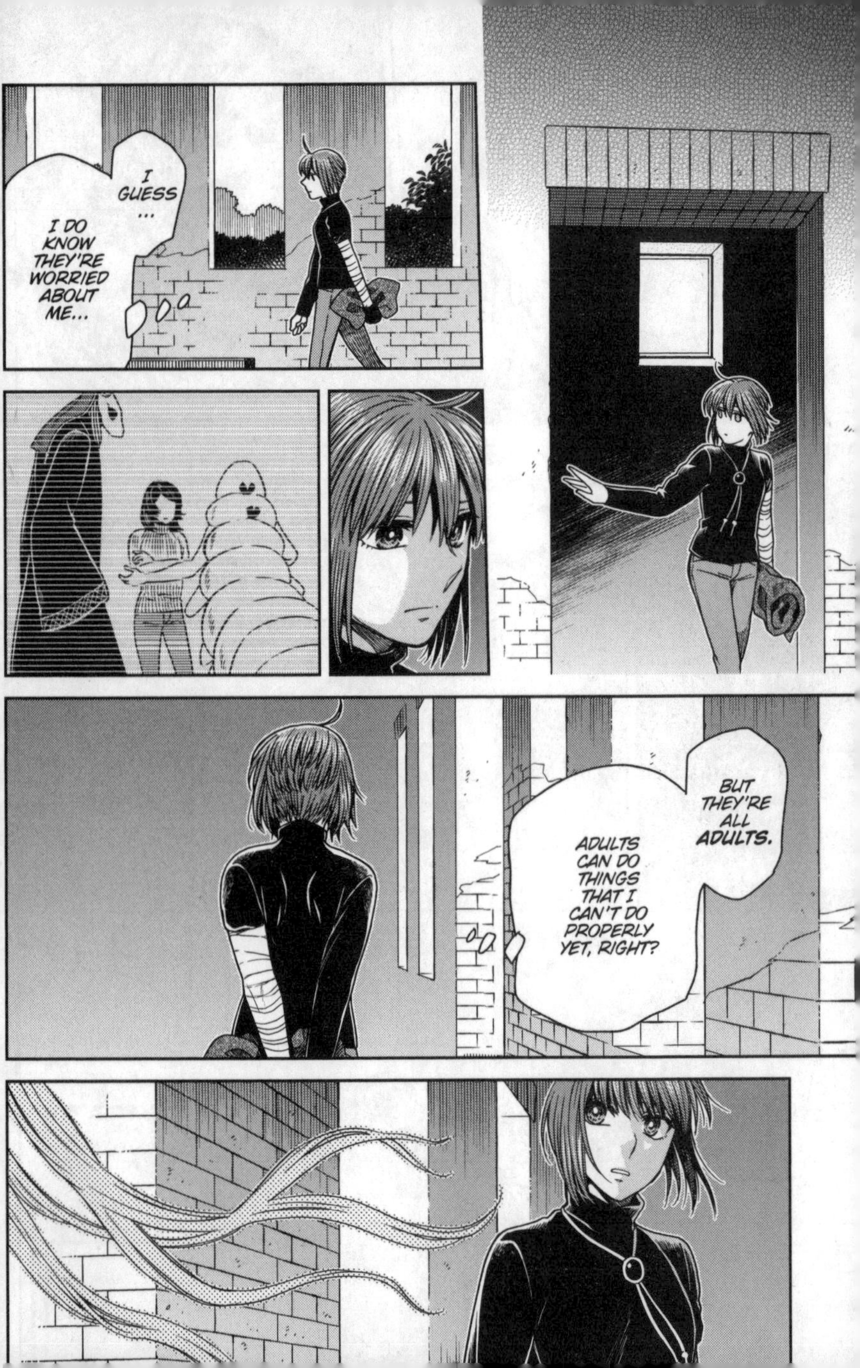
I GUESS ...
I DO KNOW THEY'RE WORRIED ABOUT ME...
BUT THEY'RE ALL ADULTS.
ADULTS CAN DO THINGS THAT I CAN'T DO PROPERLY YET, RIGHT?

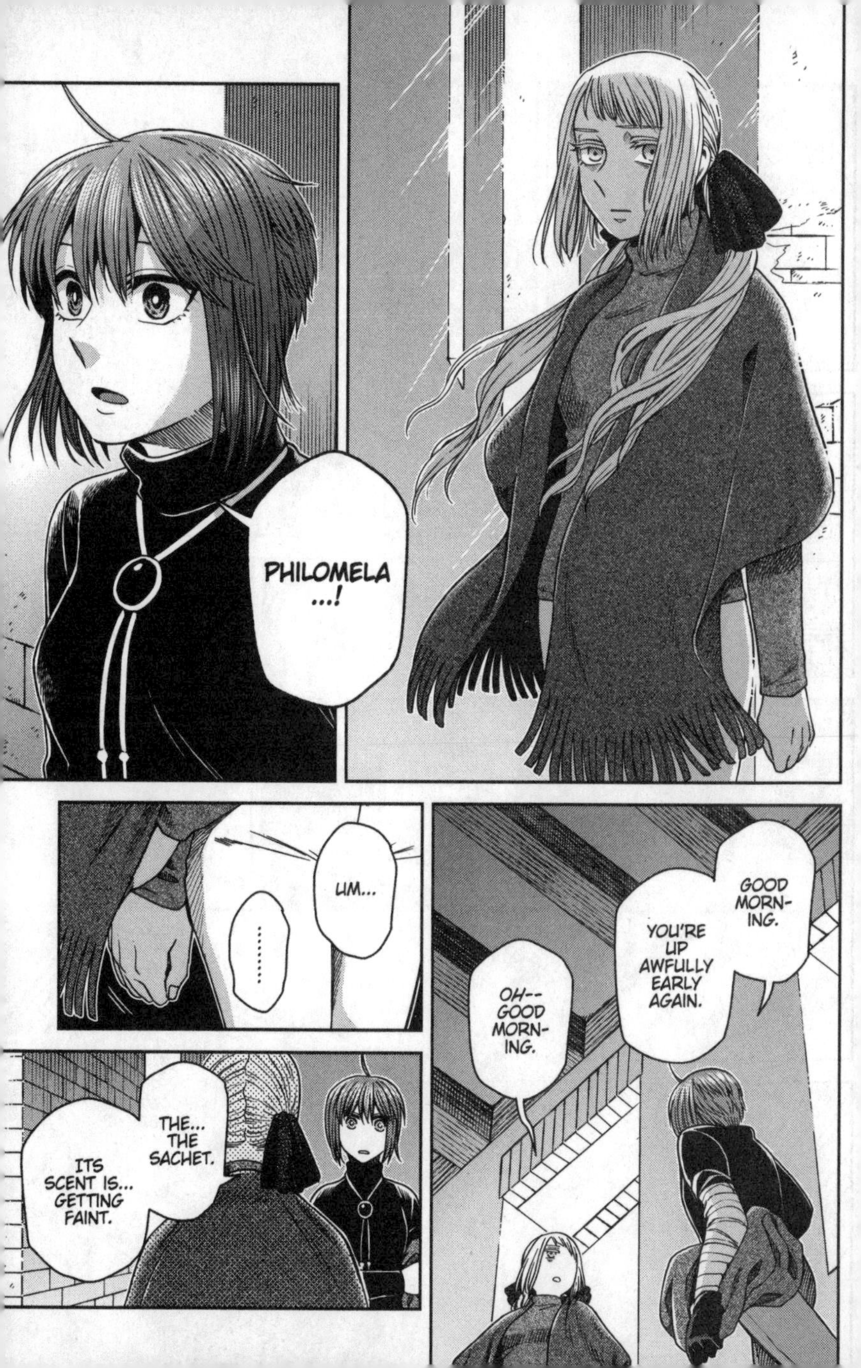
PHILOMELA...!
GOOD MORNING.
YOU'RE UP AWFULLY EARLY AGAIN.
OH-- GOOD MORNING.
UM...
......
THE... THE SACHET.
ITS SCENT IS... GETTING FAINT.

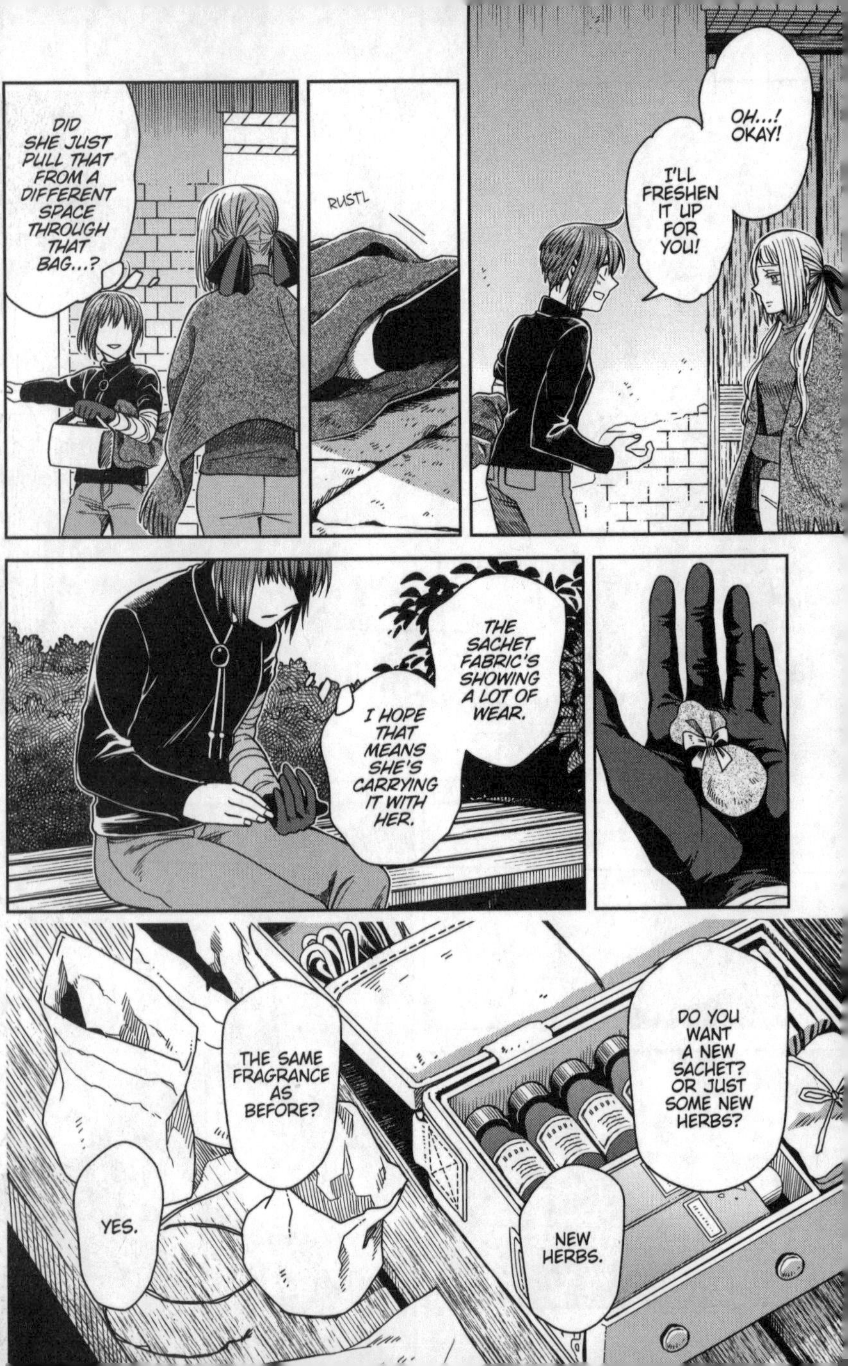
OH...! OKAY!
I'LL FRESHEN IT UP FOR YOU!
RUSTL
DID SHE JUST PULL THAT FROM A DIFFERENT SPACE THROUGH THAT BAG...?
THE SACHET FABRIC'S SHOWING A LOT OF WEAR.
I HOPE THAT MEANS SHE'S CARRYING IT WITH HER.
DO YOU WANT A NEW SACHET? OR JUST SOME NEW HERBS?
NEW HERBS.
THE SAME FRAGRANCE AS BEFORE?
YES.

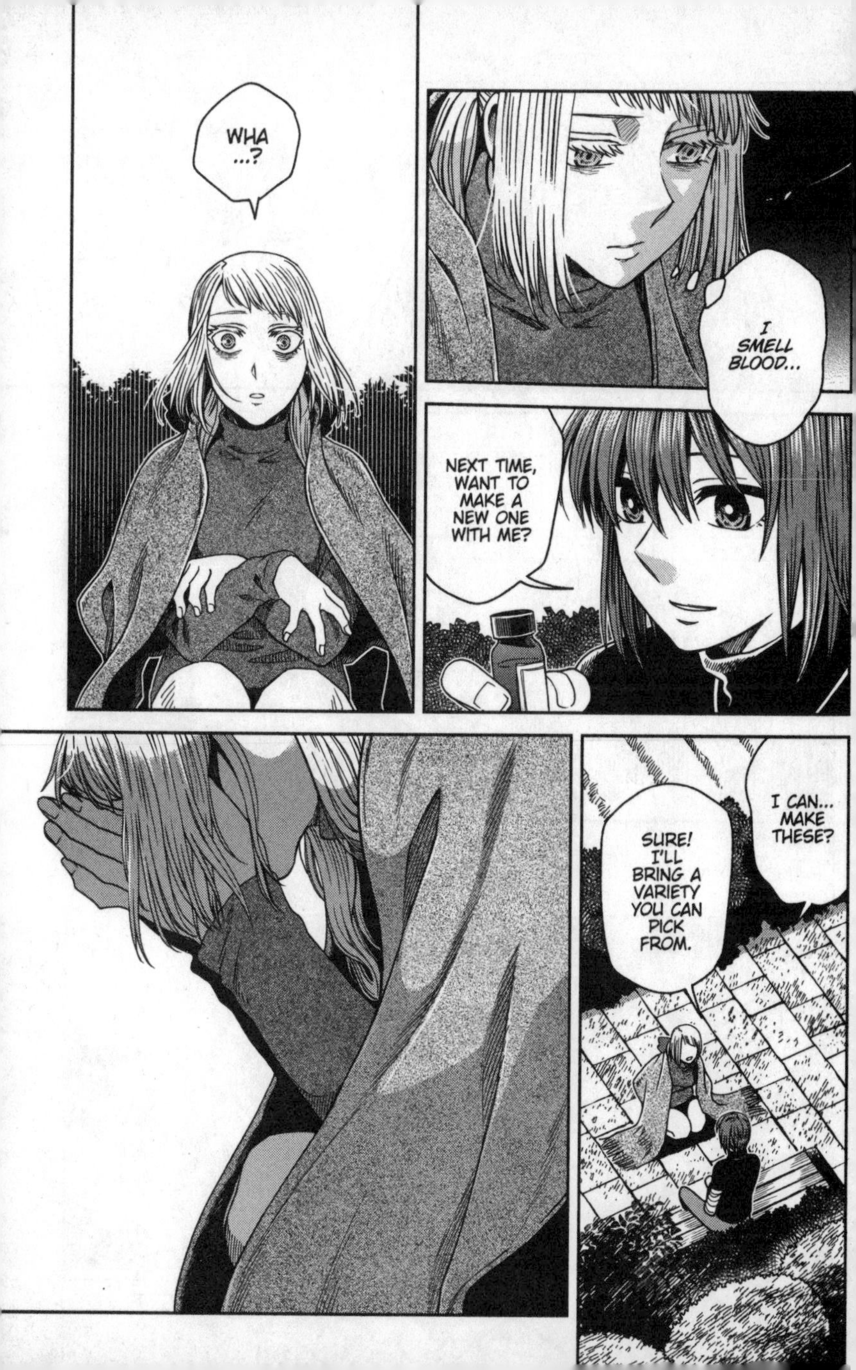
I SMELL BLOOD...
NEXT TIME, WANT TO MAKE A NEW ONE WITH ME?
WHA ...?
I CAN... MAKE THESE?
SURE! I'LL BRING A VARIETY YOU CAN PICK FROM.

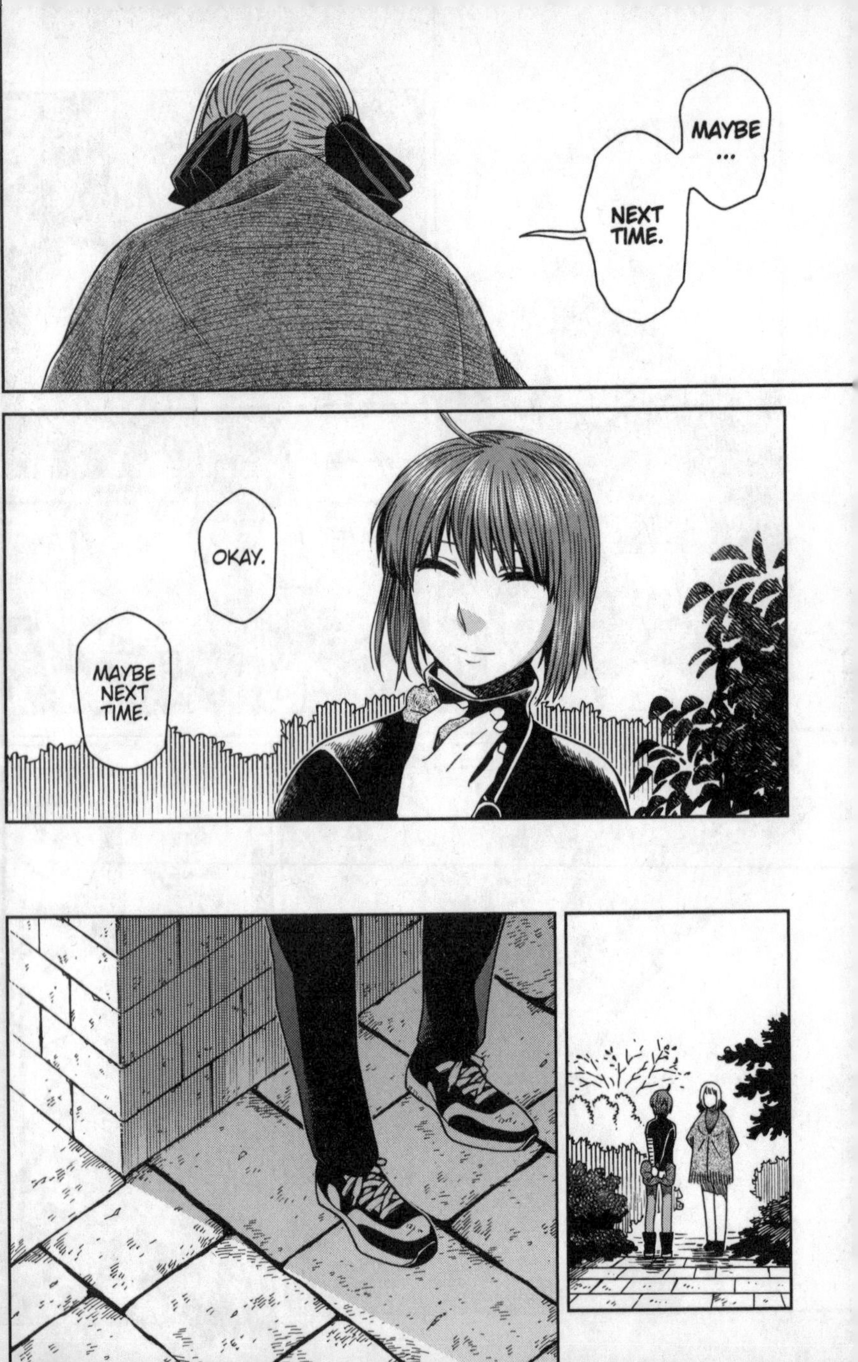
MAYBE ...
NEXT TIME.
OKAY.
MAYBE NEXT TIME.

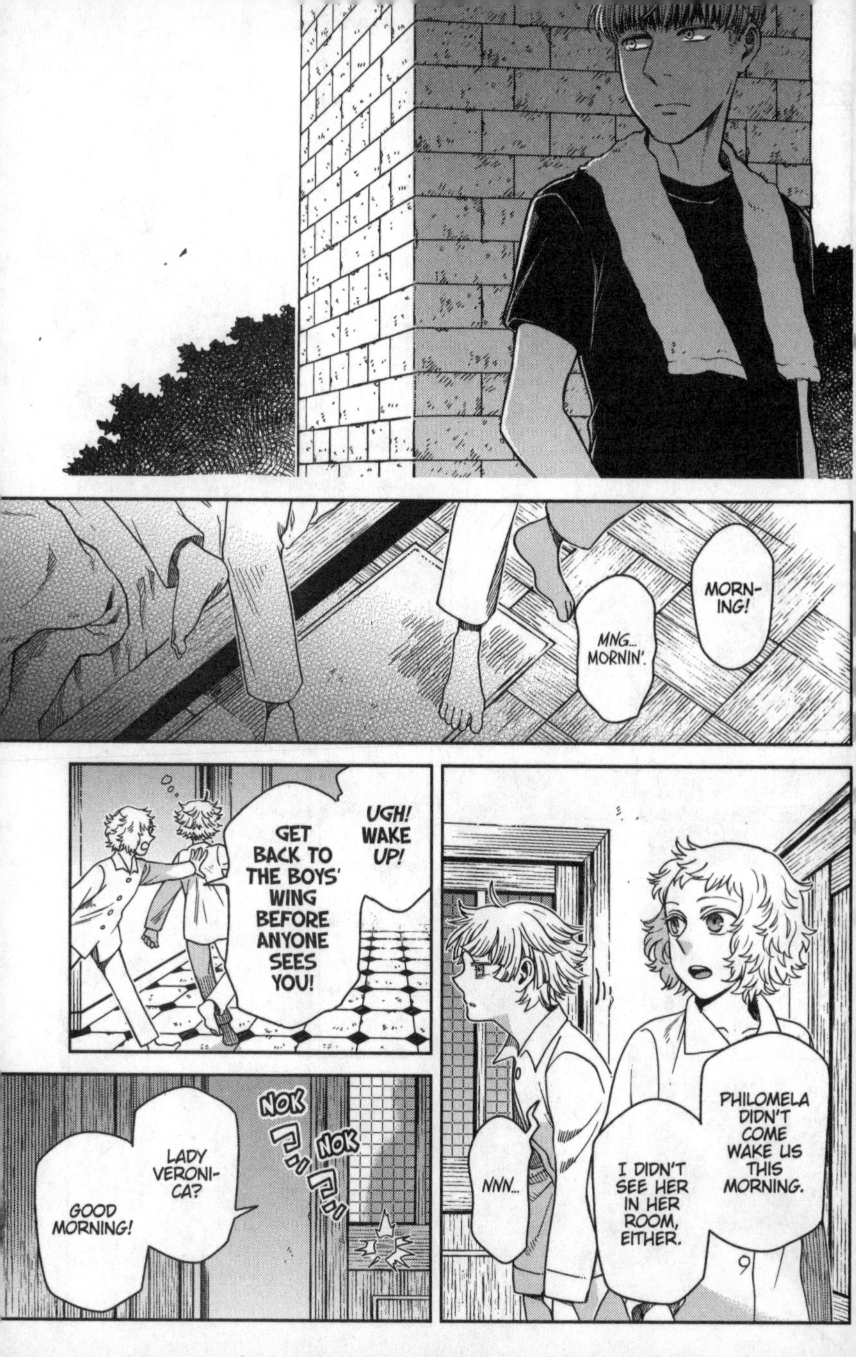
MORNING!
MNG... MORNIN'.
PHILOMELA DIDN'T COME WAKE US THIS MORNING.
I DIDN'T SEE HER IN HER ROOM, EITHER.
NNN...
UGH! WAKE UP!
GET BACK TO THE BOYS' WING BEFORE ANYONE SEES YOU!
NOK NOK
LADY VERONICA?
GOOD MORNING!

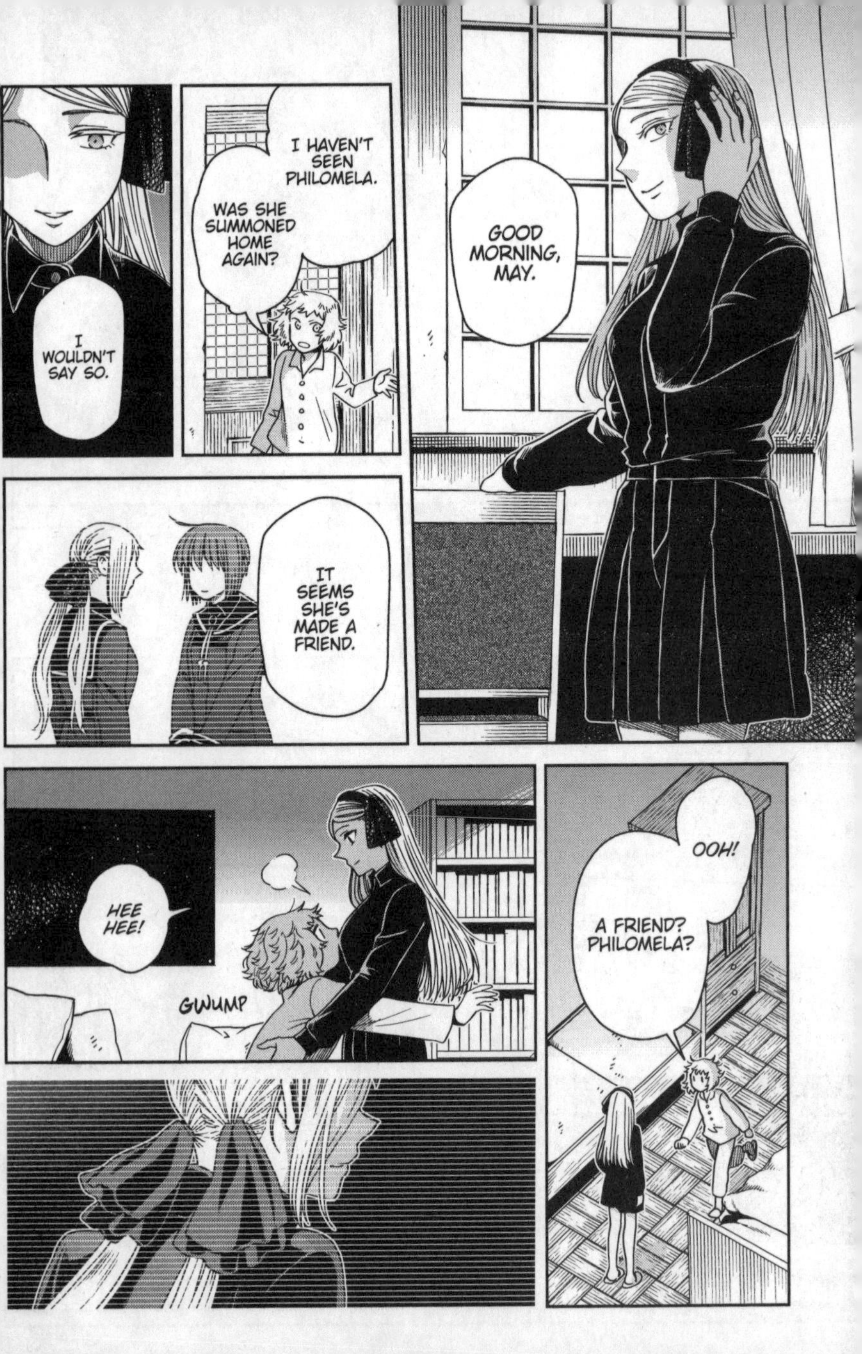
GOOD MORNING, MAY.
I HAVEN'T SEEN PHILOMELA.
WAS SHE SUMMONED HOME AGAIN?
I WOULDN'T SAY SO.
IT SEEMS SHE'S MADE A FRIEND.
OOH!
A FRIEND? PHILOMELA?
HEE HEE!
GWUMP

IT'S BEEN FOREVER SINCE I'VE SEEN HER ENJOYING HERSELF.

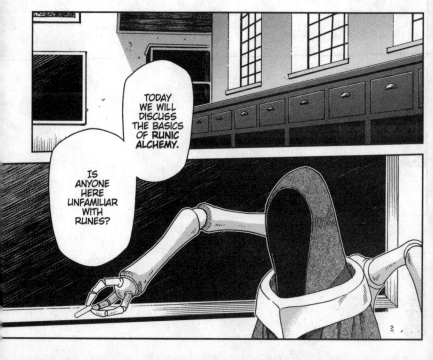

TODAY WE WILL DISCUSS THE BASICS OF RUNIC ALCHEMY.

IS ANYONE HERE UNFAMILIAR WITH RUNES?

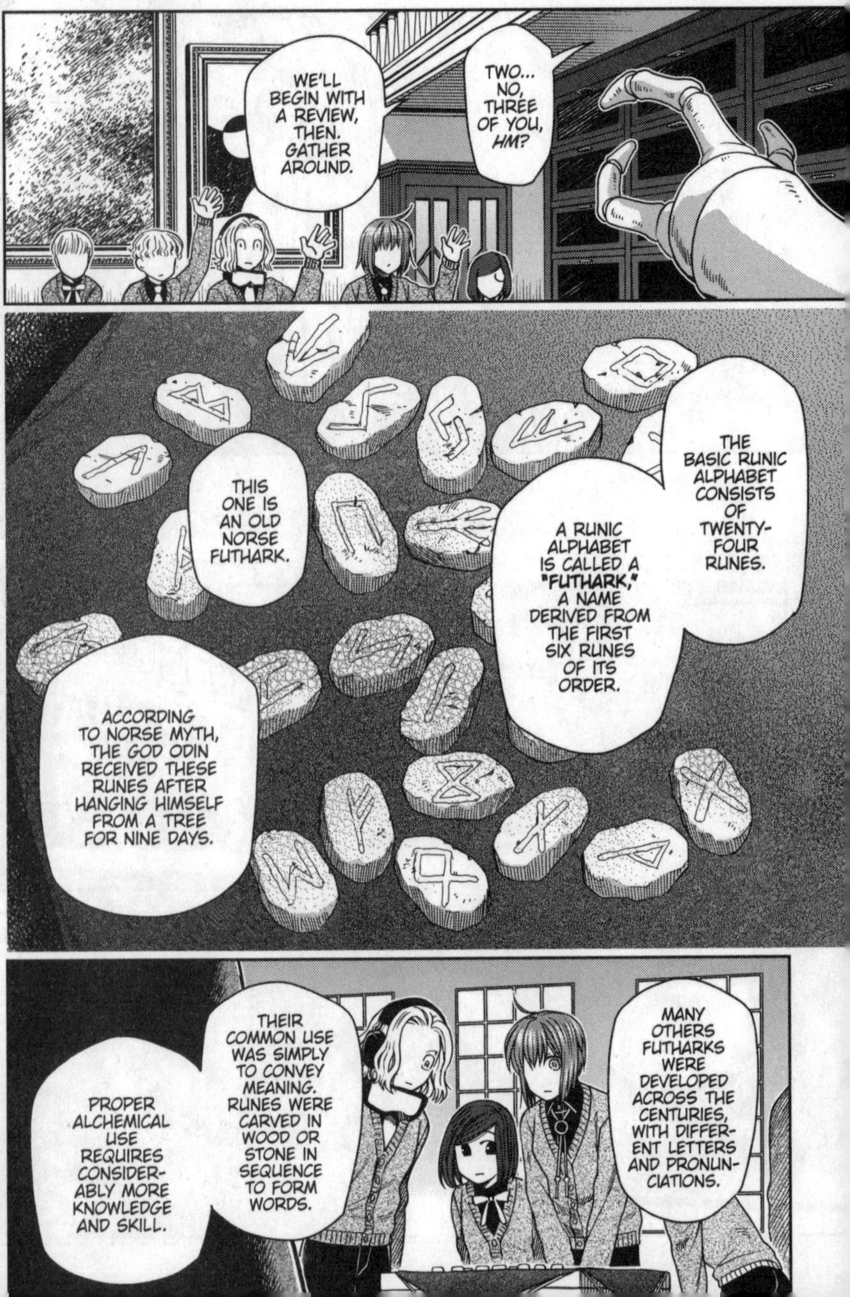
TWO... NO, THREE OF YOU, *HM?*
WE'LL BEGIN WITH A REVIEW, THEN. GATHER AROUND.
THE BASIC RUNIC ALPHABET CONSISTS OF TWENTY-FOUR RUNES.
A RUNIC ALPHABET IS CALLED A **"FUTHARK,"** A NAME DERIVED FROM THE FIRST SIX RUNES OF ITS ORDER.
THIS ONE IS AN OLD NORSE FUTHARK.
ACCORDING TO NORSE MYTH, THE GOD ODIN RECEIVED THESE RUNES AFTER HANGING HIMSELF FROM A TREE FOR NINE DAYS.
MANY OTHERS FUTHARKS WERE DEVELOPED ACROSS THE CENTURIES, WITH DIFFERENT LETTERS AND PRONUNCIATIONS.
THEIR COMMON USE WAS SIMPLY TO CONVEY MEANING. RUNES WERE CARVED IN WOOD OR STONE IN SEQUENCE TO FORM WORDS.
PROPER ALCHEMICAL USE REQUIRES CONSIDERABLY MORE KNOWLEDGE AND SKILL.

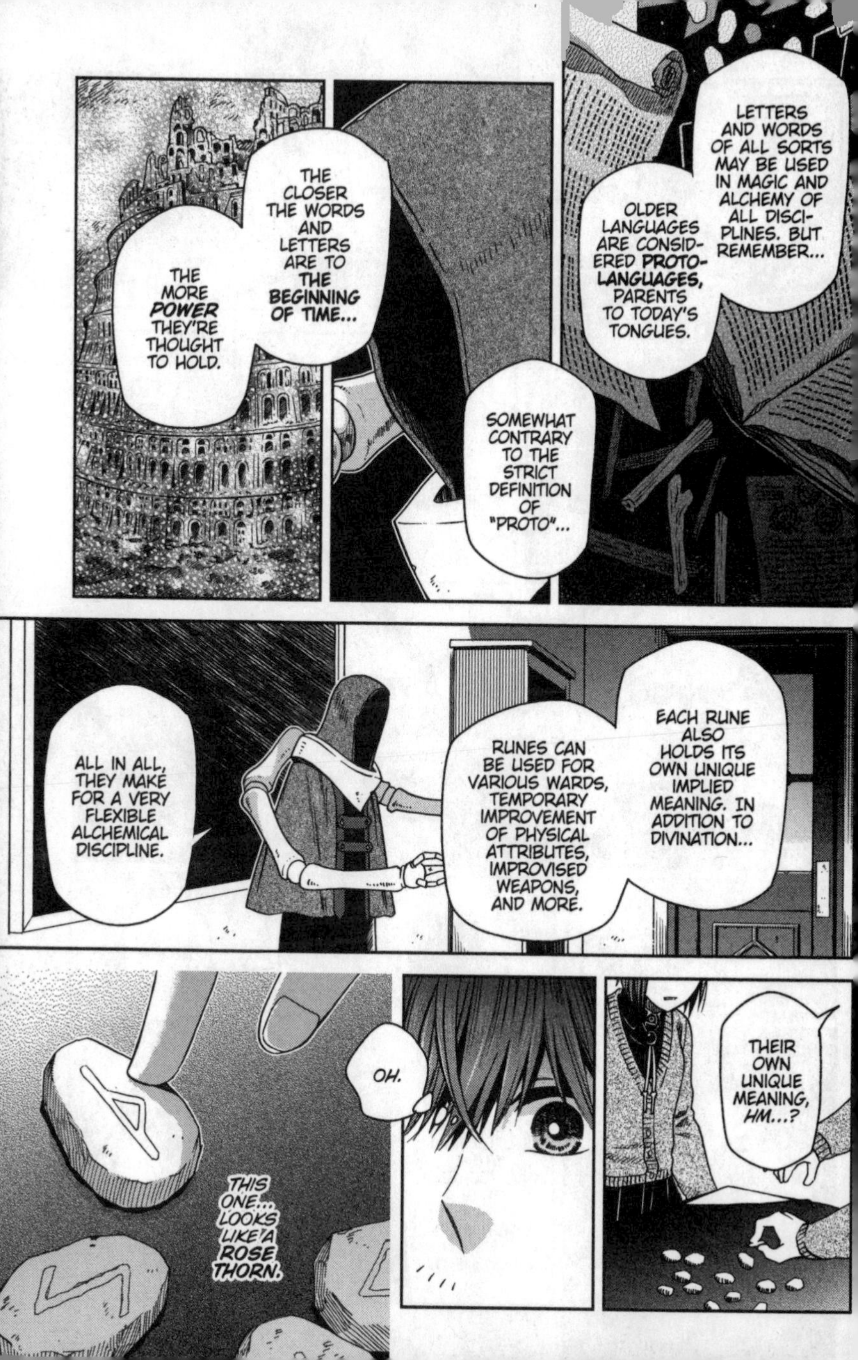
LETTERS AND WORDS OF ALL SORTS MAY BE USED IN MAGIC AND ALCHEMY OF ALL DISCI-PLINES. BUT REMEMBER...
OLDER LANGUAGES ARE CONSID-ERED **PROTO-LANGUAGES,** PARENTS TO TODAY'S TONGUES.
SOMEWHAT CONTRARY TO THE STRICT DEFINITION OF "PROTO"...
THE CLOSER THE WORDS AND LETTERS ARE TO **THE BEGINNING OF TIME...**
THE MORE ***POWER*** THEY'RE THOUGHT TO HOLD.
EACH RUNE ALSO HOLDS ITS OWN UNIQUE IMPLIED MEANING. IN ADDITION TO DIVINATION...
RUNES CAN BE USED FOR VARIOUS WARDS, TEMPORARY IMPROVEMENT OF PHYSICAL ATTRIBUTES, IMPROVISED WEAPONS, AND MORE.
ALL IN ALL, THEY MAKE FOR A VERY FLEXIBLE ALCHEMICAL DISCIPLINE.
THEIR OWN UNIQUE MEANING, *HM...?*
OH.
THIS ONE... LOOKS LIKE A ***ROSE THORN.***

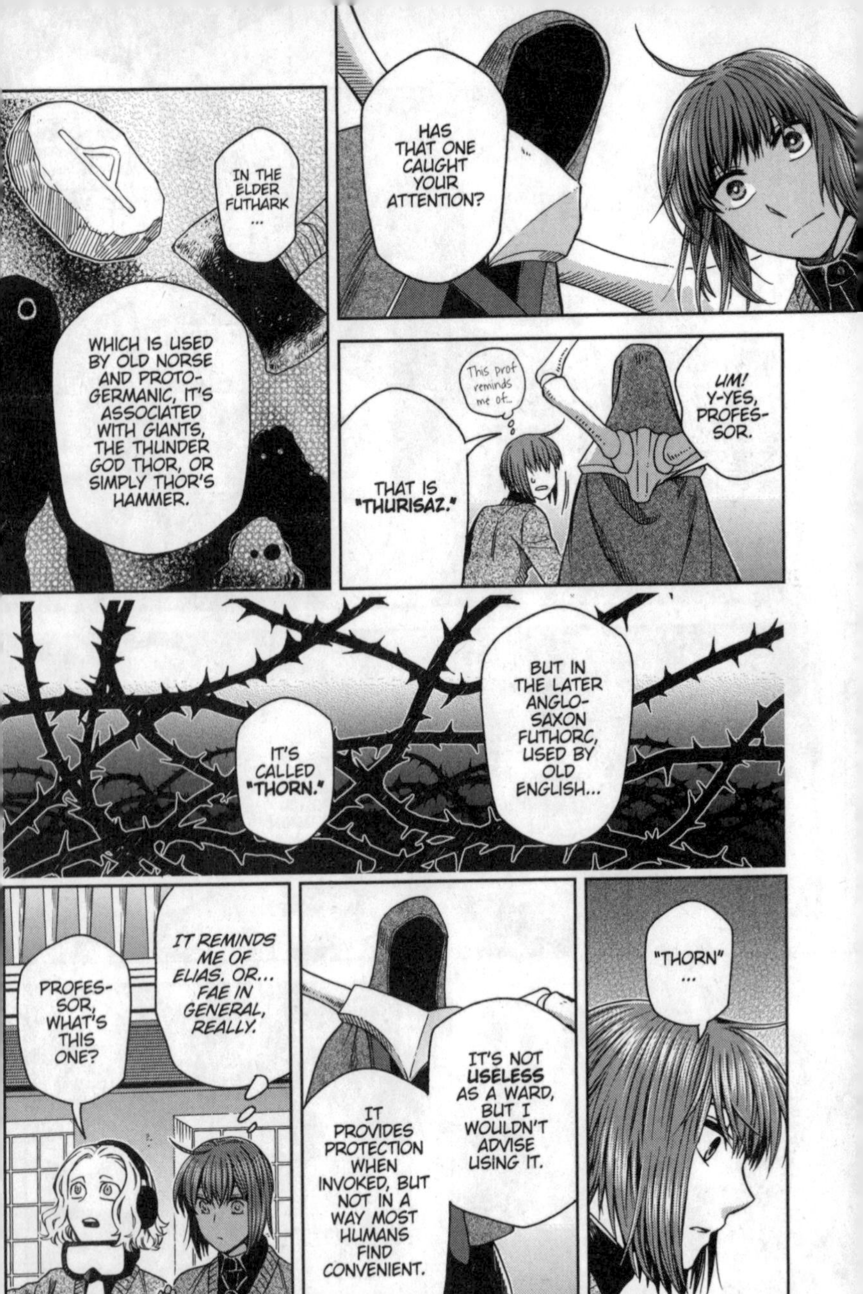
HAS THAT ONE CAUGHT YOUR ATTENTION?
UM! Y-YES, PROFESSOR.
This prof reminds me of...
THAT IS "THURISAZ."
IN THE ELDER FUTHARK...
WHICH IS USED BY OLD NORSE AND PROTO-GERMANIC, IT'S ASSOCIATED WITH GIANTS, THE THUNDER GOD THOR, OR SIMPLY THOR'S HAMMER.
BUT IN THE LATER ANGLO-SAXON FUTHORC, USED BY OLD ENGLISH...
IT'S CALLED "THORN."
"THORN"...
IT'S NOT USELESS AS A WARD, BUT I WOULDN'T ADVISE USING IT.
IT PROVIDES PROTECTION WHEN INVOKED, BUT NOT IN A WAY MOST HUMANS FIND CONVENIENT.
IT REMINDS ME OF ELIAS. OR... FAE IN GENERAL, REALLY.
PROFESSOR, WHAT'S THIS ONE?

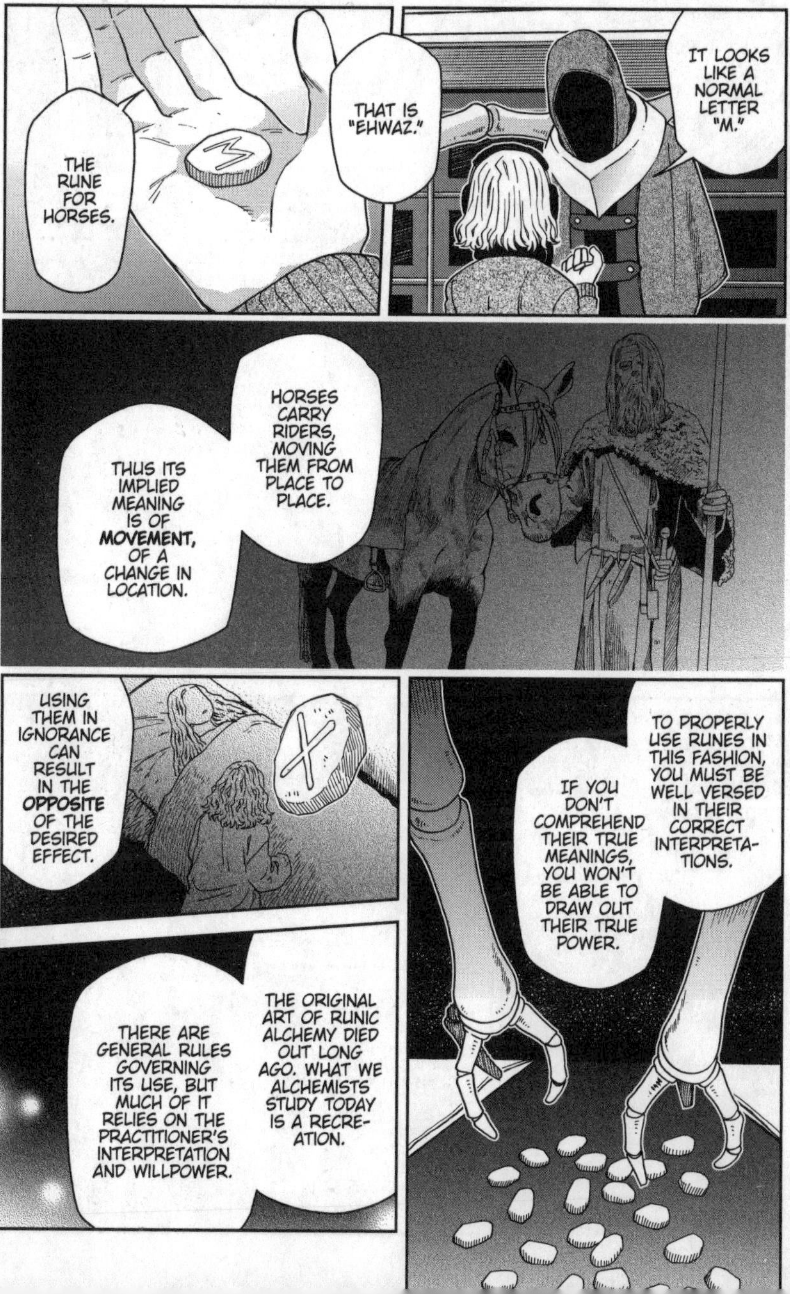
IT LOOKS LIKE A NORMAL LETTER "M."
THAT IS "EHWAZ."
THE RUNE FOR HORSES.
HORSES CARRY RIDERS, MOVING THEM FROM PLACE TO PLACE.
THUS ITS IMPLIED MEANING IS OF MOVEMENT, OF A CHANGE IN LOCATION.
TO PROPERLY USE RUNES IN THIS FASHION, YOU MUST BE WELL VERSED IN THEIR CORRECT INTERPRETATIONS.
IF YOU DON'T COMPREHEND THEIR TRUE MEANINGS, YOU WON'T BE ABLE TO DRAW OUT THEIR TRUE POWER.
USING THEM IN IGNORANCE CAN RESULT IN THE OPPOSITE OF THE DESIRED EFFECT.
THE ORIGINAL ART OF RUNIC ALCHEMY DIED OUT LONG AGO. WHAT WE ALCHEMISTS STUDY TODAY IS A RECREATION.
THERE ARE GENERAL RULES GOVERNING ITS USE, BUT MUCH OF IT RELIES ON THE PRACTITIONER'S INTERPRETATION AND WILLPOWER.

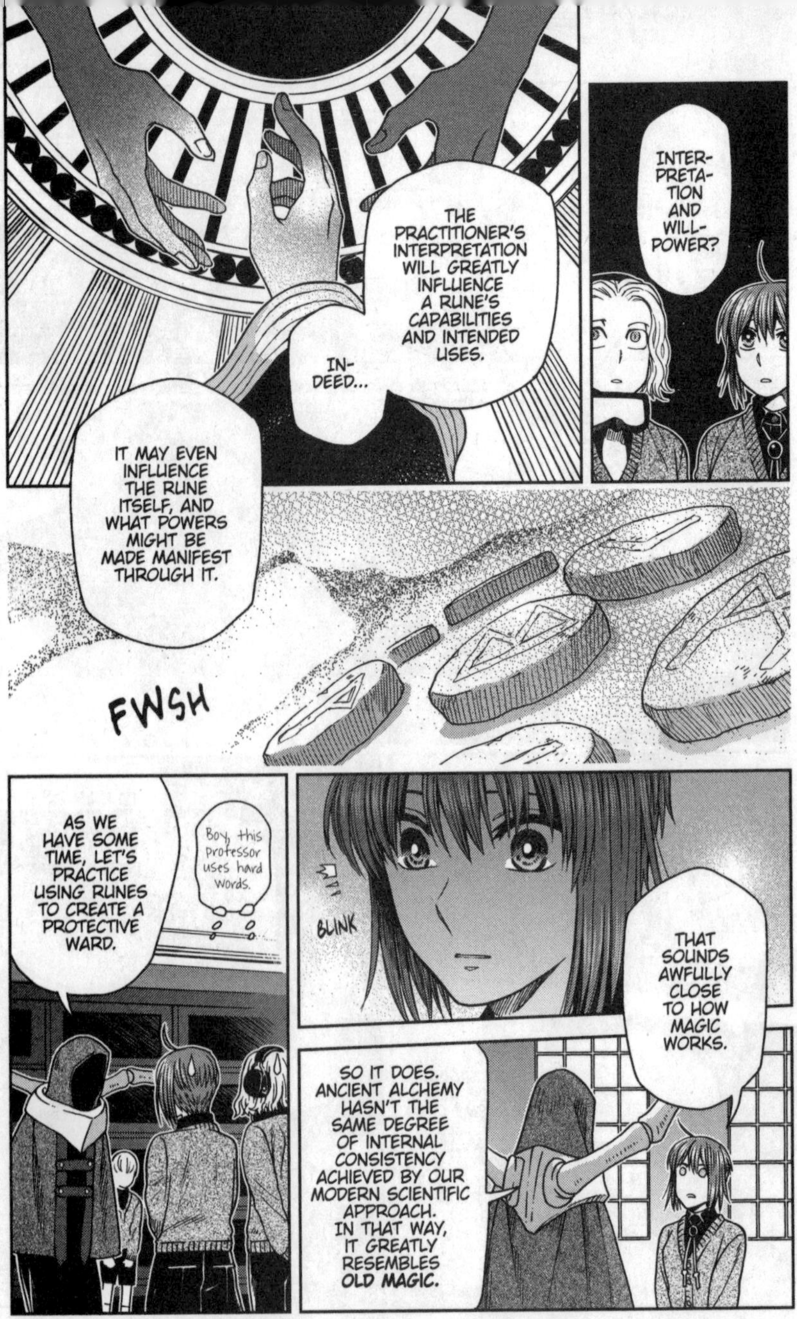
INTER-PRETA-TION AND WILL-POWER?
THE PRACTITIONER'S INTERPRETATION WILL GREATLY INFLUENCE A RUNE'S CAPABILITIES AND INTENDED USES.
IN-DEED...
IT MAY EVEN INFLUENCE THE RUNE ITSELF, AND WHAT POWERS MIGHT BE MADE MANIFEST THROUGH IT.
FWSH
BLINK
THAT SOUNDS AWFULLY CLOSE TO HOW MAGIC WORKS.
SO IT DOES. ANCIENT ALCHEMY HASN'T THE SAME DEGREE OF INTERNAL CONSISTENCY ACHIEVED BY OUR MODERN SCIENTIFIC APPROACH. IN THAT WAY, IT GREATLY RESEMBLES **OLD MAGIC.**
AS WE HAVE SOME TIME, LET'S PRACTICE USING RUNES TO CREATE A PROTECTIVE WARD.
Boy, this professor uses hard words.
Not native English speakers.

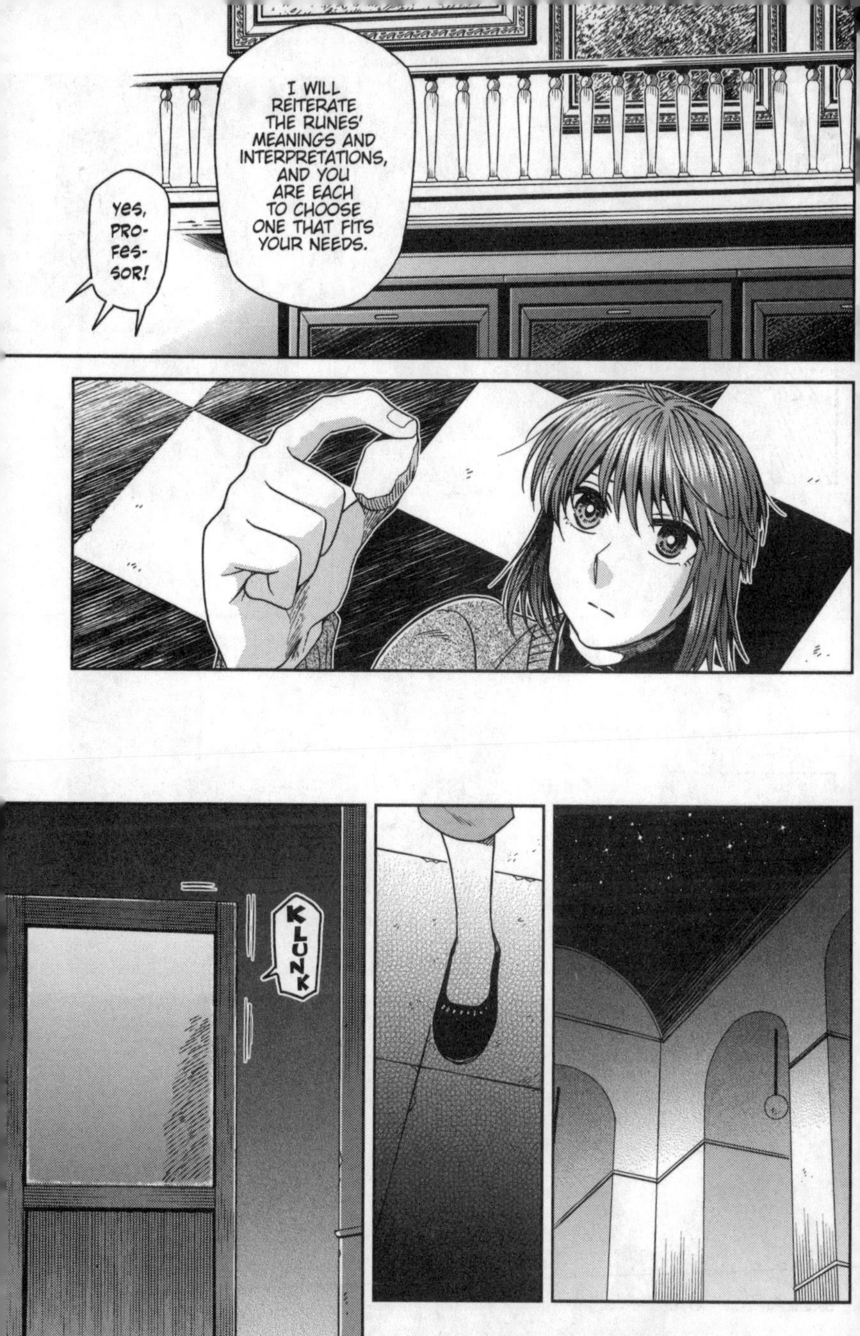
I WILL REITERATE THE RUNES' MEANINGS AND INTERPRETATIONS, AND YOU ARE EACH TO CHOOSE ONE THAT FITS YOUR NEEDS.
Yes, PRO-FES-SOR!
KLUNK

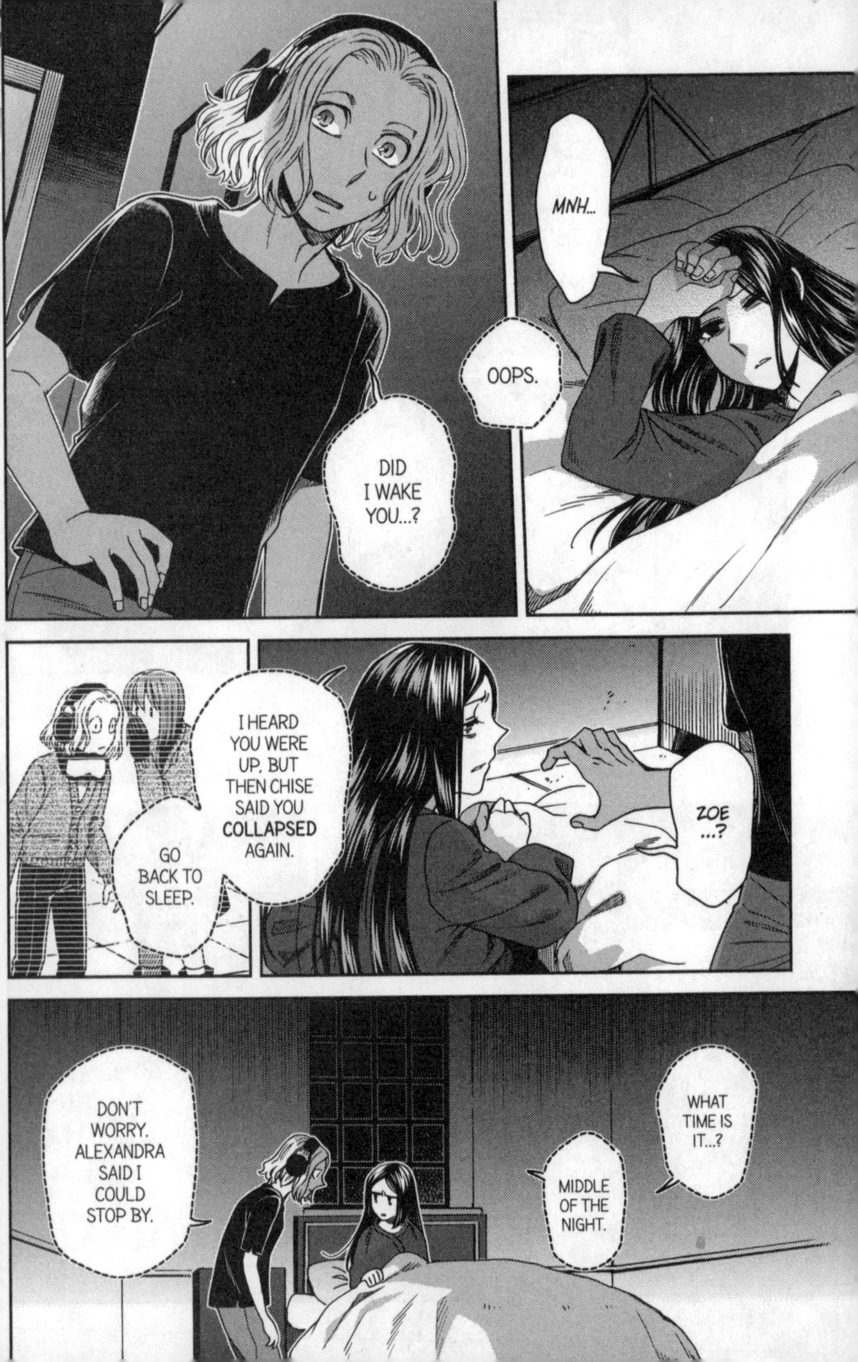
MNH...
OOPS.
DID I WAKE YOU...?
ZOE ...?
I HEARD YOU WERE UP, BUT THEN CHISE SAID YOU **COLLAPSED** AGAIN.
GO BACK TO SLEEP.
WHAT TIME IS IT...?
MIDDLE OF THE NIGHT.
DON'T WORRY. ALEXANDRA SAID I COULD STOP BY.

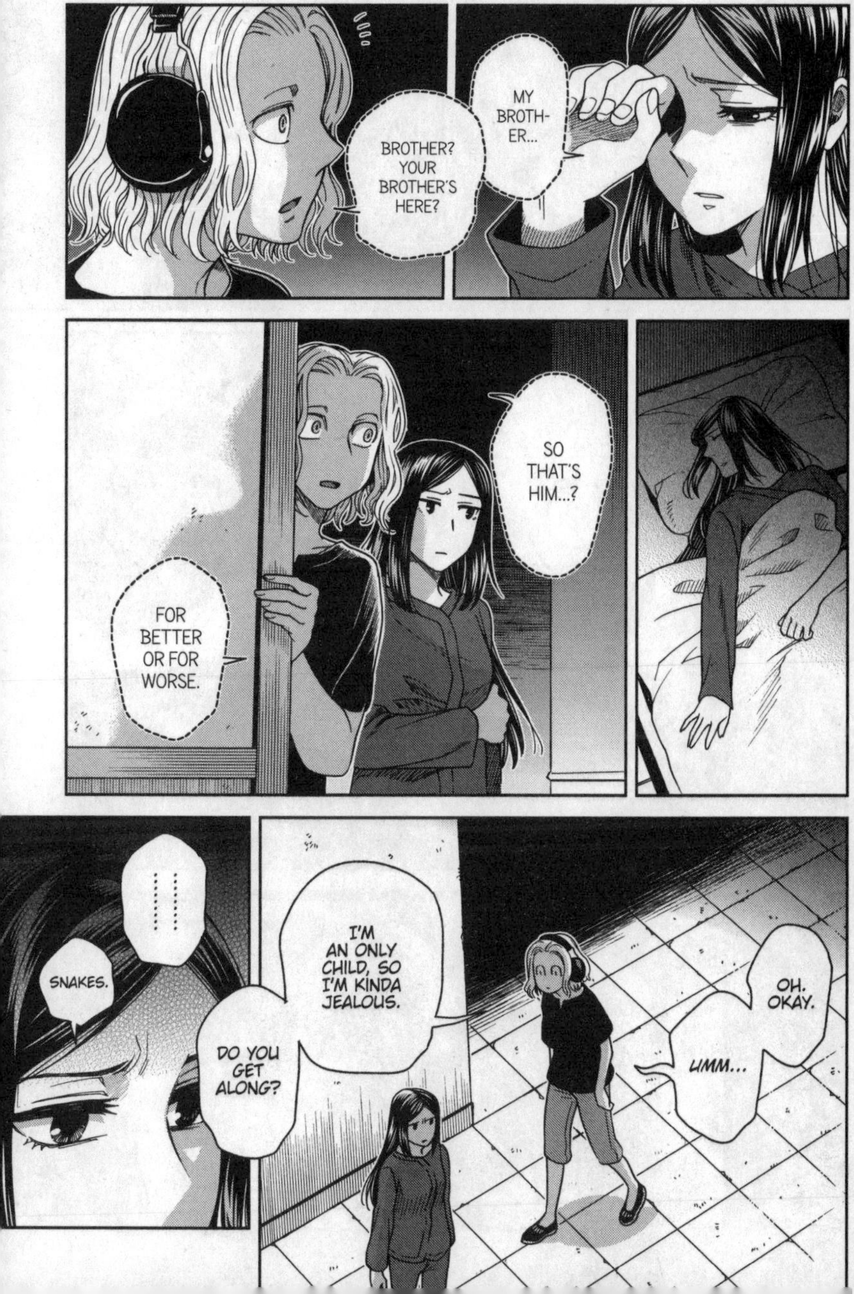
MY BROTH-ER...
BROTHER? YOUR BROTHER'S HERE?
SO THAT'S HIM...?
FOR BETTER OR FOR WORSE.
OH. OKAY.
UMM...
I'M AN ONLY CHILD, SO I'M KINDA JEALOUS.
DO YOU GET ALONG?
......
SNAKES.

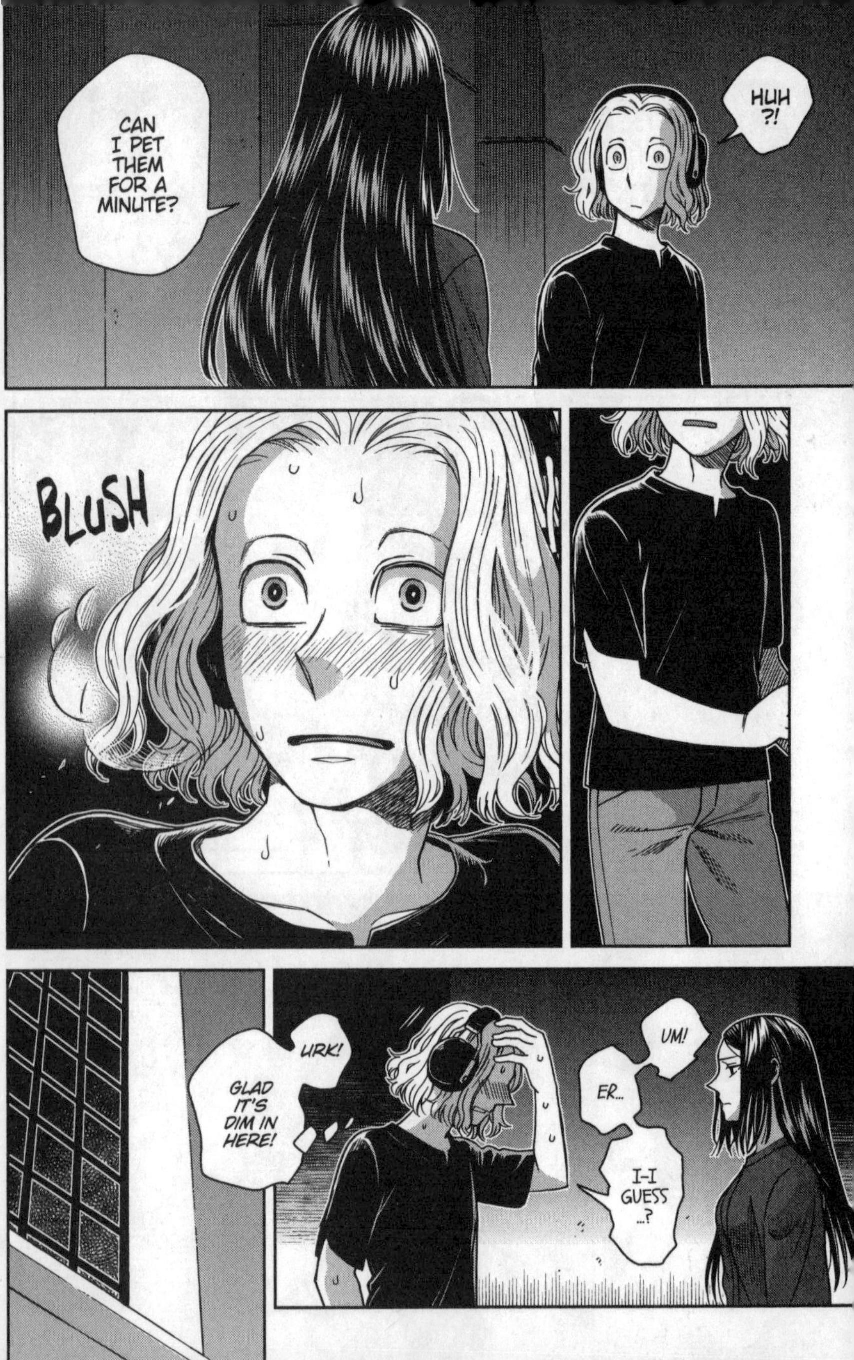
HUH ?!
CAN I PET THEM FOR A MINUTE?
BLUSH
UM!
ER...
I-I GUESS ...?
URK!
GLAD IT'S DIM IN HERE!

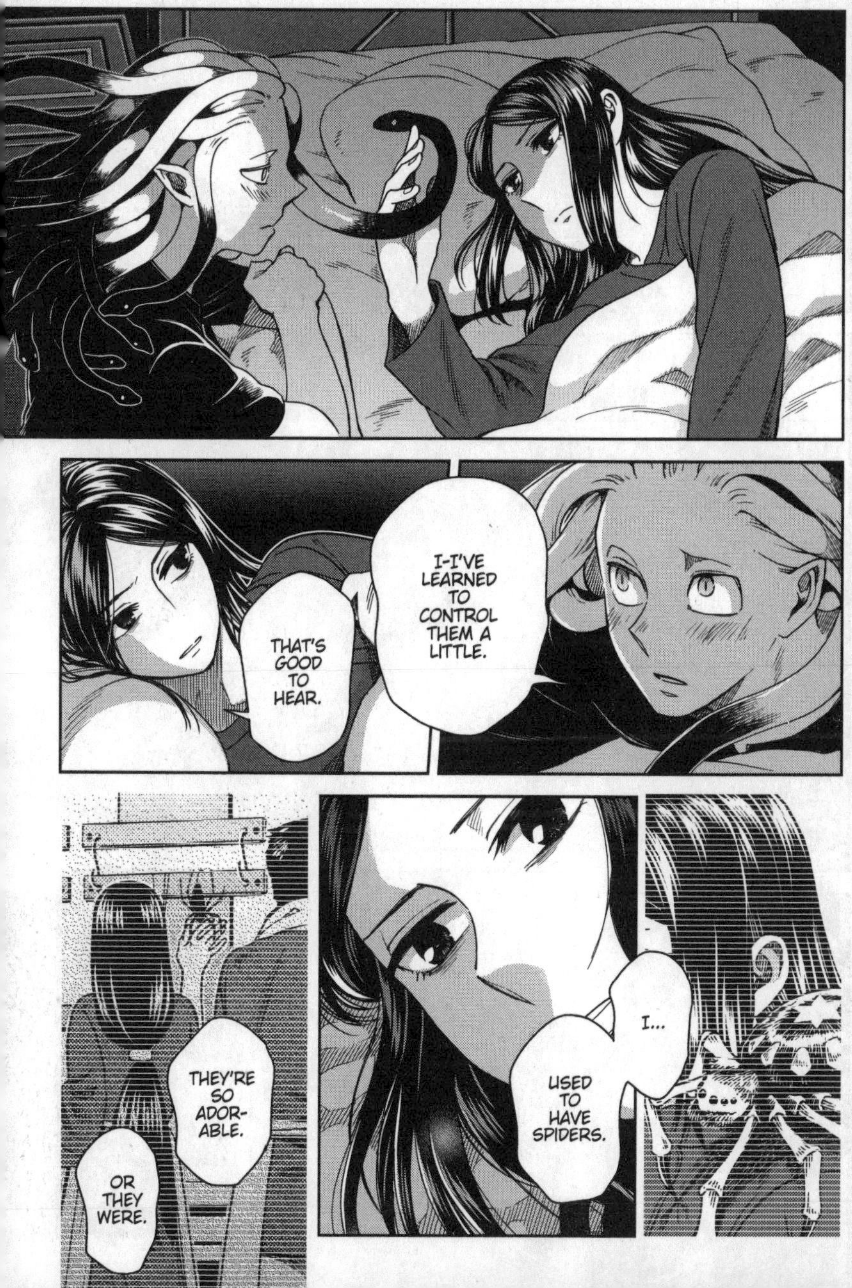
I-I'VE LEARNED TO CONTROL THEM A LITTLE.
THAT'S GOOD TO HEAR.
I...
USED TO HAVE SPIDERS.
THEY'RE SO ADORABLE.
OR THEY WERE.

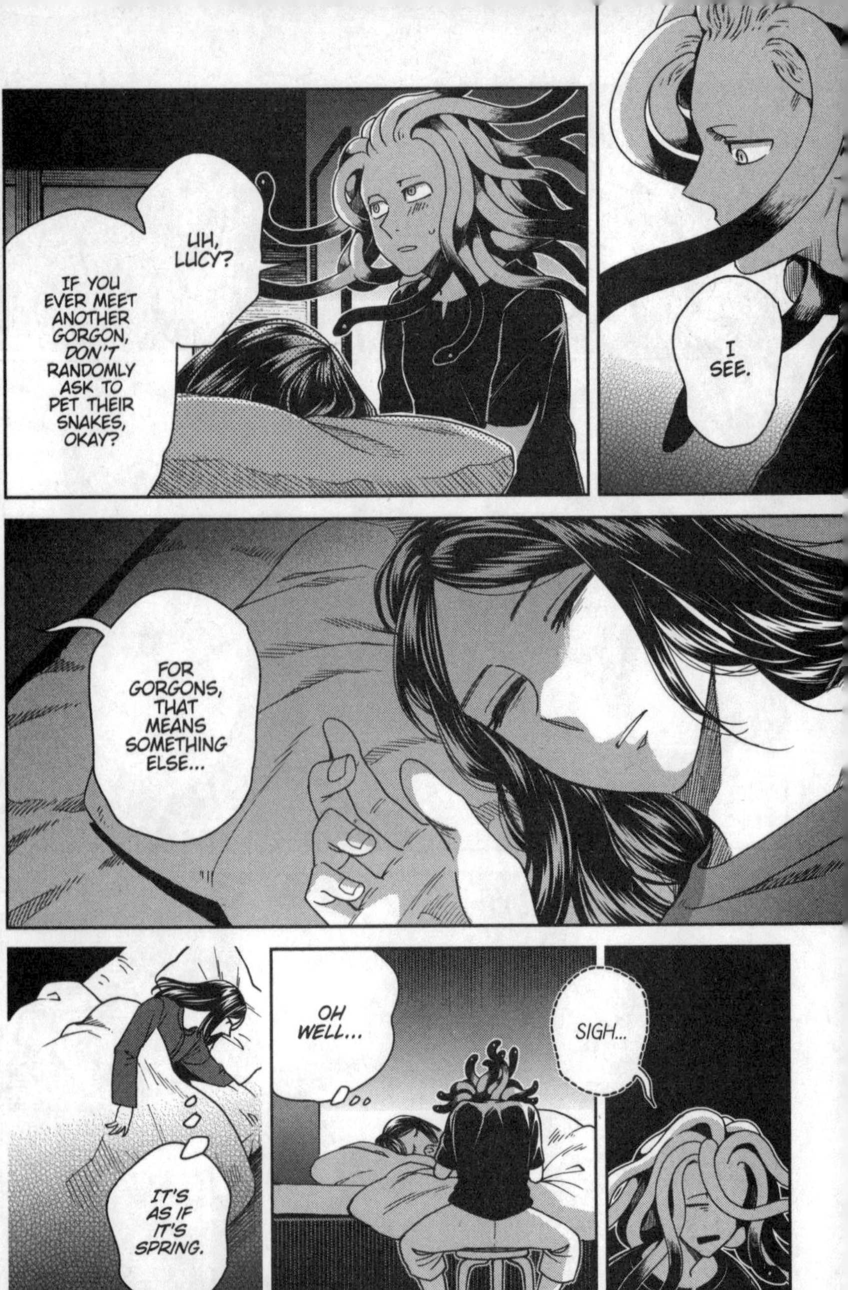
I SEE.
UH, LUCY?
IF YOU EVER MEET ANOTHER GORGON, DON'T RANDOMLY ASK TO PET THEIR SNAKES, OKAY?
FOR GORGONS, THAT MEANS SOMETHING ELSE...
SIGH...
OH WELL...
IT'S AS IF IT'S SPRING.

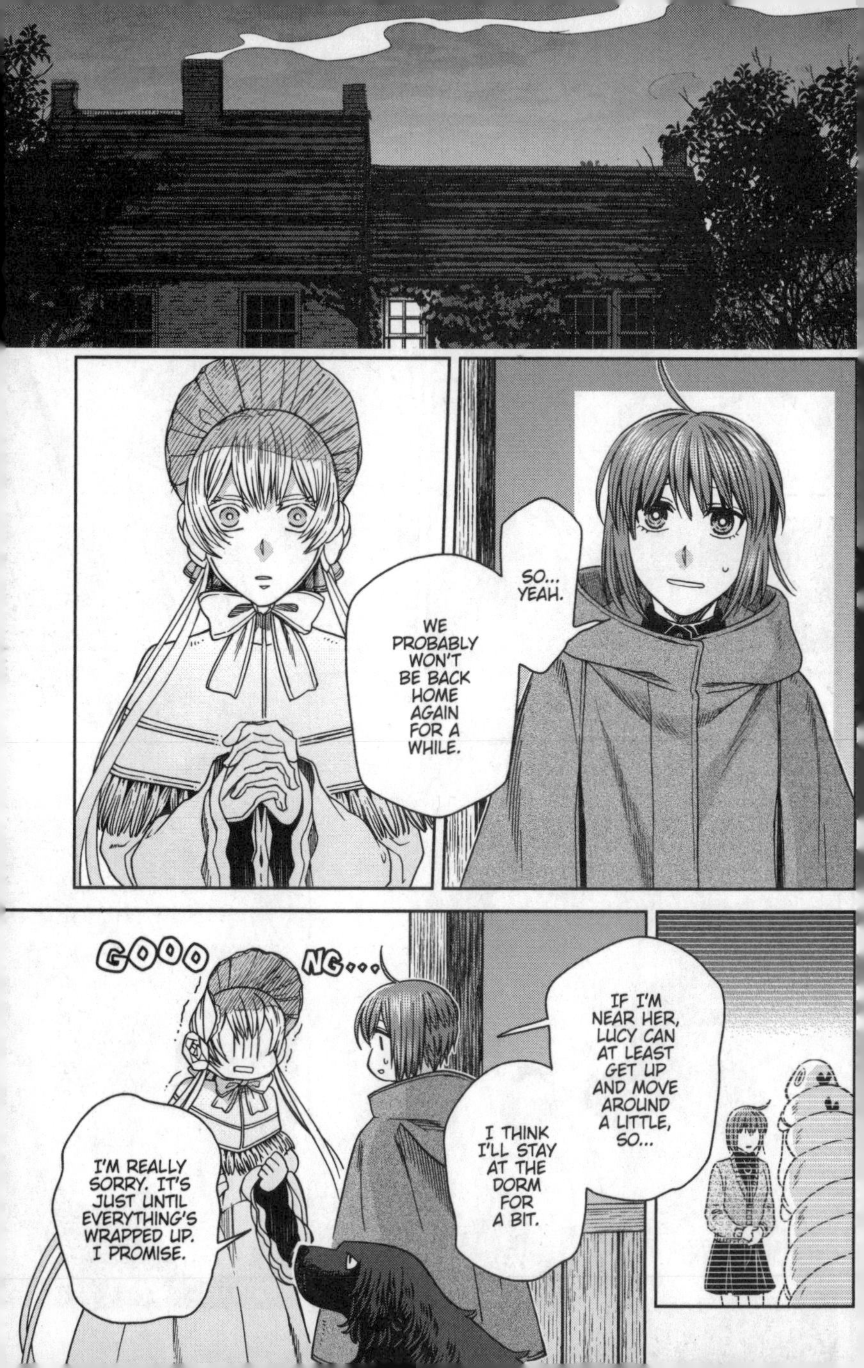
SO... YEAH.
WE PROBABLY WON'T BE BACK HOME AGAIN FOR A WHILE.
IF I'M NEAR HER, LUCY CAN AT LEAST GET UP AND MOVE AROUND A LITTLE, SO...
I THINK I'LL STAY AT THE DORM FOR A BIT.
GOOO NG...
I'M REALLY SORRY. IT'S JUST UNTIL EVERYTHING'S WRAPPED UP. I PROMISE.

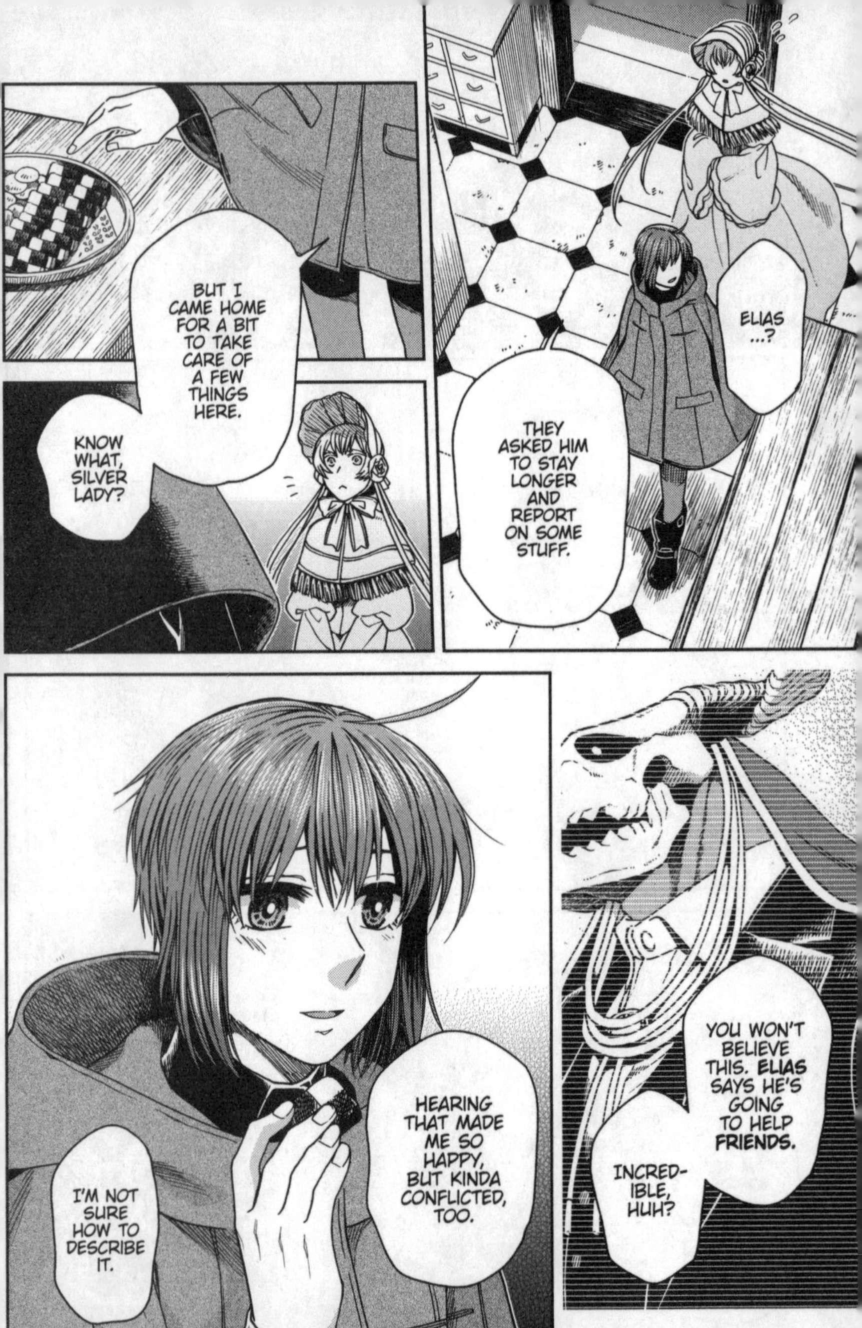
ELIAS ...?
...
THEY ASKED HIM TO STAY LONGER AND REPORT ON SOME STUFF.
BUT I CAME HOME FOR A BIT TO TAKE CARE OF A FEW THINGS HERE.
KNOW WHAT, SILVER LADY?
YOU WON'T BELIEVE THIS. ELIAS SAYS HE'S GOING TO HELP **FRIENDS**.
INCRED-IBLE, HUH?
HEARING THAT MADE ME SO HAPPY, BUT KINDA CONFLICTED, TOO.
I'M NOT SURE HOW TO DESCRIBE IT.

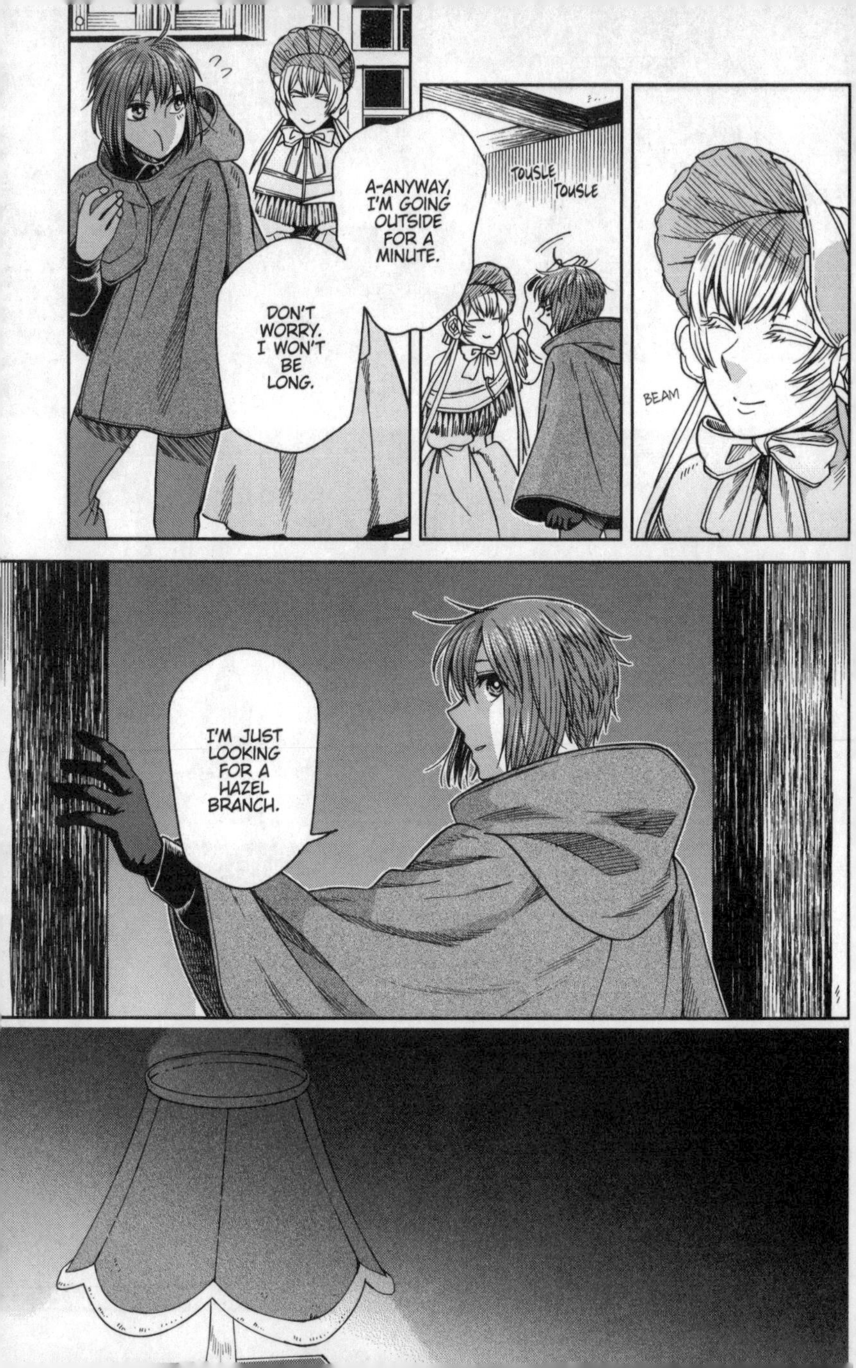
BEAM
TOUSLE
TOUSLE
A-ANYWAY, I'M GOING OUTSIDE FOR A MINUTE.
DON'T WORRY. I WON'T BE LONG.
I'M JUST LOOKING FOR A HAZEL BRANCH.

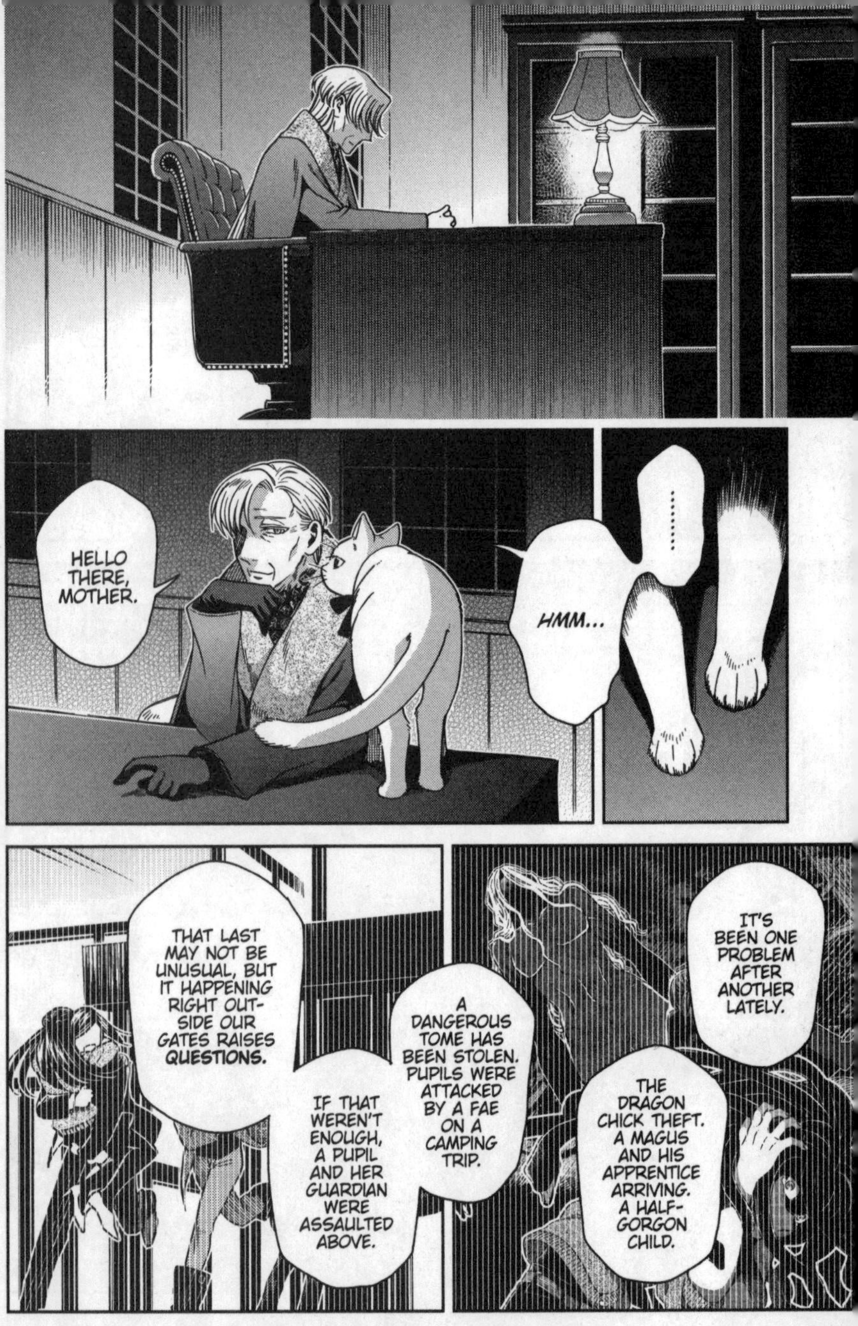
......
HMM...
HELLO THERE, MOTHER.
IT'S BEEN ONE PROBLEM AFTER ANOTHER LATELY.
THE DRAGON CHICK THEFT. A MAGUS AND HIS APPRENTICE ARRIVING. A HALF-GORGON CHILD.
A DANGEROUS TOME HAS BEEN STOLEN. PUPILS WERE ATTACKED BY A FAE ON A CAMPING TRIP.
IF THAT WEREN'T ENOUGH, A PUPIL AND HER GUARDIAN WERE ASSAULTED ABOVE.
THAT LAST MAY NOT BE UNUSUAL, BUT IT HAPPENING RIGHT OUT-SIDE OUR GATES RAISES QUESTIONS.

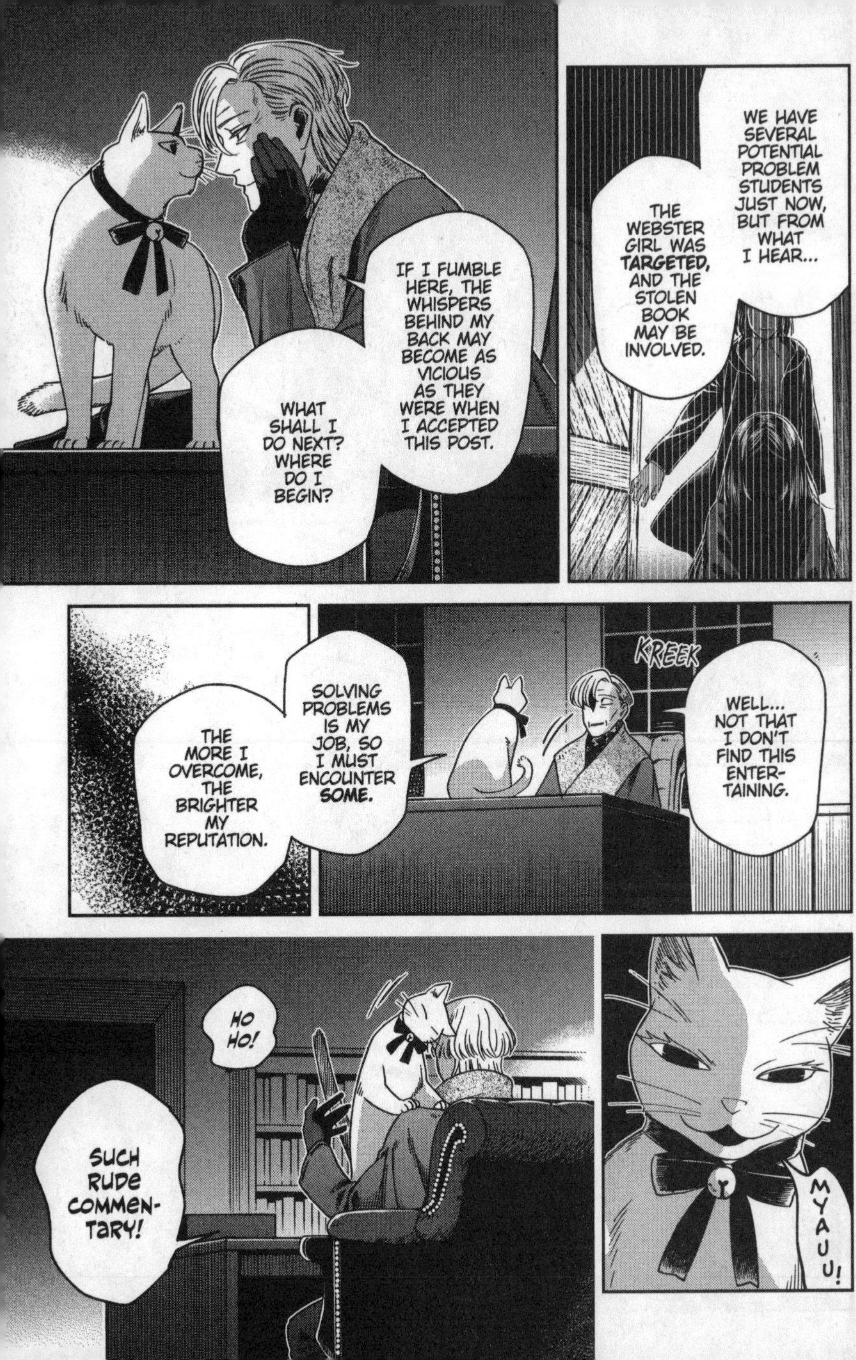
WE HAVE SEVERAL POTENTIAL PROBLEM STUDENTS JUST NOW, BUT FROM WHAT I HEAR...
THE WEBSTER GIRL WAS **TARGETED,** AND THE STOLEN BOOK MAY BE INVOLVED.
IF I FUMBLE HERE, THE WHISPERS BEHIND MY BACK MAY BECOME AS VICIOUS AS THEY WERE WHEN I ACCEPTED THIS POST.
WHAT SHALL I DO NEXT? WHERE DO I BEGIN?
KREEK
WELL... NOT THAT I DON'T FIND THIS ENTER-TAINING.
SOLVING PROBLEMS IS MY JOB, SO I MUST ENCOUNTER **SOME.**
THE MORE I OVERCOME, THE BRIGHTER MY REPUTATION.
MYAUU!
HO HO!
SUCH RUDE COMMEN-TARY!

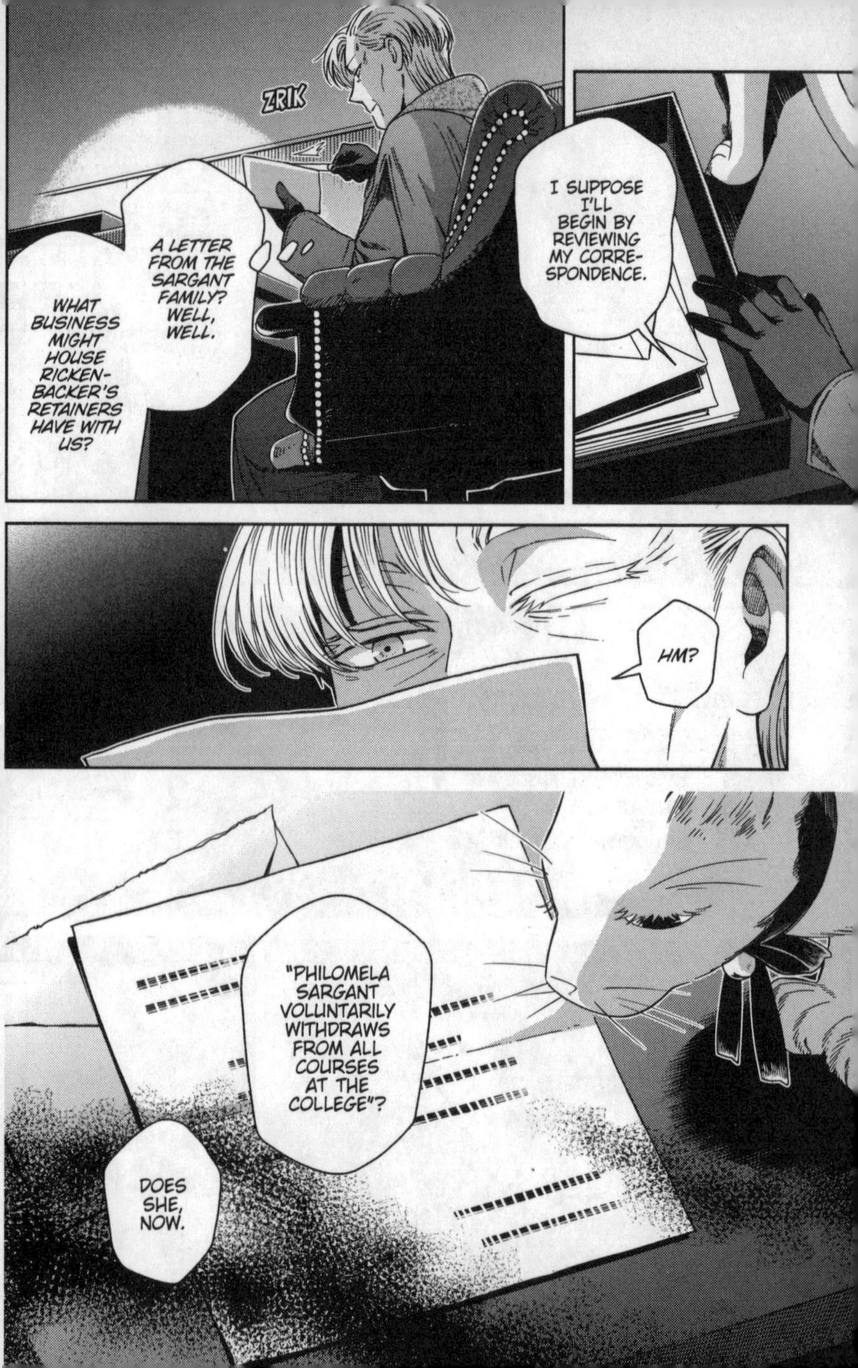
I SUPPOSE I'LL BEGIN BY REVIEWING MY CORRE-SPONDENCE.
ZRIK
A LETTER FROM THE SARGANT FAMILY? WELL, WELL.
WHAT BUSINESS MIGHT HOUSE RICKEN-BACKER'S RETAINERS HAVE WITH US?
HM?
"PHILOMELA SARGANT VOLUNTARILY WITHDRAWS FROM ALL COURSES AT THE COLLEGE"?
DOES SHE, NOW.

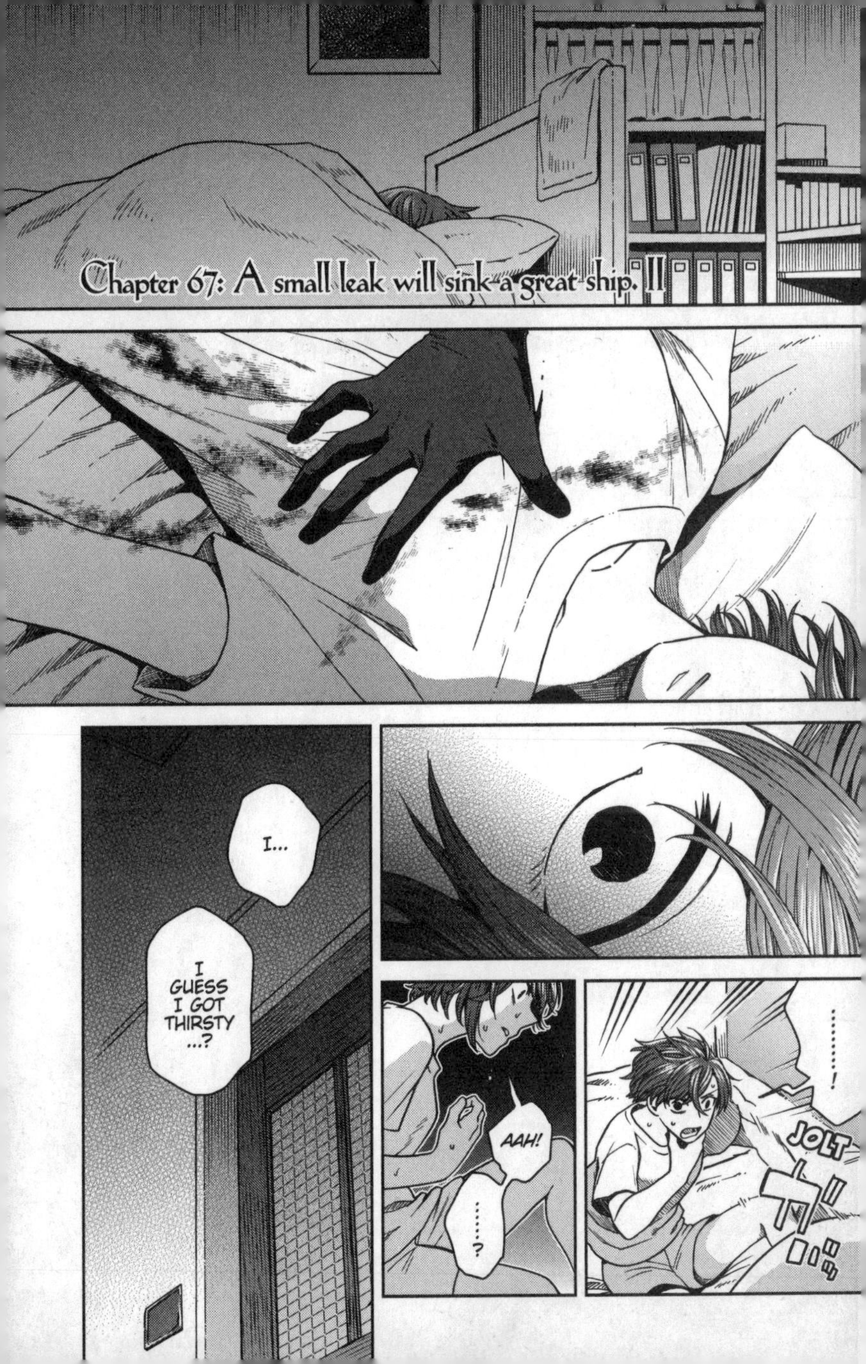
Chapter 67: A small leak will sink a great ship. II
.........!
JOLT
AAH!
......?
I...
I GUESS I GOT THIRSTY ...?

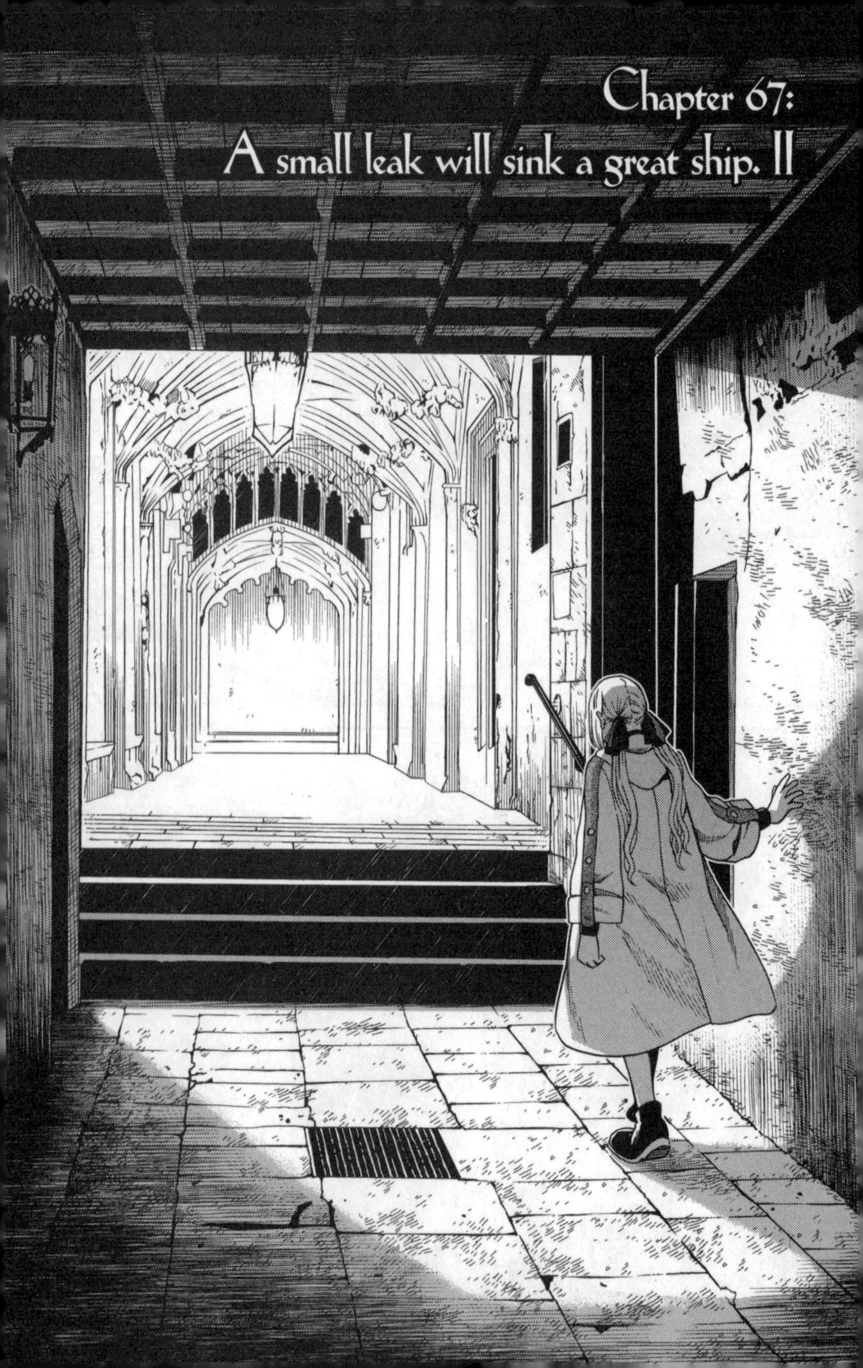
Chapter 67:
A small leak will sink a great ship. II

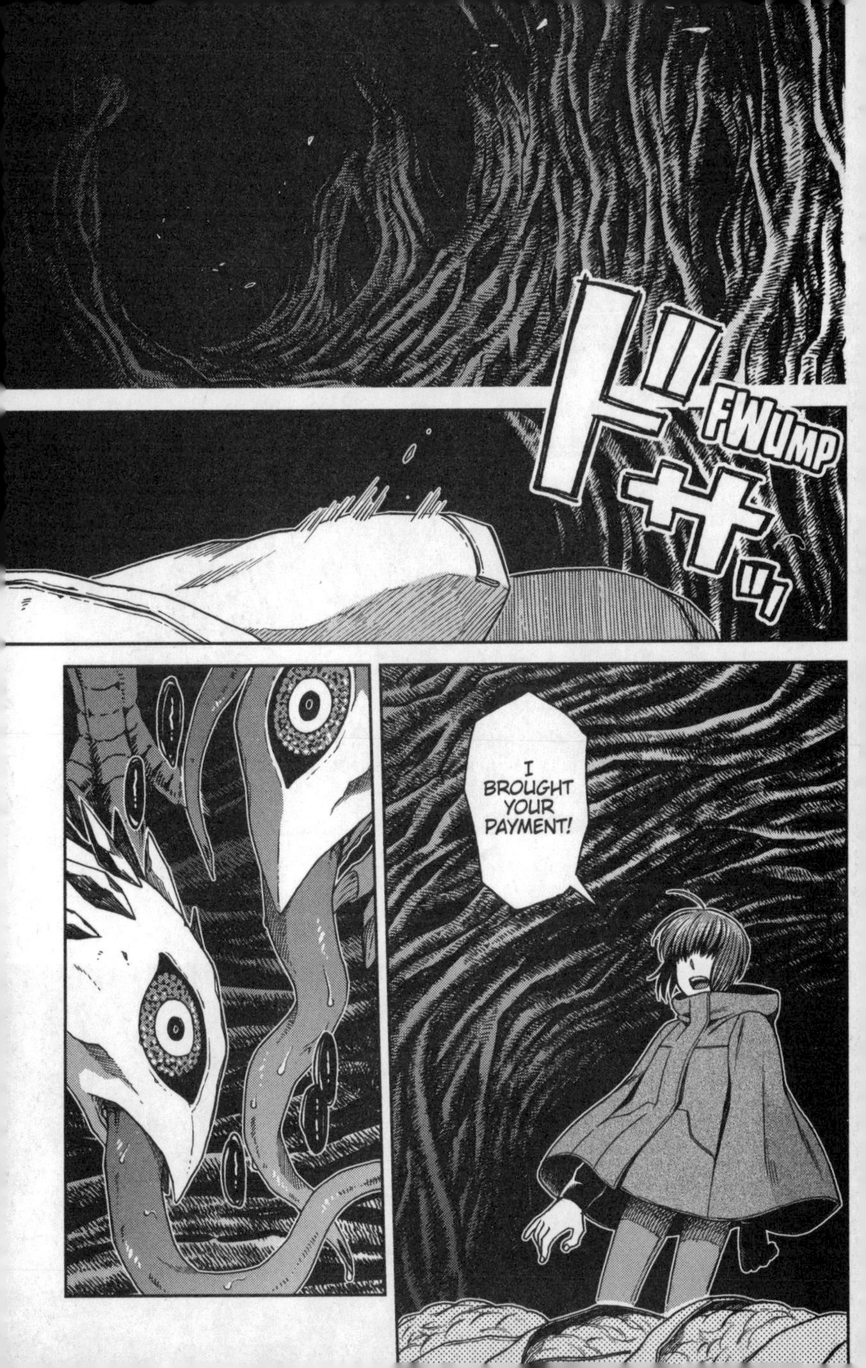
FWUMP
I BROUGHT YOUR PAYMENT!

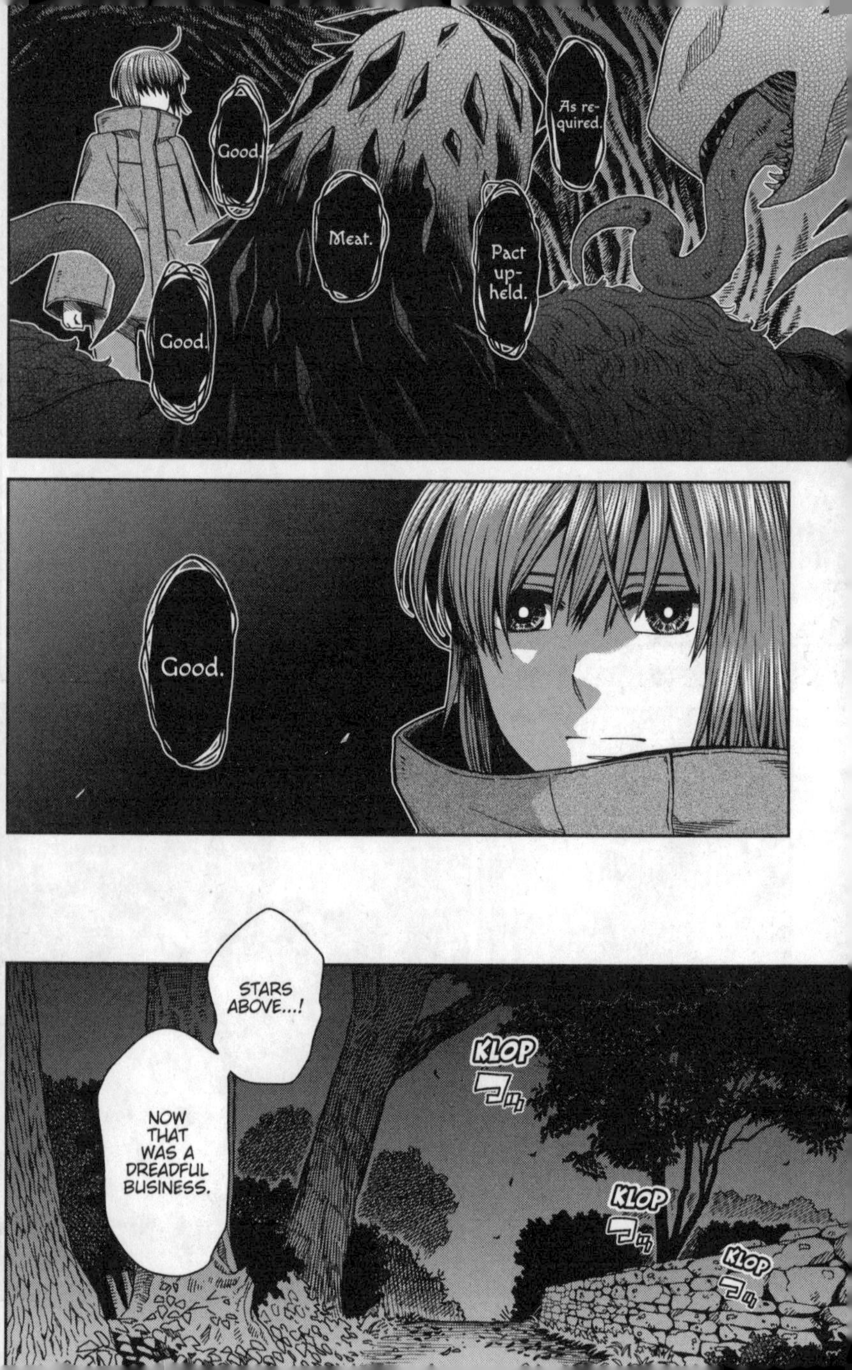
As re-quired.
Pact up-held.
Meat.
Good.
Good.
Good.
STARS ABOVE...!
NOW THAT WAS A DREADFUL BUSINESS.
KLOP
KLOP
KLOP

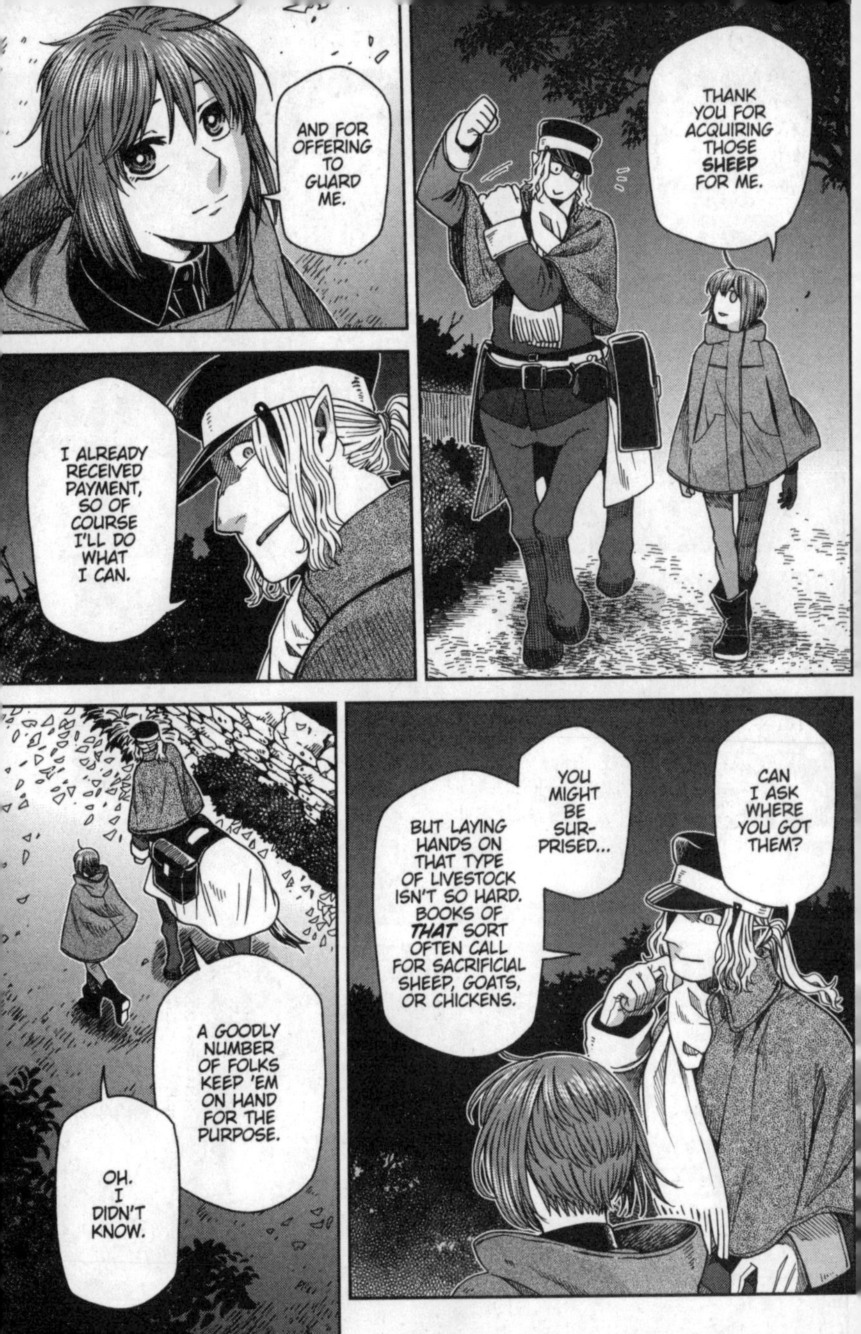
THANK YOU FOR ACQUIRING THOSE SHEEP FOR ME.
AND FOR OFFERING TO GUARD ME.
I ALREADY RECEIVED PAYMENT, SO OF COURSE I'LL DO WHAT I CAN.
CAN I ASK WHERE YOU GOT THEM?
YOU MIGHT BE SUR-PRISED...
BUT LAYING HANDS ON THAT TYPE OF LIVESTOCK ISN'T SO HARD. BOOKS OF THAT SORT OFTEN CALL FOR SACRIFICIAL SHEEP, GOATS, OR CHICKENS.
A GOODLY NUMBER OF FOLKS KEEP 'EM ON HAND FOR THE PURPOSE.
OH. I DIDN'T KNOW.

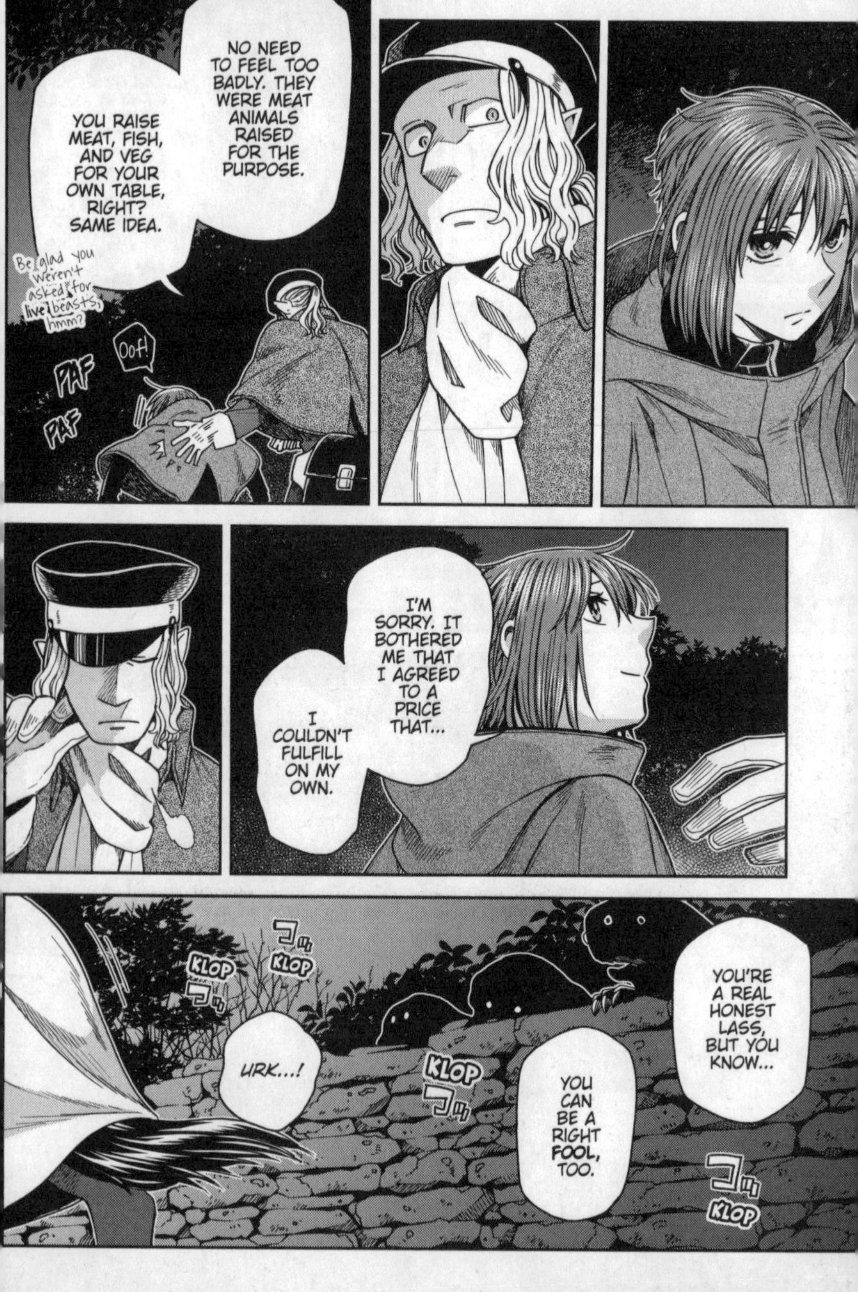
NO NEED TO FEEL TOO BADLY. THEY WERE MEAT ANIMALS RAISED FOR THE PURPOSE.
YOU RAISE MEAT, FISH, AND VEG FOR YOUR OWN TABLE, RIGHT? SAME IDEA.
Be glad you weren't asked for live beasts, hmm?
Oof!
PAF
PAF
I'M SORRY. IT BOTHERED ME THAT I AGREED TO A PRICE THAT...
I COULDN'T FULFILL ON MY OWN.
YOU'RE A REAL HONEST LASS, BUT YOU KNOW...
コッ
KLOP
YOU CAN BE A RIGHT FOOL, TOO.
コッ
KLOP
URK...!
コッ
KLOP
コッ
KLOP

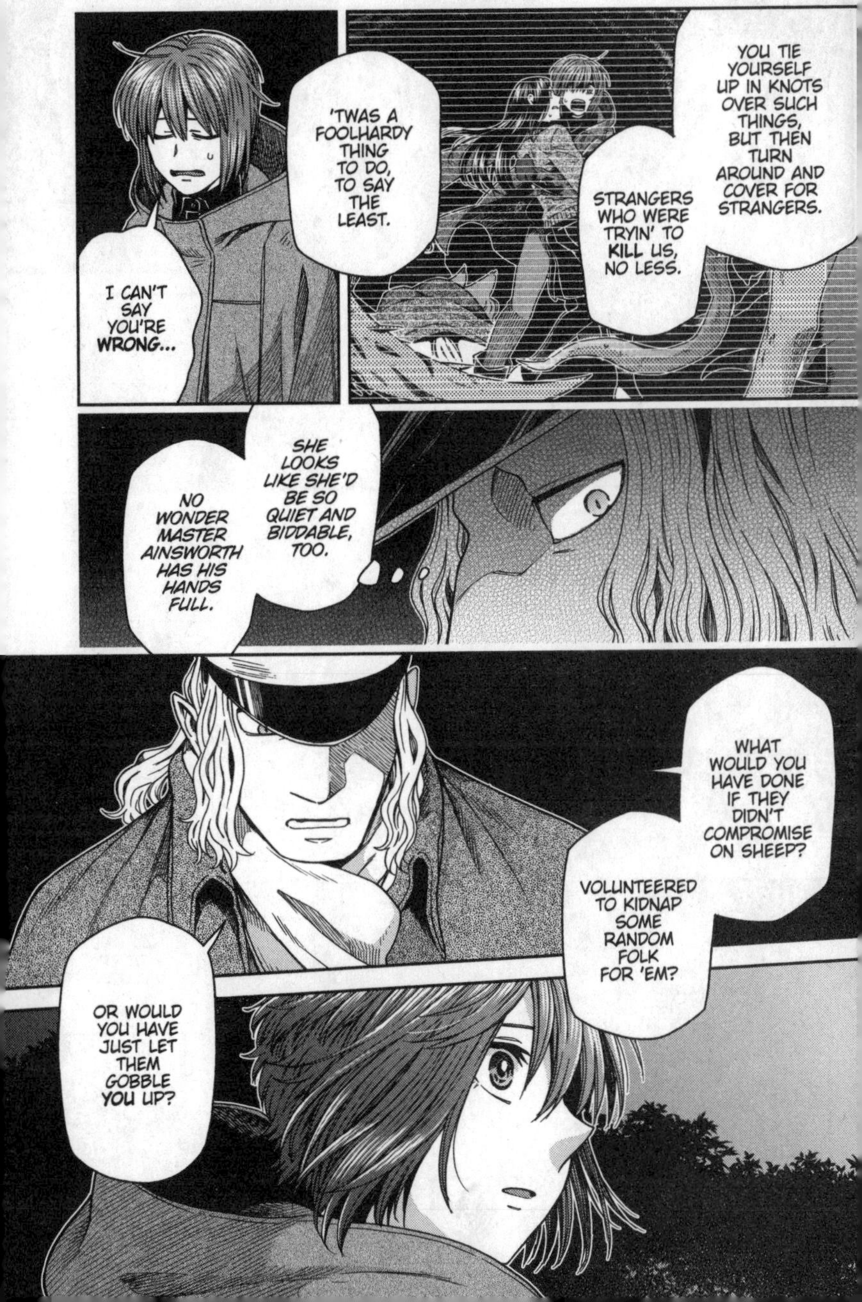
YOU TIE YOURSELF UP IN KNOTS OVER SUCH THINGS, BUT THEN TURN AROUND AND COVER FOR STRANGERS.
STRANGERS WHO WERE TRYIN' TO **KILL** US, NO LESS.
'TWAS A FOOLHARDY THING TO DO, TO SAY THE LEAST.
I CAN'T SAY YOU'RE **WRONG...**
SHE LOOKS LIKE SHE'D BE SO QUIET AND BIDDABLE, TOO.
NO WONDER MASTER AINSWORTH HAS HIS HANDS FULL.
WHAT WOULD YOU HAVE DONE IF THEY DIDN'T COMPROMISE ON SHEEP?
VOLUNTEERED TO KIDNAP SOME RANDOM FOLK FOR 'EM?
OR WOULD YOU HAVE JUST LET THEM GOBBLE **YOU UP?**

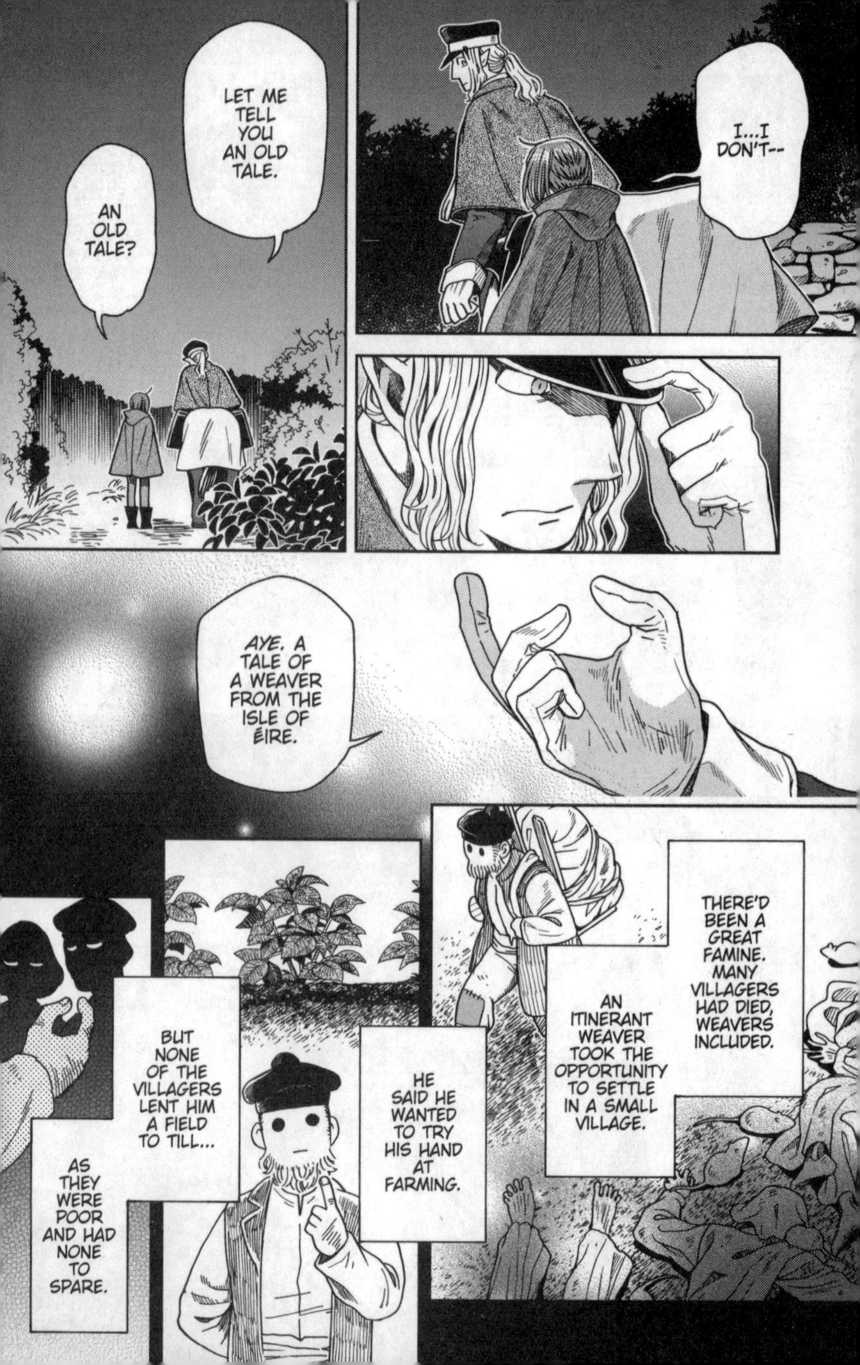
I...I DON'T--
LET ME TELL YOU AN OLD TALE.
AN OLD TALE?
AYE. A TALE OF A WEAVER FROM THE ISLE OF ÉIRE.
THERE'D BEEN A GREAT FAMINE. MANY VILLAGERS HAD DIED, WEAVERS INCLUDED.
AN ITINERANT WEAVER TOOK THE OPPORTUNITY TO SETTLE IN A SMALL VILLAGE.
HE SAID HE WANTED TO TRY HIS HAND AT FARMING.
BUT NONE OF THE VILLAGERS LENT HIM A FIELD TO TILL...
AS THEY WERE POOR AND HAD NONE TO SPARE.

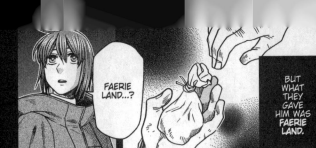

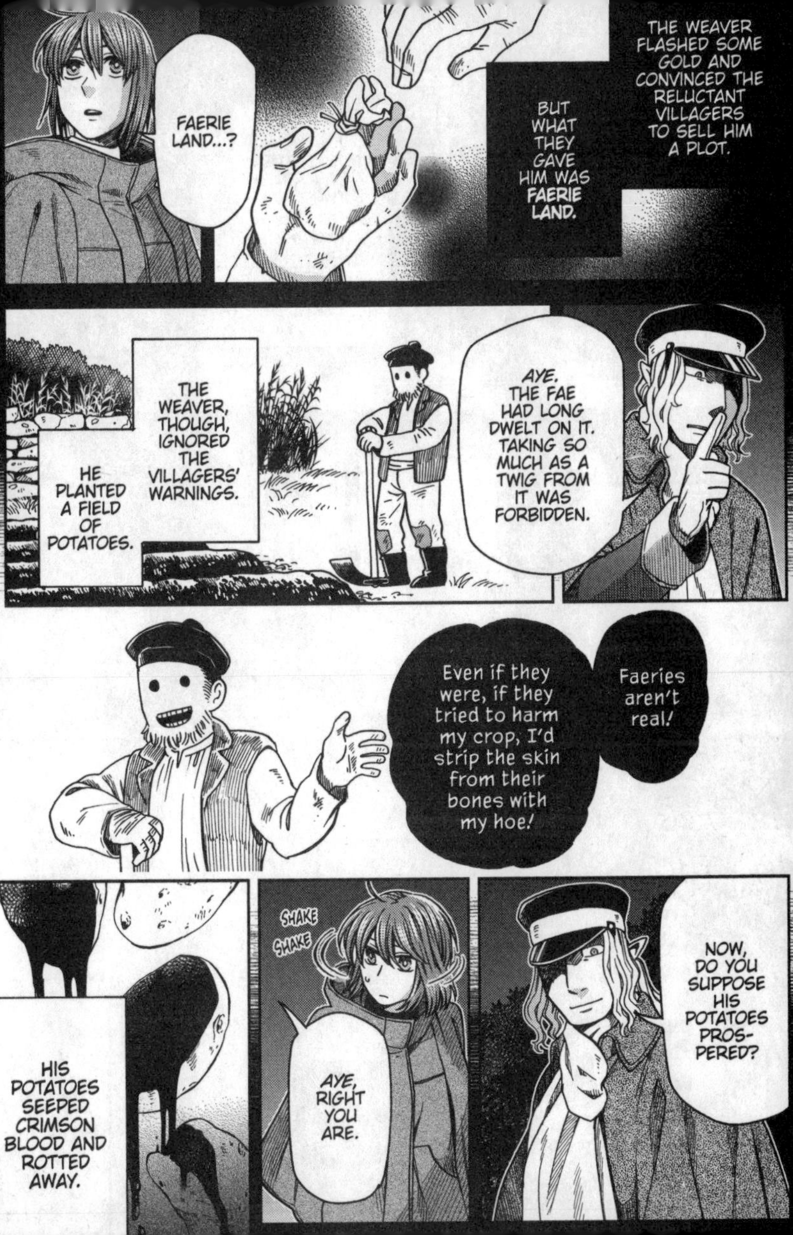
THE WEAVER FLASHED SOME GOLD AND CONVINCED THE RELUCTANT VILLAGERS TO SELL HIM A PLOT.
BUT WHAT THEY GAVE HIM WAS FAERIE LAND.
FAERIE LAND...?
AYE. THE FAE HAD LONG DWELT ON IT. TAKING SO MUCH AS A TWIG FROM IT WAS FORBIDDEN.
THE WEAVER, THOUGH, IGNORED THE VILLAGERS' WARNINGS.
HE PLANTED A FIELD OF POTATOES.
Faeries aren't real!
Even if they were, if they tried to harm my crop, I'd strip the skin from their bones with my hoe!
NOW, DO YOU SUPPOSE HIS POTATOES PROS-PERED?
SHAKE
SHAKE
AYE, RIGHT YOU ARE.
HIS POTATOES SEEPED CRIMSON BLOOD AND ROTTED AWAY.

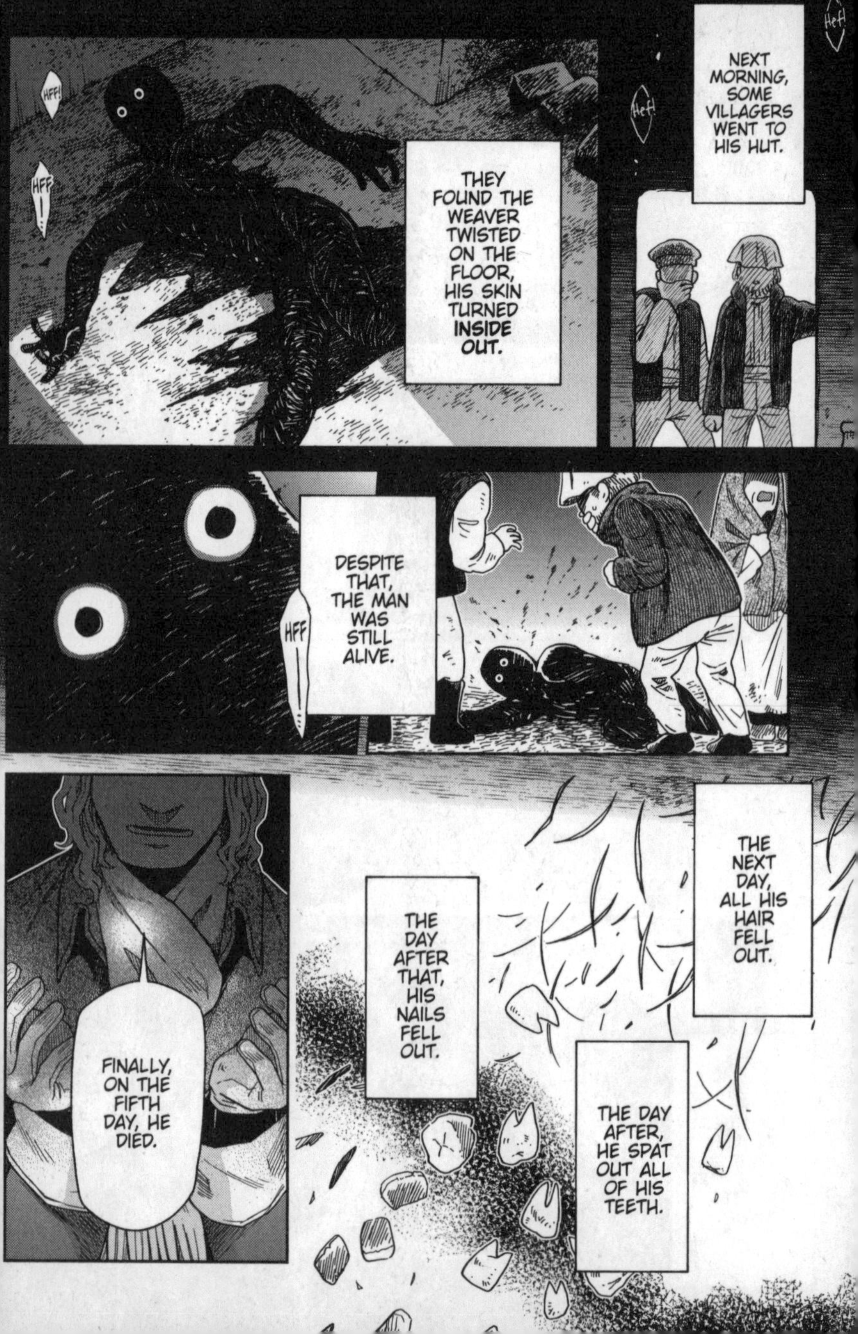
Hef!
NEXT MORNING, SOME VILLAGERS WENT TO HIS HUT.
Hef!
THEY FOUND THE WEAVER TWISTED ON THE FLOOR, HIS SKIN TURNED INSIDE OUT.
HFF!
HFF!
DESPITE THAT, THE MAN WAS STILL ALIVE.
HFF
THE NEXT DAY, ALL HIS HAIR FELL OUT.
THE DAY AFTER THAT, HIS NAILS FELL OUT.
THE DAY AFTER, HE SPAT OUT ALL OF HIS TEETH.
FINALLY, ON THE FIFTH DAY, HE DIED.

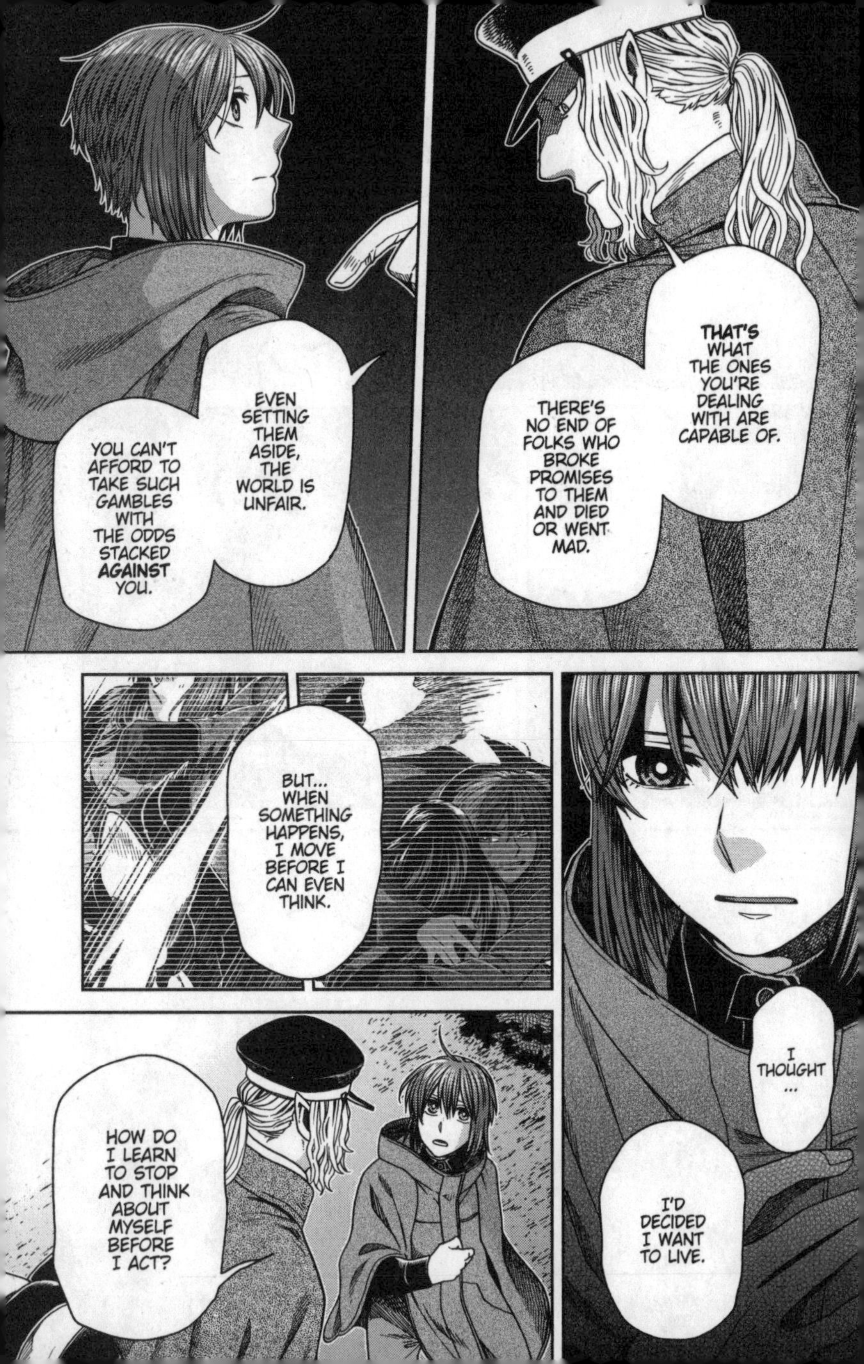
THAT'S WHAT THE ONES YOU'RE DEALING WITH ARE CAPABLE OF.
THERE'S NO END OF FOLKS WHO BROKE PROMISES TO THEM AND DIED OR WENT MAD.
EVEN SETTING THEM ASIDE, THE WORLD IS UNFAIR.
YOU CAN'T AFFORD TO TAKE SUCH GAMBLES WITH THE ODDS STACKED **AGAINST** YOU.
I THOUGHT...
I'D DECIDED I WANT TO LIVE.
BUT... WHEN SOMETHING HAPPENS, I MOVE BEFORE I CAN EVEN THINK.
HOW DO I LEARN TO STOP AND THINK ABOUT MYSELF BEFORE I ACT?

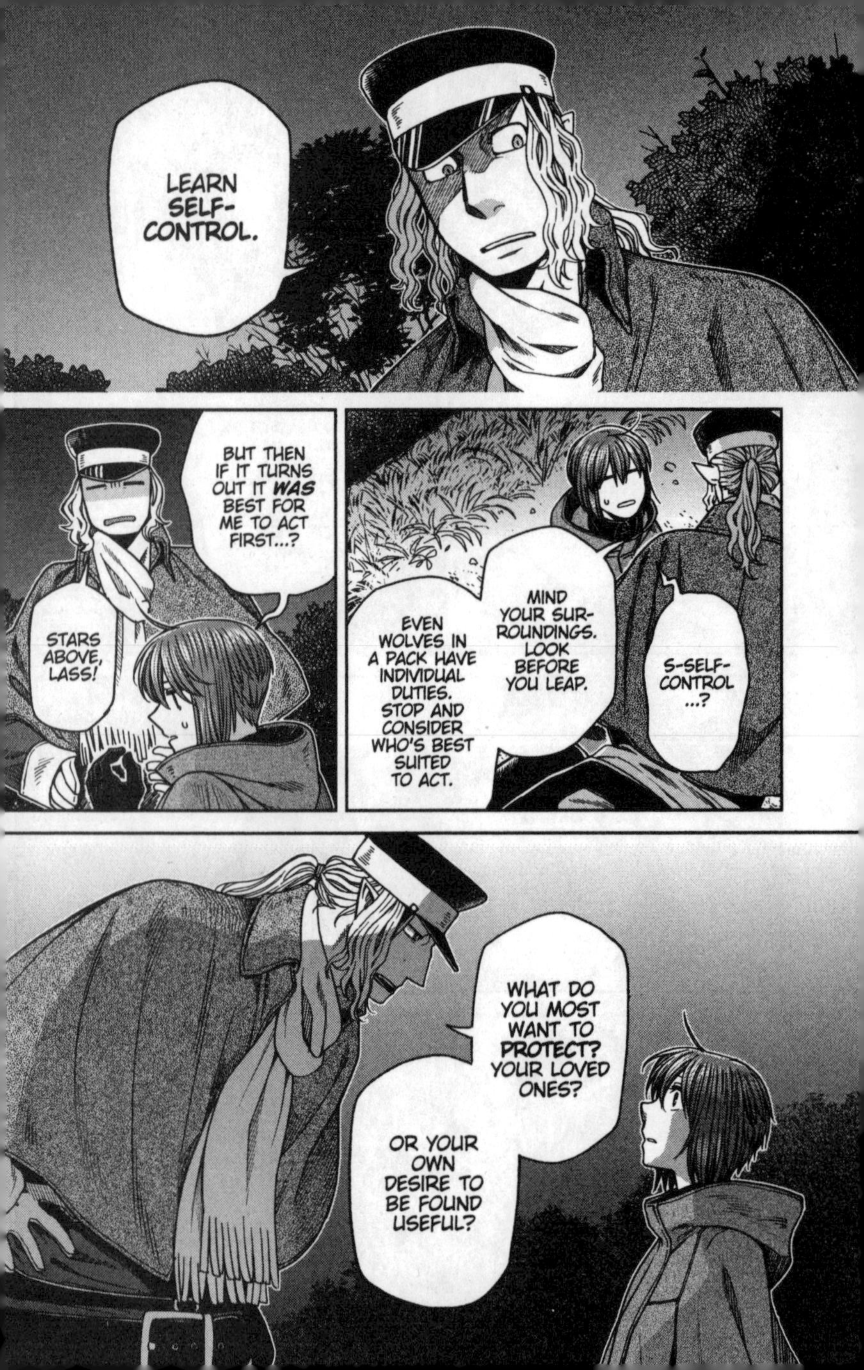
LEARN SELF-CONTROL.
S-SELF-CONTROL ...?
MIND YOUR SURROUNDINGS. LOOK BEFORE YOU LEAP.
EVEN WOLVES IN A PACK HAVE INDIVIDUAL DUTIES. STOP AND CONSIDER WHO'S BEST SUITED TO ACT.
BUT THEN IF IT TURNS OUT IT *WAS* BEST FOR ME TO ACT FIRST...?
STARS ABOVE, LASS!
WHAT DO YOU MOST WANT TO **PROTECT**? YOUR LOVED ONES?
OR YOUR OWN DESIRE TO BE FOUND USEFUL?

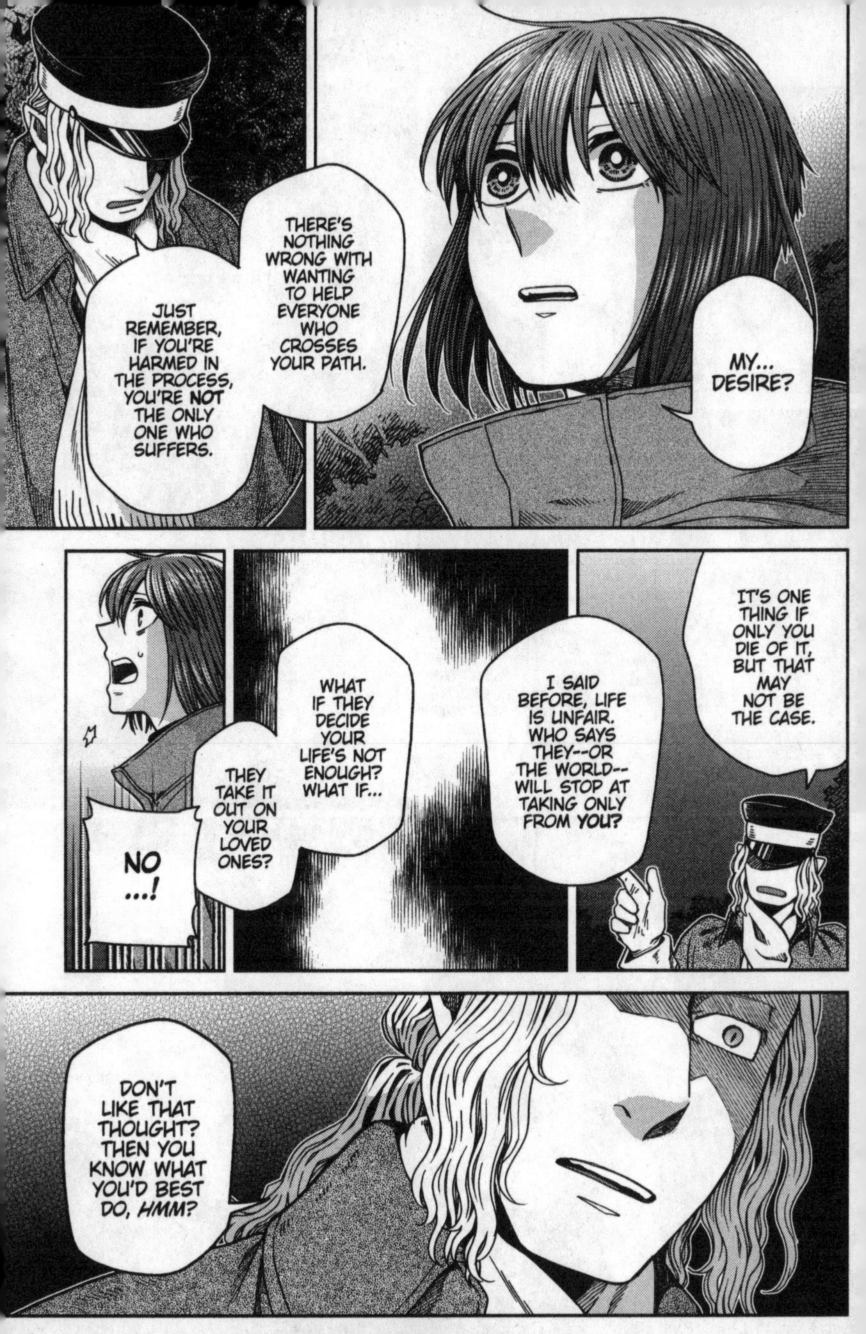
MY... DESIRE?
THERE'S NOTHING WRONG WITH WANTING TO HELP EVERYONE WHO CROSSES YOUR PATH.
JUST REMEMBER, IF YOU'RE HARMED IN THE PROCESS, YOU'RE **NOT** THE ONLY ONE WHO SUFFERS.
IT'S ONE THING IF ONLY YOU DIE OF IT, BUT THAT MAY NOT BE THE CASE.
I SAID BEFORE, LIFE IS UNFAIR. WHO SAYS THEY--OR THE WORLD--WILL STOP AT TAKING ONLY FROM **YOU**?
WHAT IF THEY DECIDE YOUR LIFE'S NOT ENOUGH? WHAT IF...
THEY TAKE IT OUT ON YOUR LOVED ONES?
NO ...!
DON'T LIKE THAT THOUGHT? THEN YOU KNOW WHAT YOU'D BEST DO, *HMM*?

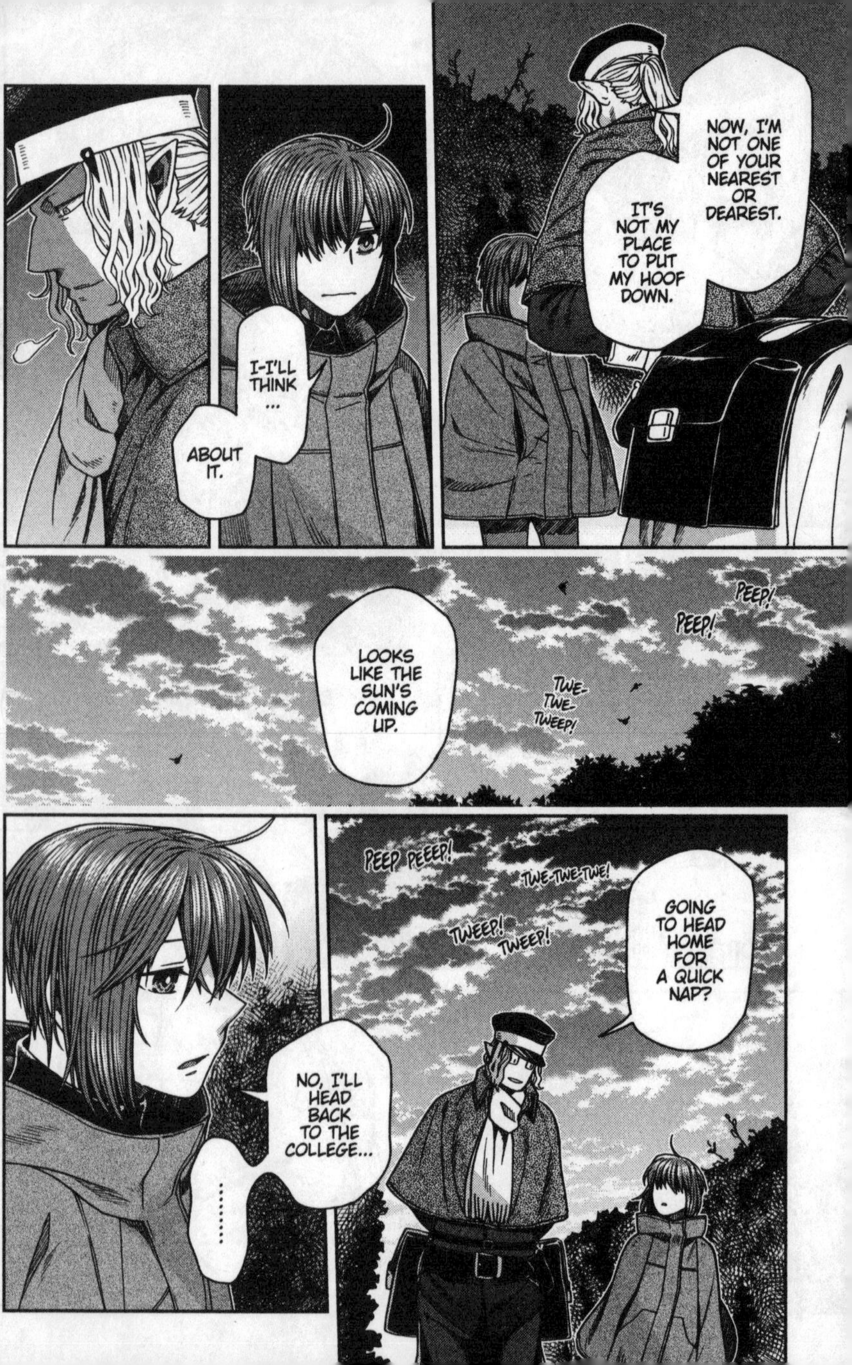
NOW, I'M NOT ONE OF YOUR NEAREST OR DEAREST.
IT'S NOT MY PLACE TO PUT MY HOOF DOWN.
I-I'LL THINK...
ABOUT IT.
PEEP!
PEEP!
TWE-TWE-TWEEP!
LOOKS LIKE THE SUN'S COMING UP.
TWE-TWE-TWE!
PEEP PEEEP!
GOING TO HEAD HOME FOR A QUICK NAP?
TWEEP!
TWEEP!
NO, I'LL HEAD BACK TO THE COLLEGE...
......

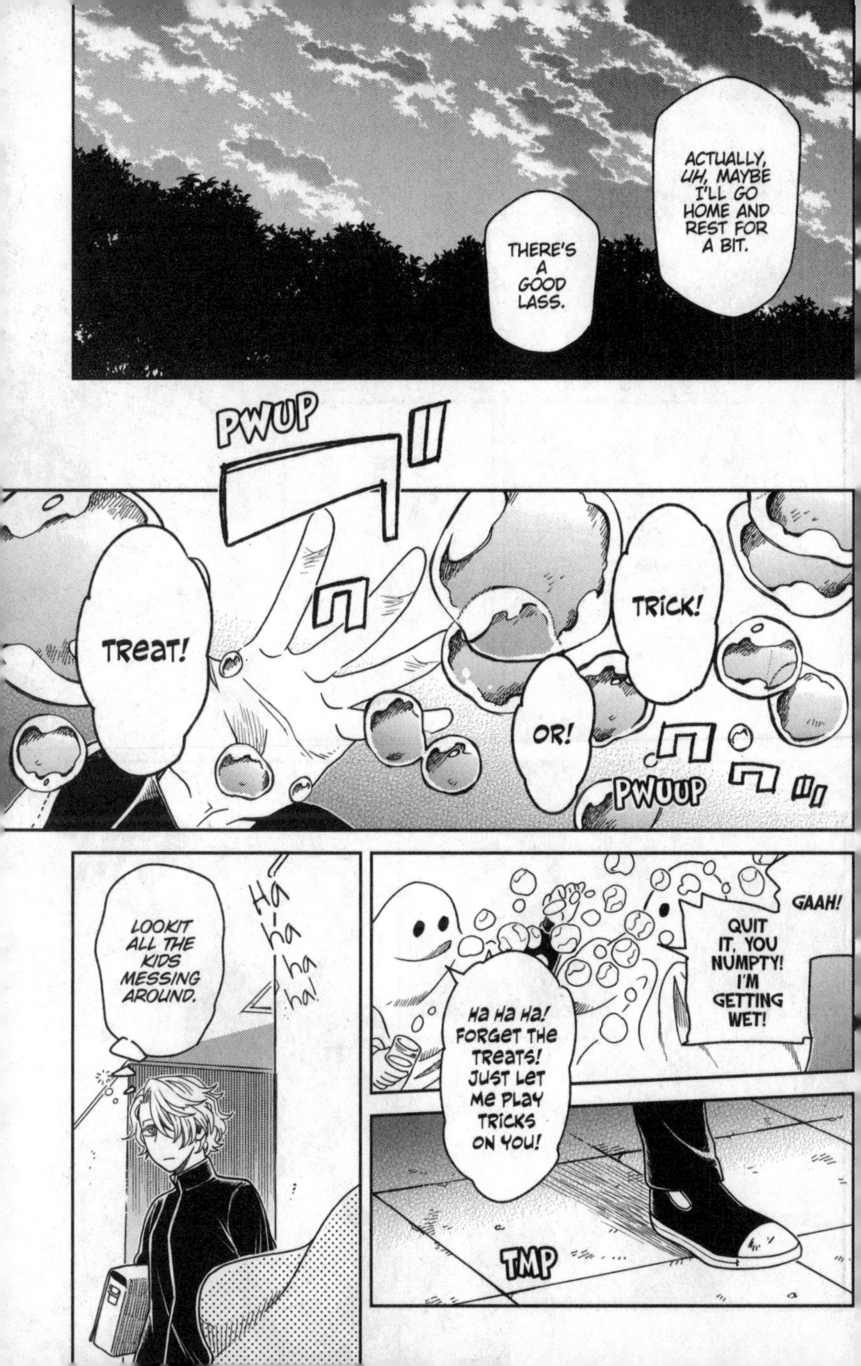
ACTUALLY, UH, MAYBE I'LL GO HOME AND REST FOR A BIT.
THERE'S A GOOD LASS.
PWUP
TRICK!
OR!
TREAT!
PWUUP
GAAH!
QUIT IT, YOU NUMPTY! I'M GETTING WET!
HA HA HA! FORGET THE TREATS! JUST LET ME PLAY TRICKS ON YOU!
TMP
Ha ha ha ha!
LOOKIT ALL THE KIDS MESSING AROUND.

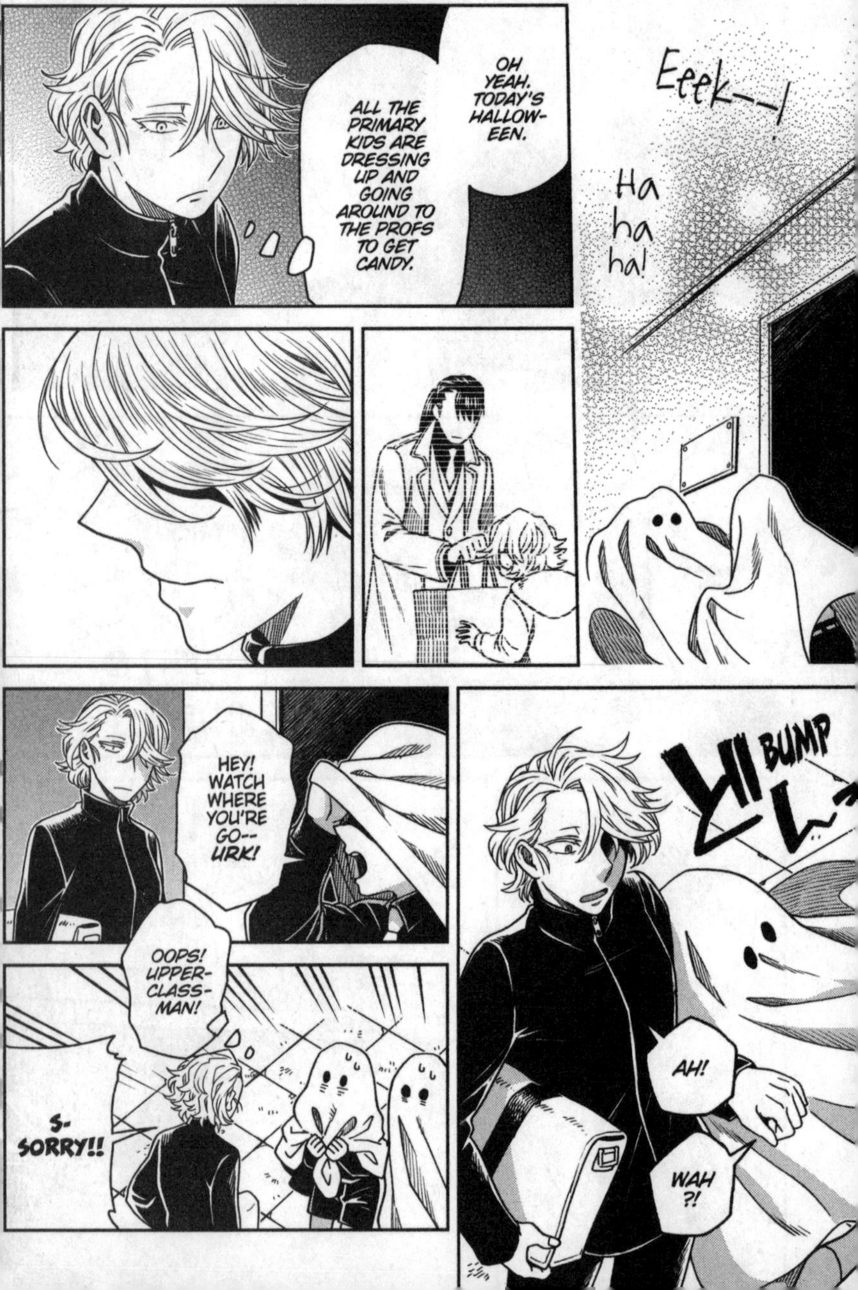
Eeek---!
Ha ha ha!
OH YEAH. TODAY'S HALLOWEEN.
ALL THE PRIMARY KIDS ARE DRESSING UP AND GOING AROUND TO THE PROFS TO GET CANDY.
BUMP
AH!
WAH?!
HEY! WATCH WHERE YOU'RE GO-- URK!
OOPS! UPPER-CLASSMAN!
S-SORRY!!

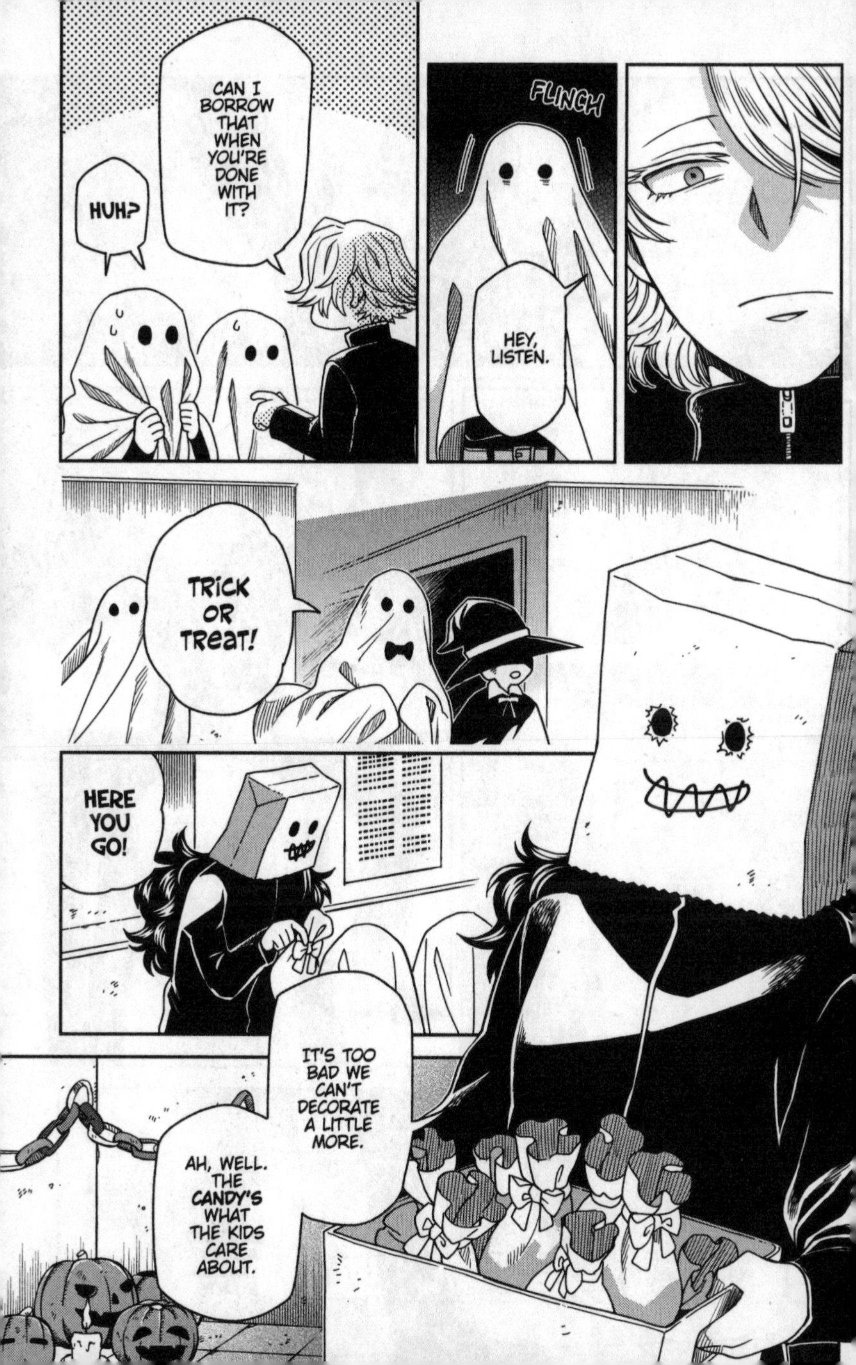
FLINCH
HEY, LISTEN.
CAN I BORROW THAT WHEN YOU'RE DONE WITH IT?
HUH?
TRICK OR TREAT!
HERE YOU GO!
IT'S TOO BAD WE CAN'T DECORATE A LITTLE MORE.
AH, WELL. THE CANDY'S WHAT THE KIDS CARE ABOUT.

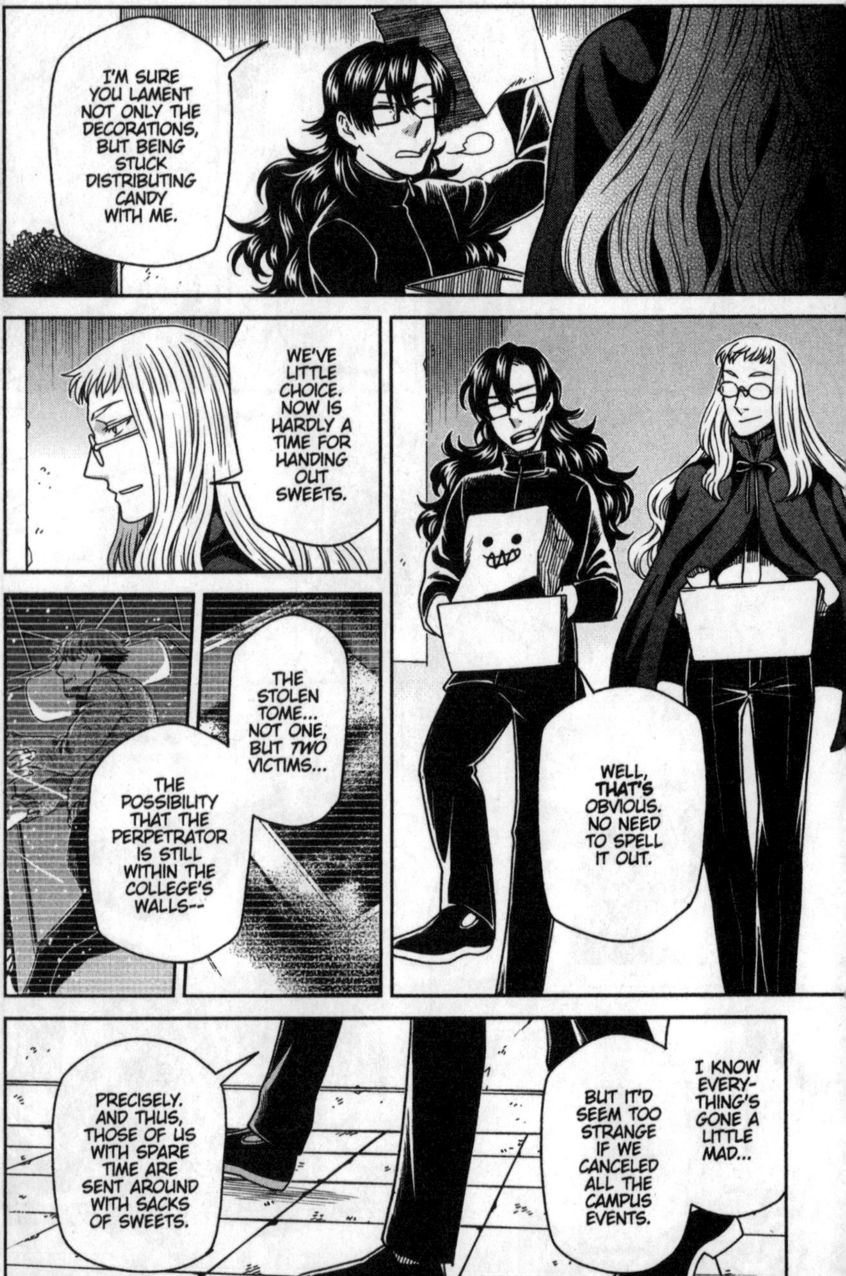
I'M SURE YOU LAMENT NOT ONLY THE DECORATIONS, BUT BEING STUCK DISTRIBUTING CANDY WITH ME.
WELL, **THAT'S** OBVIOUS. NO NEED TO SPELL IT OUT.
WE'VE LITTLE CHOICE. NOW IS HARDLY A TIME FOR HANDING OUT SWEETS.
THE STOLEN TOME... NOT ONE, BUT *TWO* VICTIMS...
THE POSSIBILITY THAT THE PERPETRATOR IS STILL WITHIN THE COLLEGE'S WALLS--
I KNOW EVERY-THING'S GONE A LITTLE MAD...
BUT IT'D SEEM TOO STRANGE IF WE CANCELED ALL THE CAMPUS EVENTS.
PRECISELY. AND THUS, THOSE OF US WITH SPARE TIME ARE SENT AROUND WITH SACKS OF SWEETS.

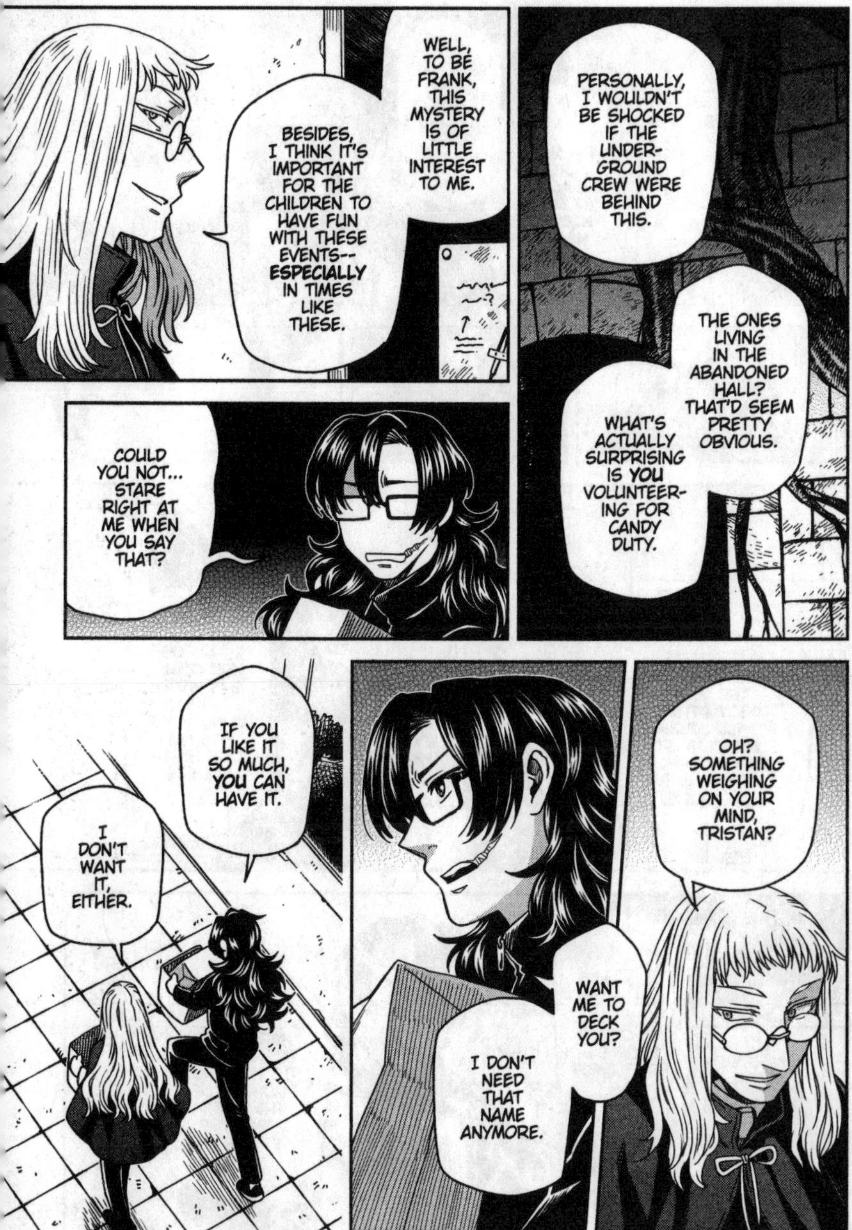
PERSONALLY, I WOULDN'T BE SHOCKED IF THE UNDER-GROUND CREW WERE BEHIND THIS.
THE ONES LIVING IN THE ABANDONED HALL? THAT'D SEEM PRETTY OBVIOUS.
WHAT'S ACTUALLY SURPRISING IS YOU VOLUNTEERING FOR CANDY DUTY.
WELL, TO BE FRANK, THIS MYSTERY IS OF LITTLE INTEREST TO ME.
BESIDES, I THINK IT'S IMPORTANT FOR THE CHILDREN TO HAVE FUN WITH THESE EVENTS-- ESPECIALLY IN TIMES LIKE THESE.
COULD YOU NOT... STARE RIGHT AT ME WHEN YOU SAY THAT?
OH? SOMETHING WEIGHING ON YOUR MIND, TRISTAN?
WANT ME TO DECK YOU?
I DON'T NEED THAT NAME ANYMORE.
IF YOU LIKE IT SO MUCH, YOU CAN HAVE IT.
I DON'T WANT IT, EITHER.

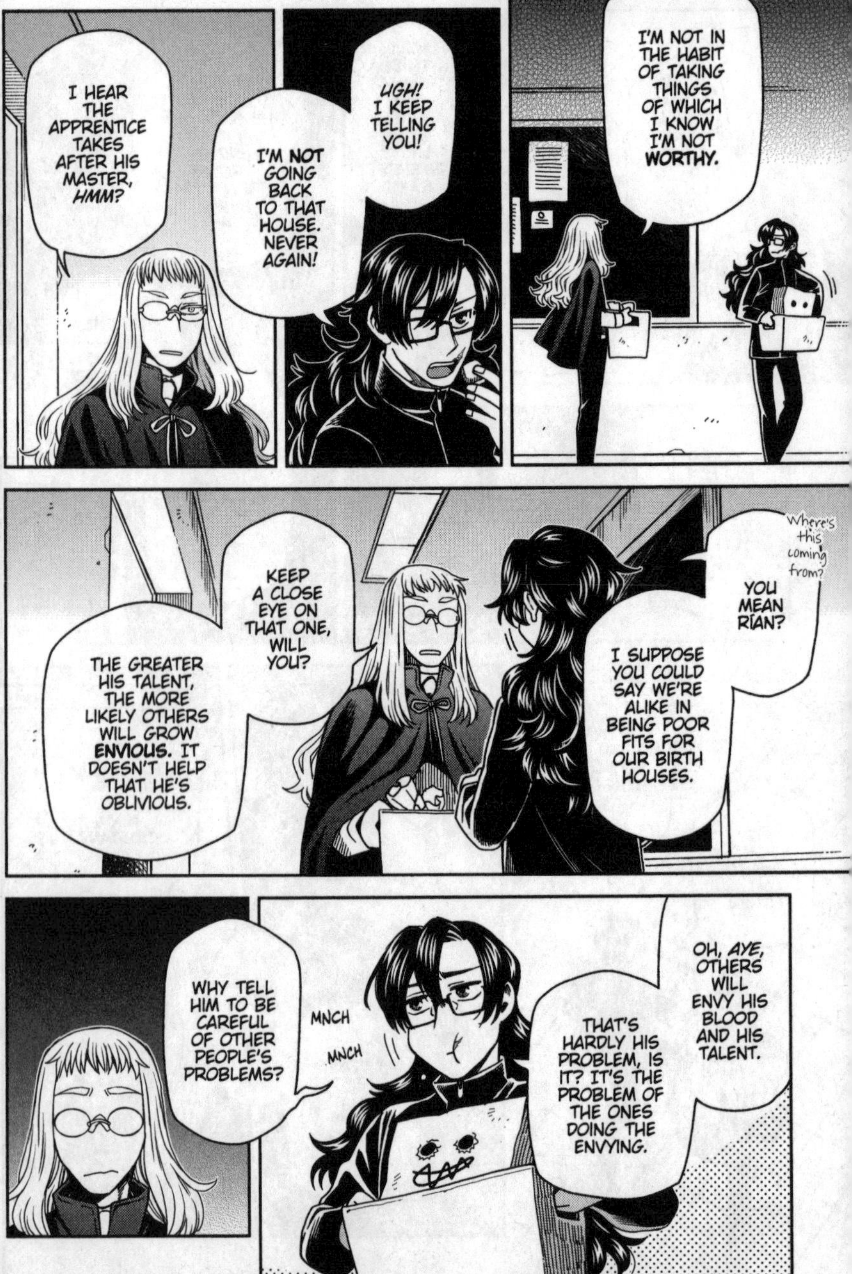
I'M NOT IN THE HABIT OF TAKING THINGS OF WHICH I KNOW I'M NOT WORTHY.
UGH! I KEEP TELLING YOU!
I'M NOT GOING BACK TO THAT HOUSE. NEVER AGAIN!
I HEAR THE APPRENTICE TAKES AFTER HIS MASTER, HMM?
Where's this coming from?
YOU MEAN RÍAN?
I SUPPOSE YOU COULD SAY WE'RE ALIKE IN BEING POOR FITS FOR OUR BIRTH HOUSES.
KEEP A CLOSE EYE ON THAT ONE, WILL YOU?
THE GREATER HIS TALENT, THE MORE LIKELY OTHERS WILL GROW ENVIOUS. IT DOESN'T HELP THAT HE'S OBLIVIOUS.
OH, AYE, OTHERS WILL ENVY HIS BLOOD AND HIS TALENT.
THAT'S HARDLY HIS PROBLEM, IS IT? IT'S THE PROBLEM OF THE ONES DOING THE ENVYING.
MNCH
MNCH
WHY TELL HIM TO BE CAREFUL OF OTHER PEOPLE'S PROBLEMS?

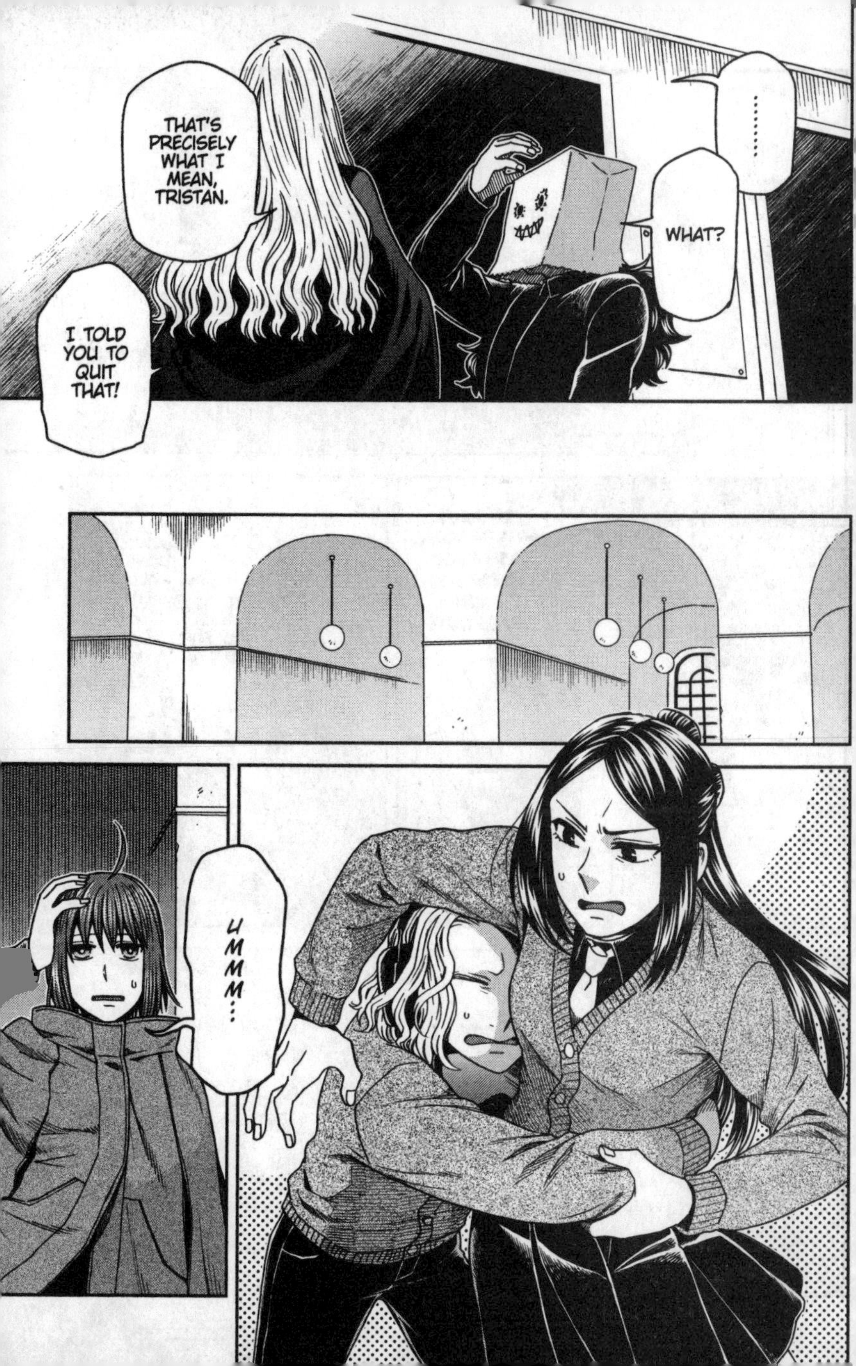
......
WHAT?
THAT'S PRECISELY WHAT I MEAN, TRISTAN.
I TOLD YOU TO QUIT THAT!
UMMM...

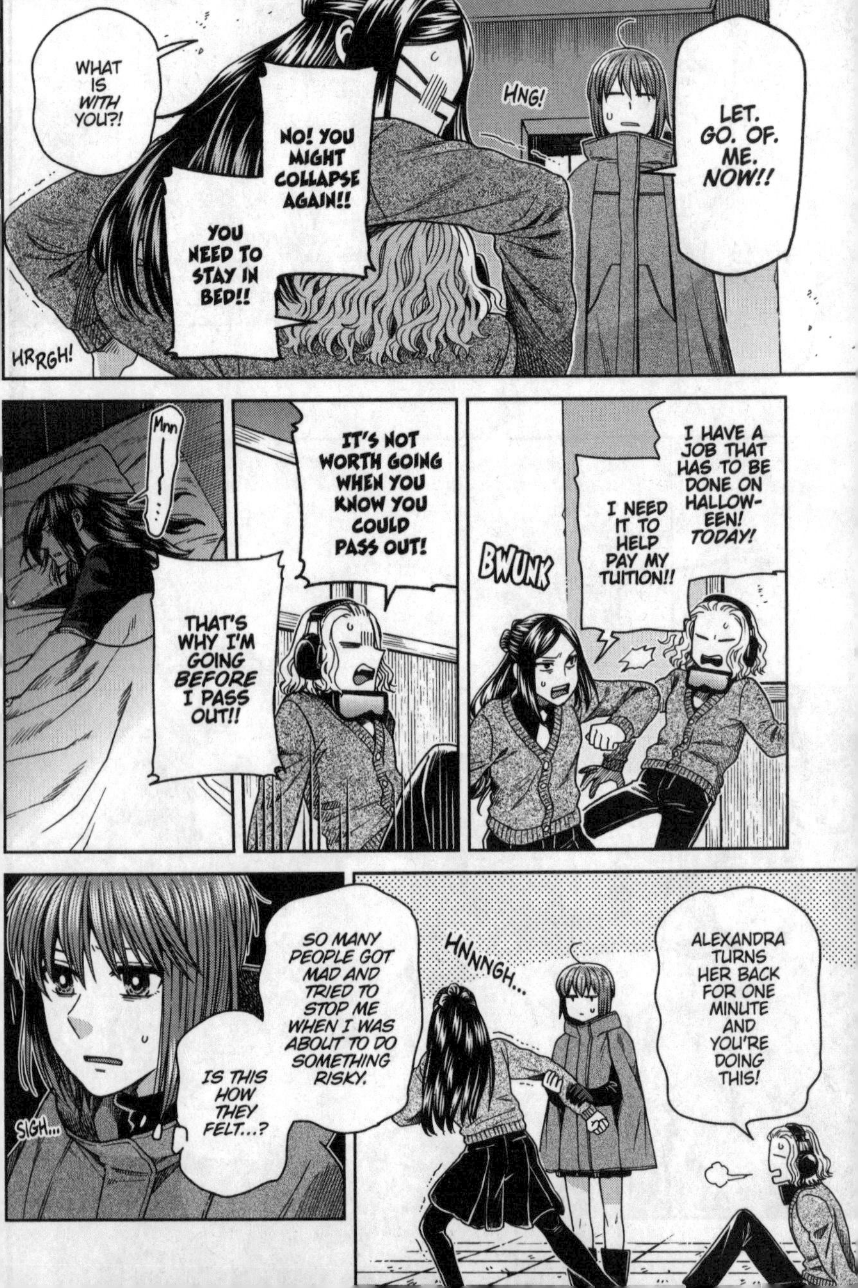
LET. GO. OF. ME. NOW!!
HNG!
NO! YOU MIGHT COLLAPSE AGAIN!!
YOU NEED TO STAY IN BED!!
WHAT IS WITH YOU?!
HRRGH!
I HAVE A JOB THAT HAS TO BE DONE ON HALLOW-EEN! TODAY!
I NEED IT TO HELP PAY MY TUITION!!
BWUNK
IT'S NOT WORTH GOING WHEN YOU KNOW YOU COULD PASS OUT!
THAT'S WHY I'M GOING BEFORE I PASS OUT!!
Mnn...
ALEXANDRA TURNS HER BACK FOR ONE MINUTE AND YOU'RE DOING THIS!
HNNNGH...
SO MANY PEOPLE GOT MAD AND TRIED TO STOP ME WHEN I WAS ABOUT TO DO SOMETHING RISKY.
IS THIS HOW THEY FELT...?
SIGH...

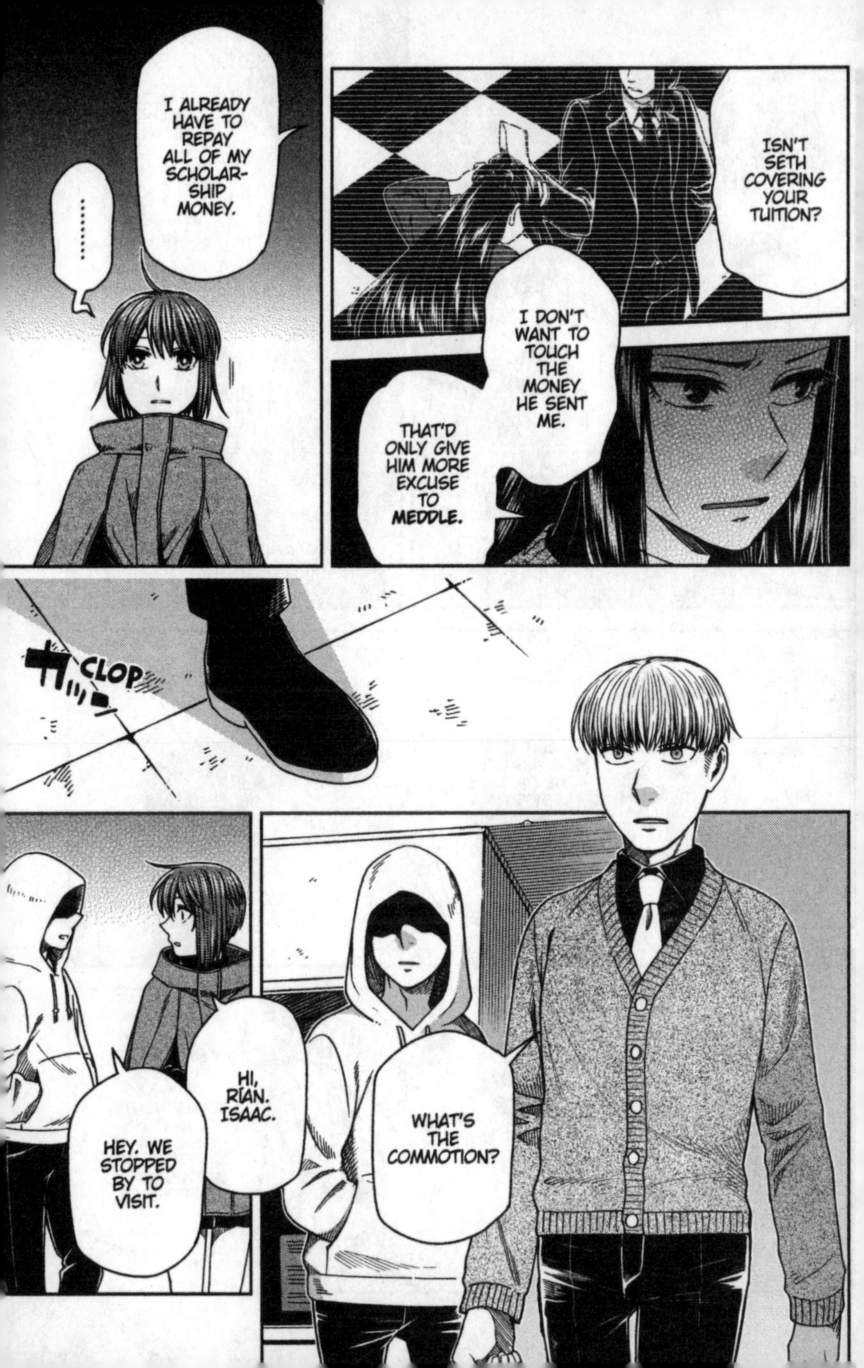
ISN'T SETH COVERING YOUR TUITION?
I DON'T WANT TO TOUCH THE MONEY HE SENT ME.
THAT'D ONLY GIVE HIM MORE EXCUSE TO MEDDLE.
I ALREADY HAVE TO REPAY ALL OF MY SCHOLARSHIP MONEY.
......
CLOP
WHAT'S THE COMMOTION?
HI, RIAN. ISAAC.
HEY. WE STOPPED BY TO VISIT.

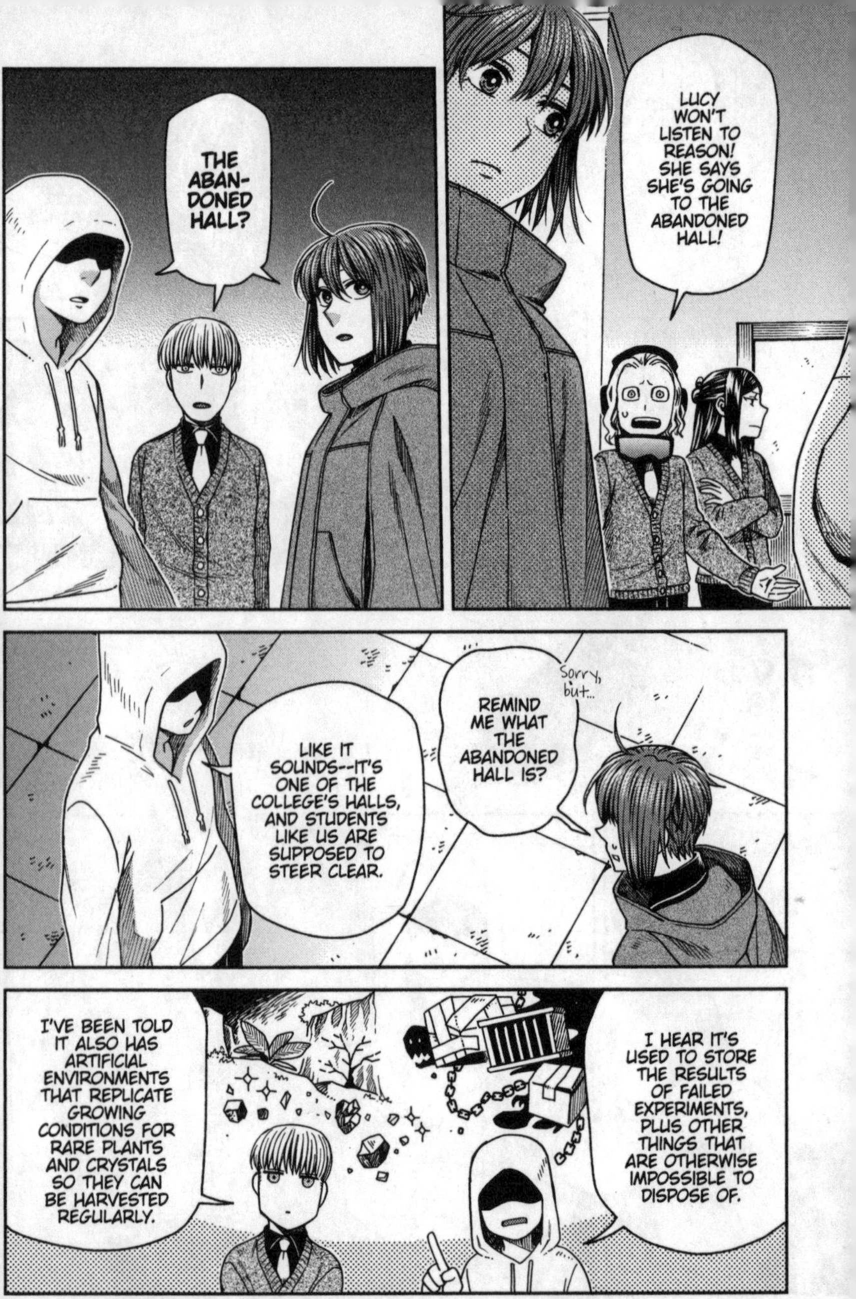
LUCY WON'T LISTEN TO REASON! SHE SAYS SHE'S GOING TO THE ABANDONED HALL!
THE ABAN-DONED HALL?
Sorry, but...
REMIND ME WHAT THE ABANDONED HALL IS?
LIKE IT SOUNDS--IT'S ONE OF THE COLLEGE'S HALLS, AND STUDENTS LIKE US ARE SUPPOSED TO STEER CLEAR.
I HEAR IT'S USED TO STORE THE RESULTS OF FAILED EXPERIMENTS, PLUS OTHER THINGS THAT ARE OTHERWISE IMPOSSIBLE TO DISPOSE OF.
I'VE BEEN TOLD IT ALSO HAS ARTIFICIAL ENVIRONMENTS THAT REPLICATE GROWING CONDITIONS FOR RARE PLANTS AND CRYSTALS SO THEY CAN BE HARVESTED REGULARLY.

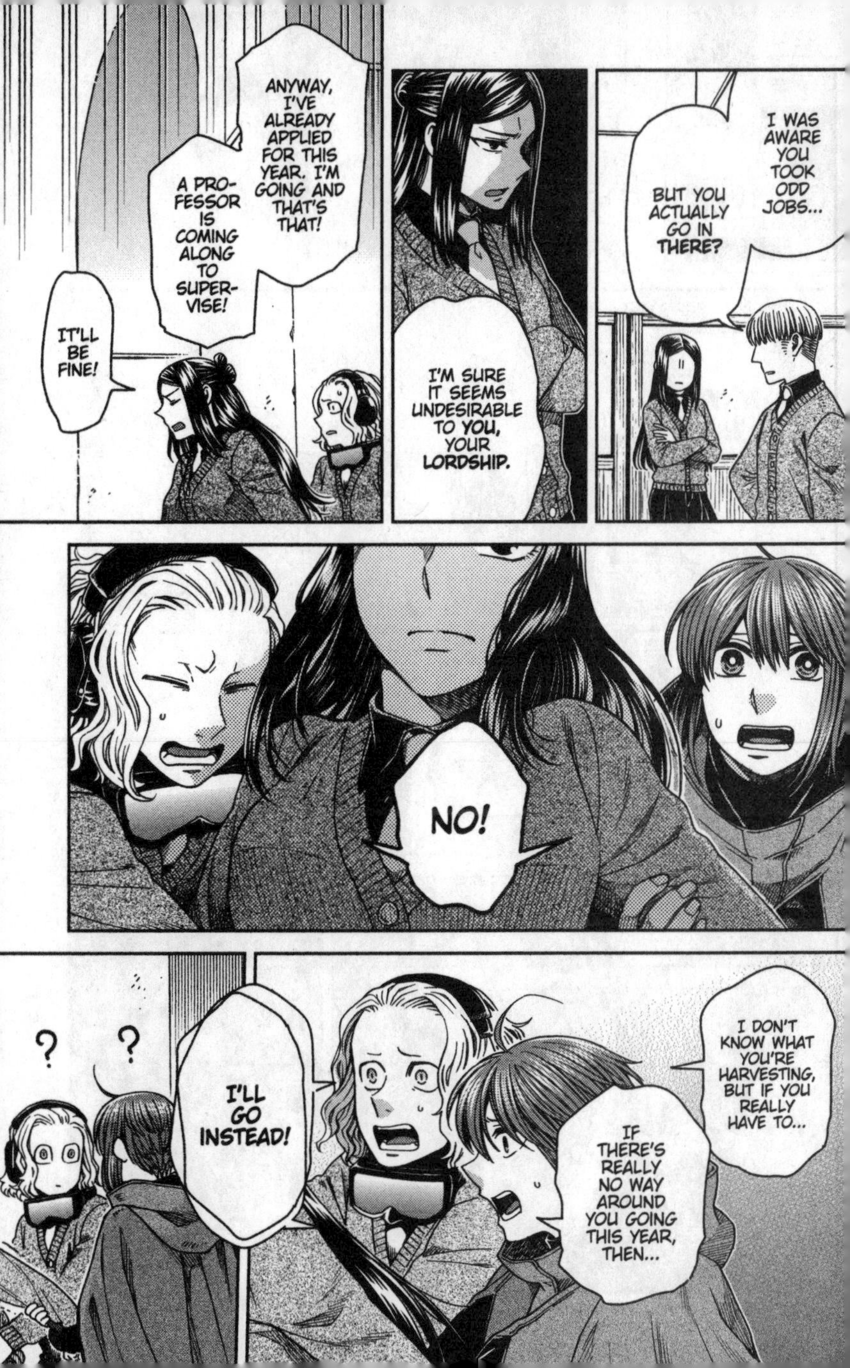

I WAS AWARE YOU TOOK ODD JOBS...
BUT YOU ACTUALLY GO IN THERE?
I'M SURE IT SEEMS UNDESIRABLE TO YOU, YOUR LORDSHIP.
ANYWAY, I'VE ALREADY APPLIED FOR THIS YEAR. I'M GOING AND THAT'S THAT!
A PRO-FESSOR IS COMING ALONG TO SUPER-VISE!
IT'LL BE FINE!
NO!
I DON'T KNOW WHAT YOU'RE HARVESTING, BUT IF YOU REALLY HAVE TO...
IF THERE'S REALLY NO WAY AROUND YOU GOING THIS YEAR, THEN...
I'LL GO INSTEAD!
?
?

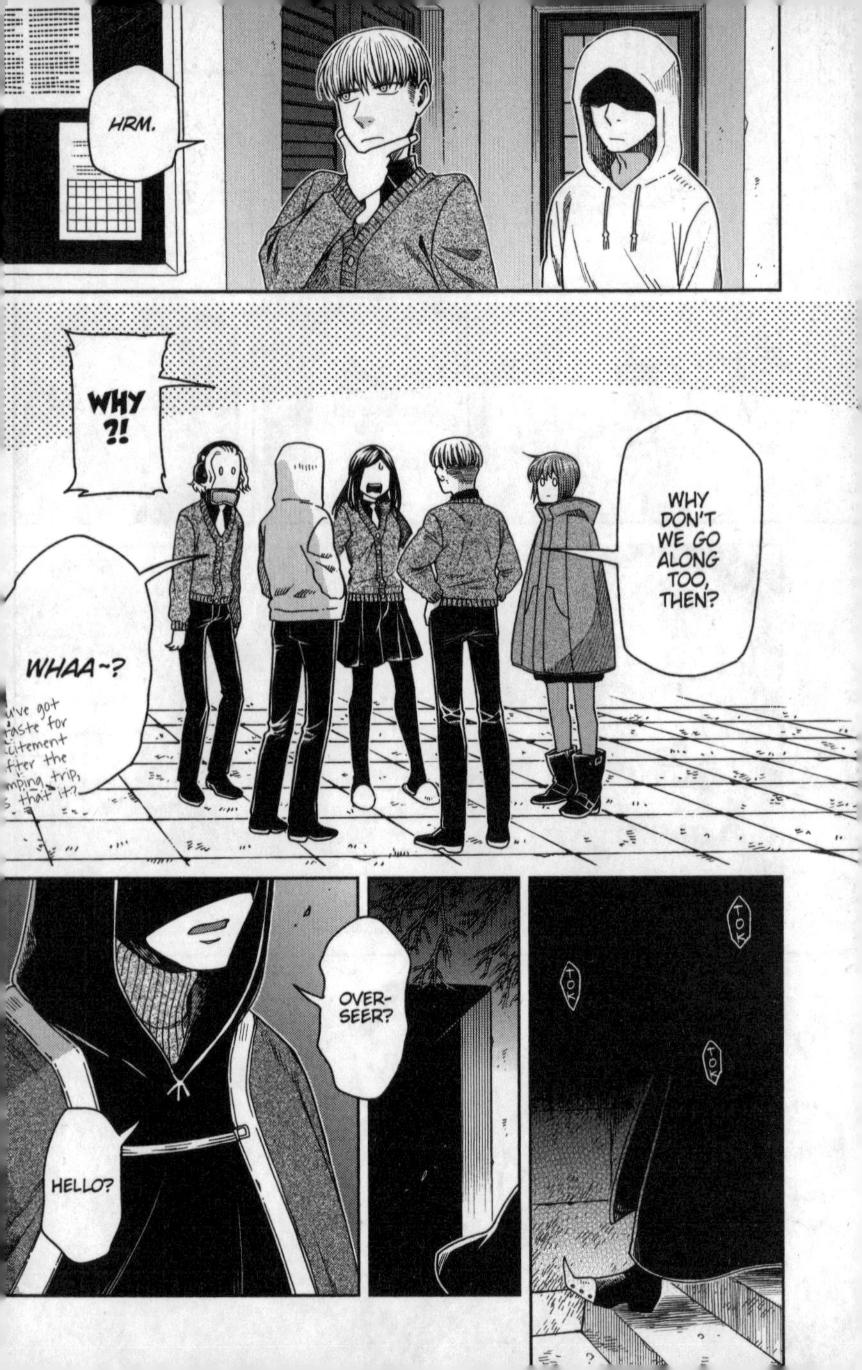
HRM.
WHY DON'T WE GO ALONG TOO, THEN?
WHY ?!
WHAA~?
u've got taste for citement fter the mping trip, s that it?
TOK
TOK
TOK
OVER-SEER?
HELLO?

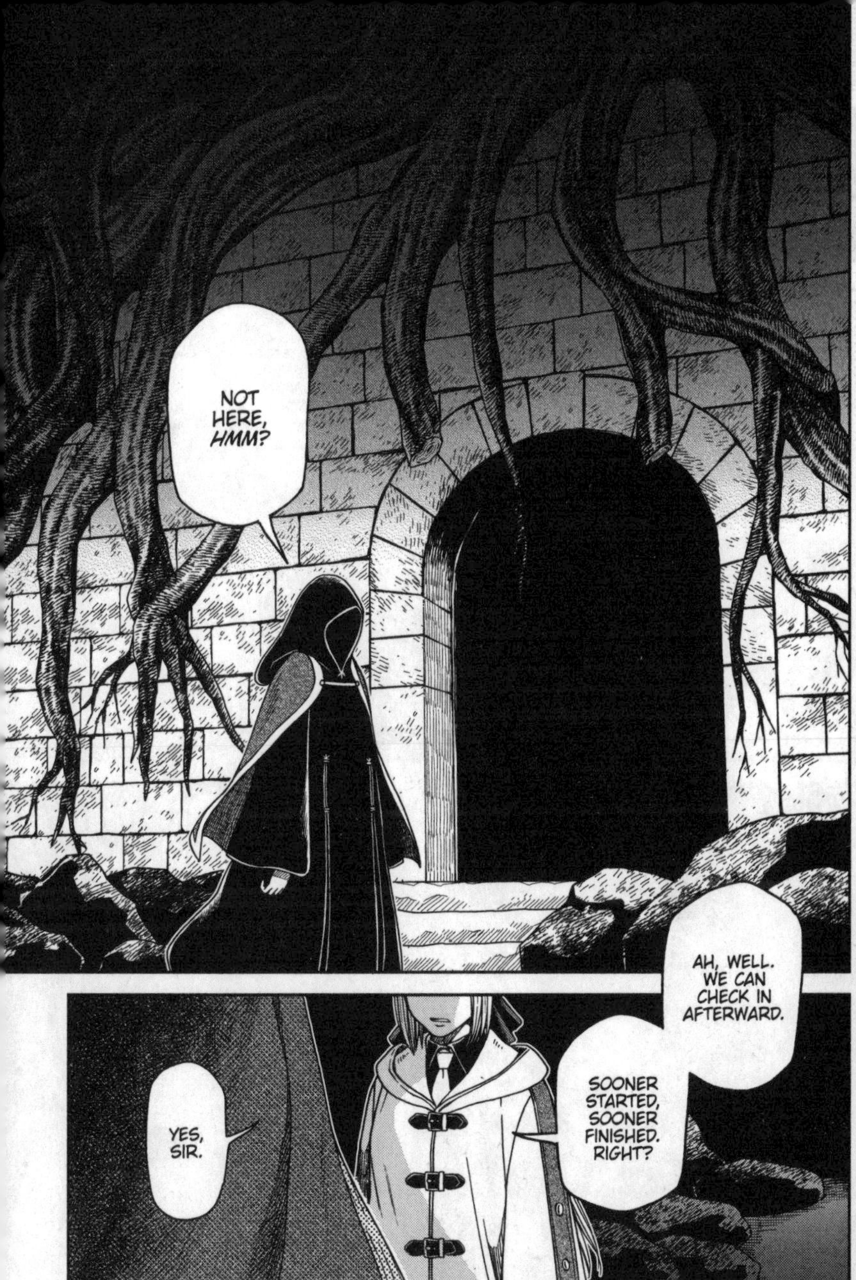
NOT HERE, HMM?
AH, WELL. WE CAN CHECK IN AFTERWARD.
SOONER STARTED, SOONER FINISHED. RIGHT?
YES, SIR.

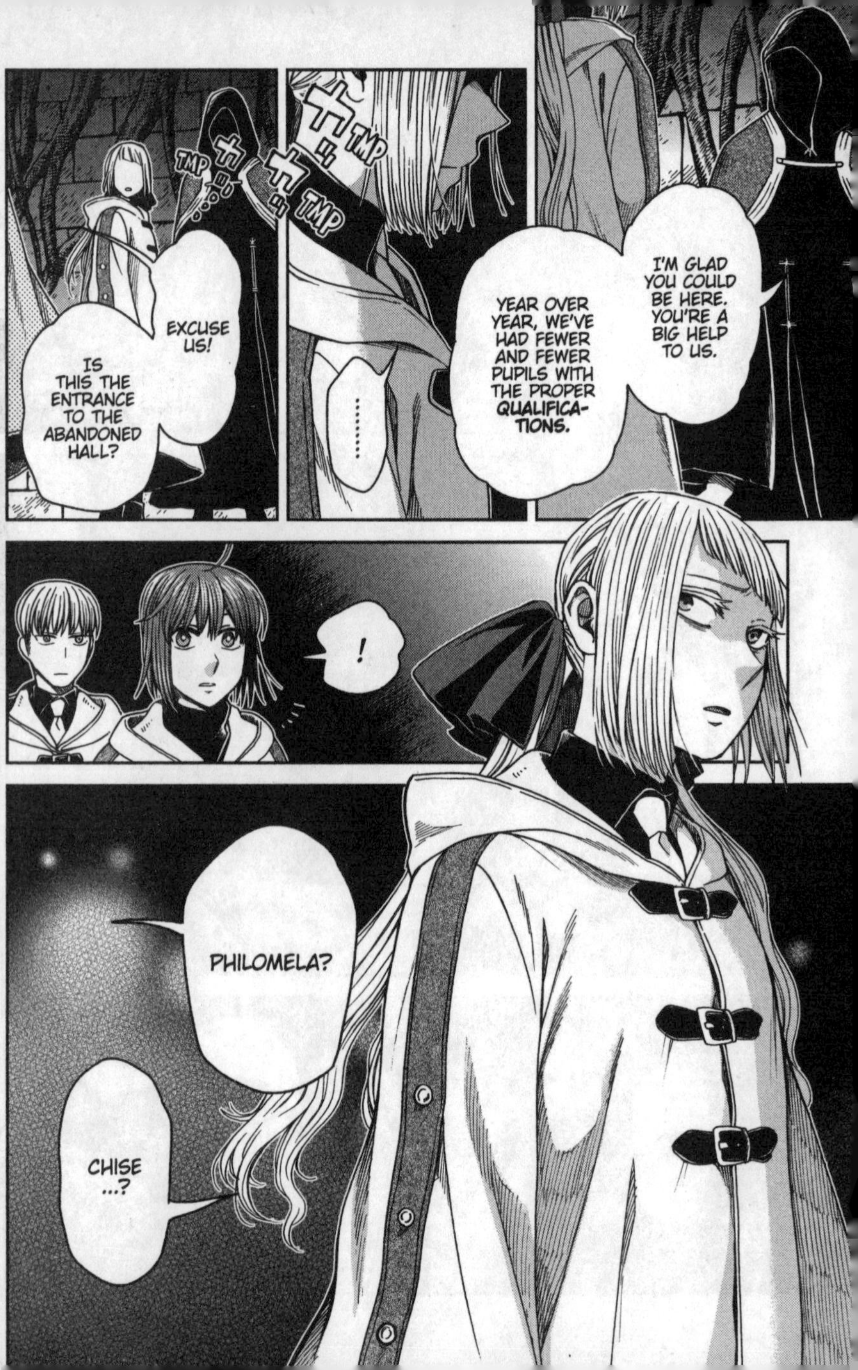
I'M GLAD YOU COULD BE HERE. YOU'RE A BIG HELP TO US.
YEAR OVER YEAR, WE'VE HAD FEWER AND FEWER PUPILS WITH THE PROPER QUALIFICATIONS.
TMP
TMP
TMP
......
EXCUSE US!
IS THIS THE ENTRANCE TO THE ABANDONED HALL?
!
PHILOMELA?
CHISE ...?

Chapter 68: A small leak will sink a great ship. III

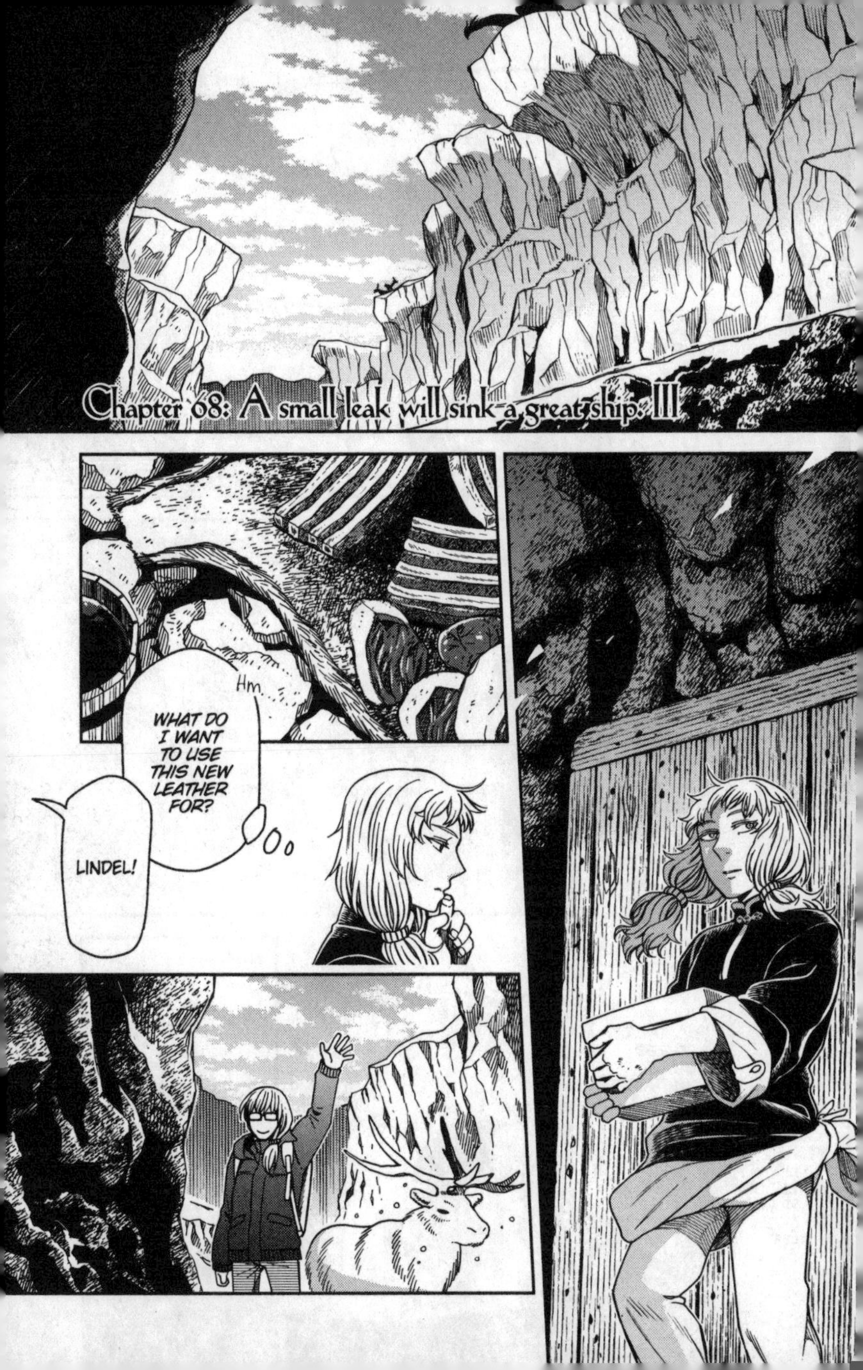
Hm...
WHAT DO I WANT TO USE THIS NEW LEATHER FOR?
LINDEL!

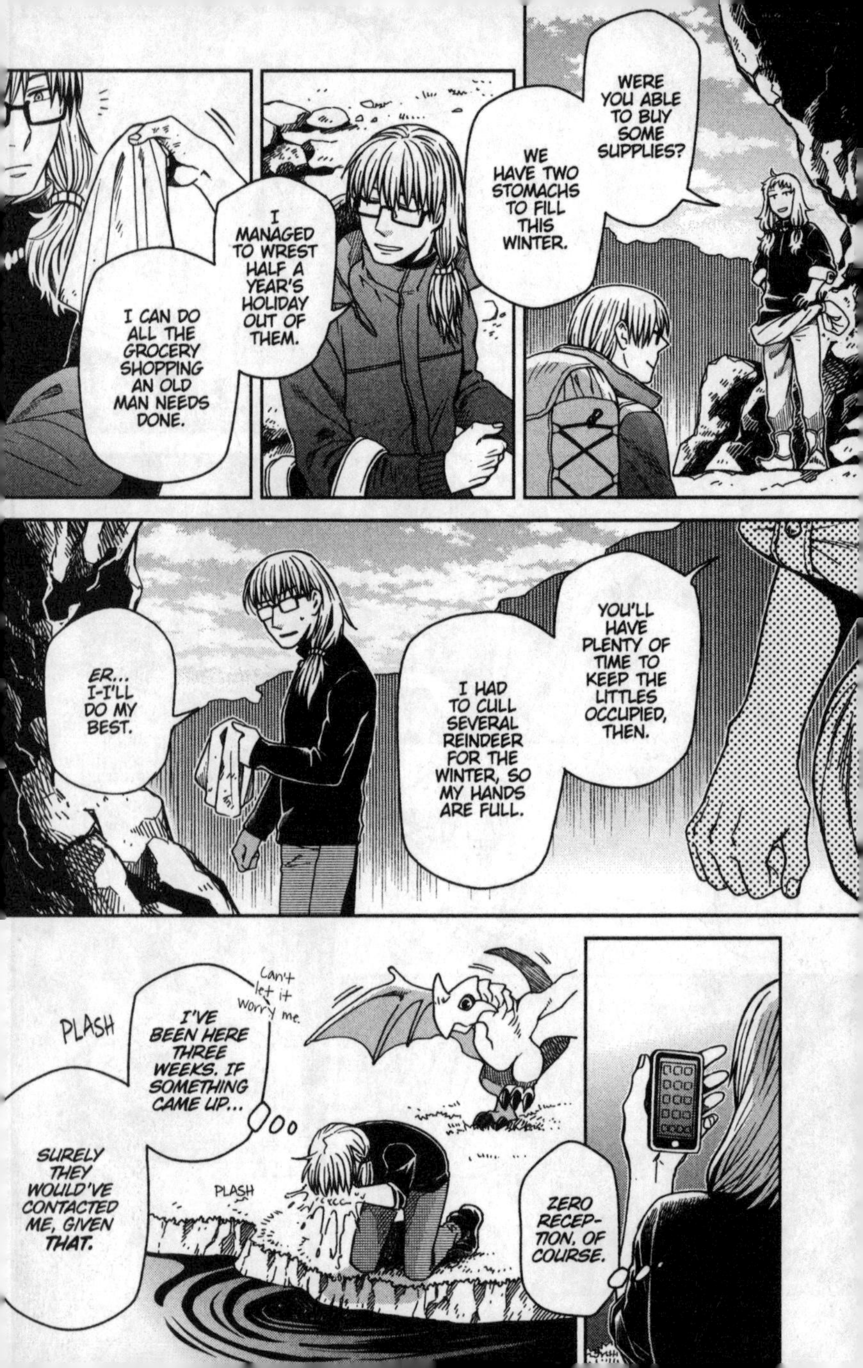
WERE YOU ABLE TO BUY SOME SUPPLIES?
WE HAVE TWO STOMACHS TO FILL THIS WINTER.
I MANAGED TO WREST HALF A YEAR'S HOLIDAY OUT OF THEM.
I CAN DO ALL THE GROCERY SHOPPING AN OLD MAN NEEDS DONE.
YOU'LL HAVE PLENTY OF TIME TO KEEP THE LITTLES OCCUPIED, THEN.
I HAD TO CULL SEVERAL REINDEER FOR THE WINTER, SO MY HANDS ARE FULL.
ER... I-I'LL DO MY BEST.
ZERO RECEPTION, OF COURSE.
Can't let it worry me.
I'VE BEEN HERE THREE WEEKS. IF SOMETHING CAME UP...
PLASH
SURELY THEY WOULD'VE CONTACTED ME, GIVEN THAT.
PLASH

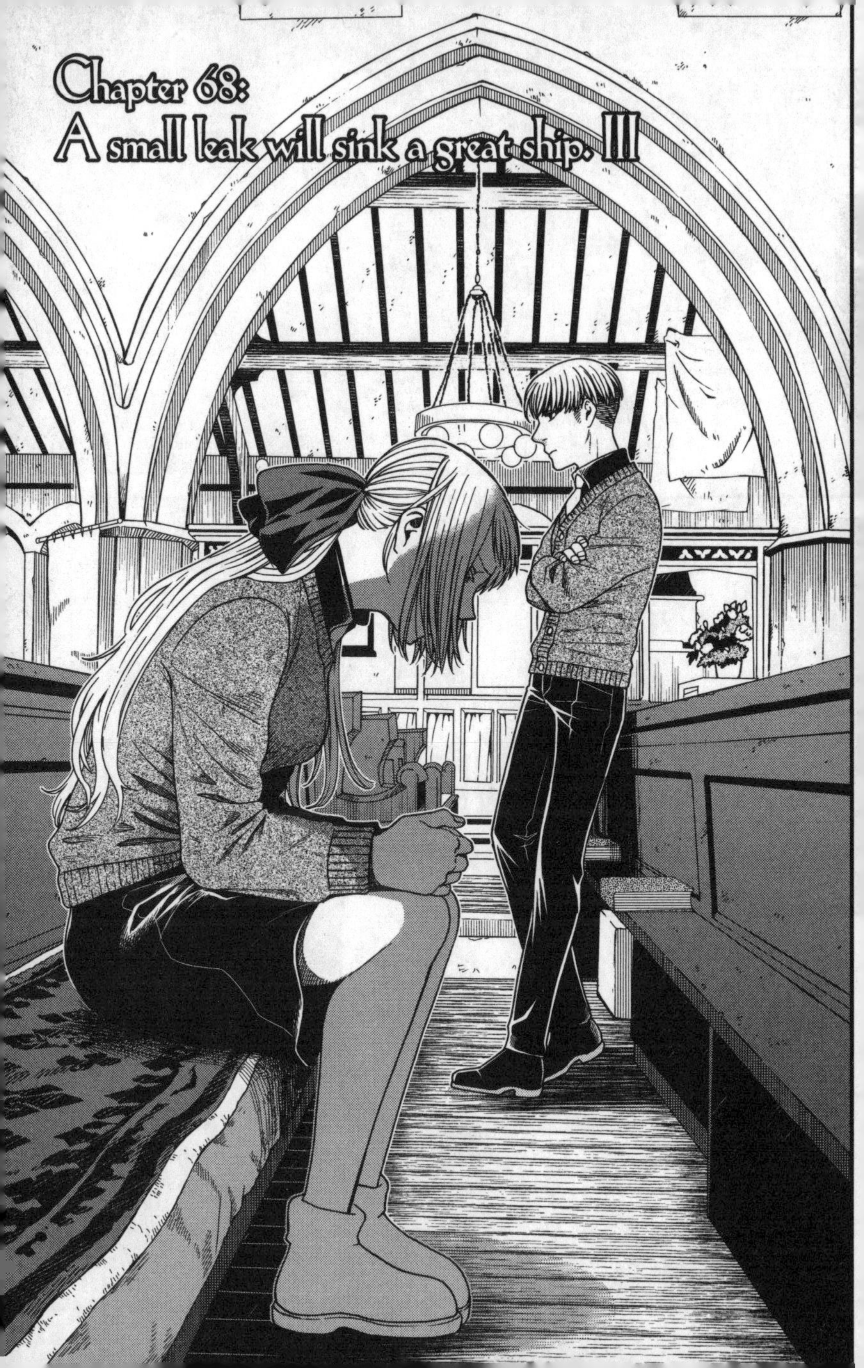
Chapter 68:
A small leak will sink a great ship. III

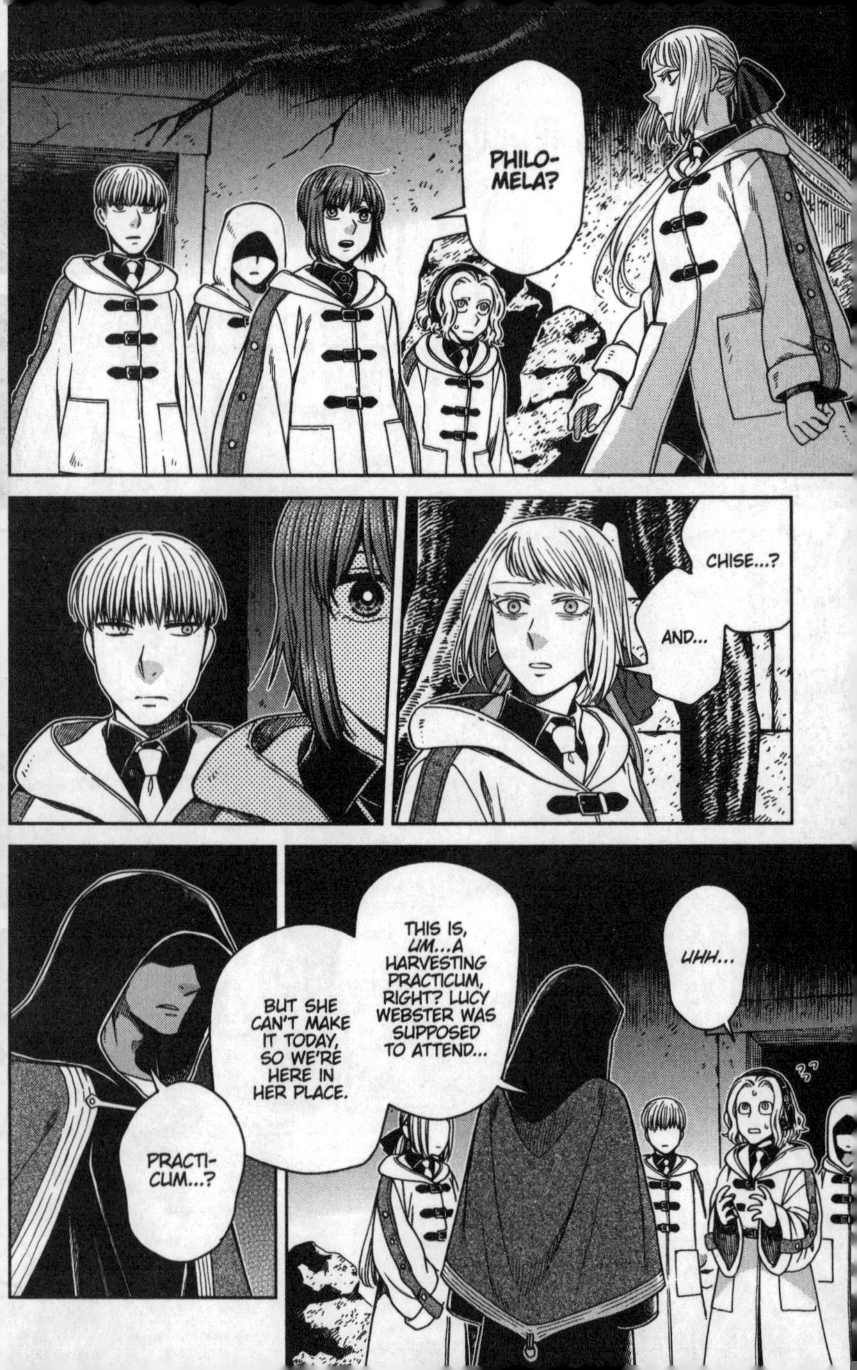
PHILO-MELA?
CHISE...?
AND...
UHH...
THIS IS, UM...A HARVESTING PRACTICUM, RIGHT? LUCY WEBSTER WAS SUPPOSED TO ATTEND...
BUT SHE CAN'T MAKE IT TODAY, SO WE'RE HERE IN HER PLACE.
PRACTI-CUM...?

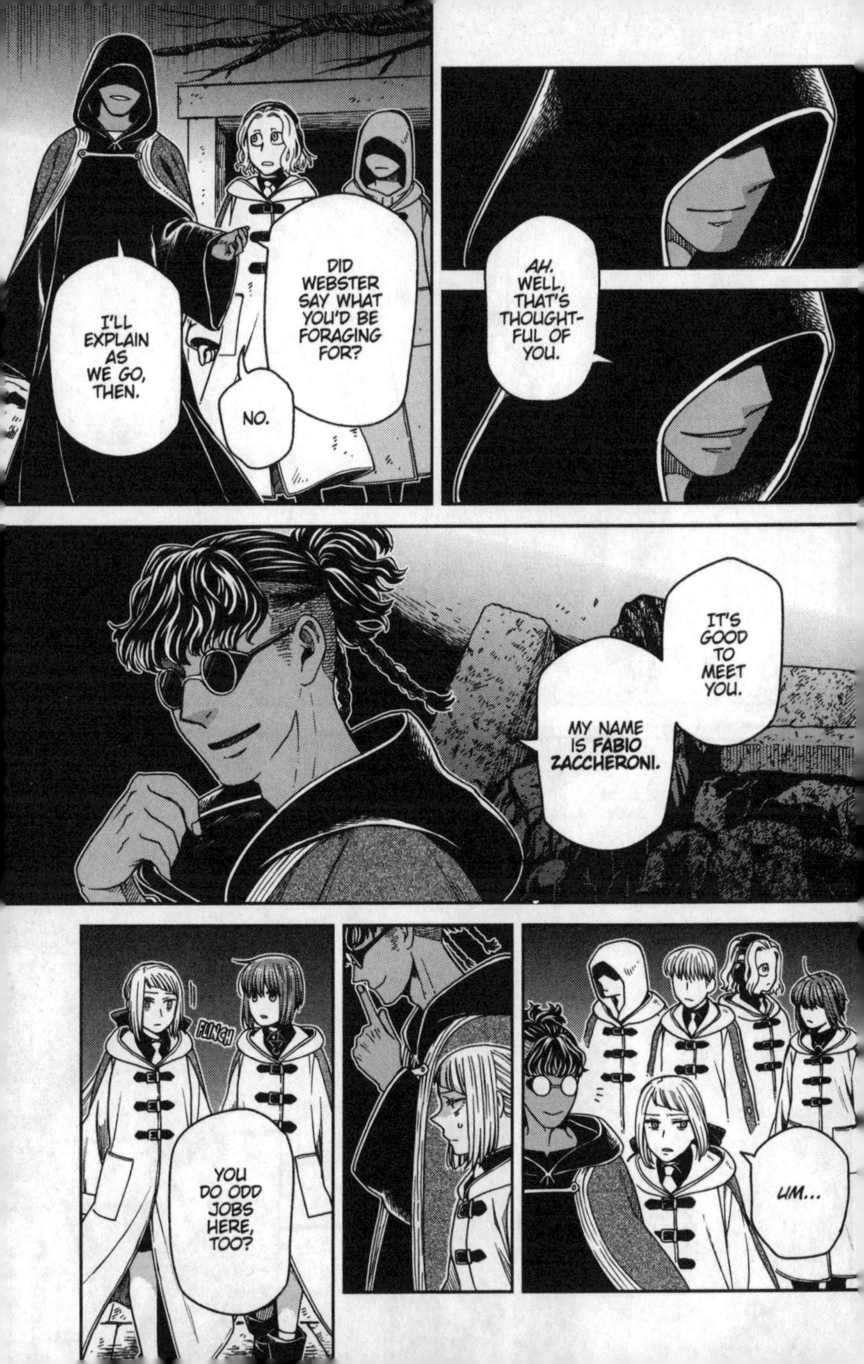
AH. WELL, THAT'S THOUGHT-FUL OF YOU.
DID WEBSTER SAY WHAT YOU'D BE FORAGING FOR?
NO.
I'LL EXPLAIN AS WE GO, THEN.
IT'S GOOD TO MEET YOU.
MY NAME IS FABIO ZACCHERONI.
UM...
FLINCH
YOU DO ODD JOBS HERE, TOO?

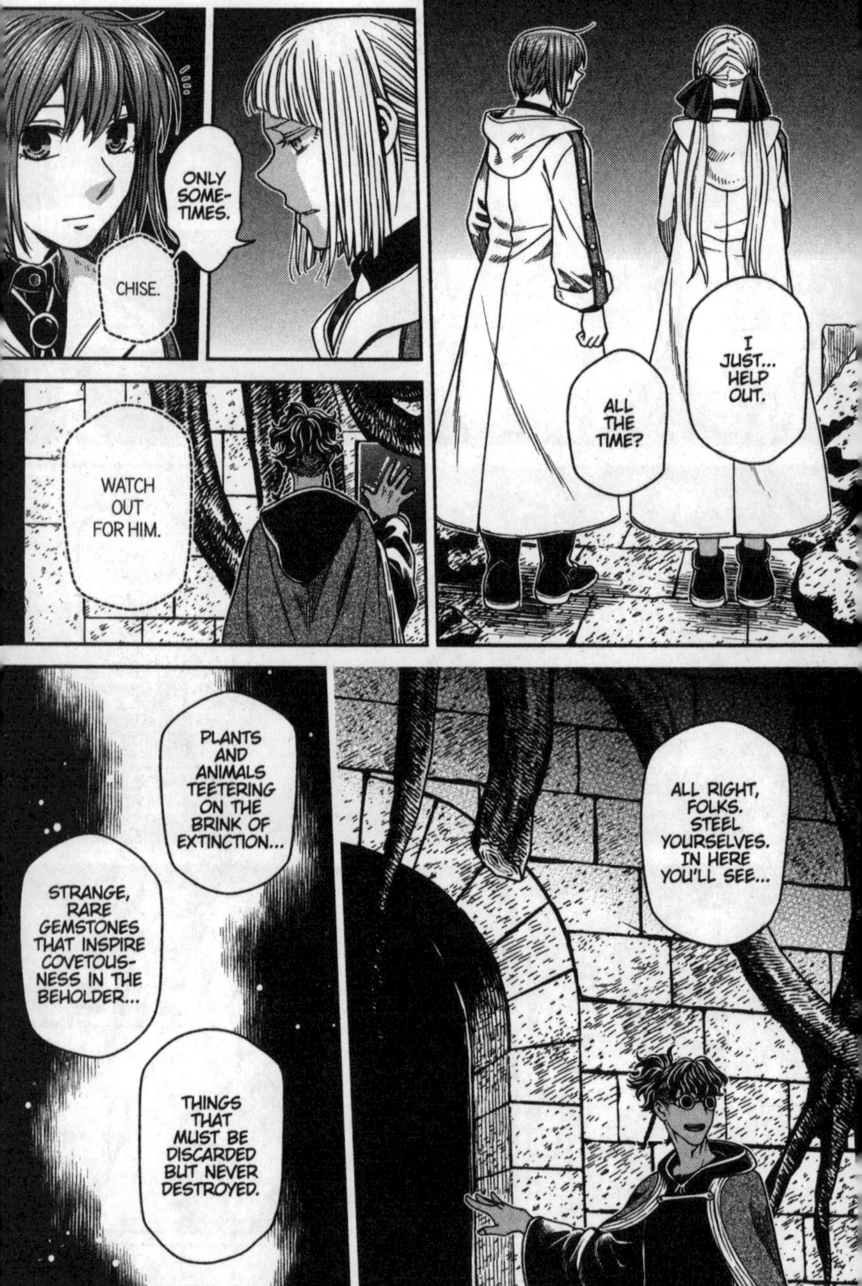
I JUST... HELP OUT.
ALL THE TIME?
ONLY SOME-TIMES.
CHISE.
WATCH OUT FOR HIM.
ALL RIGHT, FOLKS. STEEL YOURSELVES. IN HERE YOU'LL SEE...
PLANTS AND ANIMALS TEETERING ON THE BRINK OF EXTINCTION...
STRANGE, RARE GEMSTONES THAT INSPIRE COVETOUS-NESS IN THE BEHOLDER...
THINGS THAT MUST BE DISCARDED BUT NEVER DESTROYED.

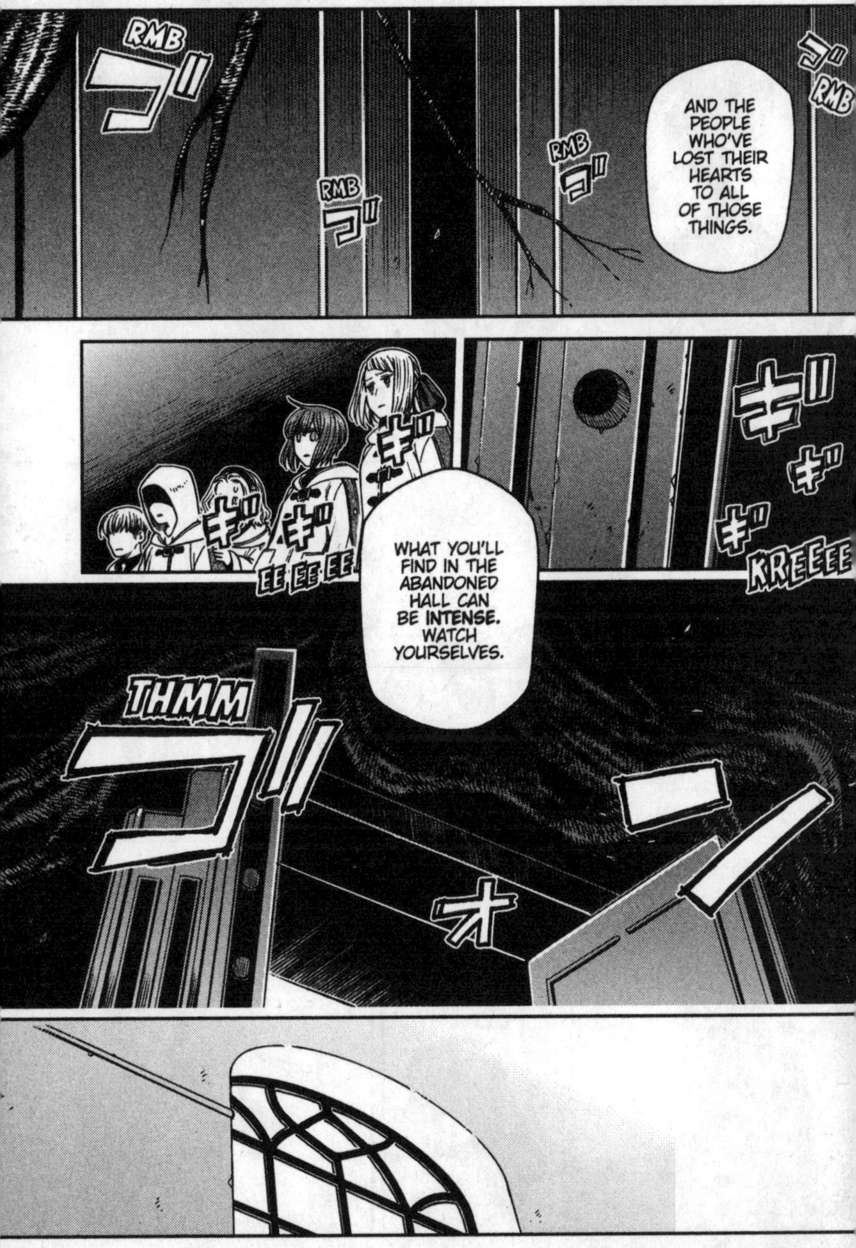
RMB
AND THE PEOPLE WHO'VE LOST THEIR HEARTS TO ALL OF THOSE THINGS.
RMB
RMB
RMB
KREEEE
EE EE EE
WHAT YOU'LL FIND IN THE ABANDONED HALL CAN BE INTENSE. WATCH YOURSELVES.
THMM

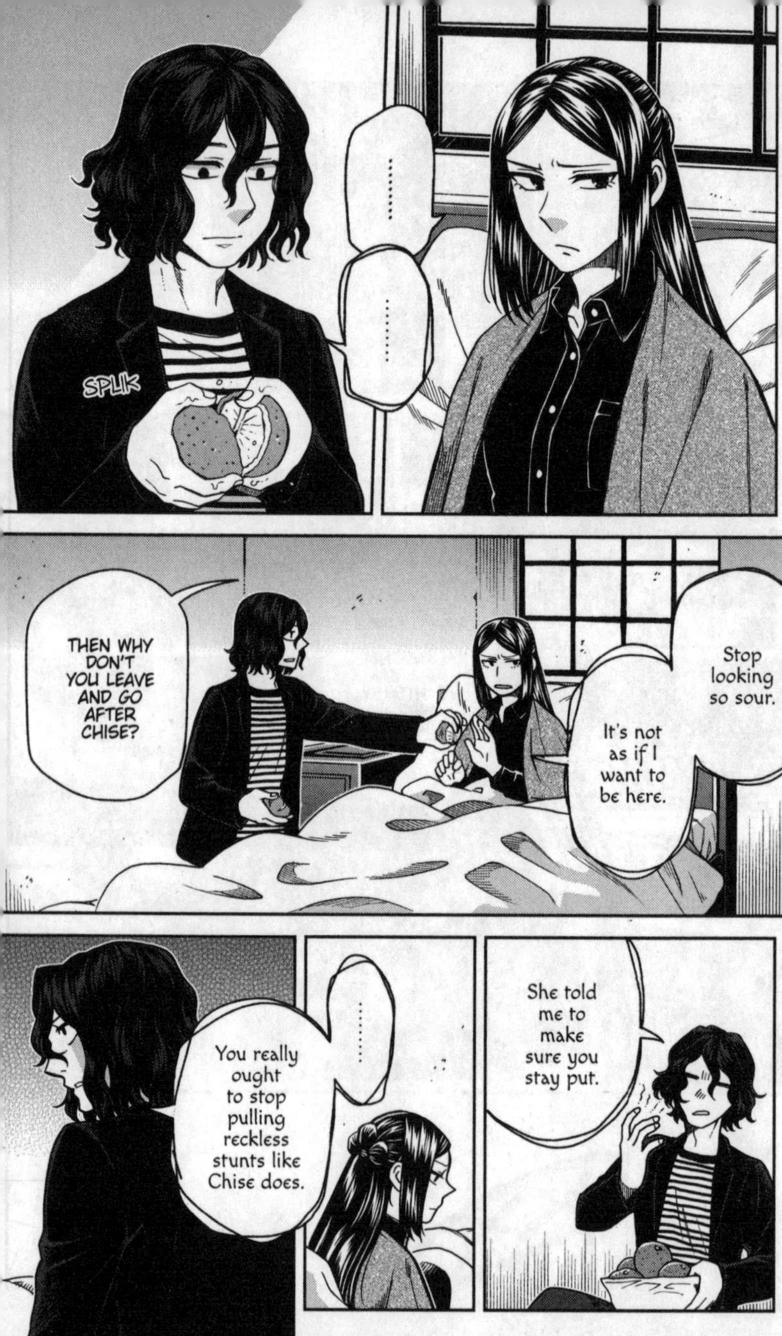
......
......
...
SPLIK
Stop looking so sour.
It's not as if I want to be here.
THEN WHY DON'T YOU LEAVE AND GO AFTER CHISE?
She told me to make sure you stay put.
......
You really ought to stop pulling reckless stunts like Chise does.

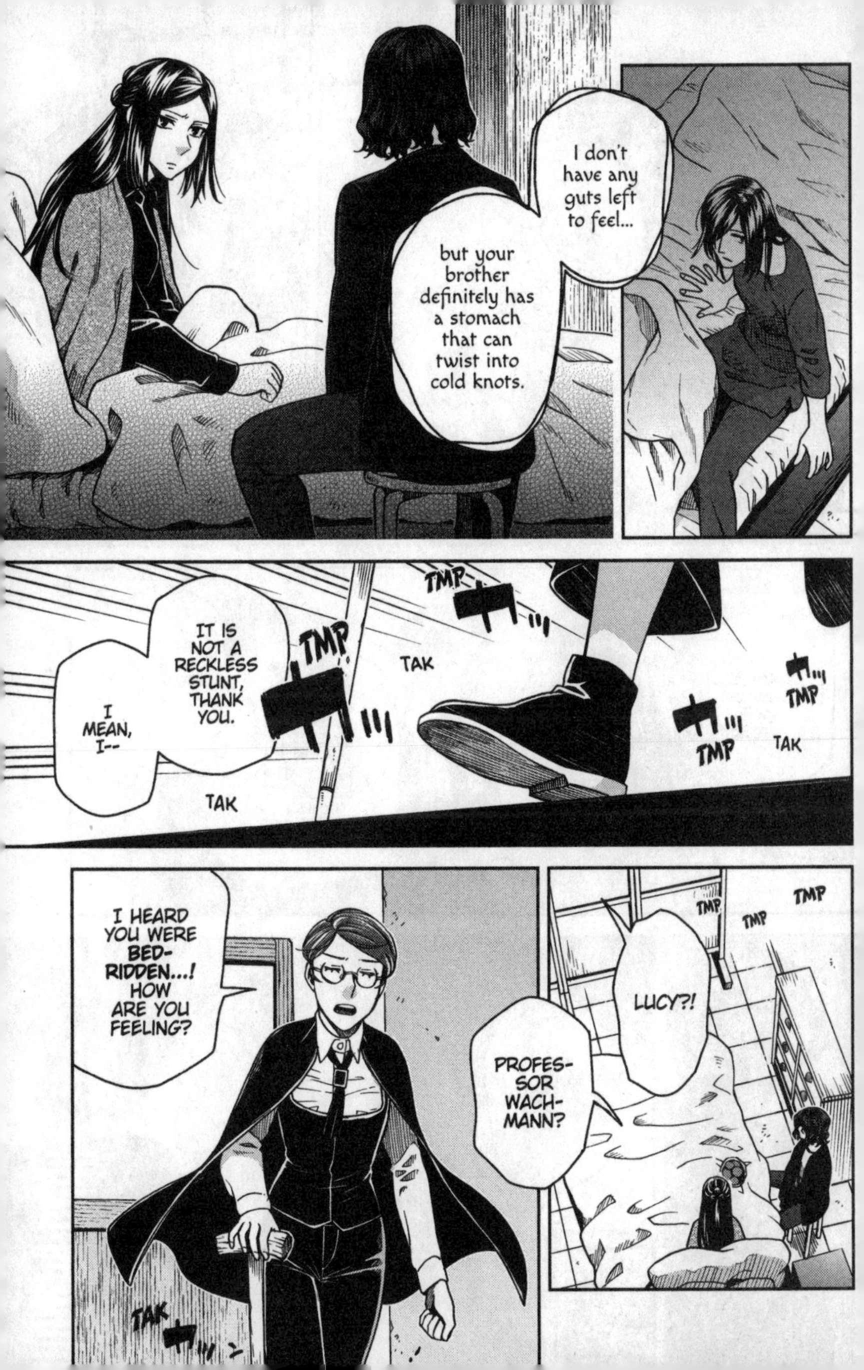
?..
I don't have any guts left to feel...
but your brother definitely has a stomach that can twist into cold knots.
TMP
TMP
TMP
TAK
TMP
TAK
TMP
IT IS NOT A RECKLESS STUNT, THANK YOU.
I MEAN, I--
TAK
TMP
TMP
TMP
LUCY?!
PROFES-SOR WACH-MANN?
I HEARD YOU WERE BED-RIDDEN...! HOW ARE YOU FEELING?
TAK

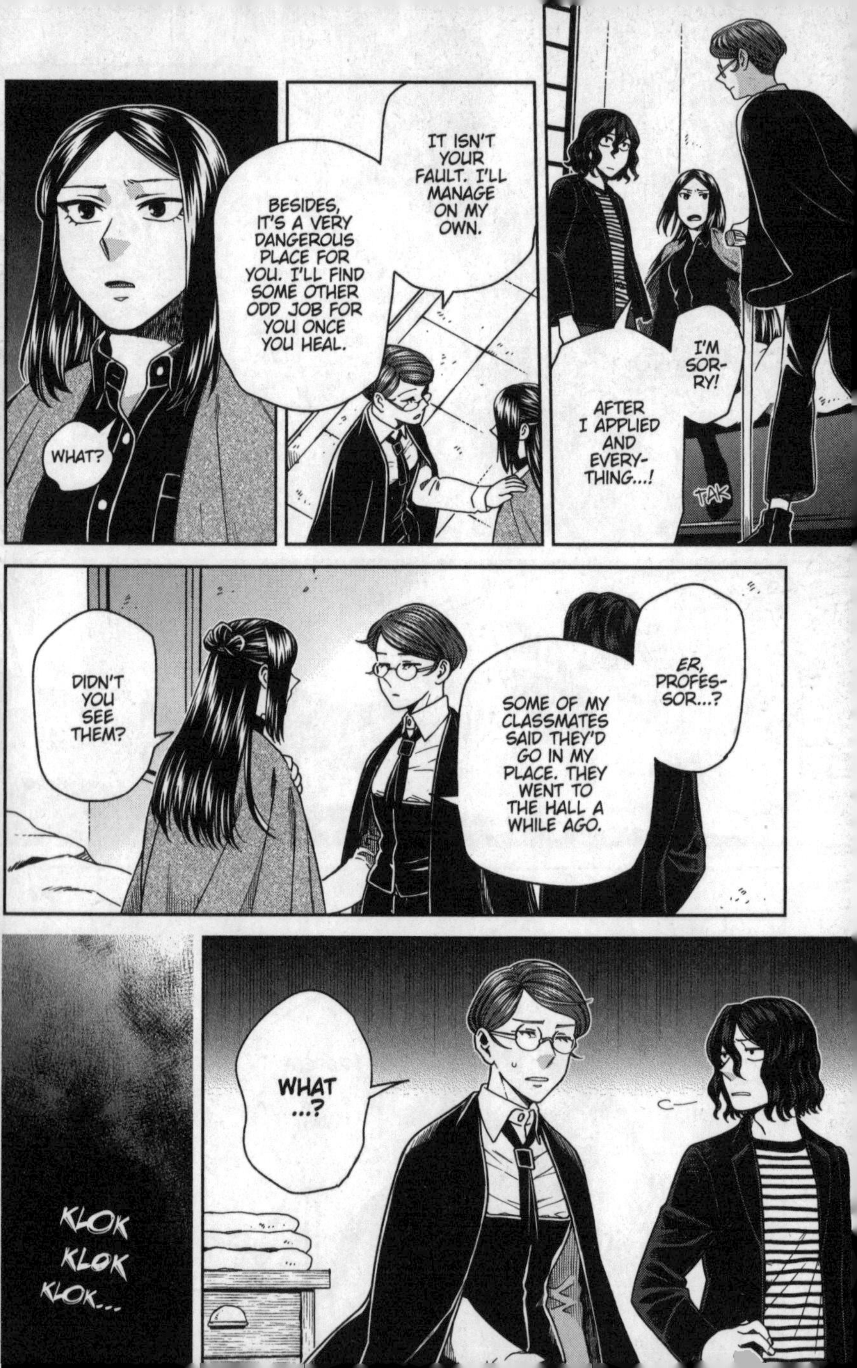
I'M SORRY!
AFTER I APPLIED AND EVERYTHING...!
TAK
IT ISN'T YOUR FAULT. I'LL MANAGE ON MY OWN.
BESIDES, IT'S A VERY DANGEROUS PLACE FOR YOU. I'LL FIND SOME OTHER ODD JOB FOR YOU ONCE YOU HEAL.
WHAT?
ER, PROFESSOR...?
SOME OF MY CLASSMATES SAID THEY'D GO IN MY PLACE. THEY WENT TO THE HALL A WHILE AGO.
DIDN'T YOU SEE THEM?
C—
WHAT ...?
KLOK
KLOK
KLOK...

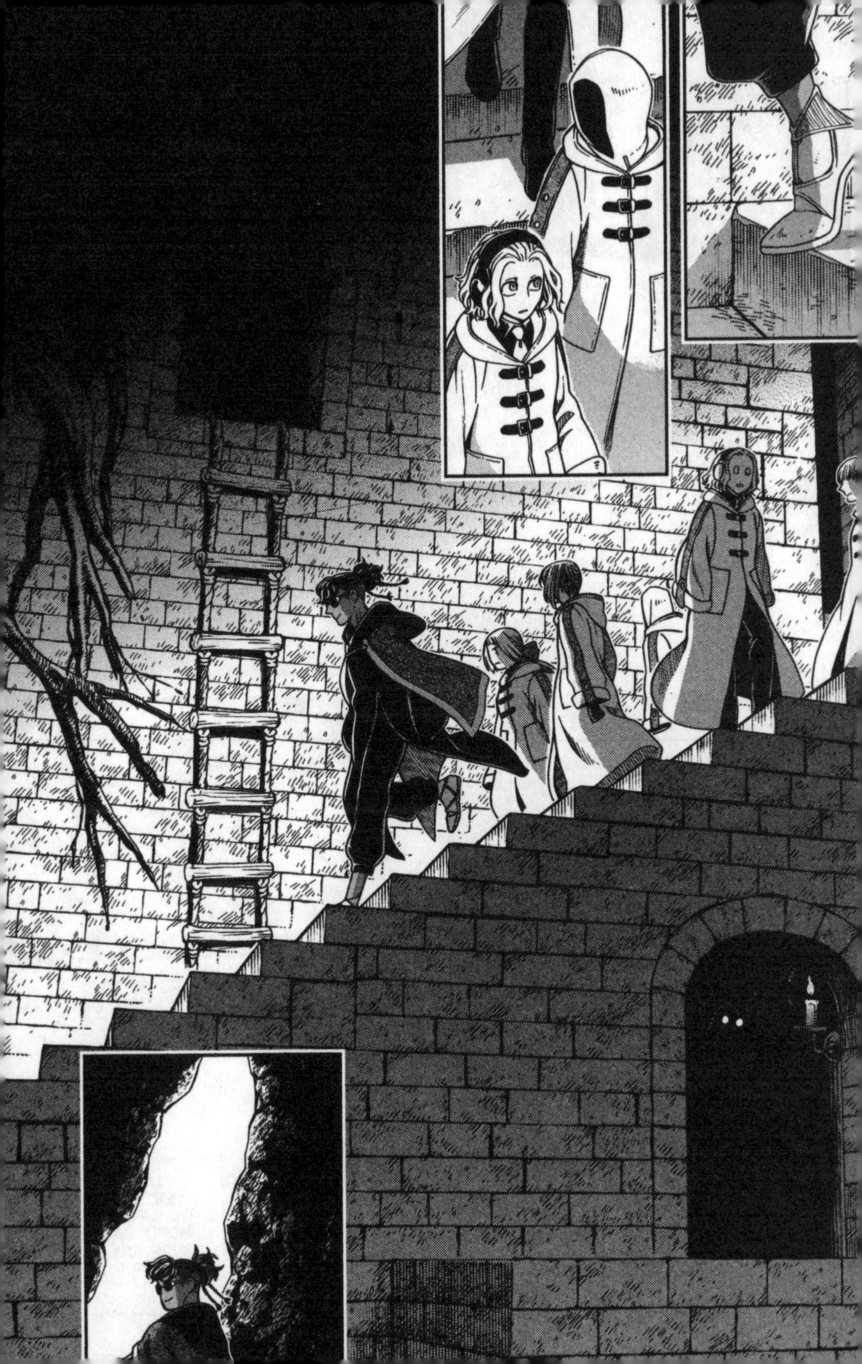

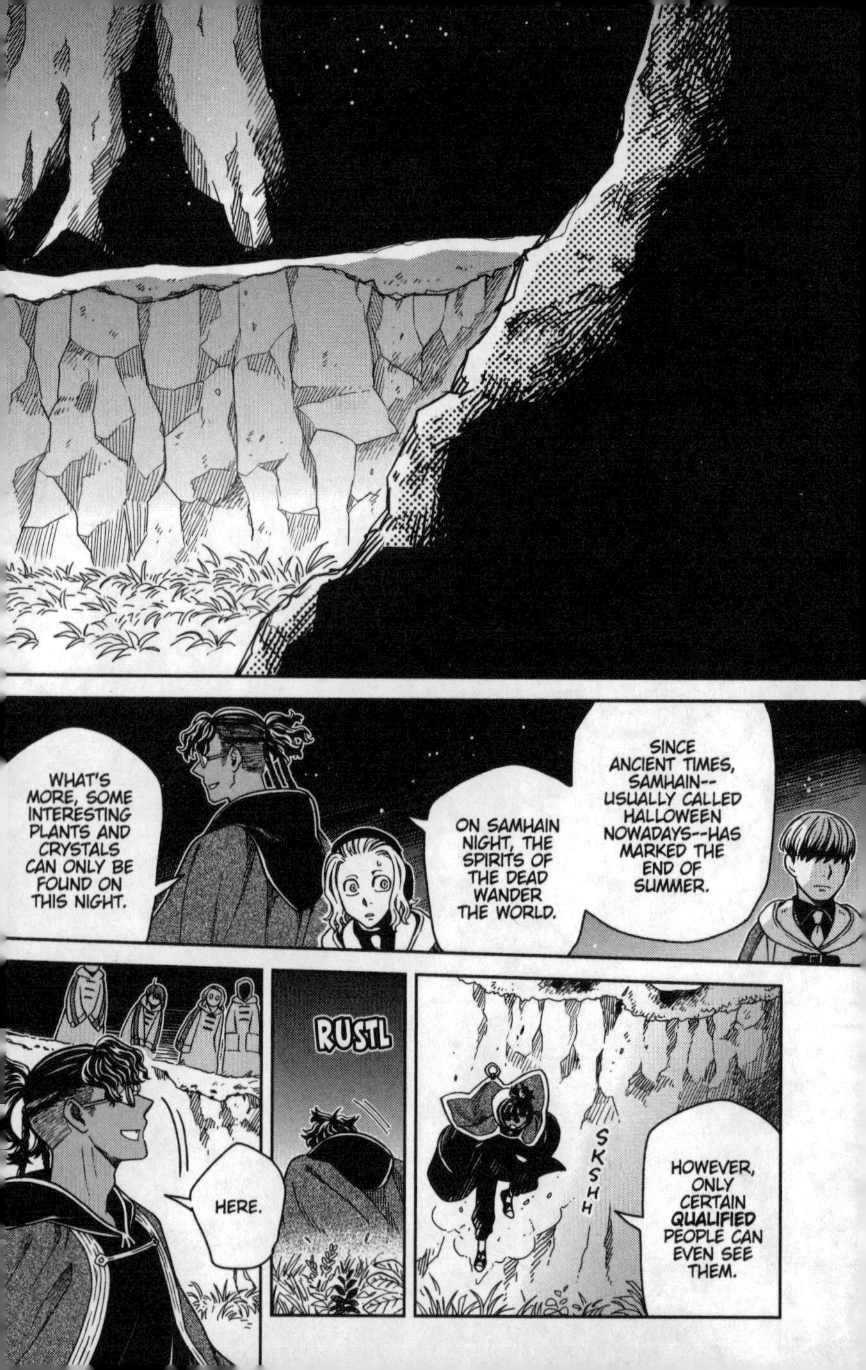
SINCE ANCIENT TIMES, SAMHAIN-- USUALLY CALLED HALLOWEEN NOWADAYS--HAS MARKED THE END OF SUMMER.
ON SAMHAIN NIGHT, THE SPIRITS OF THE DEAD WANDER THE WORLD.
WHAT'S MORE, SOME INTERESTING PLANTS AND CRYSTALS CAN ONLY BE FOUND ON THIS NIGHT.
SKSHH
HOWEVER, ONLY CERTAIN **QUALIFIED** PEOPLE CAN EVEN SEE THEM.
RUSTL
HERE.

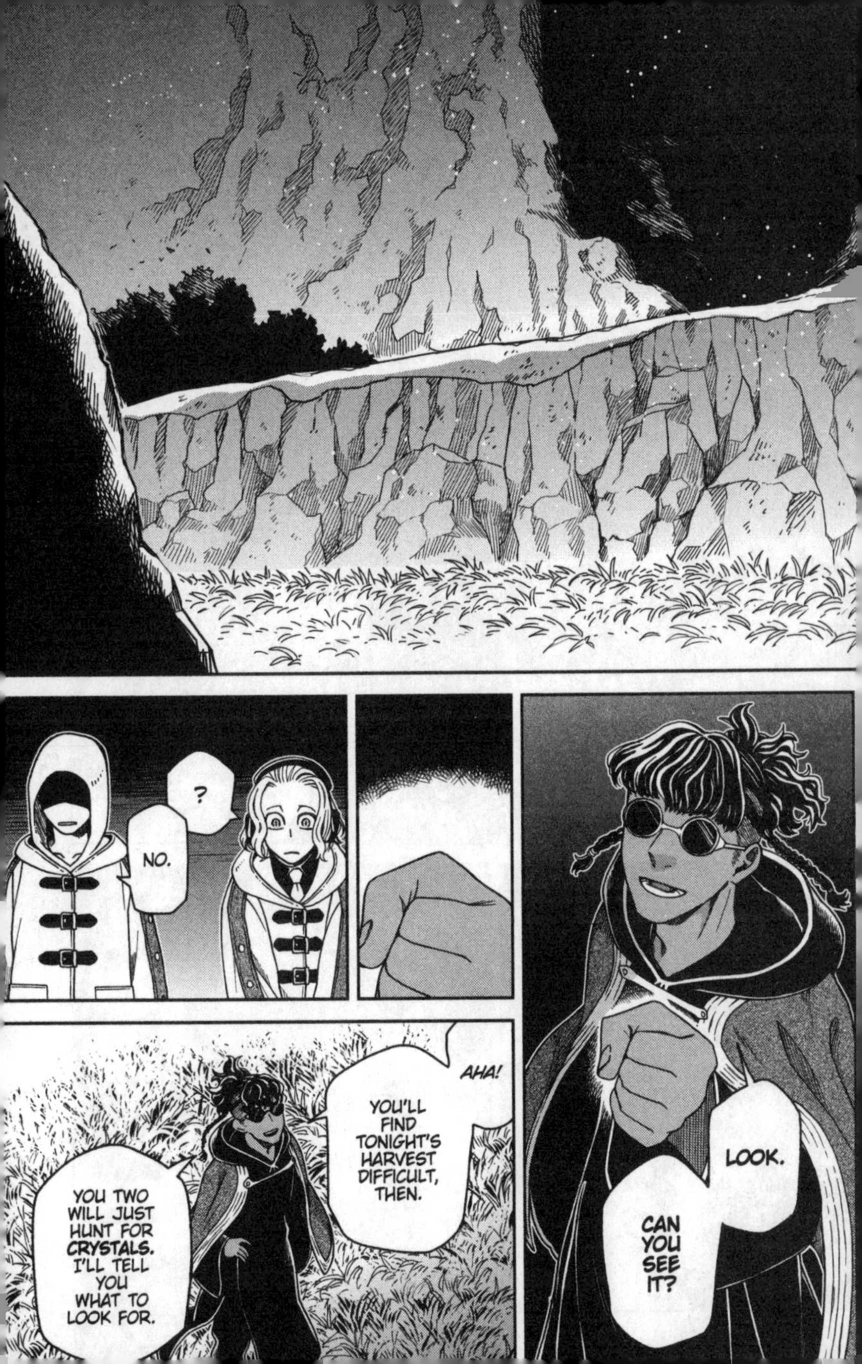
LOOK.
CAN YOU SEE IT?
?
NO.
AHA!
YOU'LL FIND TONIGHT'S HARVEST DIFFICULT, THEN.
YOU TWO WILL JUST HUNT FOR CRYSTALS. I'LL TELL YOU WHAT TO LOOK FOR.

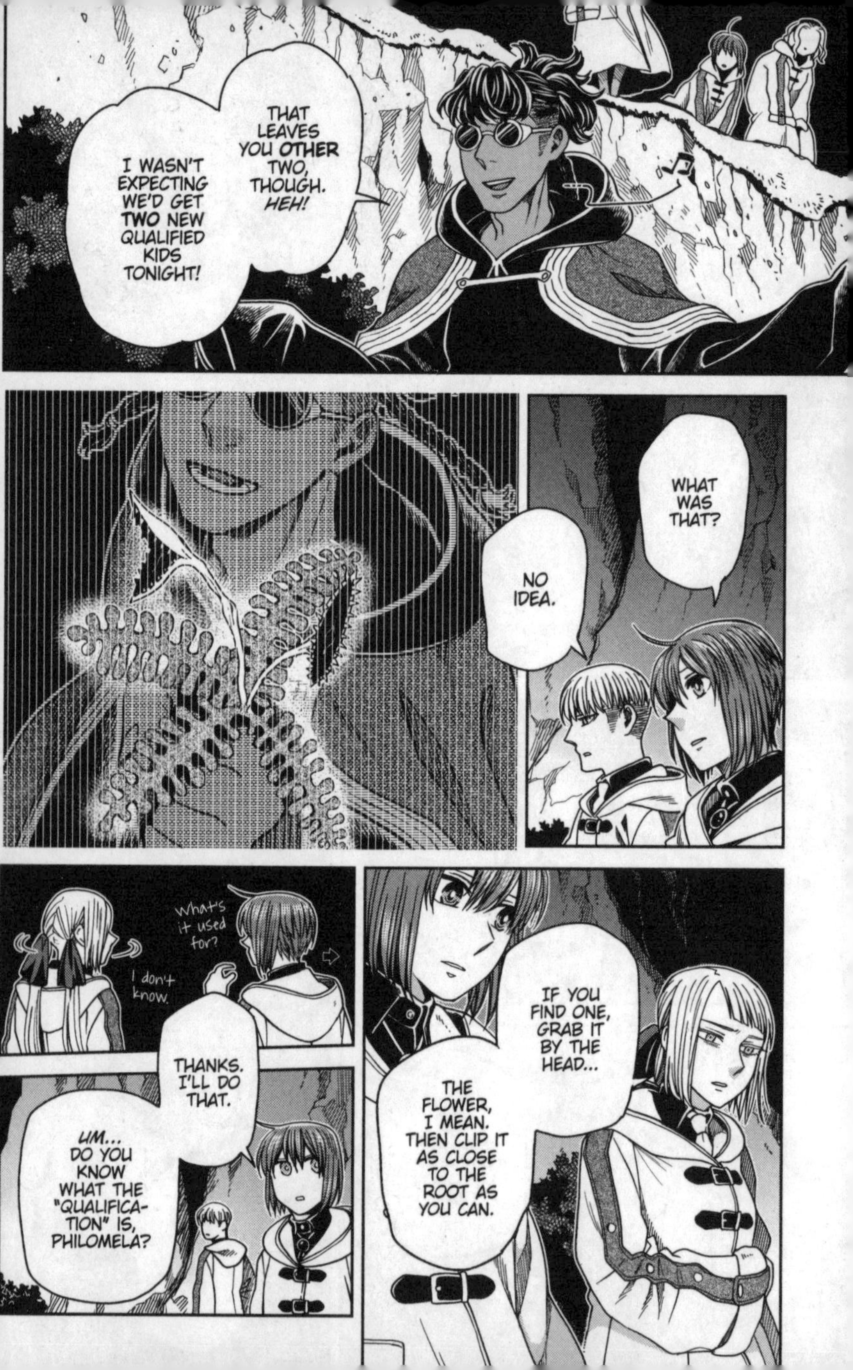
I WASN'T EXPECTING WE'D GET TWO NEW QUALIFIED KIDS TONIGHT!
THAT LEAVES YOU OTHER TWO, THOUGH. HEH!
WHAT WAS THAT?
NO IDEA.
IF YOU FIND ONE, GRAB IT BY THE HEAD...
THE FLOWER, I MEAN. THEN CLIP IT AS CLOSE TO THE ROOT AS YOU CAN.
What's it used for?
I don't know.
THANKS. I'LL DO THAT.
UM... DO YOU KNOW WHAT THE "QUALIFICATION" IS, PHILOMELA?

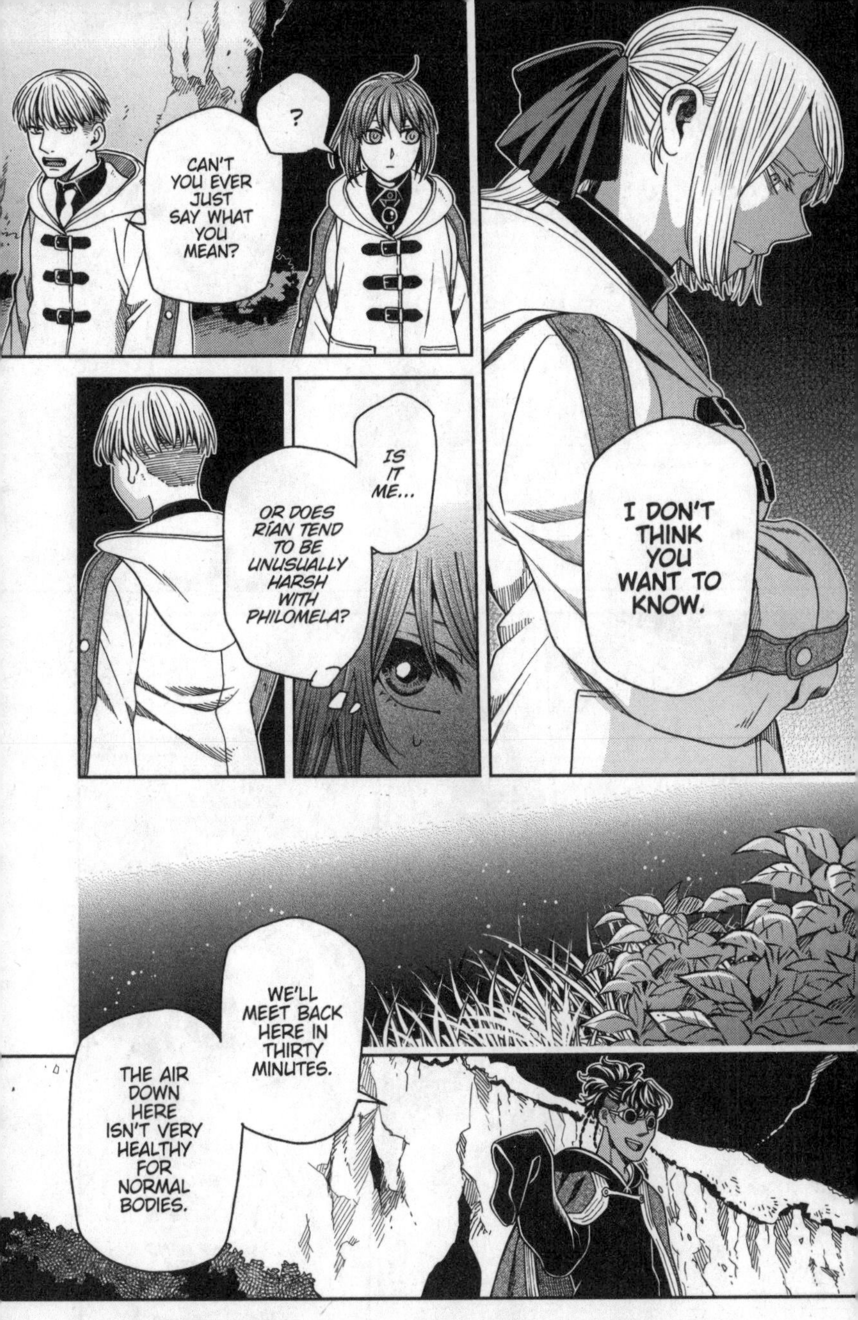
I DON'T THINK YOU WANT TO KNOW.
?
CAN'T YOU EVER JUST SAY WHAT YOU MEAN?
IS IT ME...
OR DOES RÍAN TEND TO BE UNUSUALLY HARSH WITH PHILOMELA?
WE'LL MEET BACK HERE IN THIRTY MINUTES.
THE AIR DOWN HERE ISN'T VERY HEALTHY FOR NORMAL BODIES.

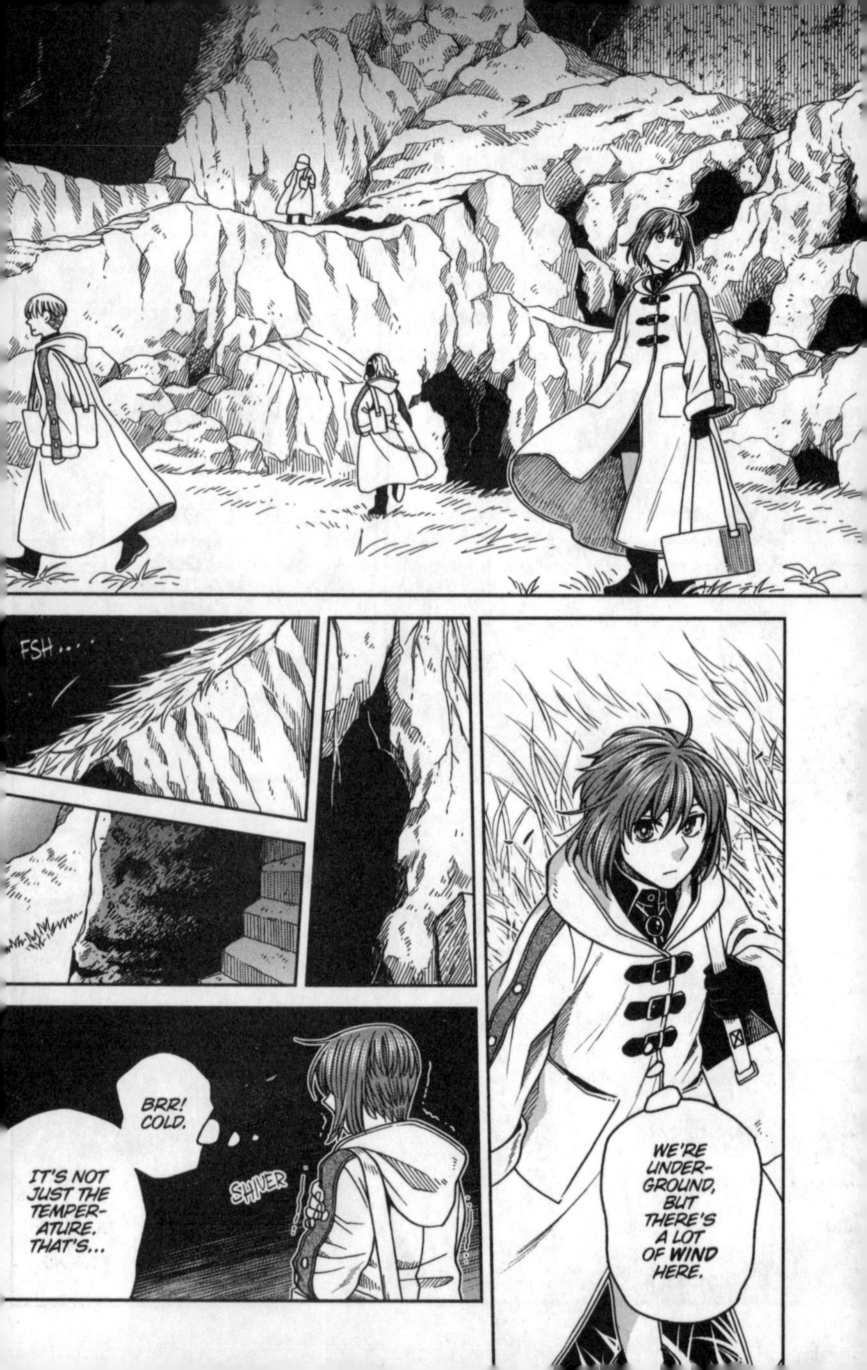
WE'RE UNDERGROUND, BUT THERE'S A LOT OF WIND HERE.
FSH...
BRR! COLD.
SHIVER
IT'S NOT JUST THE TEMPERATURE. THAT'S...

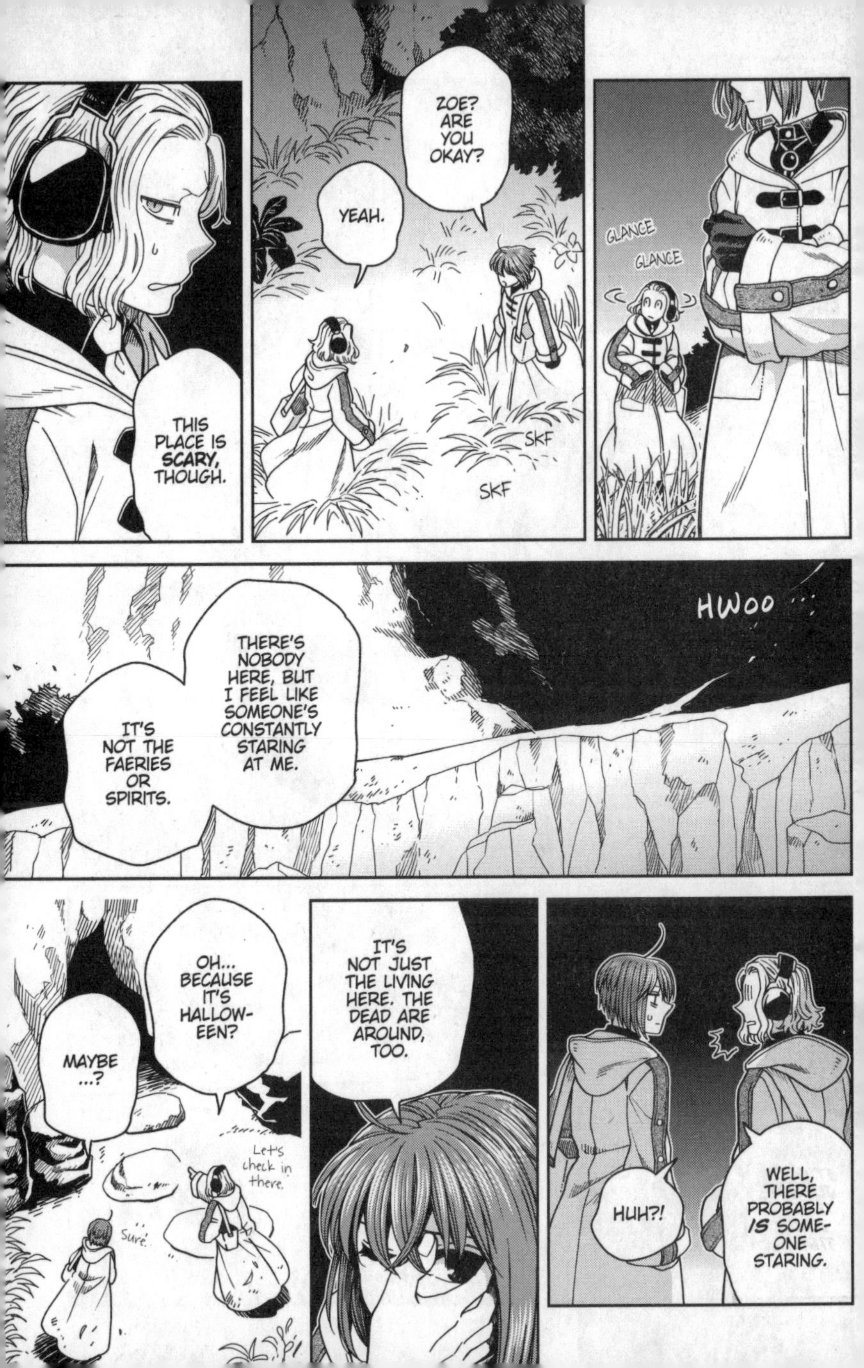
GLANCE
GLANCE
ZOE? ARE YOU OKAY?
YEAH.
SKF
SKF
THIS PLACE IS SCARY, THOUGH.
HWOO
THERE'S NOBODY HERE, BUT I FEEL LIKE SOMEONE'S CONSTANTLY STARING AT ME.
IT'S NOT THE FAERIES OR SPIRITS.
WELL, THERE PROBABLY IS SOMEONE STARING.
HUH?!
IT'S NOT JUST THE LIVING HERE. THE DEAD ARE AROUND, TOO.
OH... BECAUSE IT'S HALLOWEEN?
MAYBE ...?
Let's check in there.
Sure.

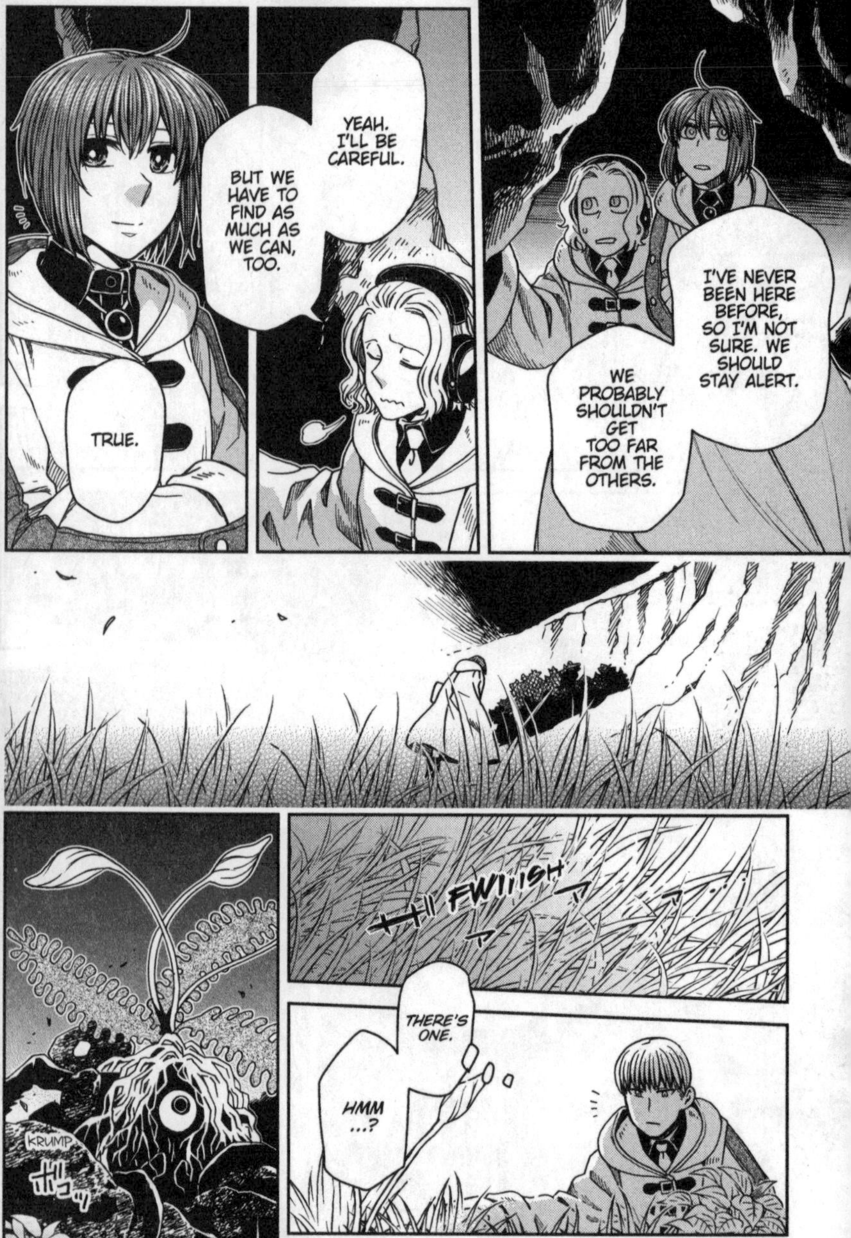
I'VE NEVER BEEN HERE BEFORE, SO I'M NOT SURE. WE SHOULD STAY ALERT.
WE PROBABLY SHOULDN'T GET TOO FAR FROM THE OTHERS.
YEAH. I'LL BE CAREFUL.
BUT WE HAVE TO FIND AS MUCH AS WE CAN, TOO.
TRUE.
FWIIISH
THERE'S ONE.
HMM ...?
KRUMP
ボコッ

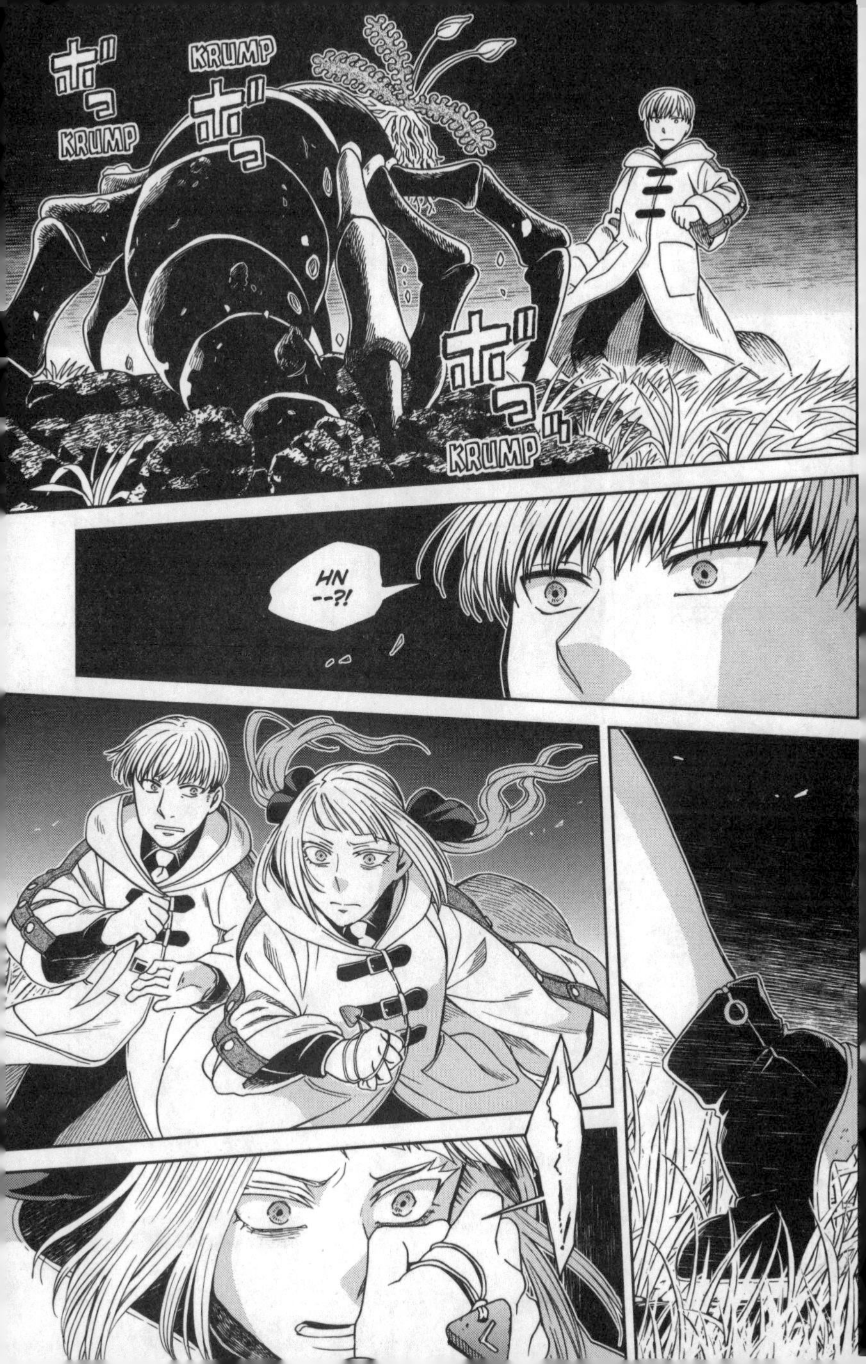
KRUMP
ボッ
ボッ
KRUMP
ボッ
KRUMP
HN --?!

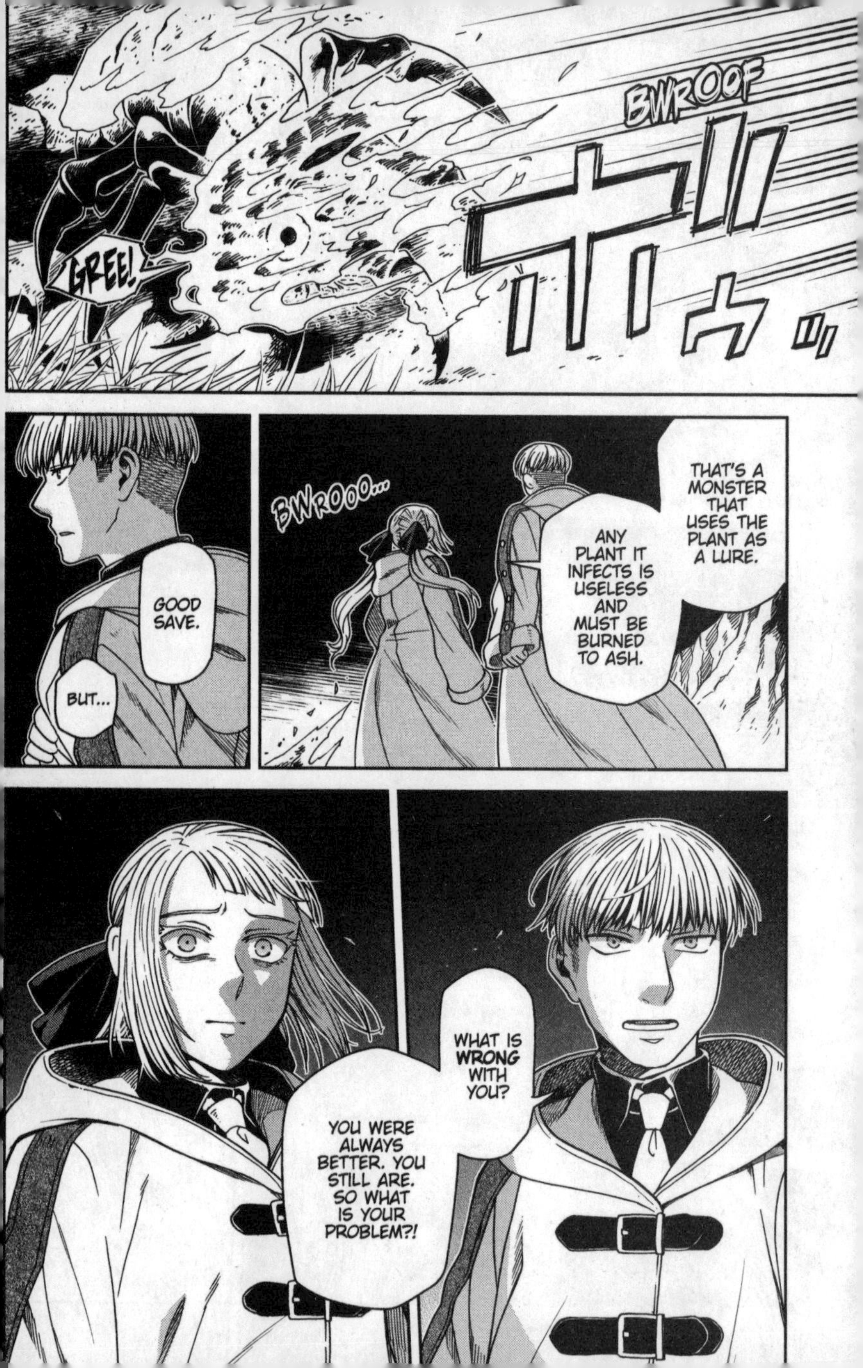
BWROOF
GREE!
THAT'S A MONSTER THAT USES THE PLANT AS A LURE.
ANY PLANT IT INFECTS IS USELESS AND MUST BE BURNED TO ASH.
BWROOO...
GOOD SAVE.
BUT...
WHAT IS **WRONG** WITH YOU?
YOU WERE ALWAYS BETTER. YOU STILL ARE. SO WHAT IS YOUR PROBLEM?!

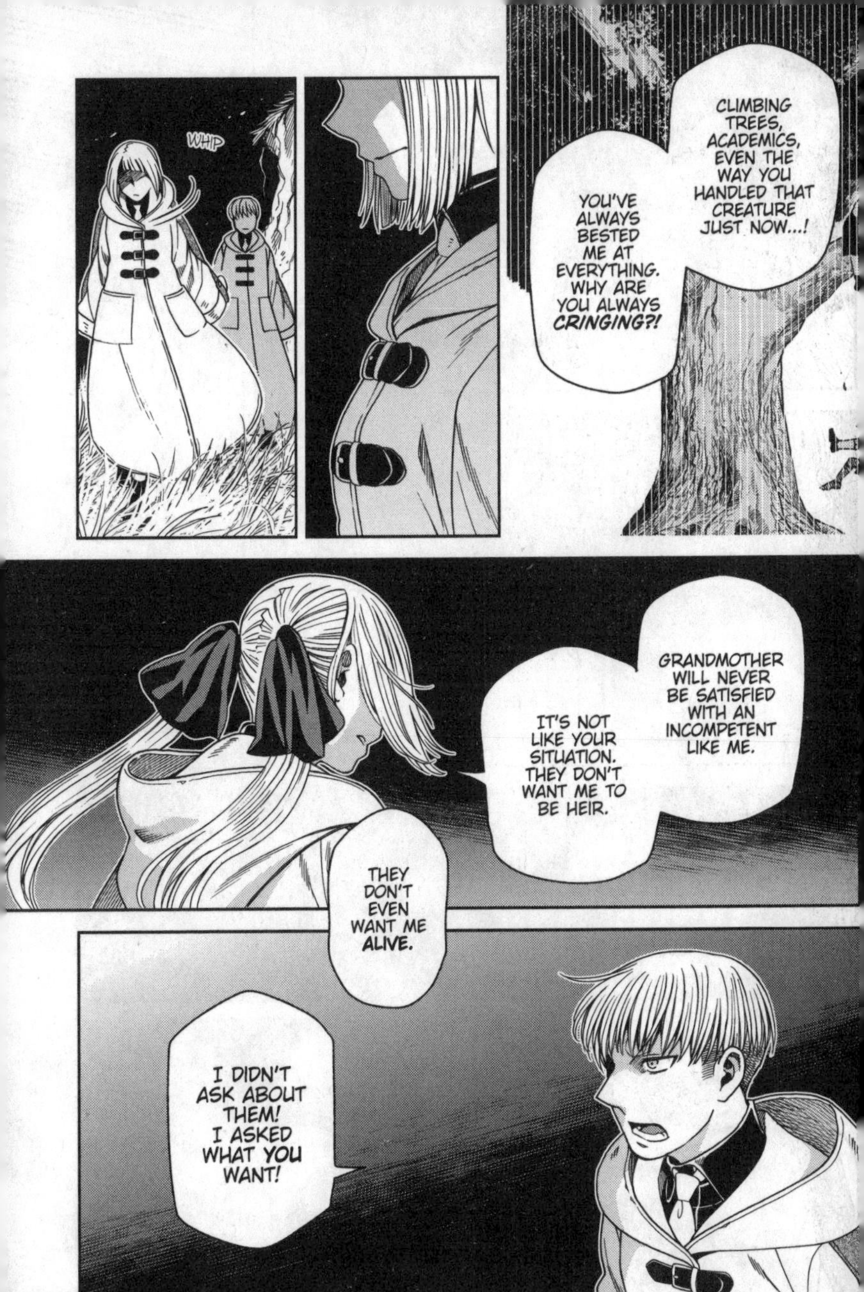
CLIMBING TREES, ACADEMICS, EVEN THE WAY YOU HANDLED THAT CREATURE JUST NOW...!
YOU'VE ALWAYS BESTED ME AT EVERYTHING. WHY ARE YOU ALWAYS CRINGING?!
WHIP
GRANDMOTHER WILL NEVER BE SATISFIED WITH AN INCOMPETENT LIKE ME.
IT'S NOT LIKE YOUR SITUATION. THEY DON'T WANT ME TO BE HEIR.
THEY DON'T EVEN WANT ME ALIVE.
I DIDN'T ASK ABOUT THEM! I ASKED WHAT YOU WANT!

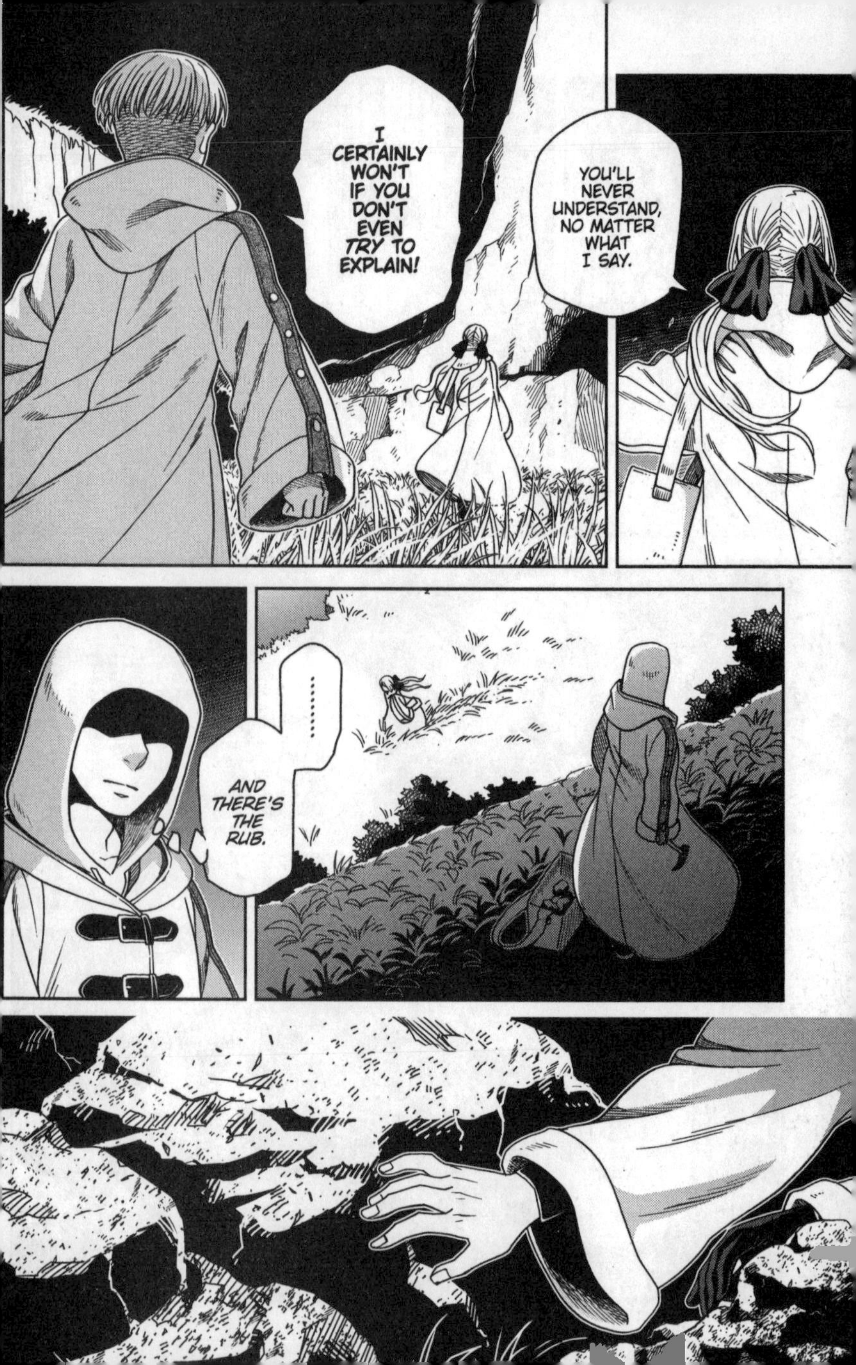
YOU'LL NEVER UNDERSTAND, NO MATTER WHAT I SAY.
I CERTAINLY WON'T IF YOU DON'T EVEN *TRY* TO EXPLAIN!
......
AND THERE'S THE RUB.

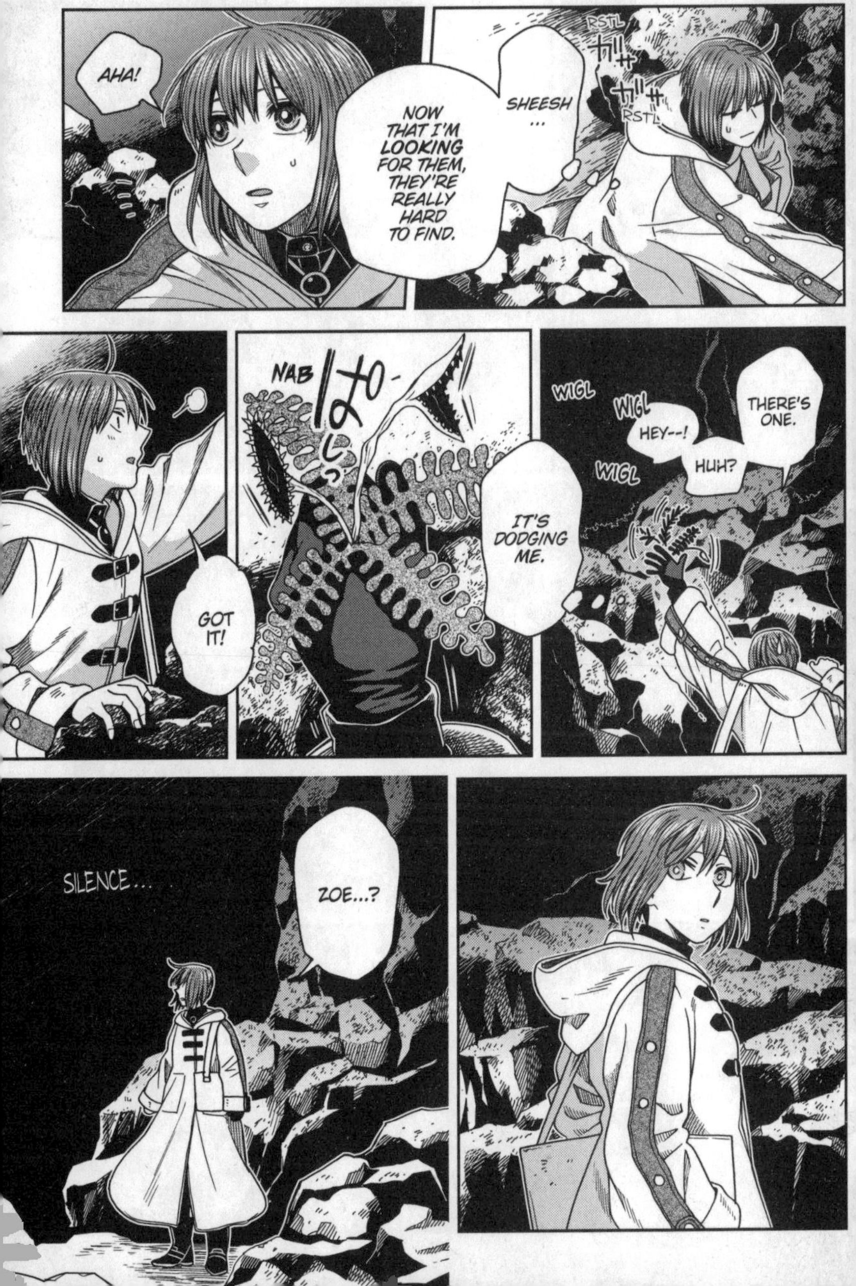
RSTL
RSTL
SHEESH ...
NOW THAT I'M LOOKING FOR THEM, THEY'RE REALLY HARD TO FIND.
AHA!
THERE'S ONE.
HUH?
HEY--!
WIGL
WIGL
WIGL
IT'S DODGING ME.
NAB
GOT IT!
ZOE...?
SILENCE...

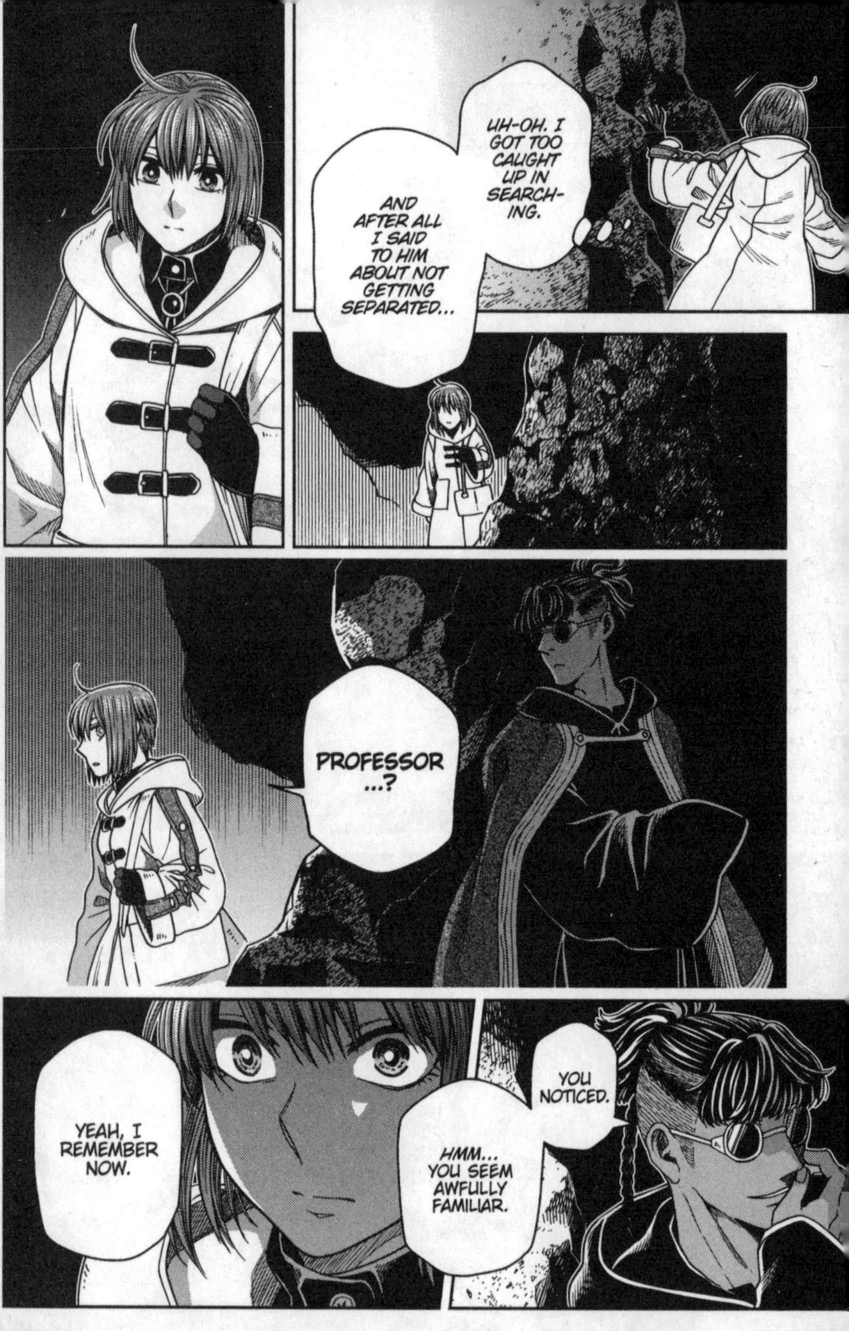
UH-OH. I GOT TOO CAUGHT UP IN SEARCH-ING.
AND AFTER ALL I SAID TO HIM ABOUT NOT GETTING SEPARATED...
PROFESSOR ...?
YOU NOTICED.
HMM... YOU SEEM AWFULLY FAMILIAR.
YEAH, I REMEMBER NOW.

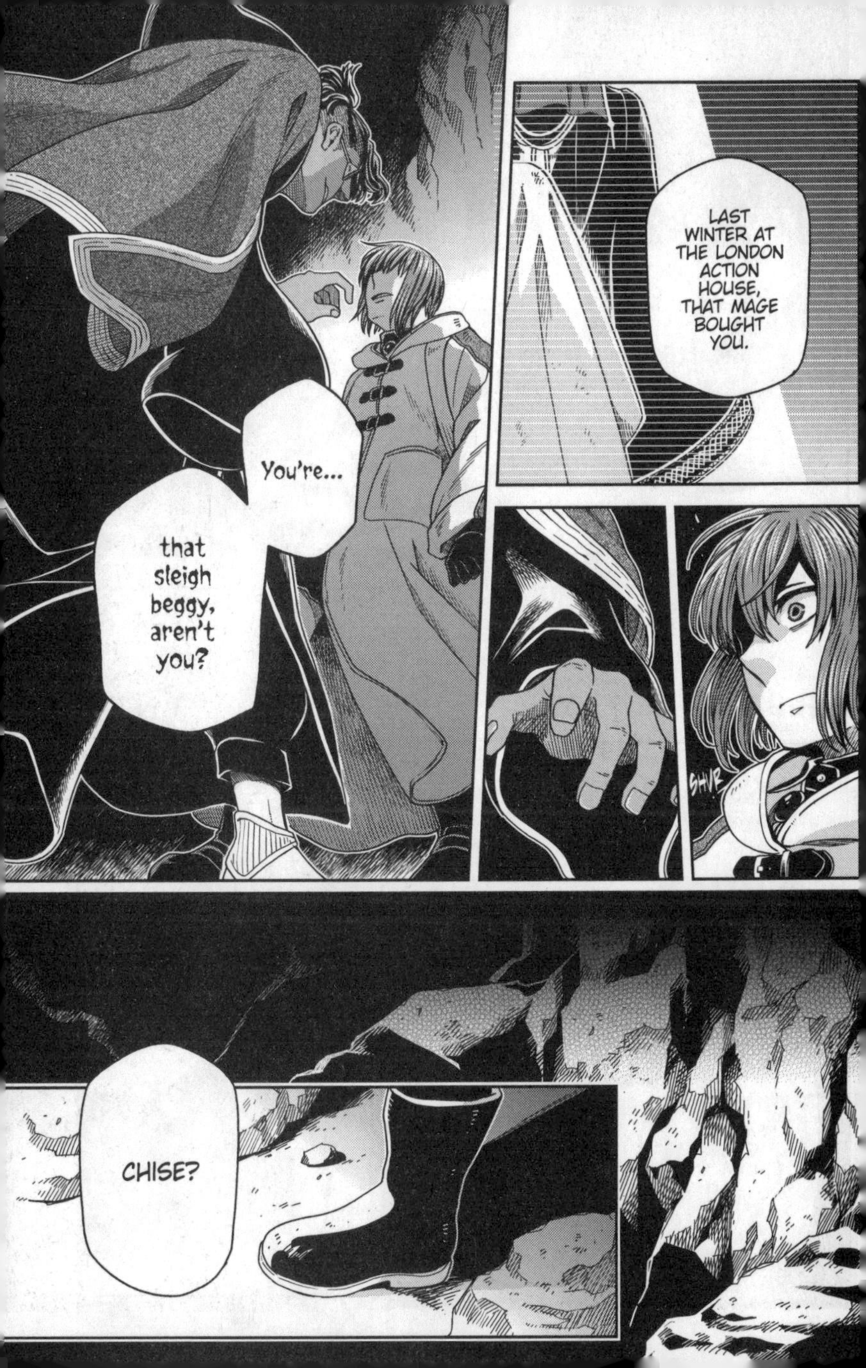
LAST WINTER AT THE LONDON ACTION HOUSE, THAT MAGE BOUGHT YOU.
SHVR
You're...
that sleigh beggy, aren't you?
CHISE?

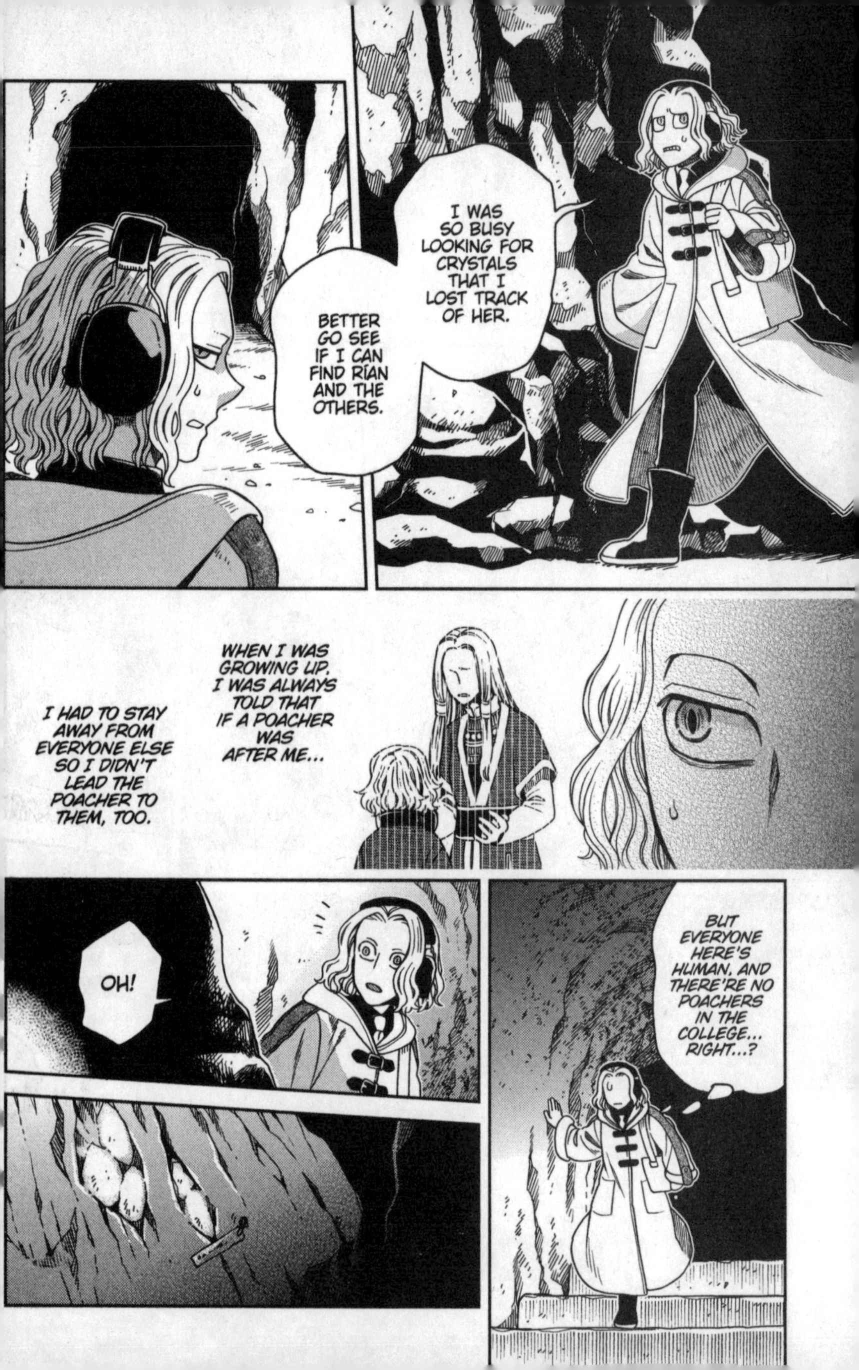
I WAS SO BUSY LOOKING FOR CRYSTALS THAT I LOST TRACK OF HER.
BETTER GO SEE IF I CAN FIND RÍAN AND THE OTHERS.
WHEN I WAS GROWING UP, I WAS ALWAYS TOLD THAT IF A POACHER WAS AFTER ME...
I HAD TO STAY AWAY FROM EVERYONE ELSE SO I DIDN'T LEAD THE POACHER TO THEM, TOO.
BUT EVERYONE HERE'S HUMAN, AND THERE'RE NO POACHERS IN THE COLLEGE... RIGHT...?
OH!

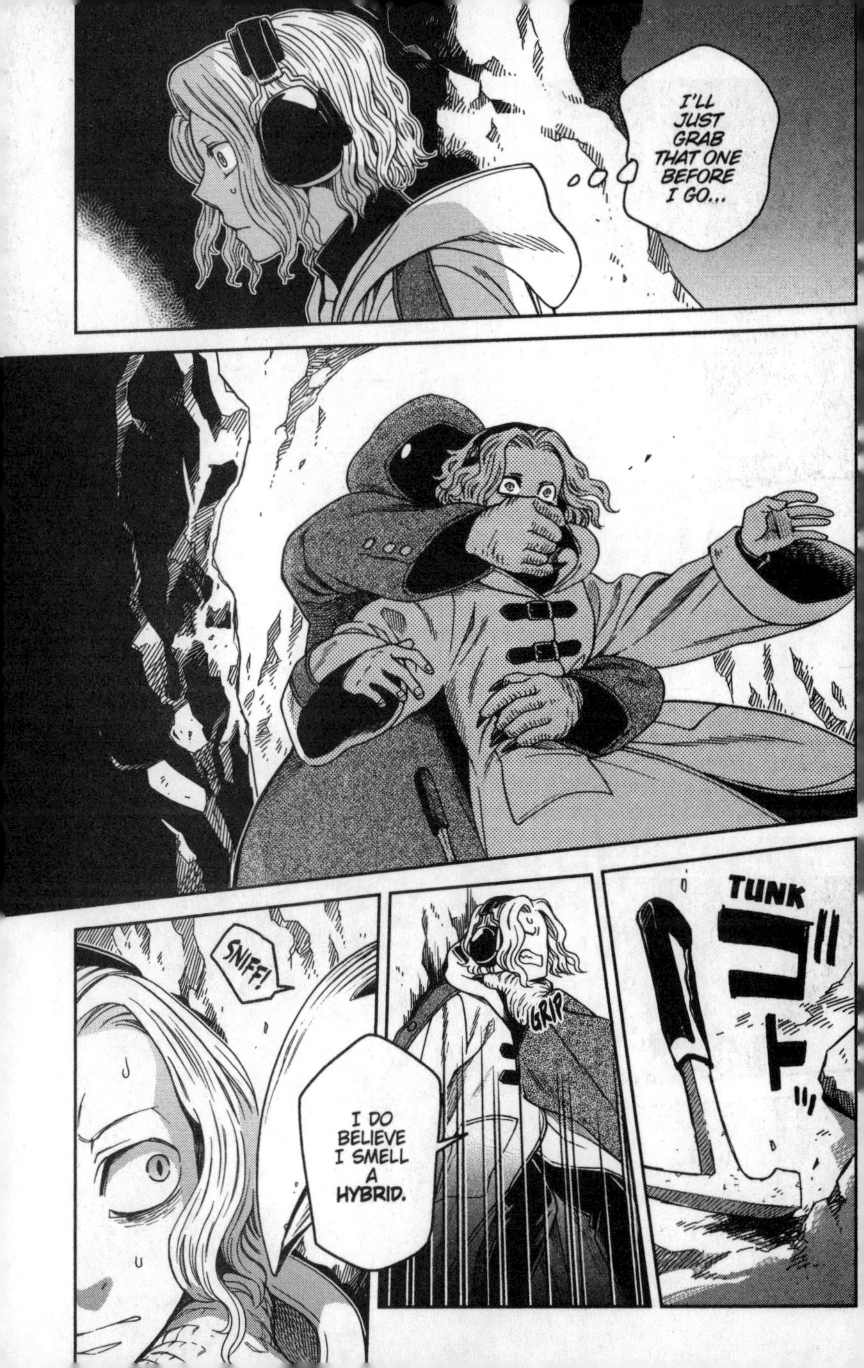
I'LL JUST GRAB THAT ONE BEFORE I GO...
TUNK
GRIP
I DO BELIEVE I SMELL A HYBRID.
SNIFF!

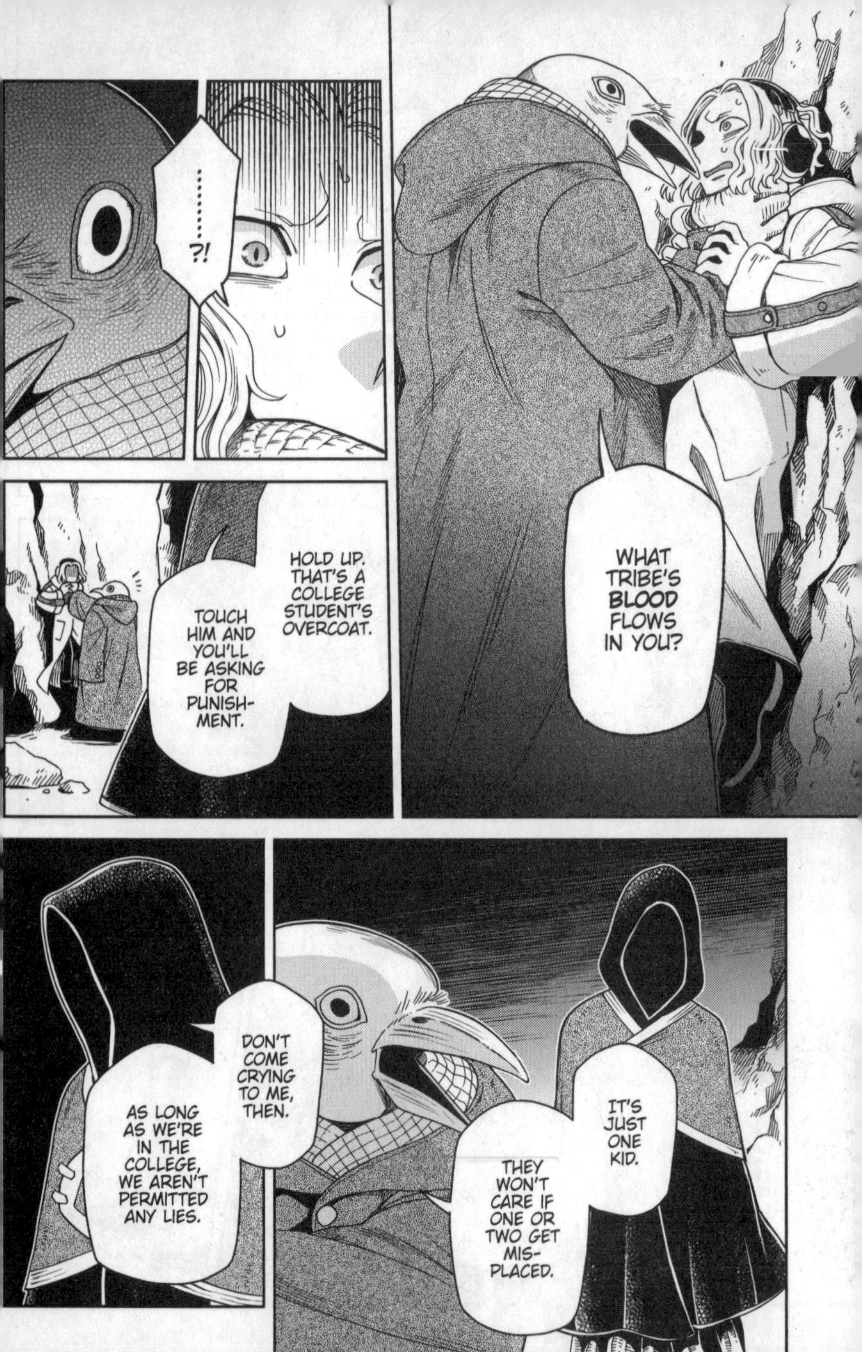
WHAT TRIBE'S BLOOD FLOWS IN YOU?
......?!
HOLD UP. THAT'S A COLLEGE STUDENT'S OVERCOAT.
TOUCH HIM AND YOU'LL BE ASKING FOR PUNISHMENT.
IT'S JUST ONE KID.
THEY WON'T CARE IF ONE OR TWO GET MIS-PLACED.
DON'T COME CRYING TO ME, THEN.
AS LONG AS WE'RE IN THE COLLEGE, WE AREN'T PERMITTED ANY LIES.

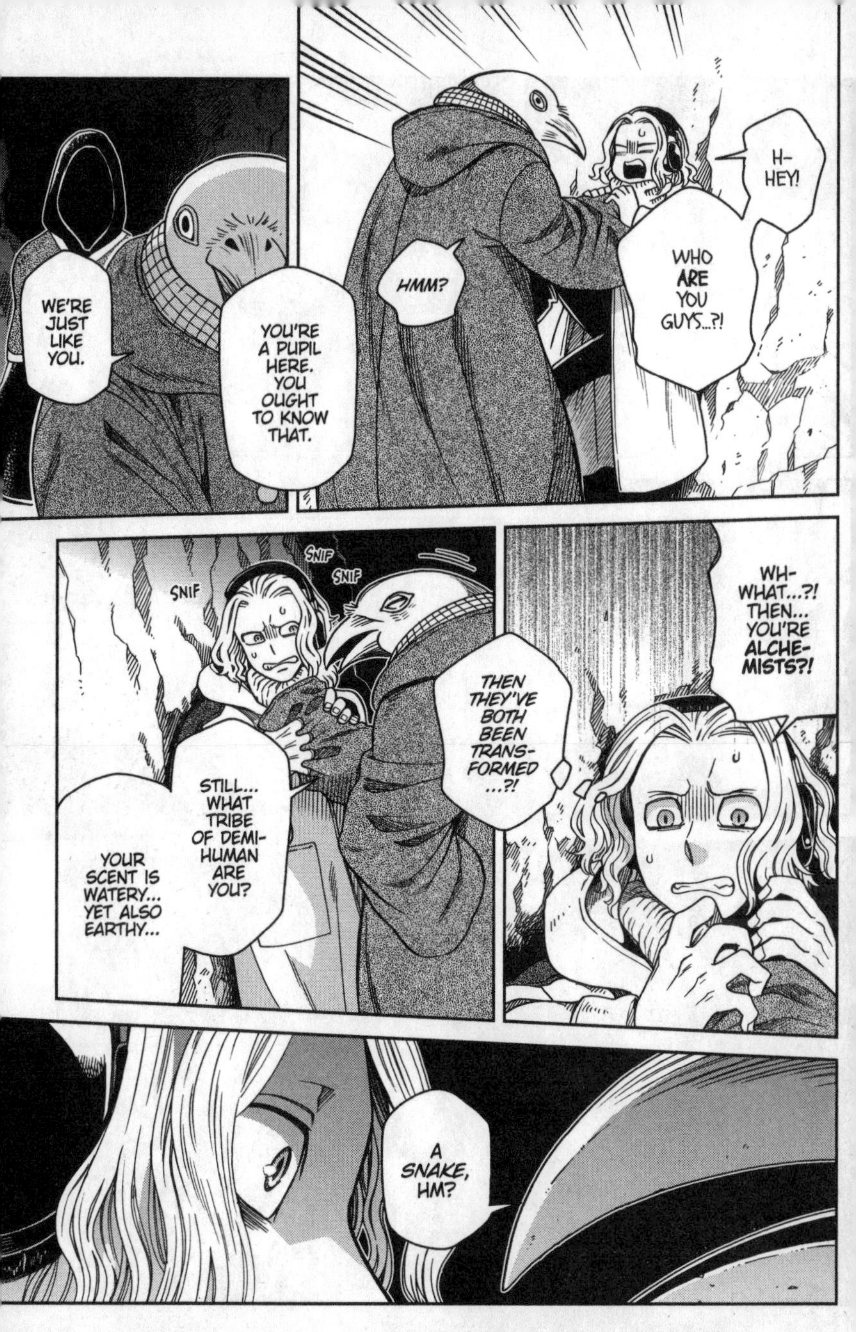
H-HEY!
WHO ARE YOU GUYS...?!
HMM?
YOU'RE A PUPIL HERE. YOU OUGHT TO KNOW THAT.
WE'RE JUST LIKE YOU.
WH-WHAT...?! THEN... YOU'RE ALCHEMISTS?!
THEN THEY'VE BOTH BEEN TRANSFORMED...?!
SNIF
SNIF
SNIF
STILL... WHAT TRIBE OF DEMI-HUMAN ARE YOU?
YOUR SCENT IS WATERY... YET ALSO EARTHY...
A SNAKE, HM?

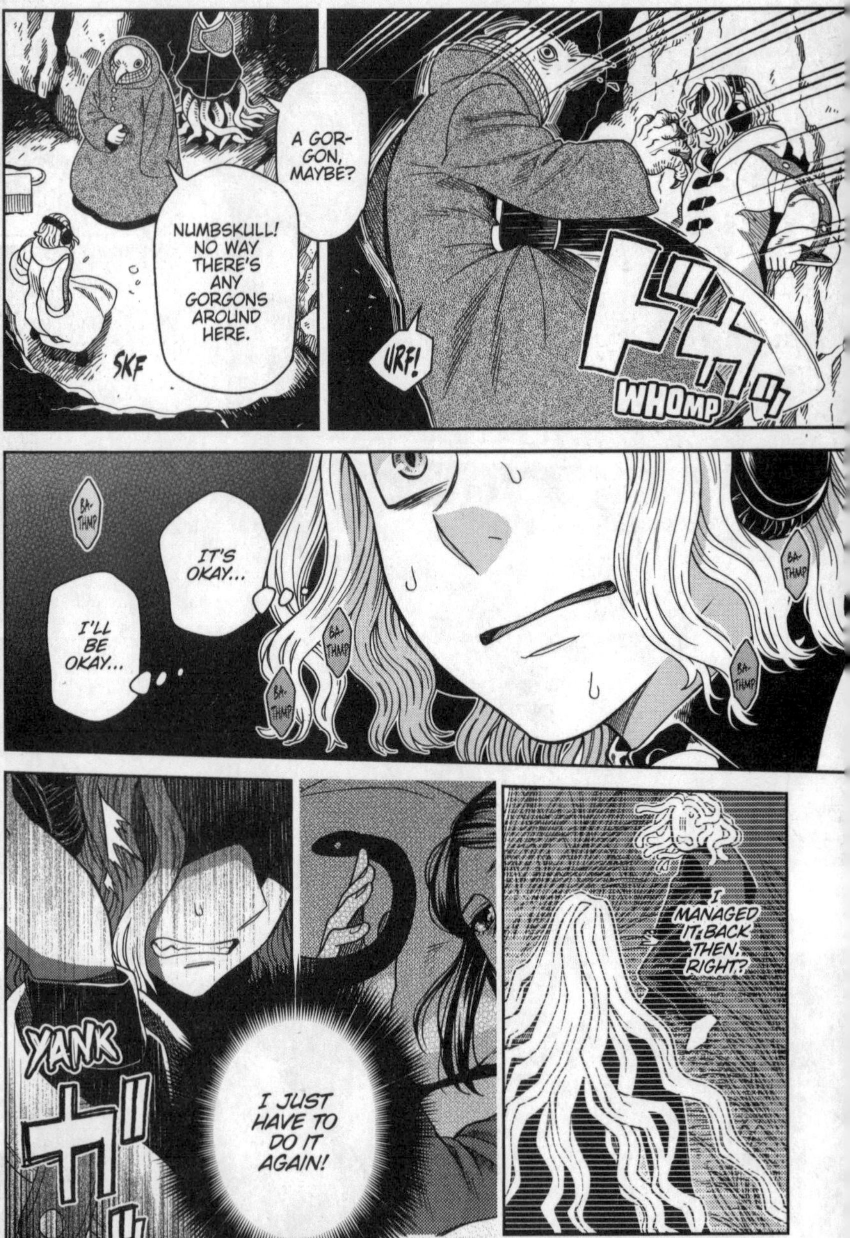
WHOMP
URF!
A GORGON, MAYBE?
NUMBSKULL! NO WAY THERE'S ANY GORGONS AROUND HERE.
SKF
BA-THMP
IT'S OKAY...
I'LL BE OKAY...
BA-THMP
BA-THMP
BA-THMP
BA-THMP
I MANAGED IT BACK THEN, RIGHT?
I JUST HAVE TO DO IT AGAIN!
YANK

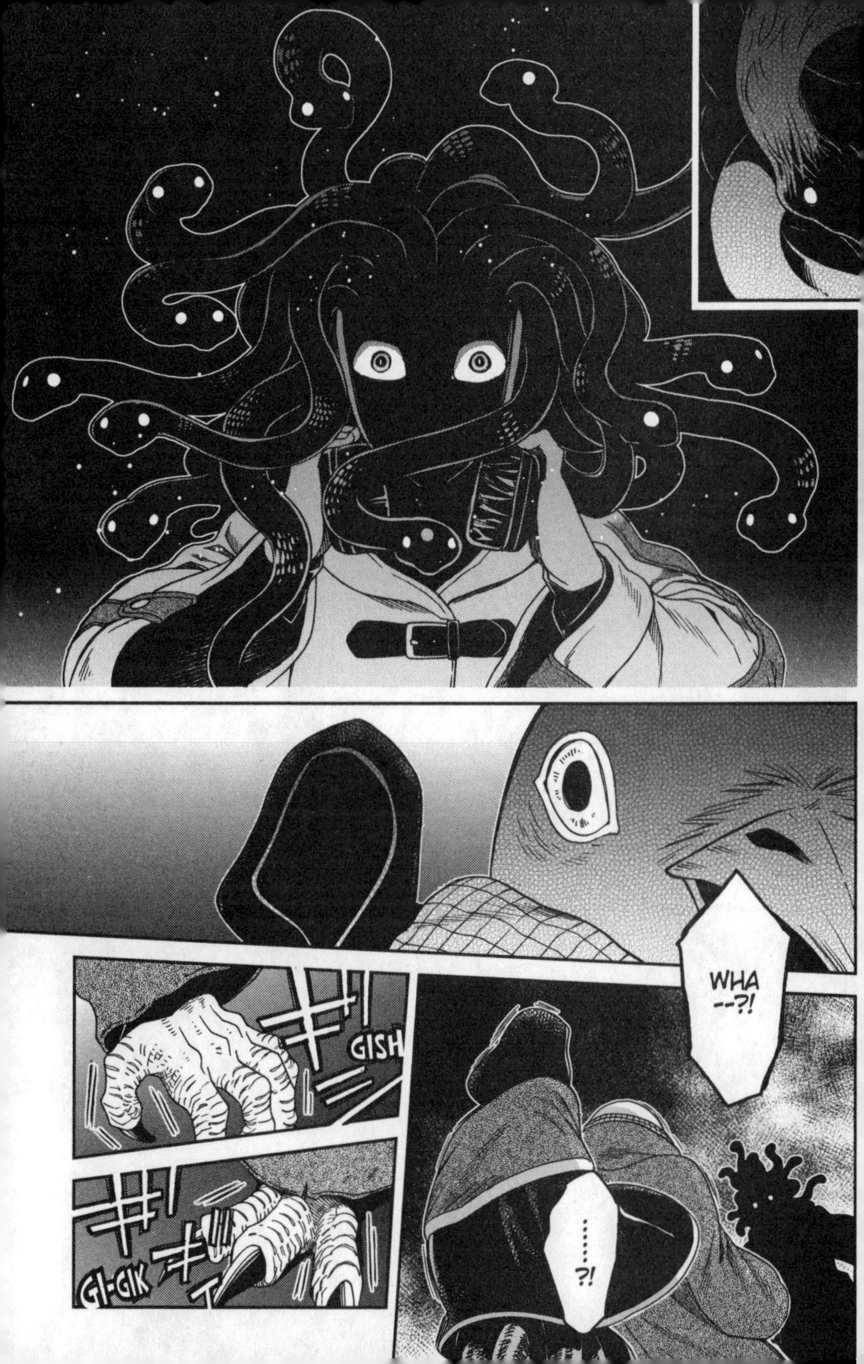
WHA--?!
GISH
GI-GIK
......?!

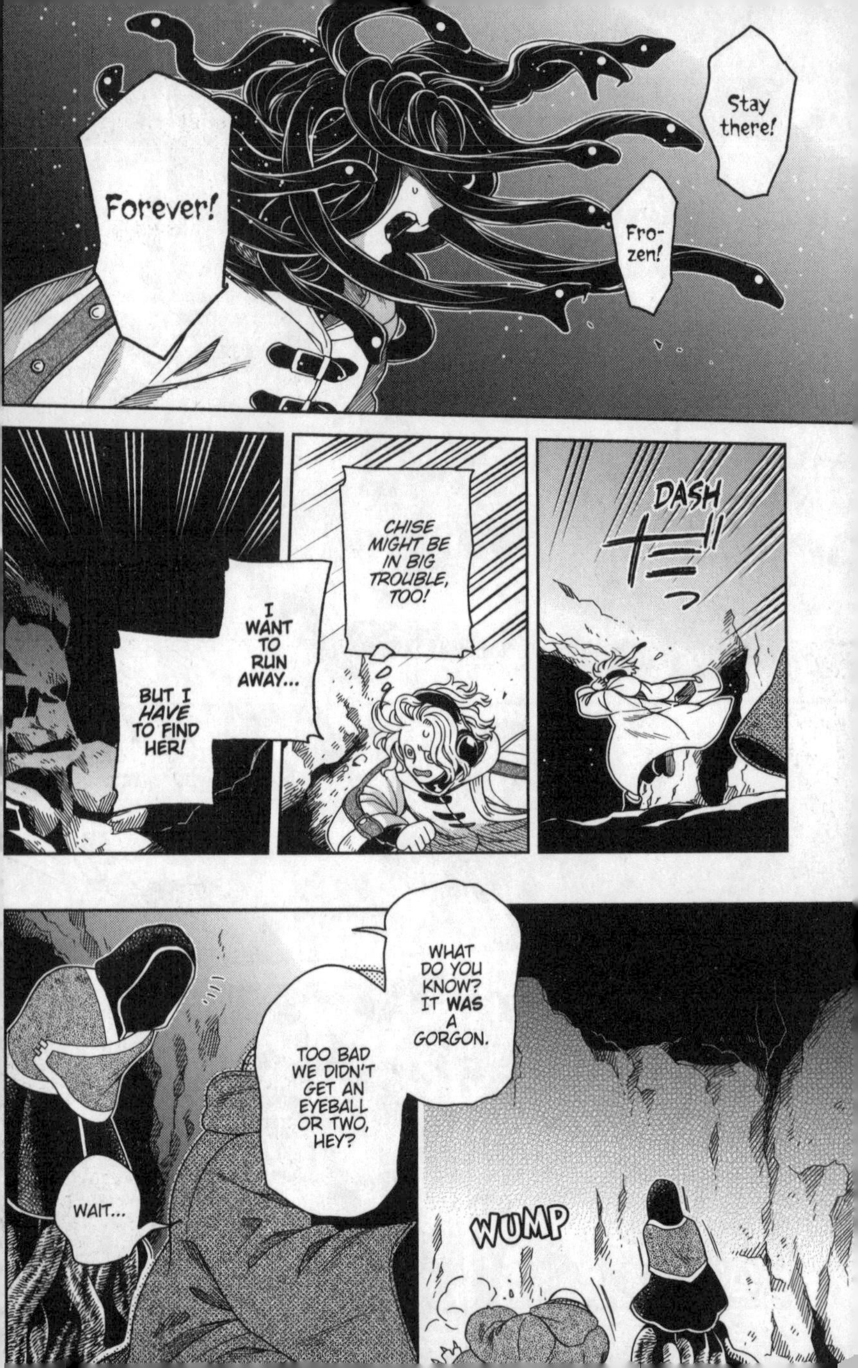
Stay there!
Fro-zen!
Forever!
DASH
CHISE MIGHT BE IN BIG TROUBLE, TOO!
I WANT TO RUN AWAY...
BUT I *HAVE* TO FIND HER!
WHAT DO YOU KNOW? IT WAS A GORGON.
TOO BAD WE DIDN'T GET AN EYEBALL OR TWO, HEY?
WUMP
WAIT...

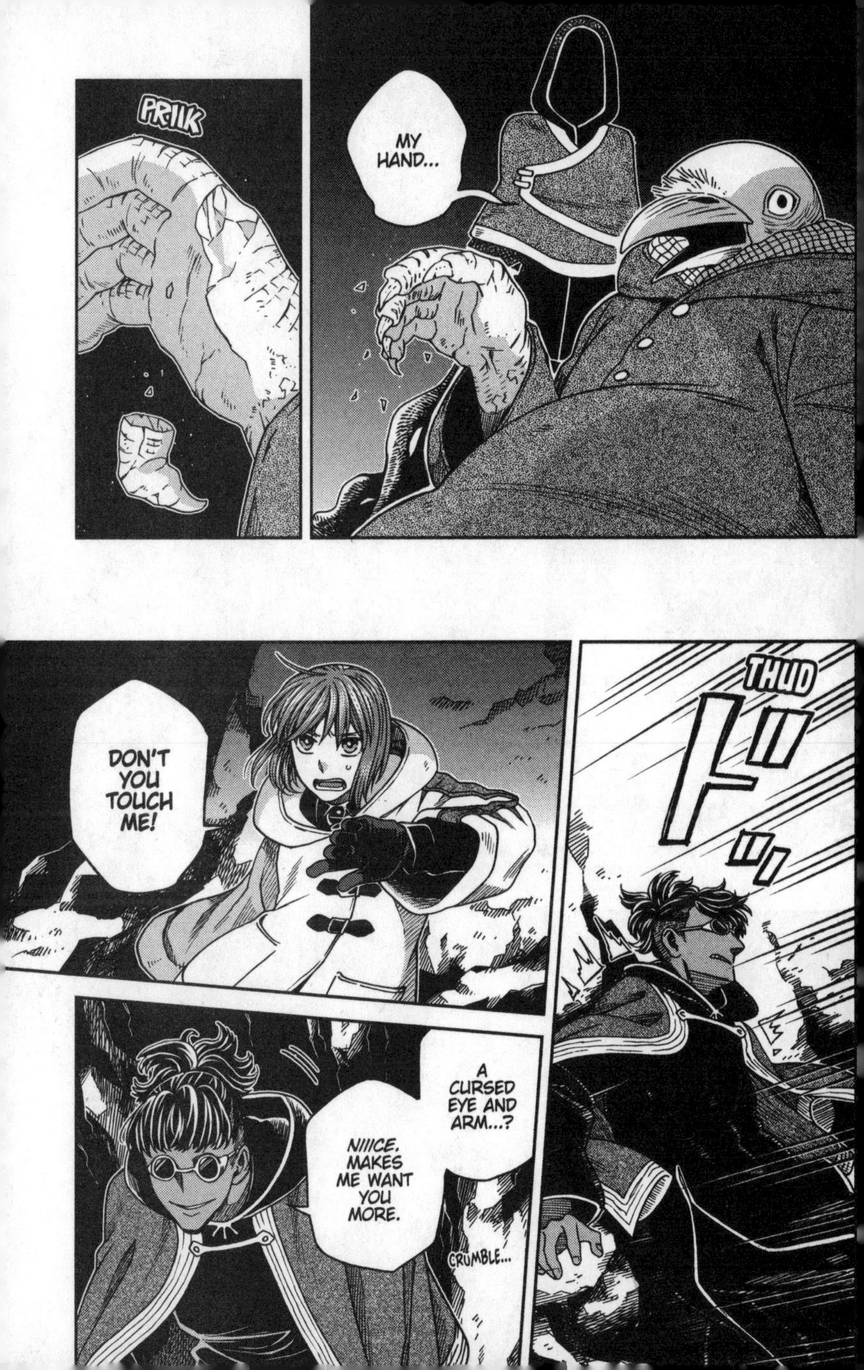
MY HAND...
PRIIK
THUD
ドッ
DON'T YOU TOUCH ME!
A CURSED EYE AND ARM...?
NIIICE. MAKES ME WANT YOU MORE.
CRUMBLE...

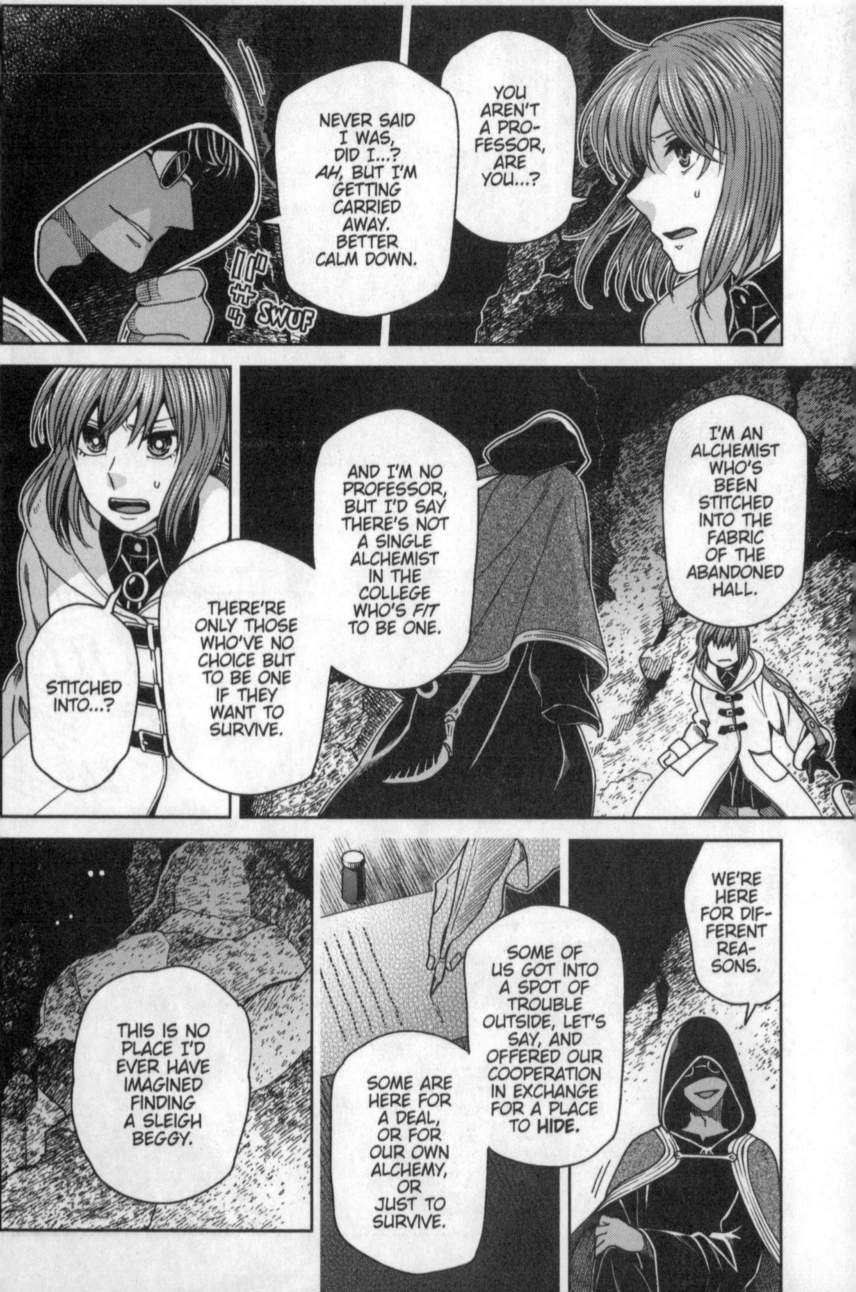
YOU AREN'T A PROFESSOR, ARE YOU...?
NEVER SAID I WAS, DID I...? *AH*, BUT I'M GETTING CARRIED AWAY. BETTER CALM DOWN.
SWUF
I'M AN ALCHEMIST WHO'S BEEN STITCHED INTO THE FABRIC OF THE ABANDONED HALL.
AND I'M NO PROFESSOR, BUT I'D SAY THERE'S NOT A SINGLE ALCHEMIST IN THE COLLEGE WHO'S *FIT* TO BE ONE.
THERE'RE ONLY THOSE WHO'VE NO CHOICE BUT TO BE ONE IF THEY WANT TO SURVIVE.
STITCHED INTO...?
WE'RE HERE FOR DIFFERENT REASONS.
SOME OF US GOT INTO A SPOT OF TROUBLE OUTSIDE, LET'S SAY, AND OFFERED OUR COOPERATION IN EXCHANGE FOR A PLACE TO **HIDE**.
SOME ARE HERE FOR A DEAL, OR FOR OUR OWN ALCHEMY, OR JUST TO SURVIVE.
THIS IS NO PLACE I'D EVER HAVE IMAGINED FINDING A SLEIGH BEGGY.

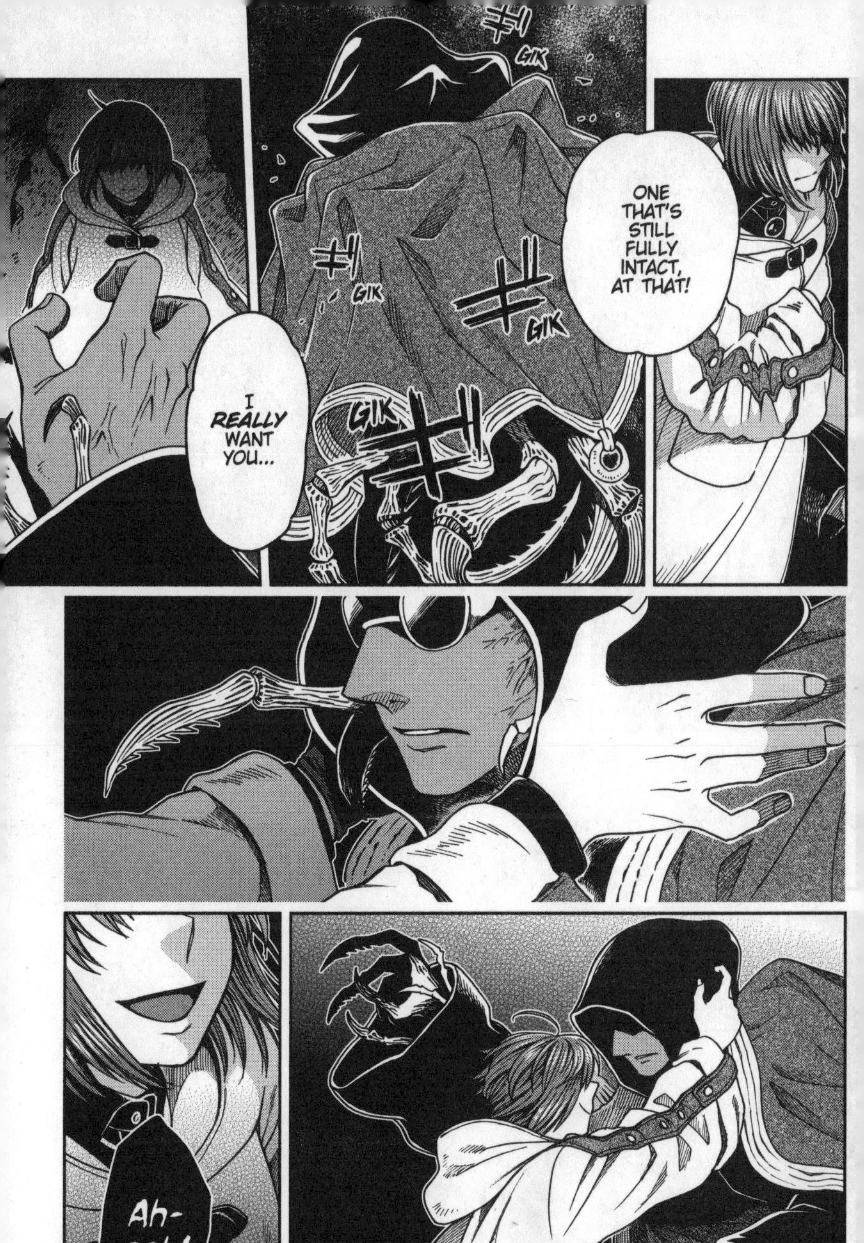
ONE THAT'S STILL FULLY INTACT, AT THAT!
GIK
GIK
GIK
GIK
I *REALLY* WANT YOU...
Ah-aah!

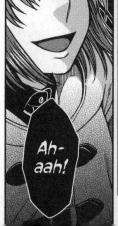

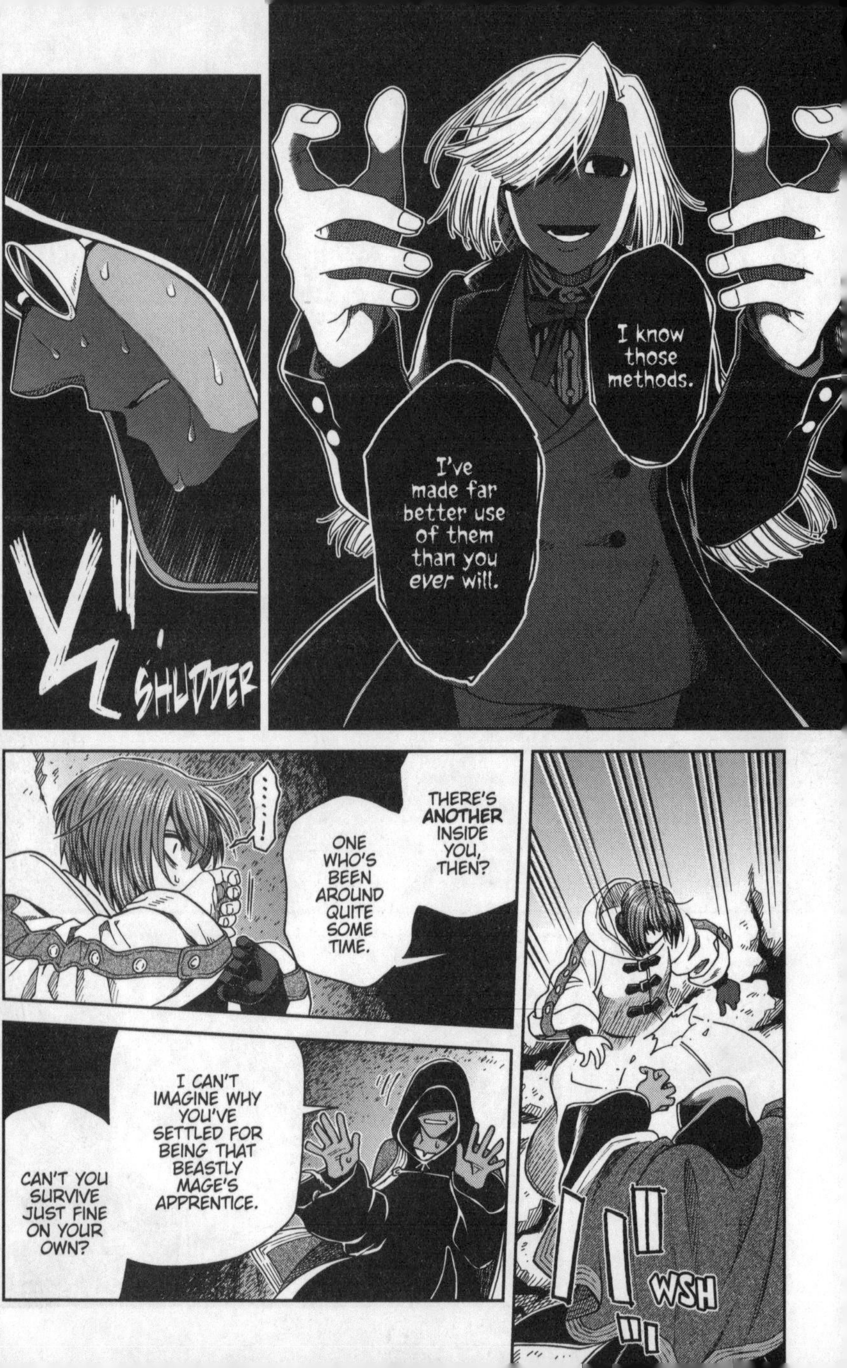
I know those methods.
I've made far better use of them than you *ever* will.
SHUDDER
WSH
THERE'S **ANOTHER** INSIDE YOU, THEN?
ONE WHO'S BEEN AROUND QUITE SOME TIME.
......!
I CAN'T IMAGINE WHY YOU'VE SETTLED FOR BEING THAT BEASTLY MAGE'S APPRENTICE.
CAN'T YOU SURVIVE JUST FINE ON YOUR OWN?

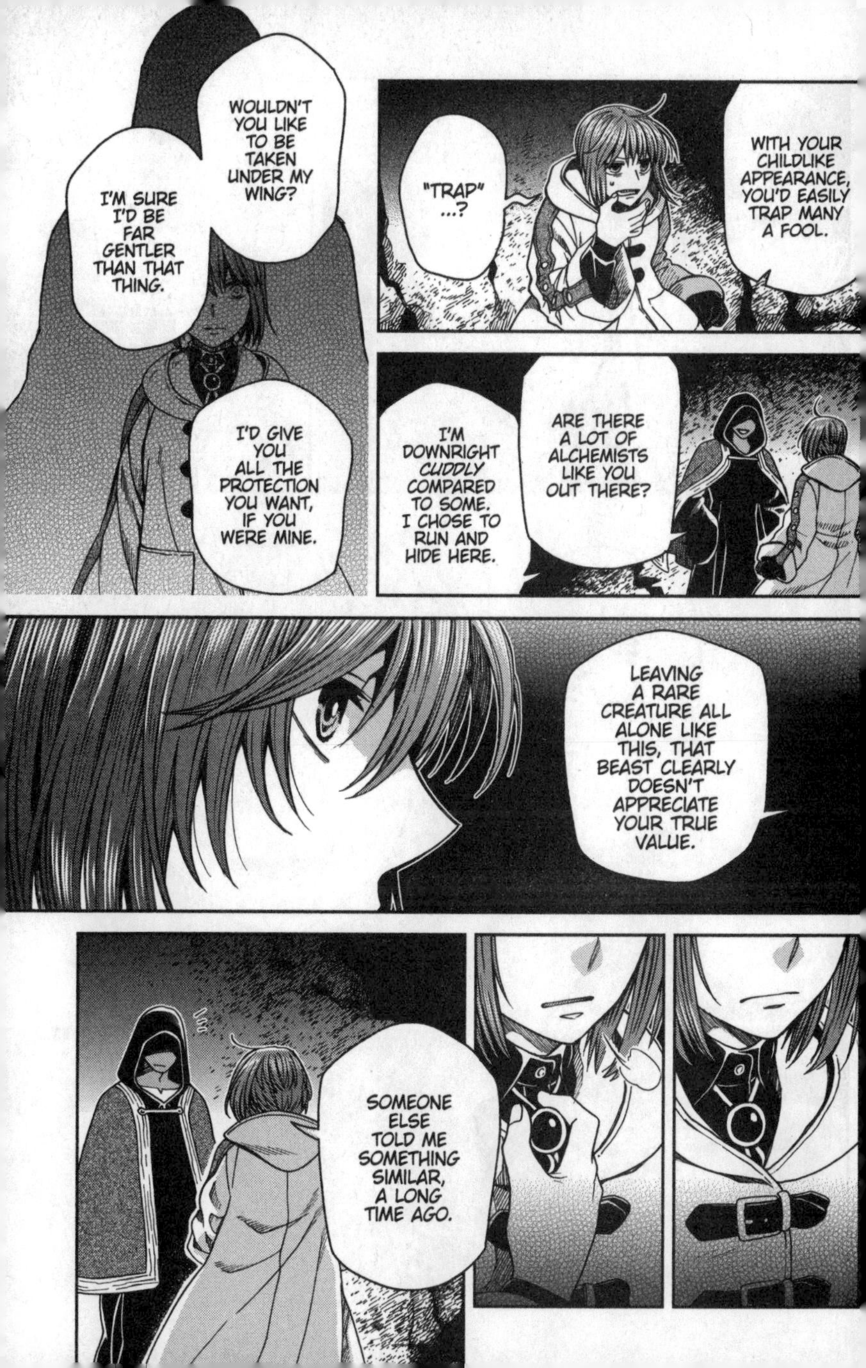
WITH YOUR CHILDLIKE APPEARANCE, YOU'D EASILY TRAP MANY A FOOL.
"TRAP" ...?
ARE THERE A LOT OF ALCHEMISTS LIKE YOU OUT THERE?
I'M DOWNRIGHT *CUDDLY* COMPARED TO SOME. I CHOSE TO RUN AND HIDE HERE.
WOULDN'T YOU LIKE TO BE TAKEN UNDER MY WING?
I'M SURE I'D BE FAR GENTLER THAN THAT THING.
I'D GIVE YOU ALL THE PROTECTION YOU WANT, IF YOU WERE MINE.
LEAVING A RARE CREATURE ALL ALONE LIKE THIS, THAT BEAST CLEARLY DOESN'T APPRECIATE YOUR TRUE VALUE.
SOMEONE ELSE TOLD ME SOMETHING SIMILAR, A LONG TIME AGO.

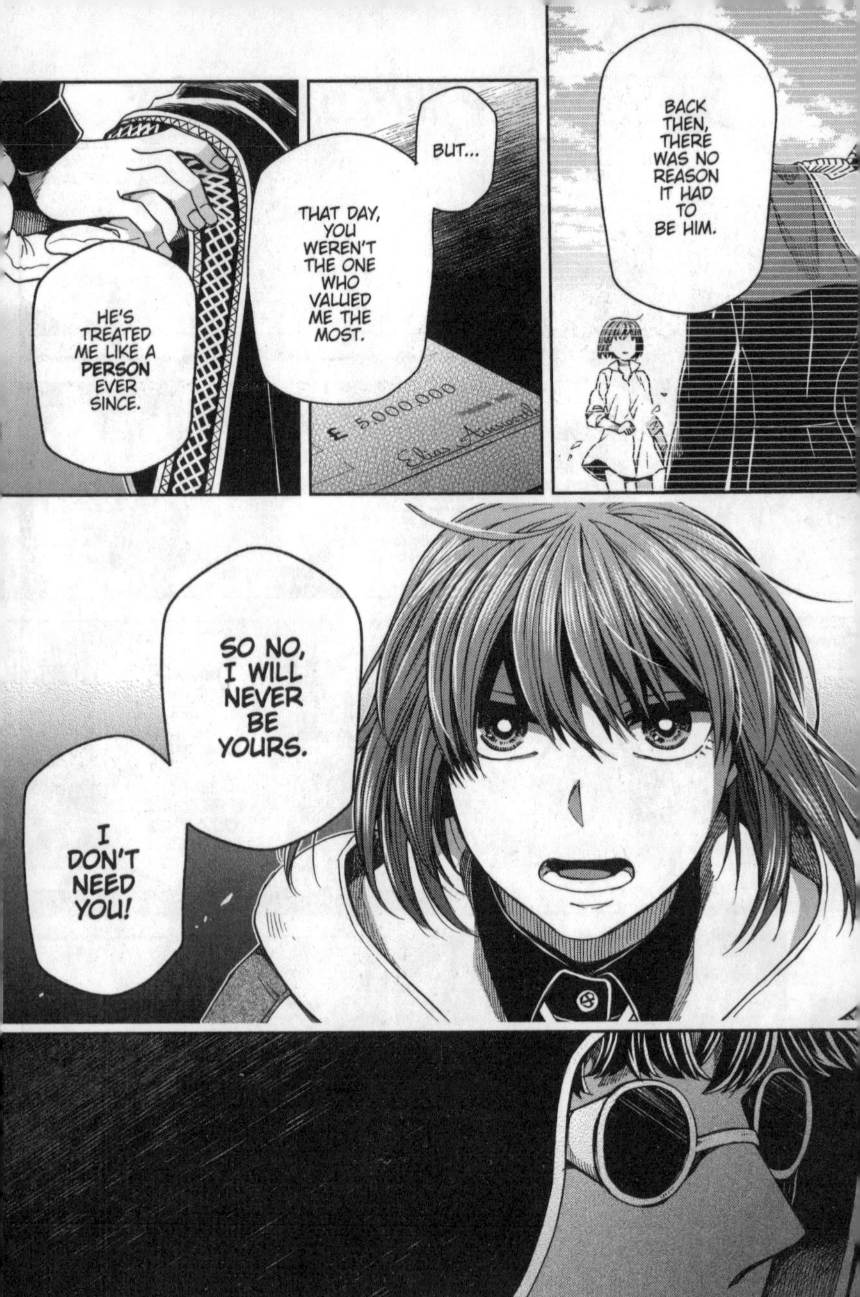
BACK THEN, THERE WAS NO REASON IT HAD TO BE HIM.
BUT...
THAT DAY, YOU WEREN'T THE ONE WHO VALUED ME THE MOST.
£ 5,000,000
HE'S TREATED ME LIKE A PERSON EVER SINCE.
SO NO, I WILL NEVER BE YOURS.
I DON'T NEED YOU!

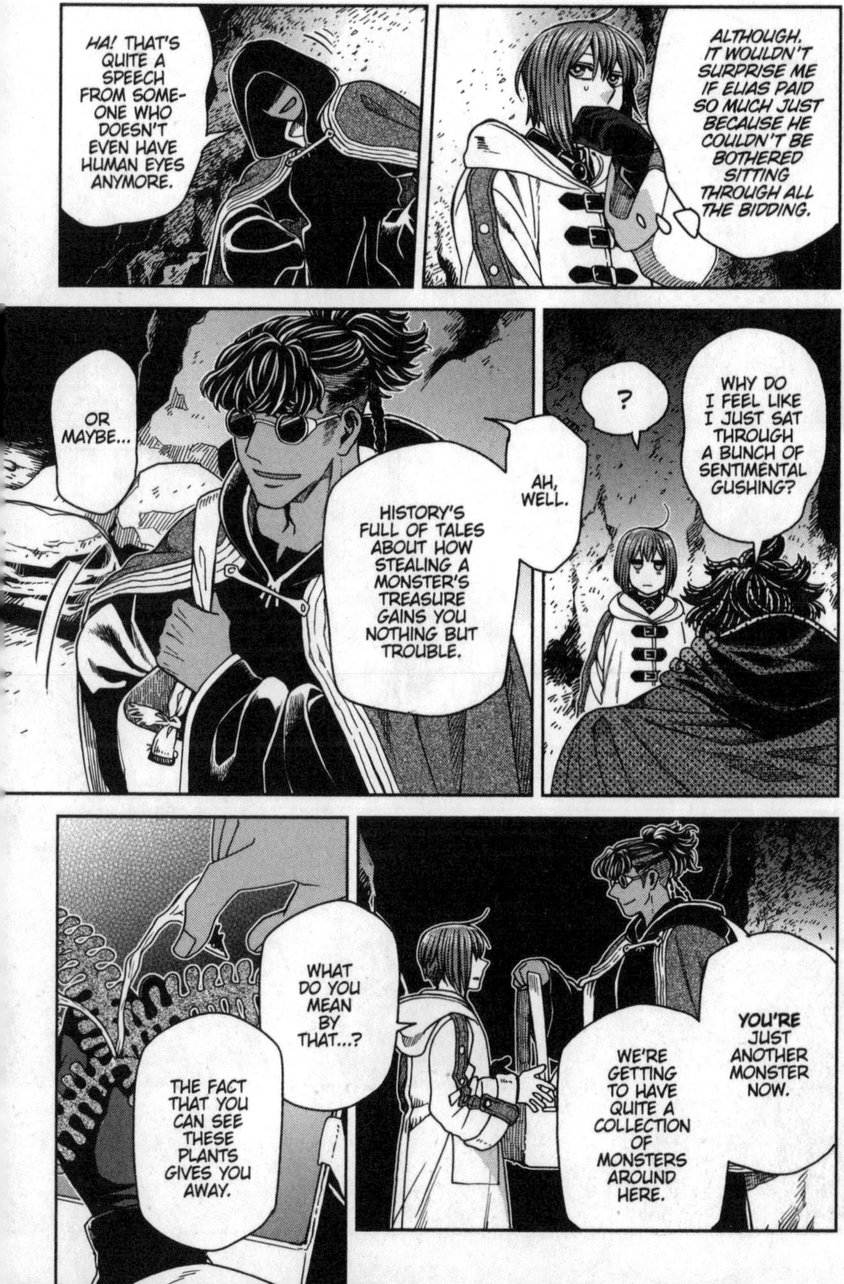
ALTHOUGH. IT WOULDN'T SURPRISE ME IF ELIAS PAID SO MUCH JUST BECAUSE HE COULDN'T BE BOTHERED SITTING THROUGH ALL THE BIDDING.
HA! THAT'S QUITE A SPEECH FROM SOME-ONE WHO DOESN'T EVEN HAVE HUMAN EYES ANYMORE.
WHY DO I FEEL LIKE I JUST SAT THROUGH A BUNCH OF SENTIMENTAL GUSHING?
?
AH, WELL.
HISTORY'S FULL OF TALES ABOUT HOW STEALING A MONSTER'S TREASURE GAINS YOU NOTHING BUT TROUBLE.
OR MAYBE...
YOU'RE JUST ANOTHER MONSTER NOW.
WE'RE GETTING TO HAVE QUITE A COLLECTION OF MONSTERS AROUND HERE.
WHAT DO YOU MEAN BY THAT...?
THE FACT THAT YOU CAN SEE THESE PLANTS GIVES YOU AWAY.

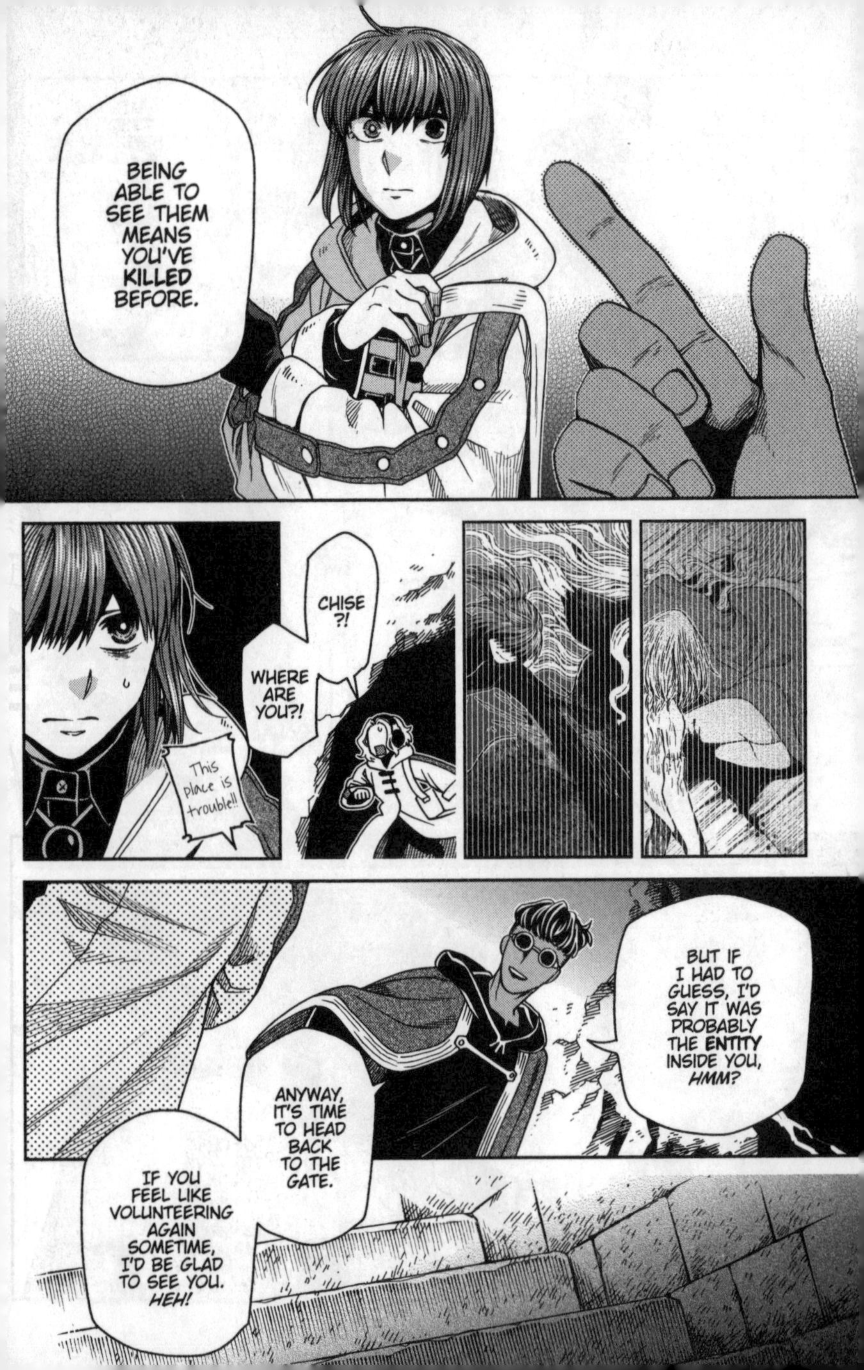
BEING ABLE TO SEE THEM MEANS YOU'VE KILLED BEFORE.
CHISE?!
WHERE ARE YOU?!
This place is trouble!!
BUT IF I HAD TO GUESS, I'D SAY IT WAS PROBABLY THE ENTITY INSIDE YOU, HMM?
ANYWAY, IT'S TIME TO HEAD BACK TO THE GATE.
IF YOU FEEL LIKE VOLUNTEERING AGAIN SOMETIME, I'D BE GLAD TO SEE YOU. HEH!

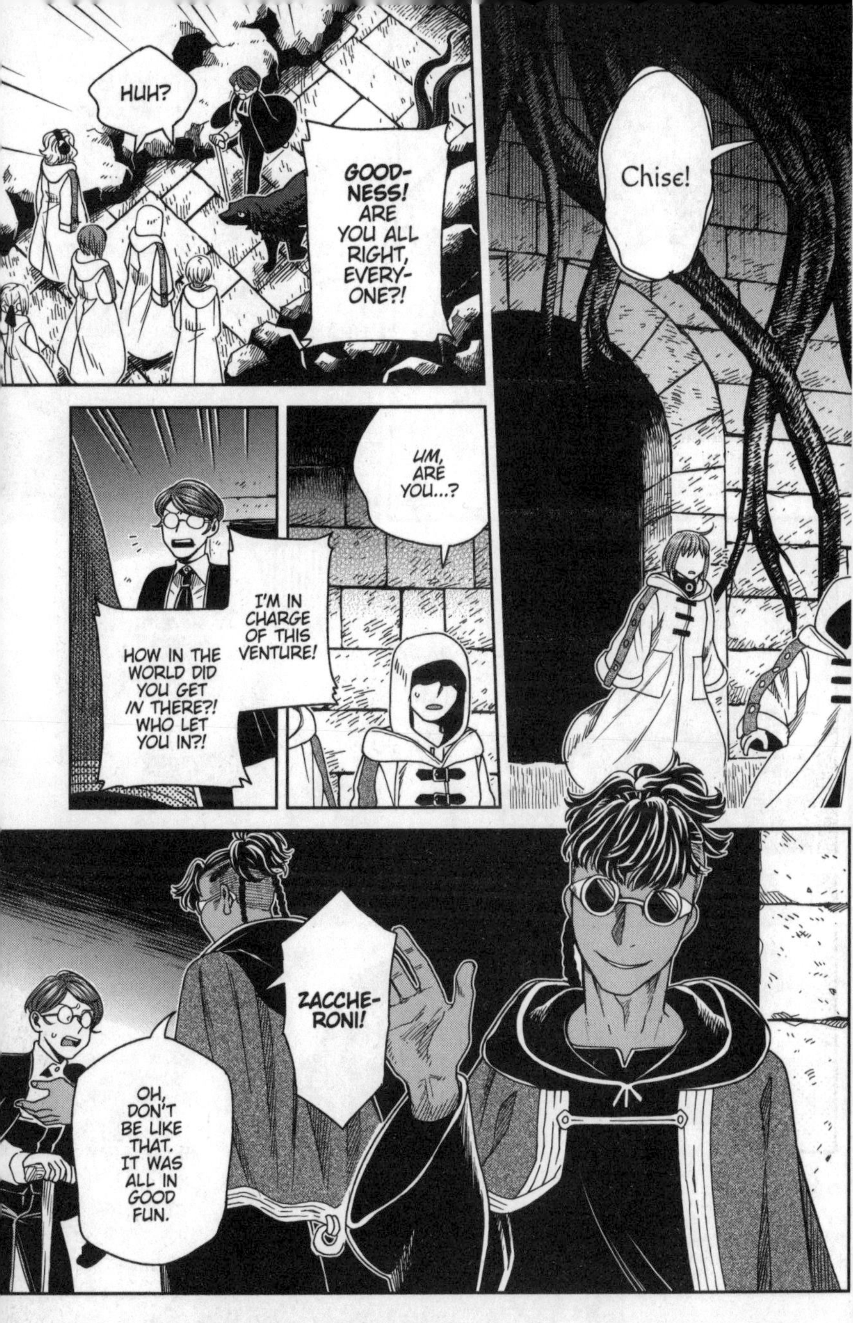
Chise!
GOOD-NESS! ARE YOU ALL RIGHT, EVERY-ONE?!
HUH?
UM, ARE YOU...?
I'M IN CHARGE OF THIS VENTURE!
HOW IN THE WORLD DID YOU GET IN THERE?! WHO LET YOU IN?!
ZACCHE-RONI!
OH, DON'T BE LIKE THAT. IT WAS ALL IN GOOD FUN.

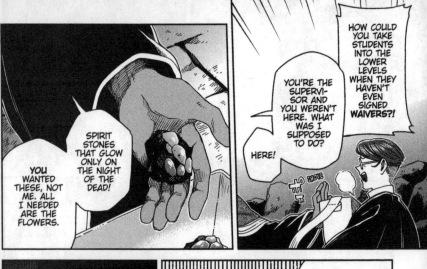

HOW COULD YOU TAKE STUDENTS INTO THE LOWER LEVELS WHEN THEY HAVEN'T EVEN SIGNED WAIVERS?!
YOU'RE THE SUPERVI-SOR AND YOU WEREN'T HERE. WHAT WAS I SUPPOSED TO DO?
HERE!
SHOVE
SPIRIT STONES THAT GLOW ONLY ON THE NIGHT OF THE DEAD!
YOU WANTED THESE, NOT ME. ALL I NEEDED ARE THE FLOWERS.
BUT I WENT OUT OF MY WAY TO HAVE THESE HARVESTED FOR YOU. SHOW SOME APPRECIATION, HM?
HNGR-RRRR ...!
MY SUPERIORS WILL BE HEARING ABOUT THIS!!
WHIRL
IF YOU WANT.
ISN'T THERE SOMEONE WAY NASTIER THAN ME WHO YOU SHOULD PAY ATTENTION TO, THOUGH?
RIGHT INSIDE THE COL-LEGE?
......!
?

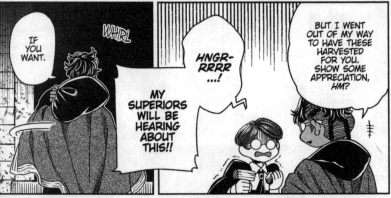

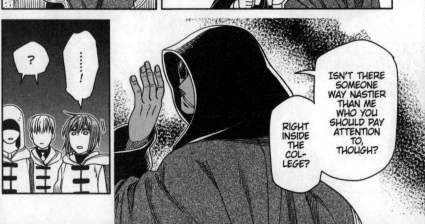

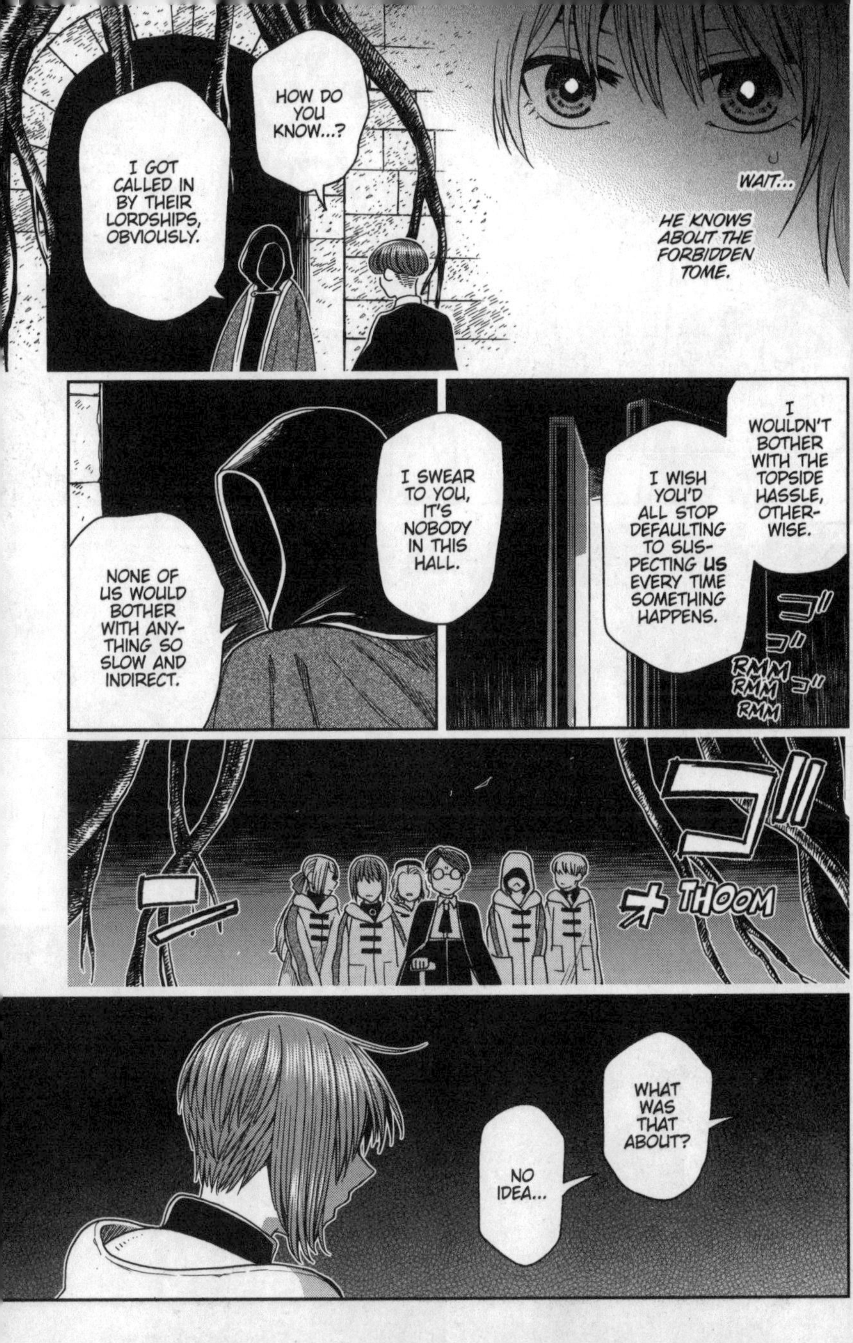
WAIT...
HE KNOWS ABOUT THE FORBIDDEN TOME.
HOW DO YOU KNOW...?
I GOT CALLED IN BY THEIR LORDSHIPS, OBVIOUSLY.
I WOULDN'T BOTHER WITH THE TOPSIDE HASSLE, OTHERWISE.
I WISH YOU'D ALL STOP DEFAULTING TO SUSPECTING US EVERY TIME SOMETHING HAPPENS.
RMM RMM RMM
I SWEAR TO YOU, IT'S NOBODY IN THIS HALL.
NONE OF US WOULD BOTHER WITH ANYTHING SO SLOW AND INDIRECT.
THOOM
WHAT WAS THAT ABOUT?
NO IDEA...

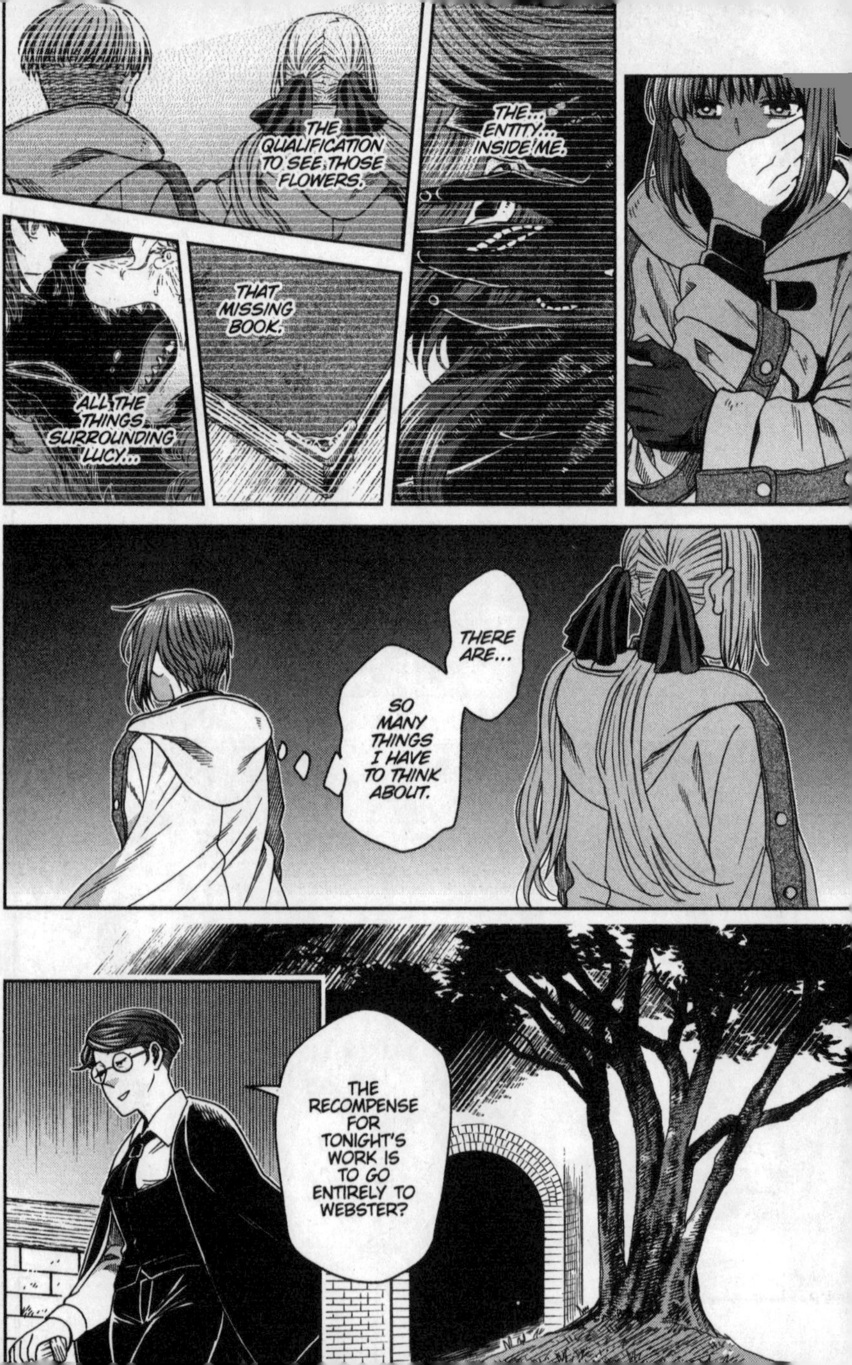
THE... ENTITY... INSIDE ME.
THE QUALIFICATION TO SEE THOSE FLOWERS.
THAT MISSING BOOK.
ALL THE THINGS SURROUNDING LUCY...
THERE ARE...
SO MANY THINGS I HAVE TO THINK ABOUT.
THE RECOMPENSE FOR TONIGHT'S WORK IS TO GO ENTIRELY TO WEBSTER?

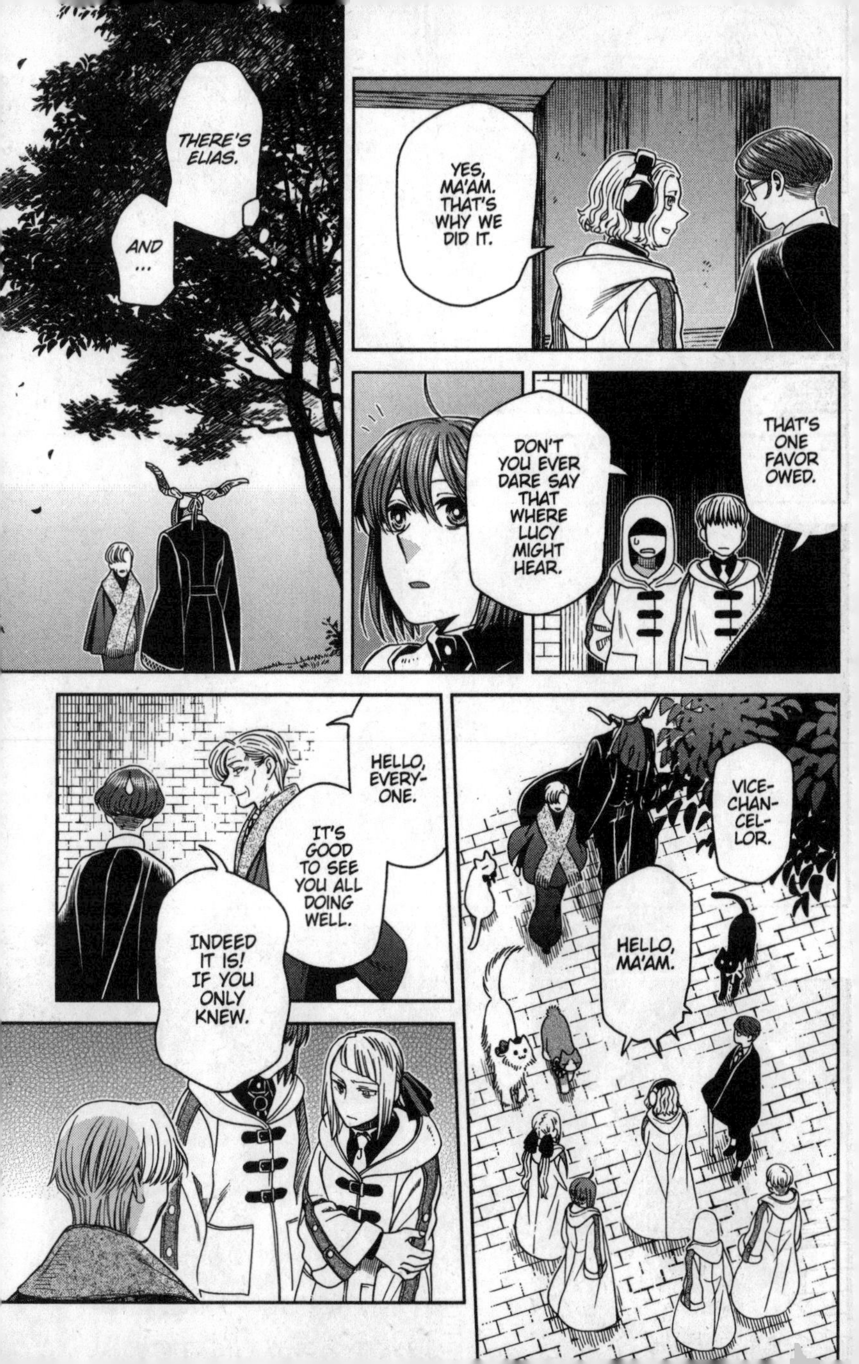
YES, MA'AM. THAT'S WHY WE DID IT.
THAT'S ONE FAVOR OWED.
DON'T YOU EVER DARE SAY THAT WHERE LUCY MIGHT HEAR.
THERE'S ELIAS.
AND ...
VICE-CHANCELLOR.
HELLO, MA'AM.
HELLO, EVERYONE.
IT'S GOOD TO SEE YOU ALL DOING WELL.
INDEED IT IS! IF YOU ONLY KNEW.

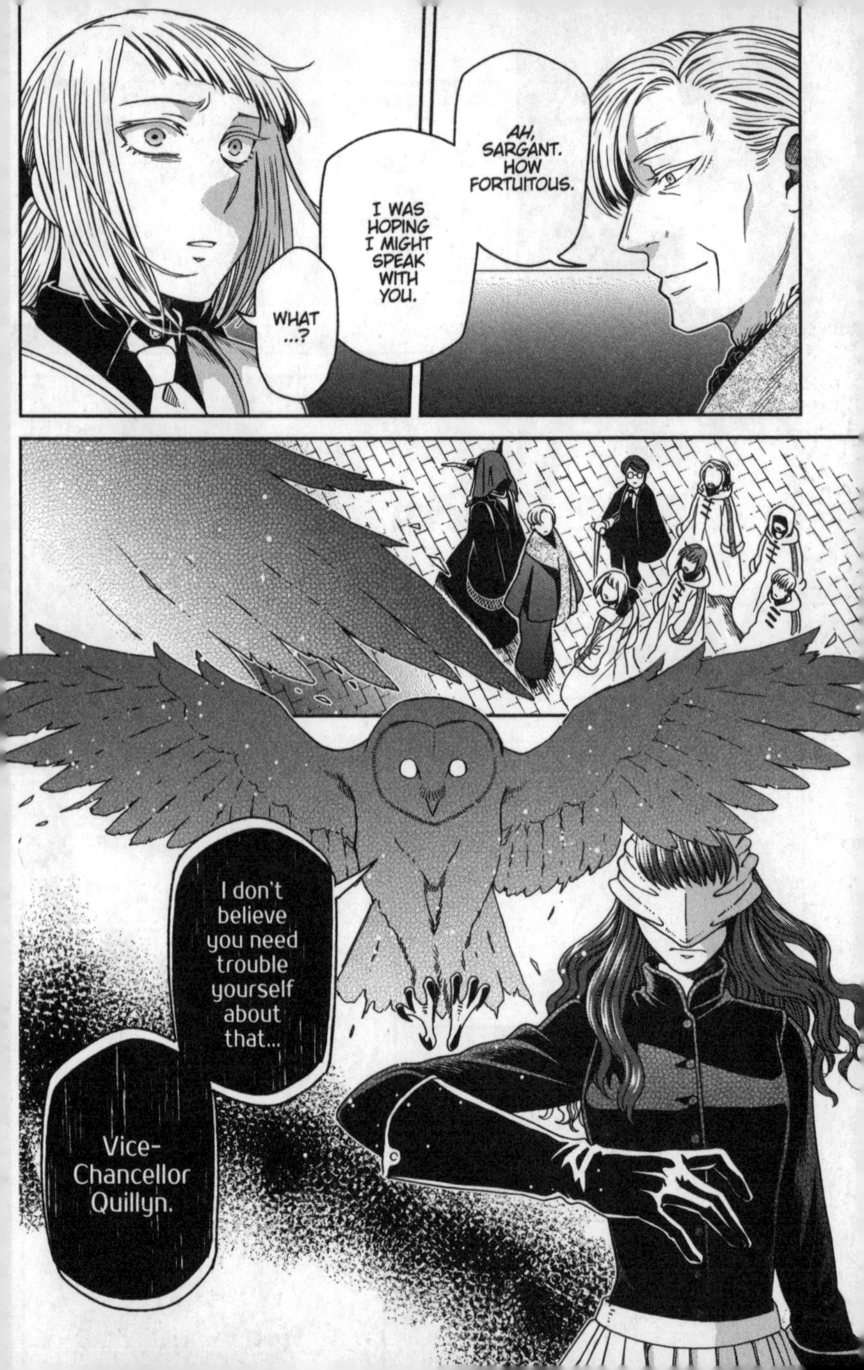
AH, SARGANT. HOW FORTUITOUS.
I WAS HOPING I MIGHT SPEAK WITH YOU.
WHAT ...?
I don't believe you need trouble yourself about that...
Vice-Chancellor Quillyn.

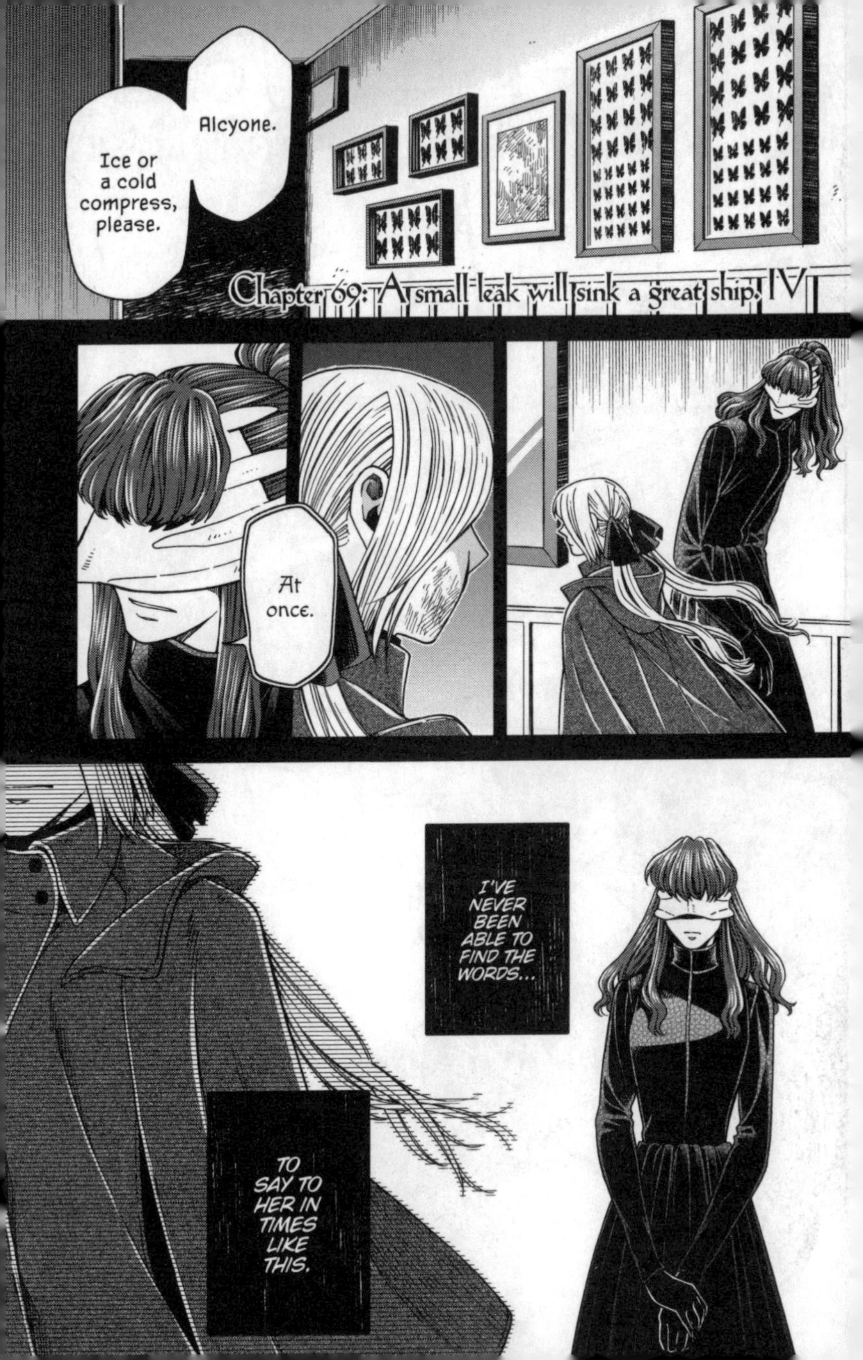
Alcyone.
Ice or a cold compress, please.
Chapter 69: A small leak will sink a great ship. IV
At once.
I'VE NEVER BEEN ABLE TO FIND THE WORDS...
TO SAY TO HER IN TIMES LIKE THIS.

Chapter 69:
A small leak will sink a great ship. IV

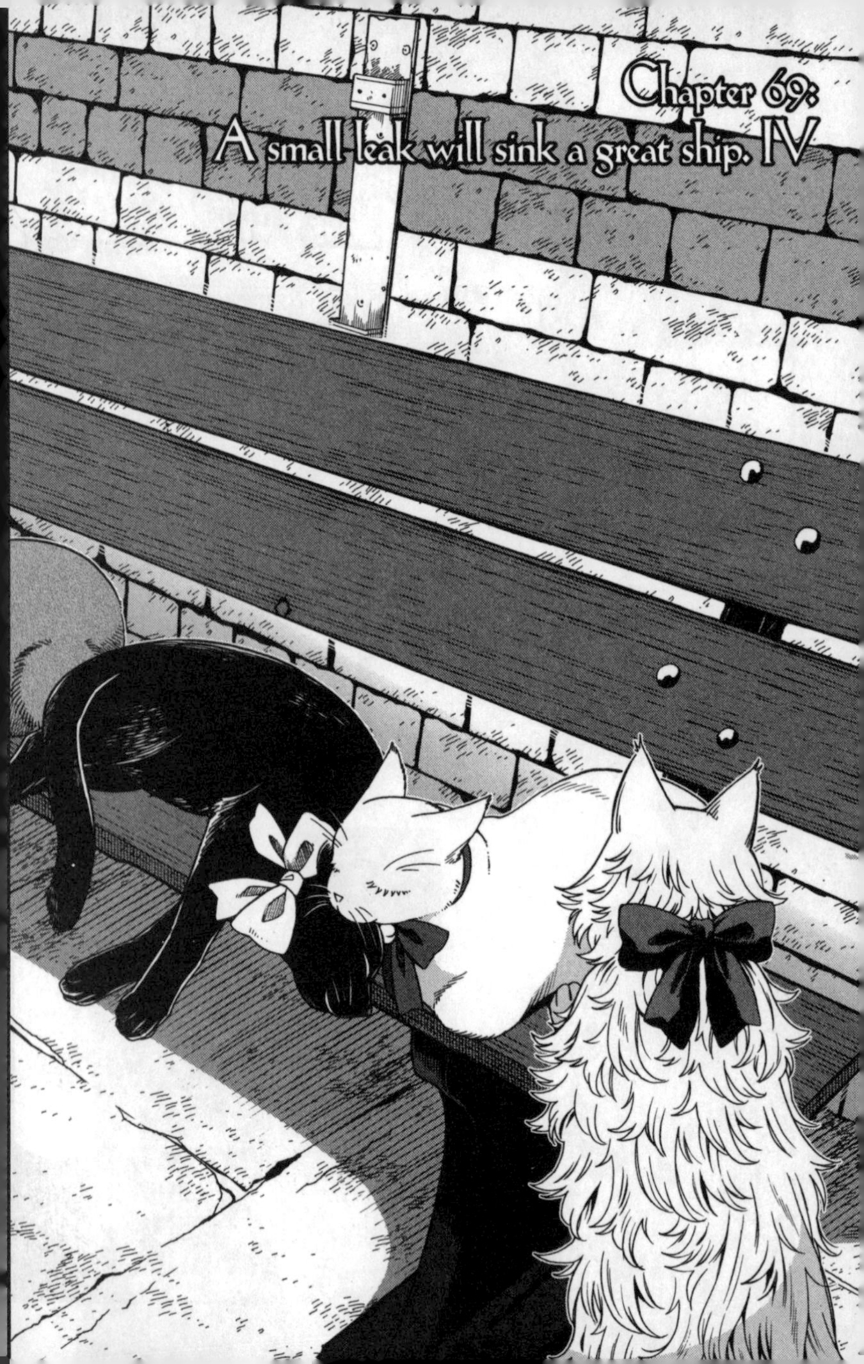

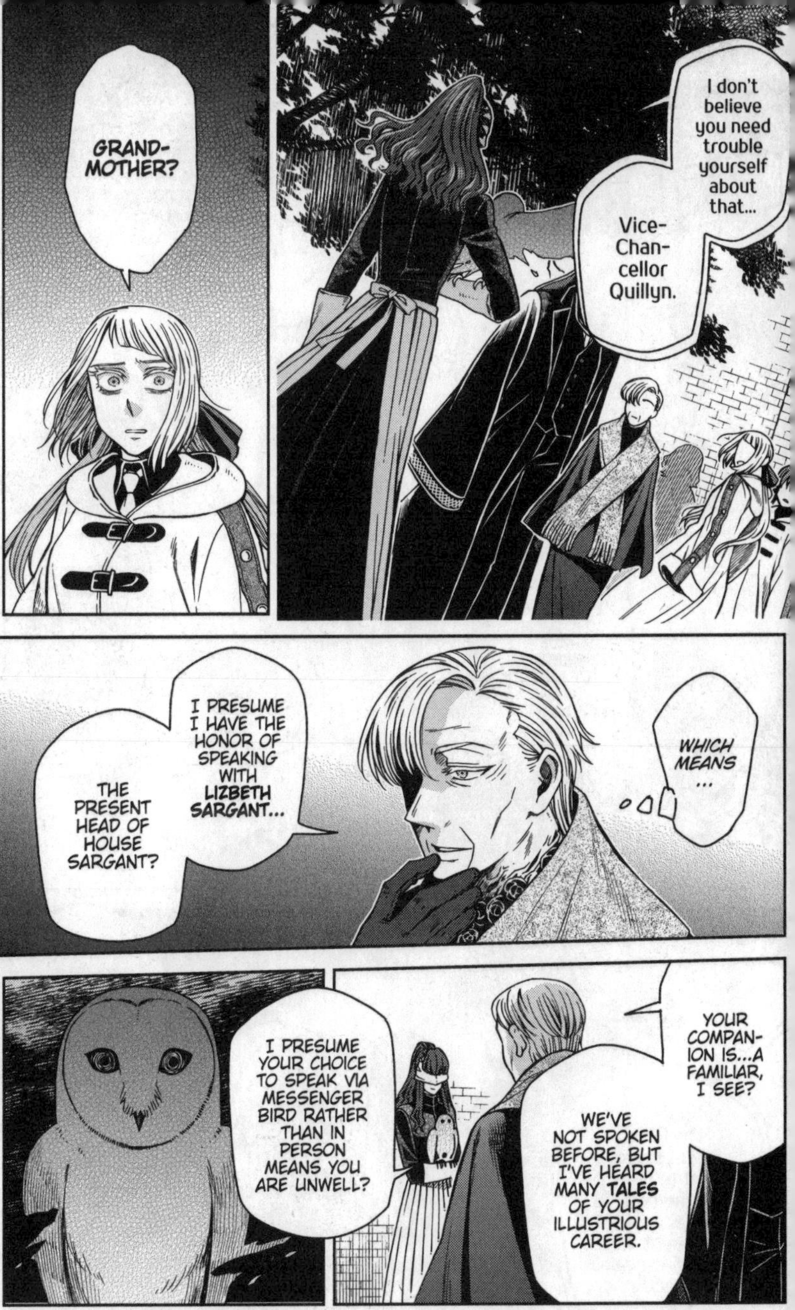
I don't believe you need trouble yourself about that...
Vice-Chancellor Quillyn.
GRAND-MOTHER?
WHICH MEANS ...
I PRESUME I HAVE THE HONOR OF SPEAKING WITH LIZBETH SARGANT...
THE PRESENT HEAD OF HOUSE SARGANT?
YOUR COMPANION IS...A FAMILIAR, I SEE?
WE'VE NOT SPOKEN BEFORE, BUT I'VE HEARD MANY TALES OF YOUR ILLUSTRIOUS CAREER.
I PRESUME YOUR CHOICE TO SPEAK VIA MESSENGER BIRD RATHER THAN IN PERSON MEANS YOU ARE UNWELL?

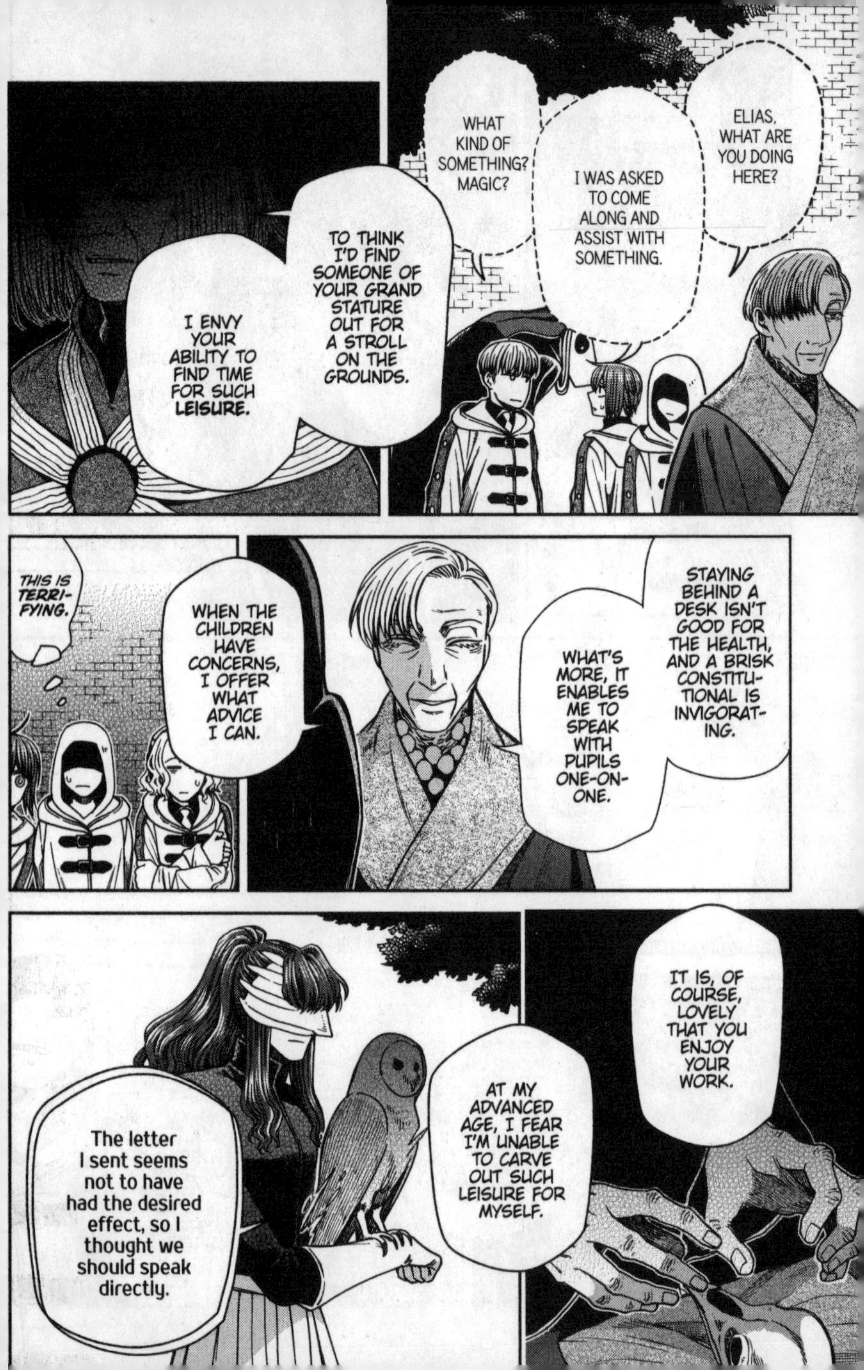
ELIAS, WHAT ARE YOU DOING HERE?
I WAS ASKED TO COME ALONG AND ASSIST WITH SOMETHING.
WHAT KIND OF SOMETHING? MAGIC?
TO THINK I'D FIND SOMEONE OF YOUR GRAND STATURE OUT FOR A STROLL ON THE GROUNDS.
I ENVY YOUR ABILITY TO FIND TIME FOR SUCH LEISURE.
STAYING BEHIND A DESK ISN'T GOOD FOR THE HEALTH, AND A BRISK CONSTITUTIONAL IS INVIGORATING.
WHAT'S MORE, IT ENABLES ME TO SPEAK WITH PUPILS ONE-ON-ONE.
WHEN THE CHILDREN HAVE CONCERNS, I OFFER WHAT ADVICE I CAN.
THIS IS TERRIFYING.
IT IS, OF COURSE, LOVELY THAT YOU ENJOY YOUR WORK.
AT MY ADVANCED AGE, I FEAR I'M UNABLE TO CARVE OUT SUCH LEISURE FOR MYSELF.
The letter I sent seems not to have had the desired effect, so I thought we should speak directly.

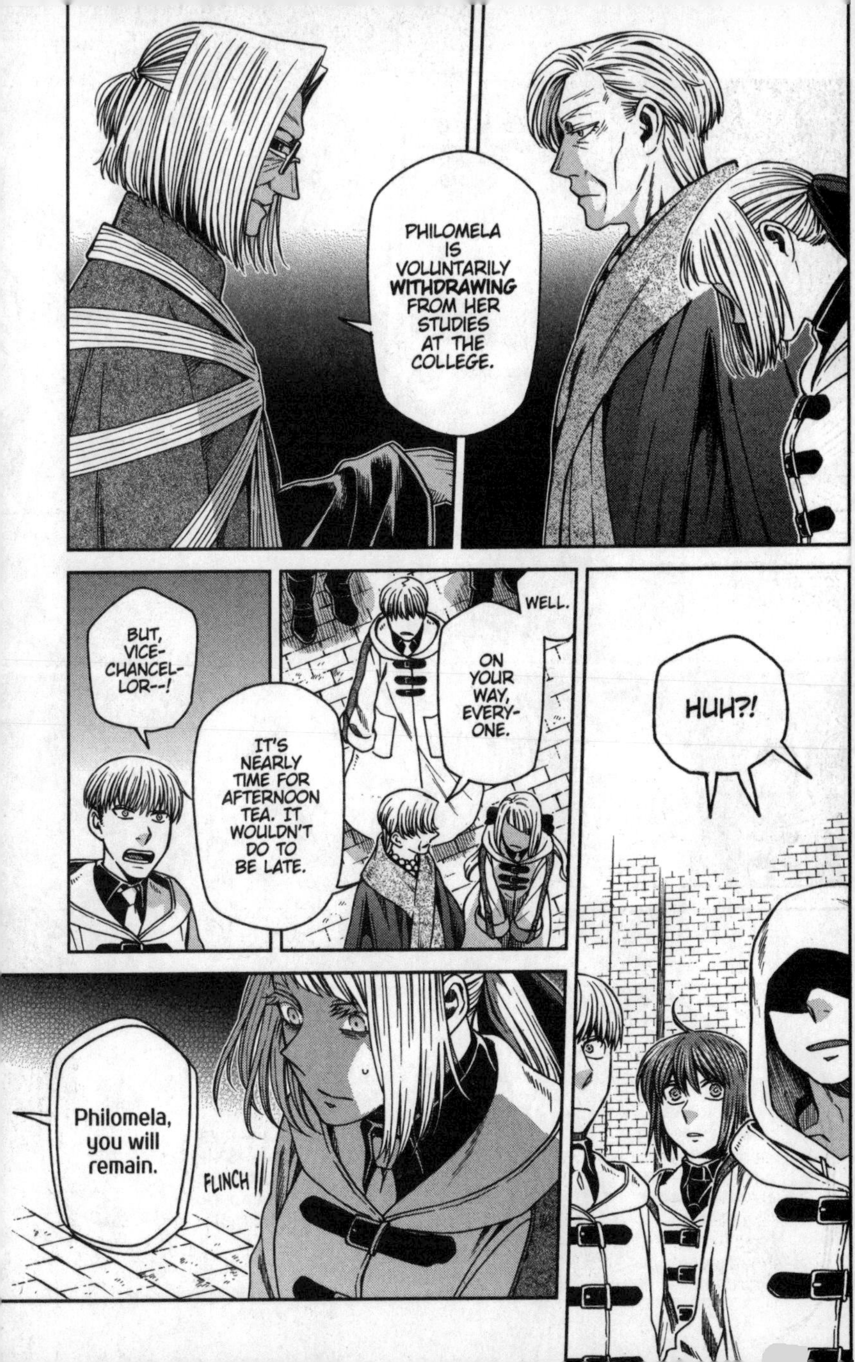
PHILOMELA IS VOLUNTARILY WITHDRAWING FROM HER STUDIES AT THE COLLEGE.
HUH?!
WELL.
ON YOUR WAY, EVERYONE.
IT'S NEARLY TIME FOR AFTERNOON TEA. IT WOULDN'T DO TO BE LATE.
BUT, VICE-CHANCELLOR--!
Philomela, you will remain.
FLINCH

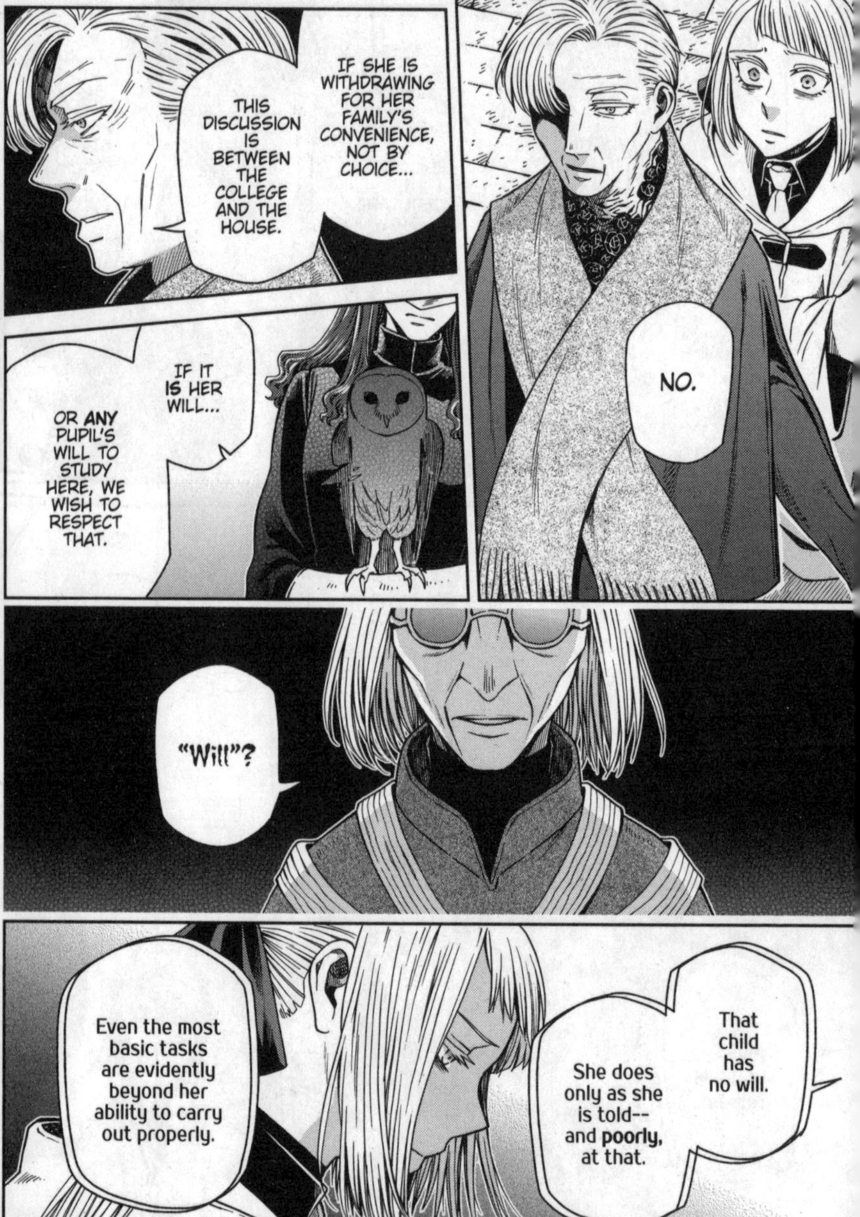
NO.
IF SHE IS WITHDRAWING FOR HER FAMILY'S CONVENIENCE, NOT BY CHOICE...
THIS DISCUSSION IS BETWEEN THE COLLEGE AND THE HOUSE.
IF IT IS HER WILL...
OR **ANY** PUPIL'S WILL TO STUDY HERE, WE WISH TO RESPECT THAT.
"Will"?
That child has no will.
She does only as she is told-- and **poorly,** at that.
Even the most basic tasks are evidently beyond her ability to carry out properly.

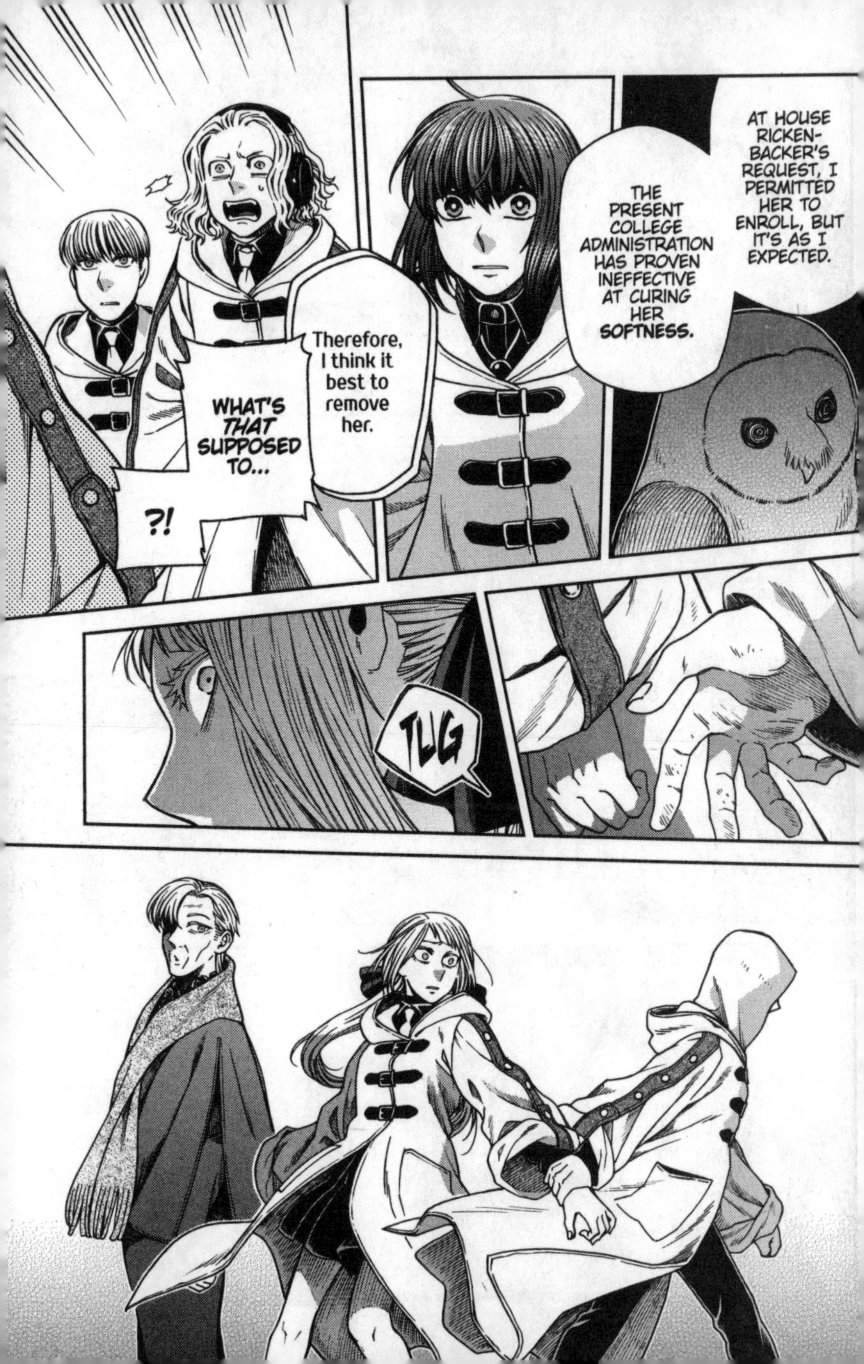
AT HOUSE RICKEN-BACKER'S REQUEST, I PERMITTED HER TO ENROLL, BUT IT'S AS I EXPECTED.
THE PRESENT COLLEGE ADMINISTRATION HAS PROVEN INEFFECTIVE AT CURING HER SOFTNESS.
Therefore, I think it best to remove her.
WHAT'S THAT SUPPOSED TO...
?!
TUG

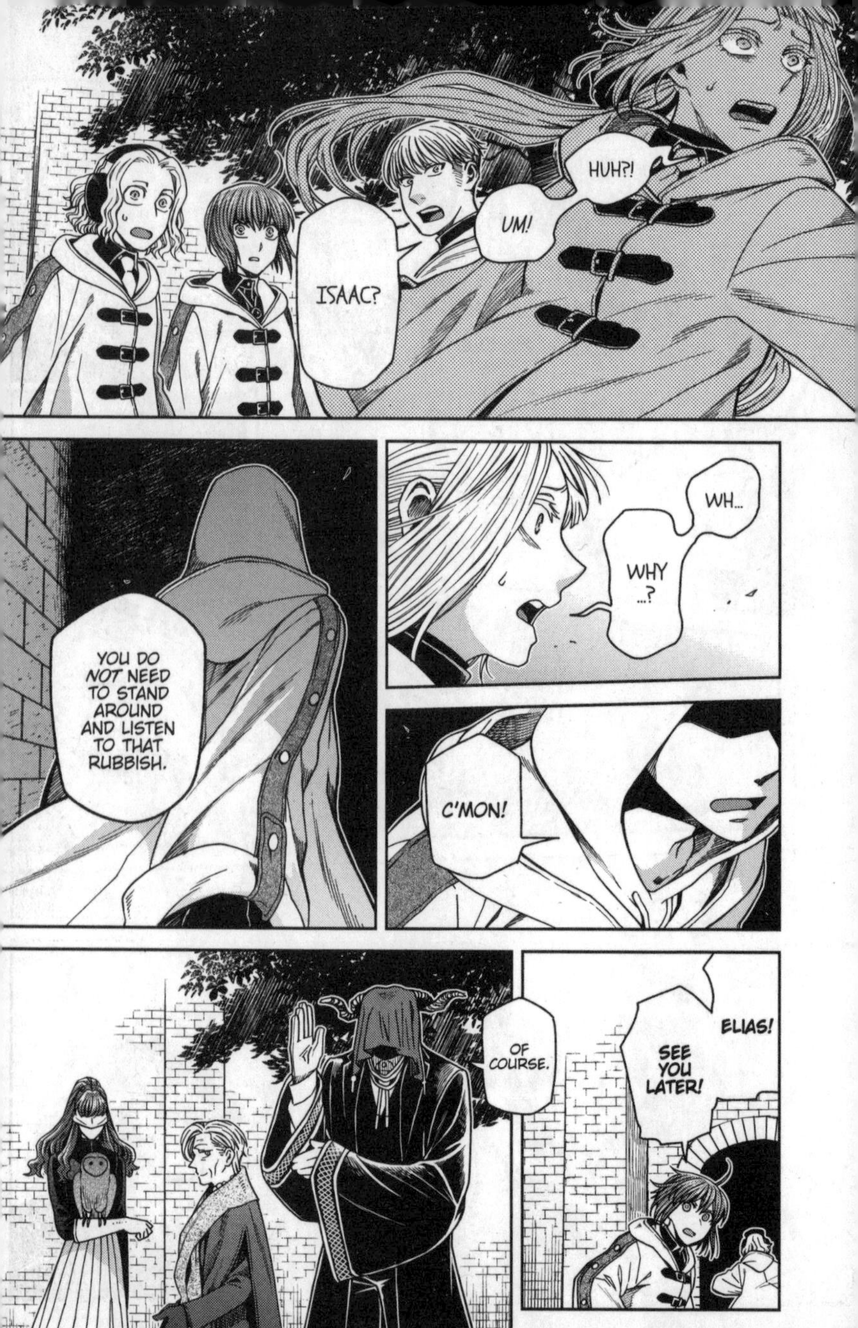
HUH?!
UM!
ISAAC?
WH...
WHY ...?
C'MON!
YOU DO *NOT* NEED TO STAND AROUND AND LISTEN TO THAT RUBBISH.
ELIAS!
SEE YOU LATER!
OF COURSE.

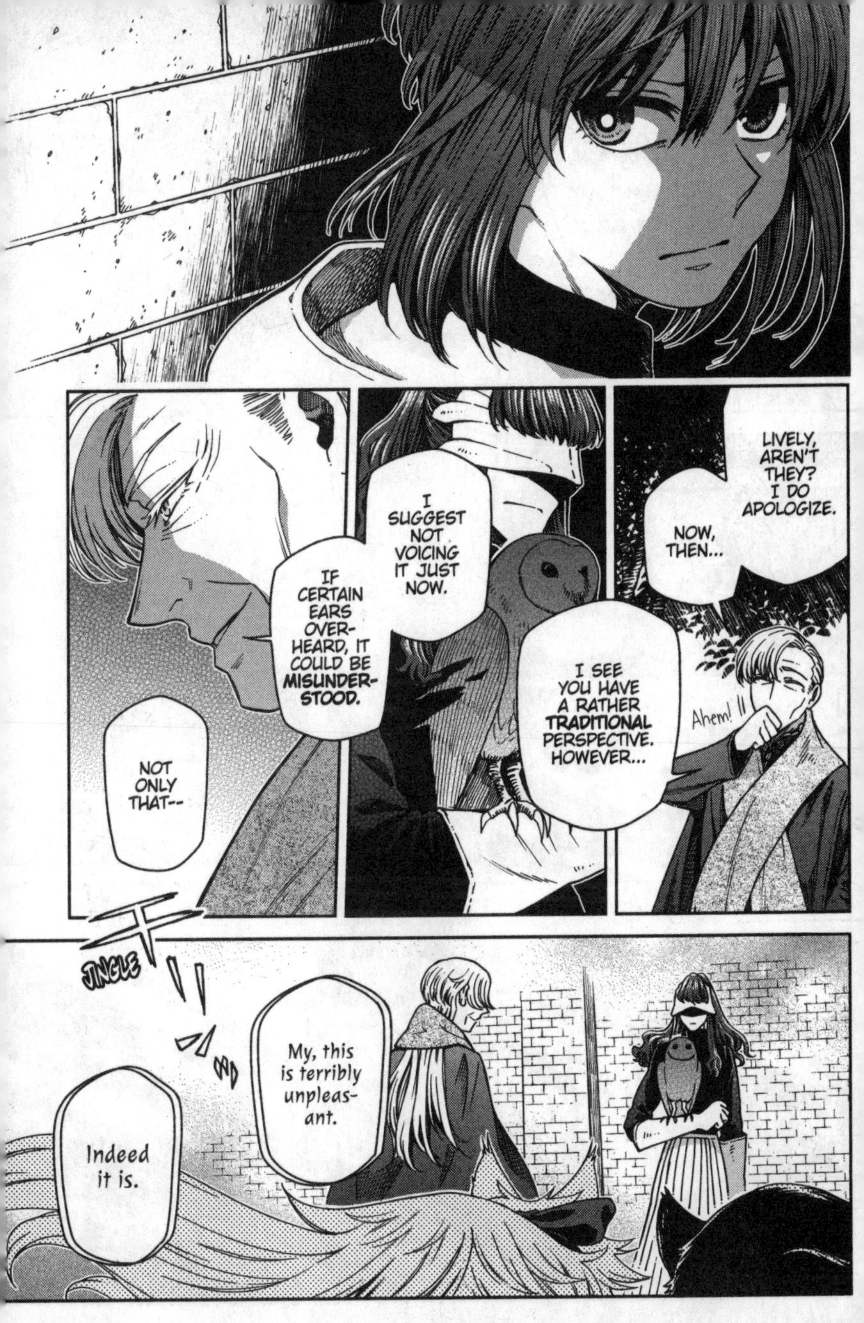
LIVELY, AREN'T THEY? I DO APOLOGIZE.
NOW, THEN...
Ahem!
I SEE YOU HAVE A RATHER TRADITIONAL PERSPECTIVE. HOWEVER...
I SUGGEST NOT VOICING IT JUST NOW.
IF CERTAIN EARS OVERHEARD, IT COULD BE MISUNDERSTOOD.
NOT ONLY THAT--
JINGLE
My, this is terribly unpleasant.
Indeed it is.

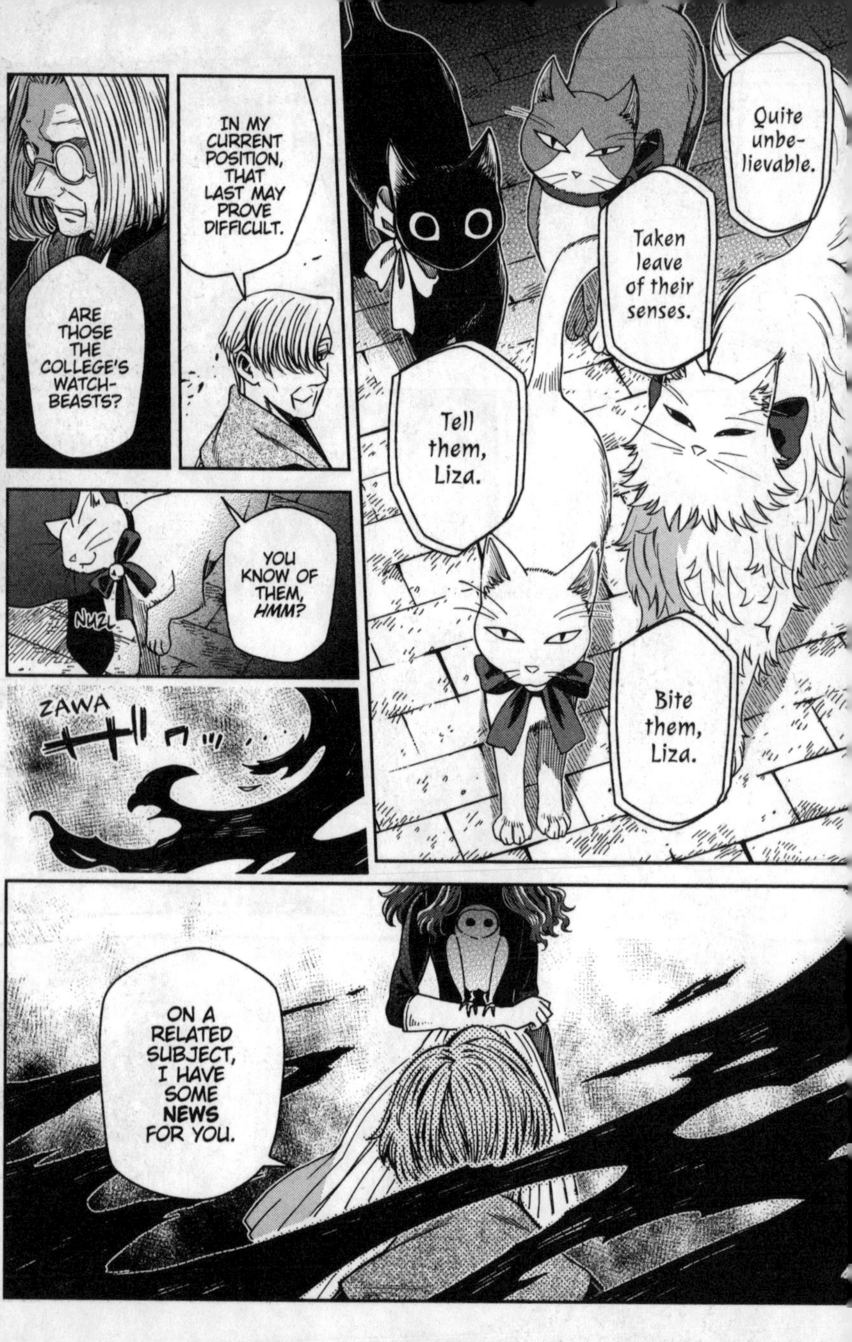
Quite unbe-lievable.
Taken leave of their senses.
Tell them, Liza.
Bite them, Liza.
IN MY CURRENT POSITION, THAT LAST MAY PROVE DIFFICULT.
ARE THOSE THE COLLEGE'S WATCH-BEASTS?
YOU KNOW OF THEM, *HMM?*
NUZL
ZAWA
ON A RELATED SUBJECT, I HAVE SOME NEWS FOR YOU.

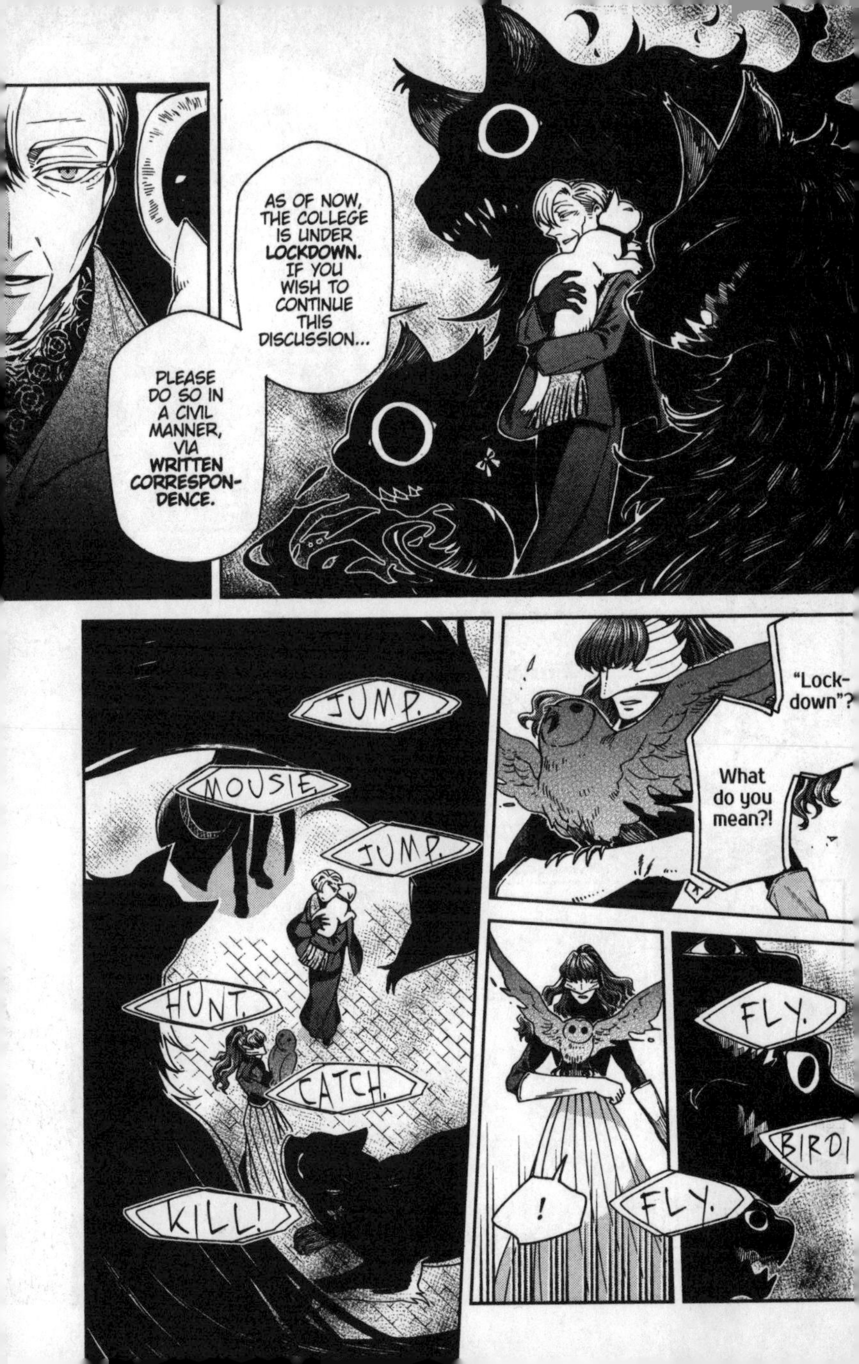
AS OF NOW, THE COLLEGE IS UNDER LOCKDOWN. IF YOU WISH TO CONTINUE THIS DISCUSSION...
PLEASE DO SO IN A CIVIL MANNER, VIA WRITTEN CORRESPON-DENCE.
"Lock-down"?
What do you mean?!
FLY.
BIRD!
!
FLY.
JUMP.
MOUSIE.
JUMP.
HUNT.
CATCH.
KILL!

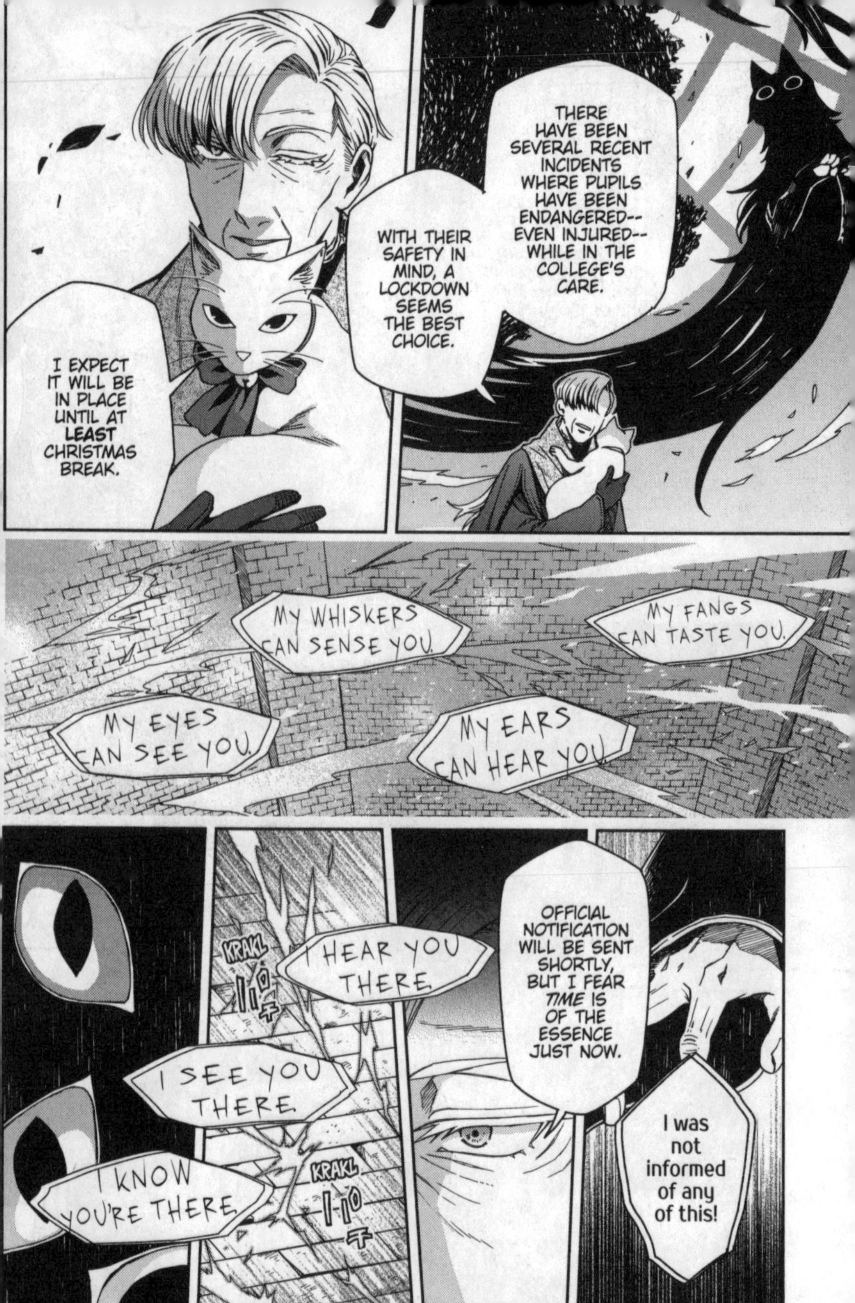
THERE HAVE BEEN SEVERAL RECENT INCIDENTS WHERE PUPILS HAVE BEEN ENDANGERED-- EVEN INJURED-- WHILE IN THE COLLEGE'S CARE.
WITH THEIR SAFETY IN MIND, A LOCKDOWN SEEMS THE BEST CHOICE.
I EXPECT IT WILL BE IN PLACE UNTIL AT **LEAST** CHRISTMAS BREAK.
MY FANGS CAN TASTE YOU.
MY WHISKERS CAN SENSE YOU.
MY EARS CAN HEAR YOU.
MY EYES CAN SEE YOU.
OFFICIAL NOTIFICATION WILL BE SENT SHORTLY, BUT I FEAR *TIME* IS OF THE ESSENCE JUST NOW.
I was not informed of any of this!
I HEAR YOU THERE.
KRAKL
I SEE YOU THERE.
KRAKL
I KNOW YOU'RE THERE.

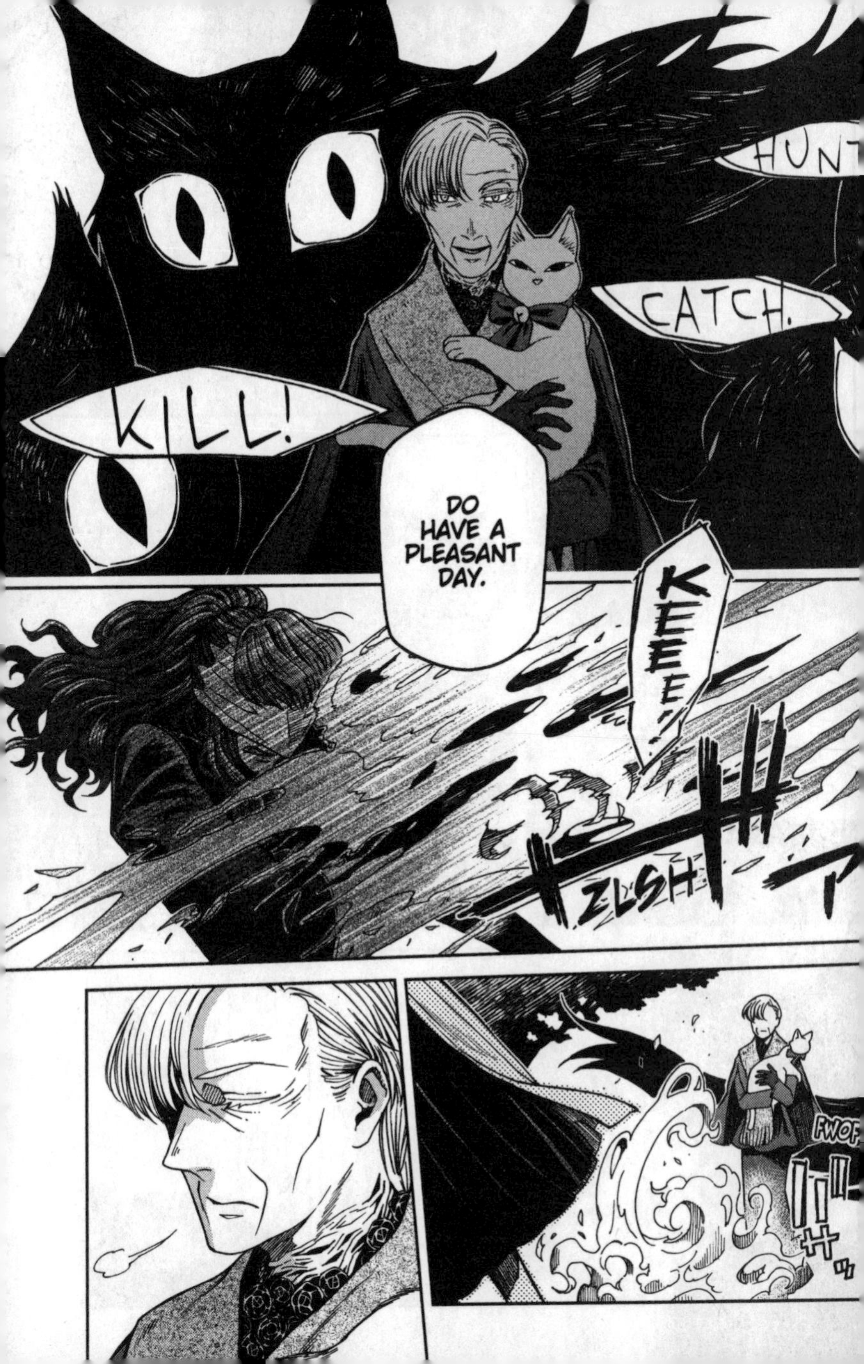
HUNT
CATCH.
KILL!
DO HAVE A PLEASANT DAY.
KEEEE!!
ZLSH
FWOF

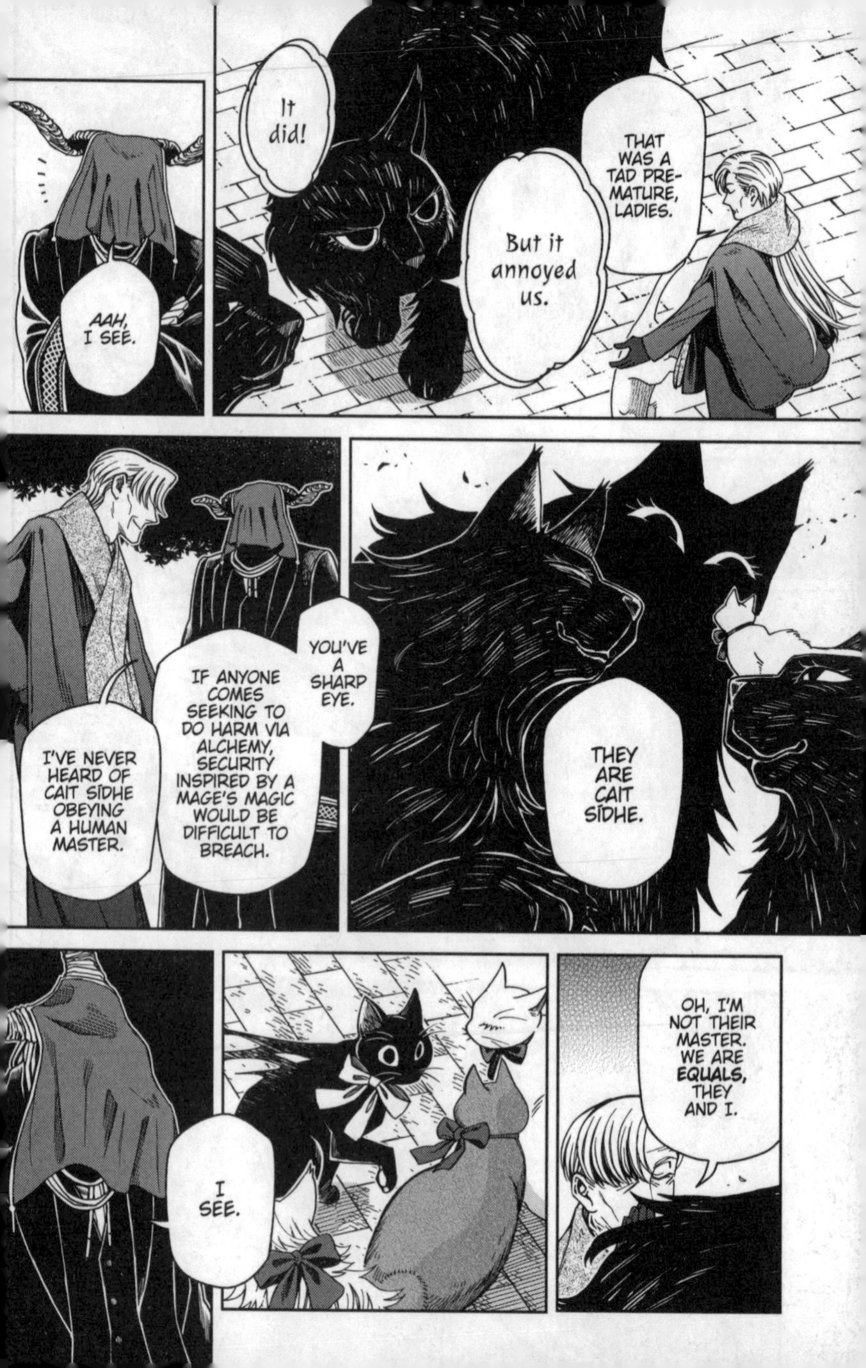
THAT WAS A TAD PRE-MATURE, LADIES.
It did!
But it annoyed us.
AAH, I SEE.
THEY ARE CAIT SÍDHE.
YOU'VE A SHARP EYE.
IF ANYONE COMES SEEKING TO DO HARM VIA ALCHEMY, SECURITY INSPIRED BY A MAGE'S MAGIC WOULD BE DIFFICULT TO BREACH.
I'VE NEVER HEARD OF CAIT SÍDHE OBEYING A HUMAN MASTER.
OH, I'M NOT THEIR MASTER. WE ARE EQUALS, THEY AND I.
I SEE.

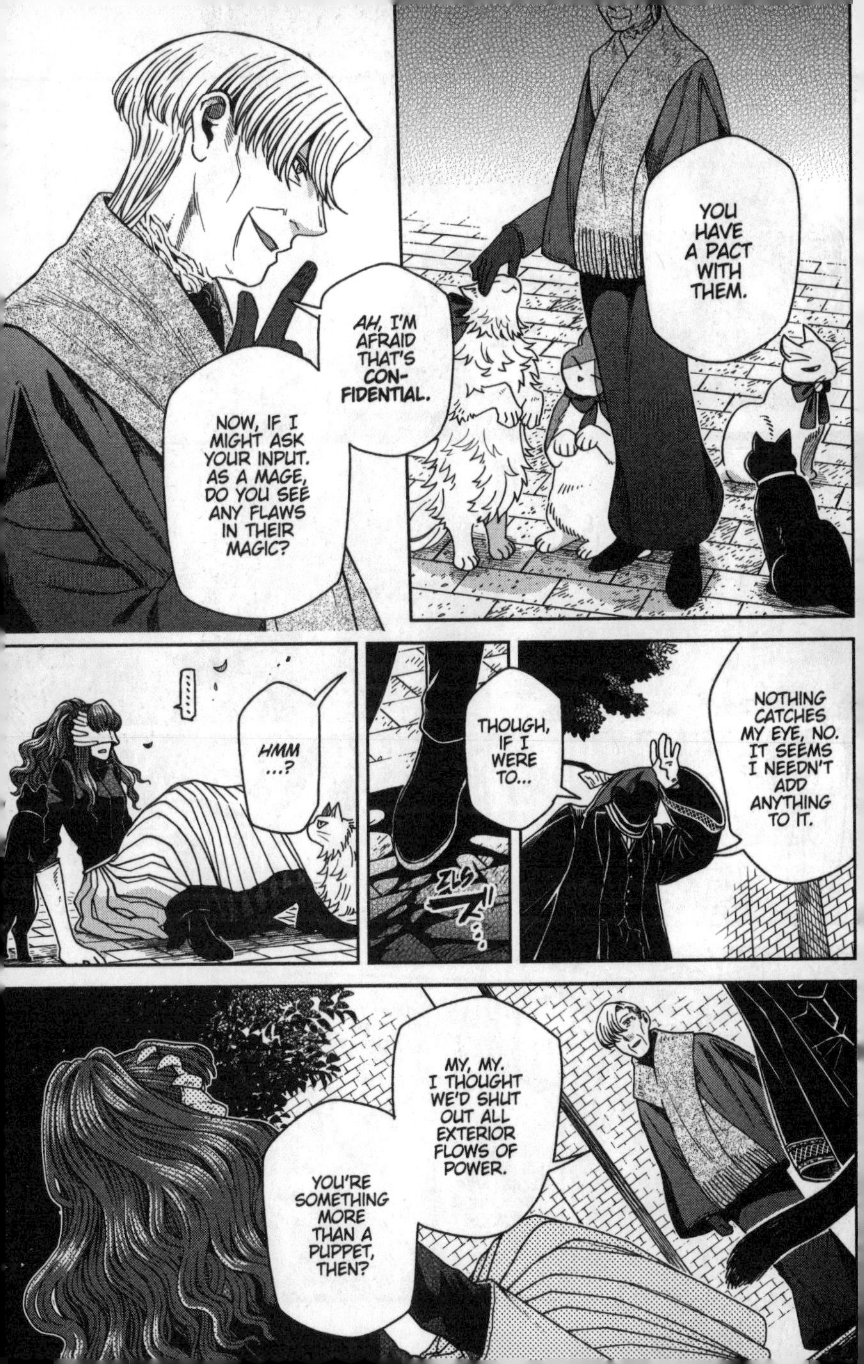
YOU HAVE A PACT WITH THEM.
AH, I'M AFRAID THAT'S CON-FIDENTIAL.
NOW, IF I MIGHT ASK YOUR INPUT. AS A MAGE, DO YOU SEE ANY FLAWS IN THEIR MAGIC?
NOTHING CATCHES MY EYE, NO. IT SEEMS I NEEDN'T ADD ANYTHING TO IT.
THOUGH, IF I WERE TO...
......
HMM ...?
MY, MY. I THOUGHT WE'D SHUT OUT ALL EXTERIOR FLOWS OF POWER.
YOU'RE SOMETHING MORE THAN A PUPPET, THEN?

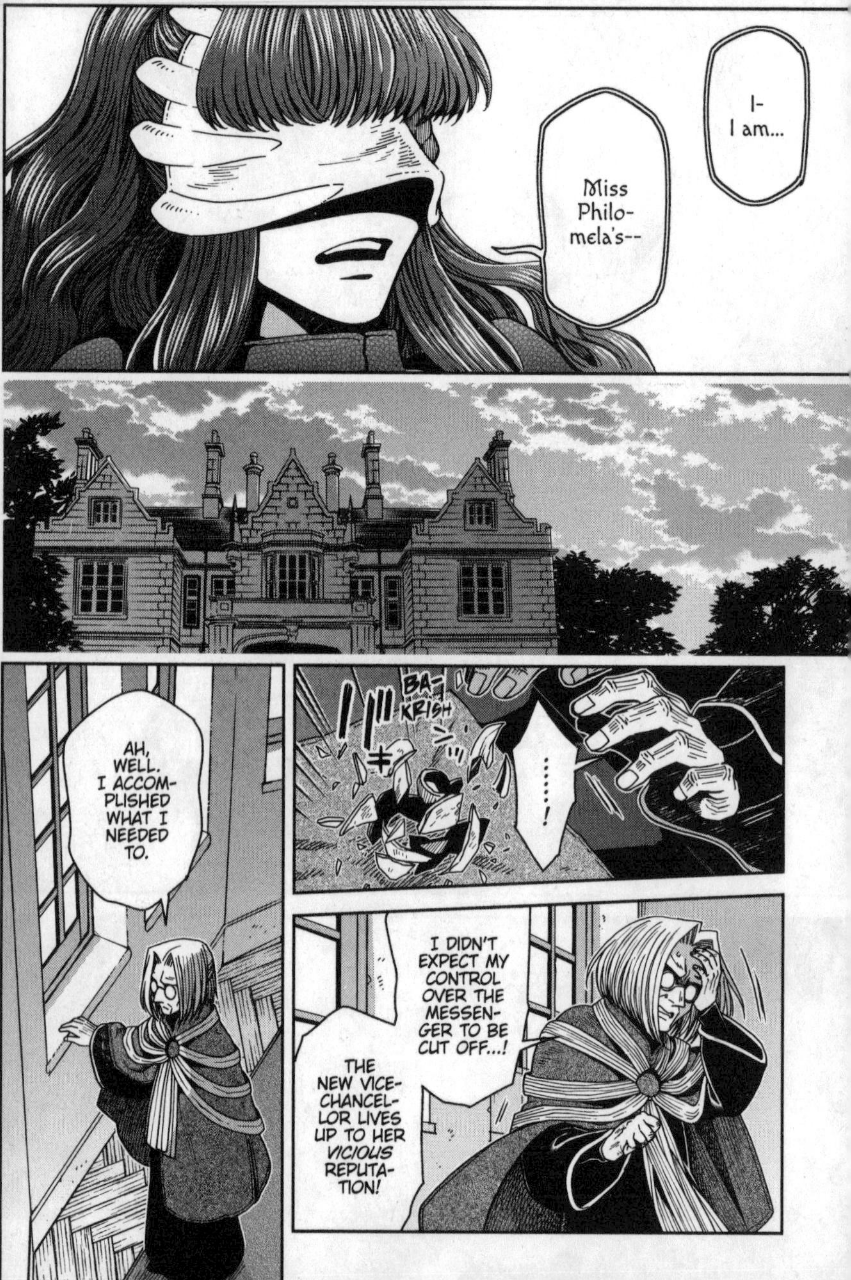
I-
I am...
Miss Philo-
mela's--
BA-
KRISH
......!
I DIDN'T EXPECT MY CONTROL OVER THE MESSEN-GER TO BE CUT OFF...!
THE NEW VICE-CHANCEL-LOR LIVES UP TO HER *VICIOUS* REPUTA-TION!
AH, WELL. I ACCOM-PLISHED WHAT I NEEDED TO.

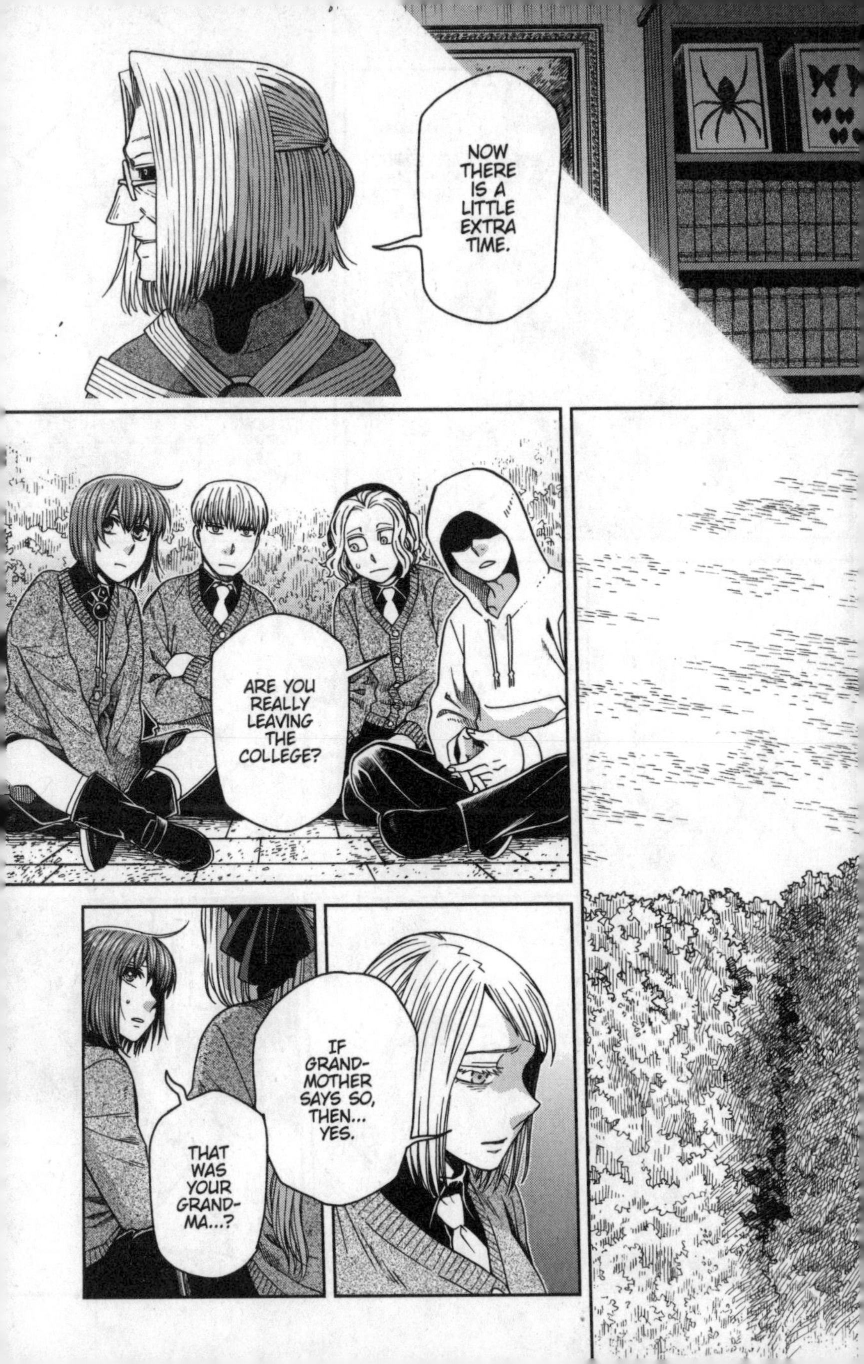
NOW THERE IS A LITTLE EXTRA TIME.
ARE YOU REALLY LEAVING THE COLLEGE?
IF GRANDMOTHER SAYS SO, THEN... YES.
THAT WAS YOUR GRANDMA...?

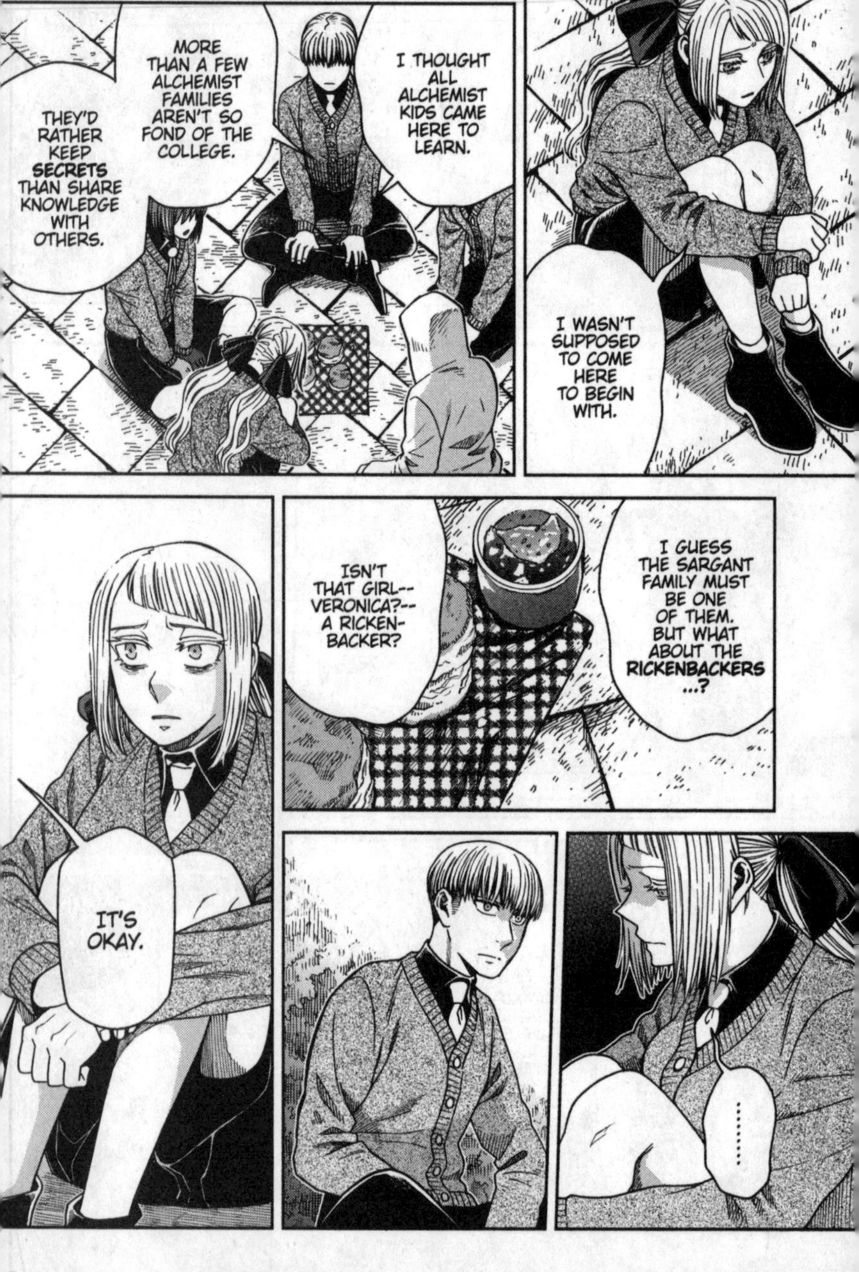
I WASN'T SUPPOSED TO COME HERE TO BEGIN WITH.
I THOUGHT ALL ALCHEMIST KIDS CAME HERE TO LEARN.
MORE THAN A FEW ALCHEMIST FAMILIES AREN'T SO FOND OF THE COLLEGE.
THEY'D RATHER KEEP **SECRETS** THAN SHARE KNOWLEDGE WITH OTHERS.
I GUESS THE SARGANT FAMILY MUST BE ONE OF THEM. BUT WHAT ABOUT THE **RICKENBACKERS** ...?
ISN'T THAT GIRL-- VERONICA?-- A RICKEN-BACKER?
......
IT'S OKAY.

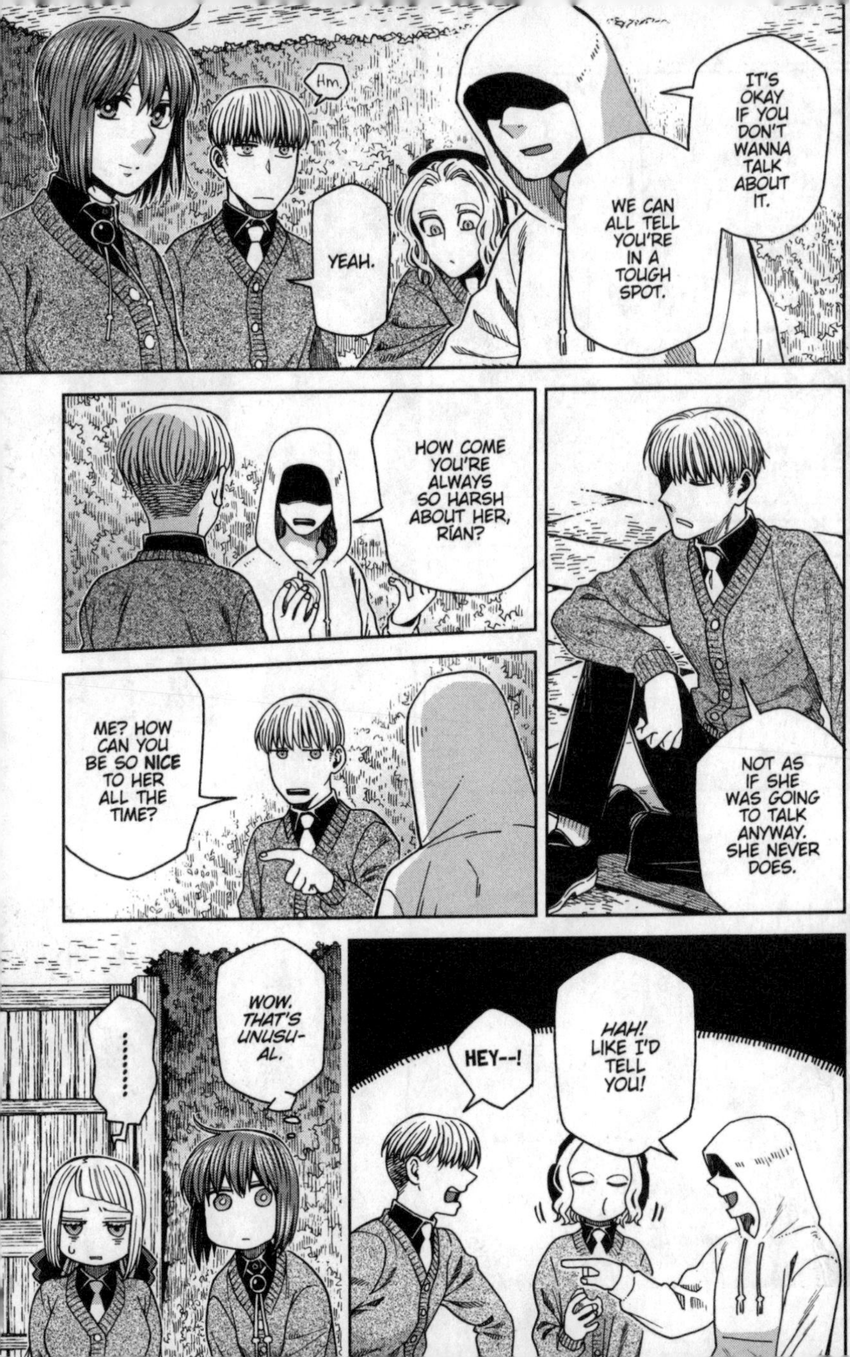
IT'S OKAY IF YOU DON'T WANNA TALK ABOUT IT.
WE CAN ALL TELL YOU'RE IN A TOUGH SPOT.
Hm.
YEAH.
NOT AS IF SHE WAS GOING TO TALK ANYWAY. SHE NEVER DOES.
HOW COME YOU'RE ALWAYS SO HARSH ABOUT HER, RÍAN?
ME? HOW CAN YOU BE SO NICE TO HER ALL THE TIME?
HAH! LIKE I'D TELL YOU!
HEY--!
WOW. THAT'S UNUSU-AL.
....

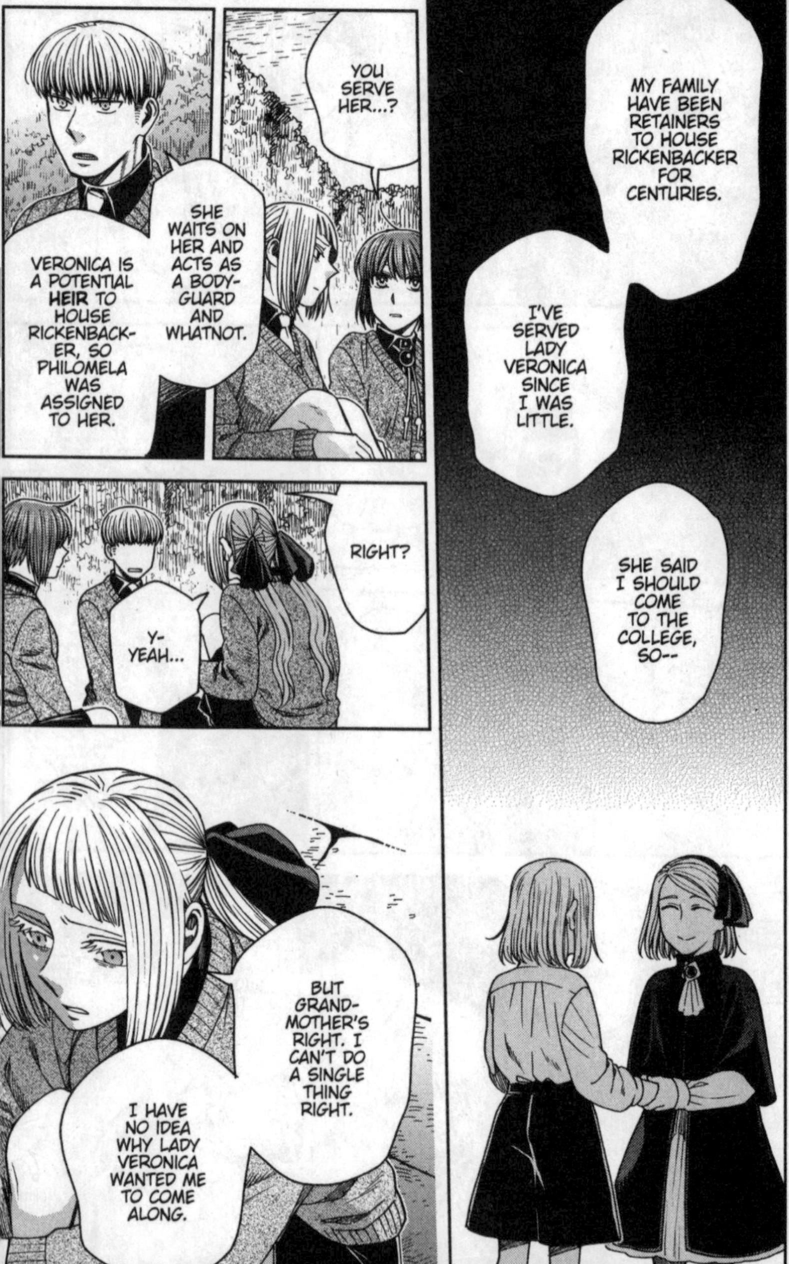
MY FAMILY HAVE BEEN RETAINERS TO HOUSE RICKENBACKER FOR CENTURIES.
I'VE SERVED LADY VERONICA SINCE I WAS LITTLE.
SHE SAID I SHOULD COME TO THE COLLEGE, SO--
YOU SERVE HER...?
SHE WAITS ON HER AND ACTS AS A BODY-GUARD AND WHATNOT.
VERONICA IS A POTENTIAL **HEIR** TO HOUSE RICKENBACK-ER, SO PHILOMELA WAS ASSIGNED TO HER.
RIGHT?
Y-YEAH...
BUT GRAND-MOTHER'S RIGHT. I CAN'T DO A SINGLE THING RIGHT.
I HAVE NO IDEA WHY LADY VERONICA WANTED ME TO COME ALONG.

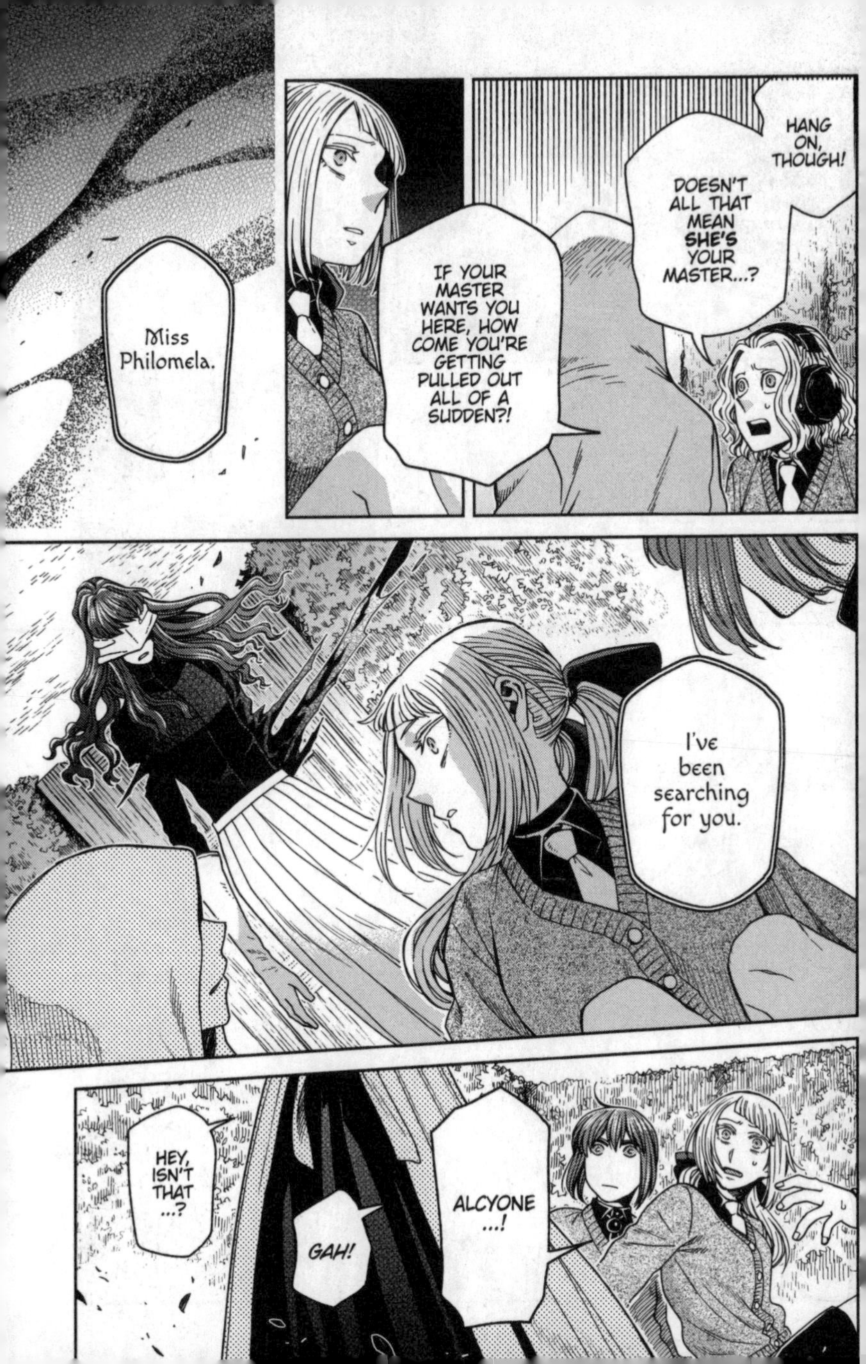
HANG ON, THOUGH!
DOESN'T ALL THAT MEAN SHE'S YOUR MASTER...?
IF YOUR MASTER WANTS YOU HERE, HOW COME YOU'RE GETTING PULLED OUT ALL OF A SUDDEN?!
Miss Philomela.
I've been searching for you.
ALCYONE ...!
HEY, ISN'T THAT ...?
GAH!

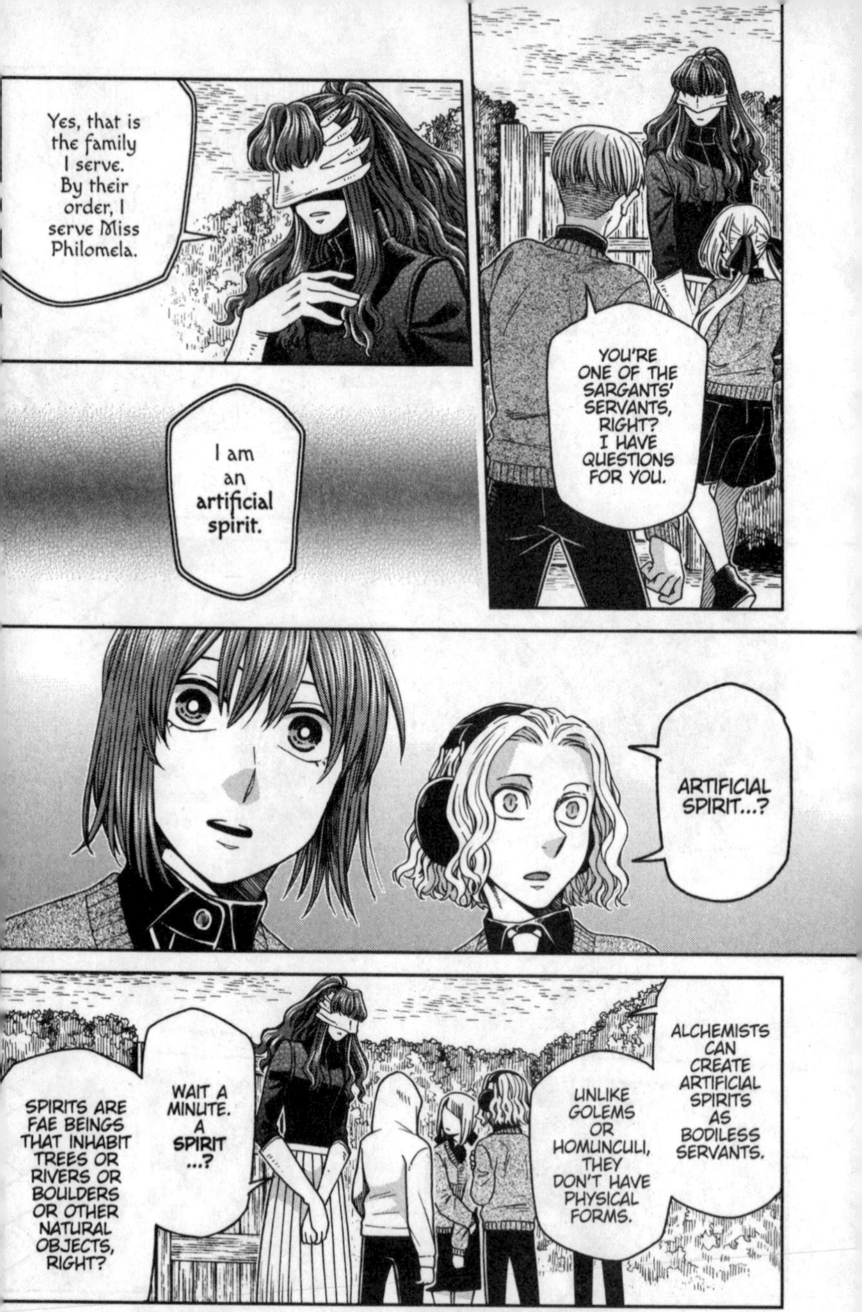
YOU'RE ONE OF THE SARGANTS' SERVANTS, RIGHT? I HAVE QUESTIONS FOR YOU.
Yes, that is the family I serve. By their order, I serve Miss Philomela.
I am an artificial spirit.
ARTIFICIAL SPIRIT...?
ALCHEMISTS CAN CREATE ARTIFICIAL SPIRITS AS BODILESS SERVANTS.
UNLIKE GOLEMS OR HOMUNCULI, THEY DON'T HAVE PHYSICAL FORMS.
WAIT A MINUTE. A SPIRIT ...?
SPIRITS ARE FAE BEINGS THAT INHABIT TREES OR RIVERS OR BOULDERS OR OTHER NATURAL OBJECTS, RIGHT?

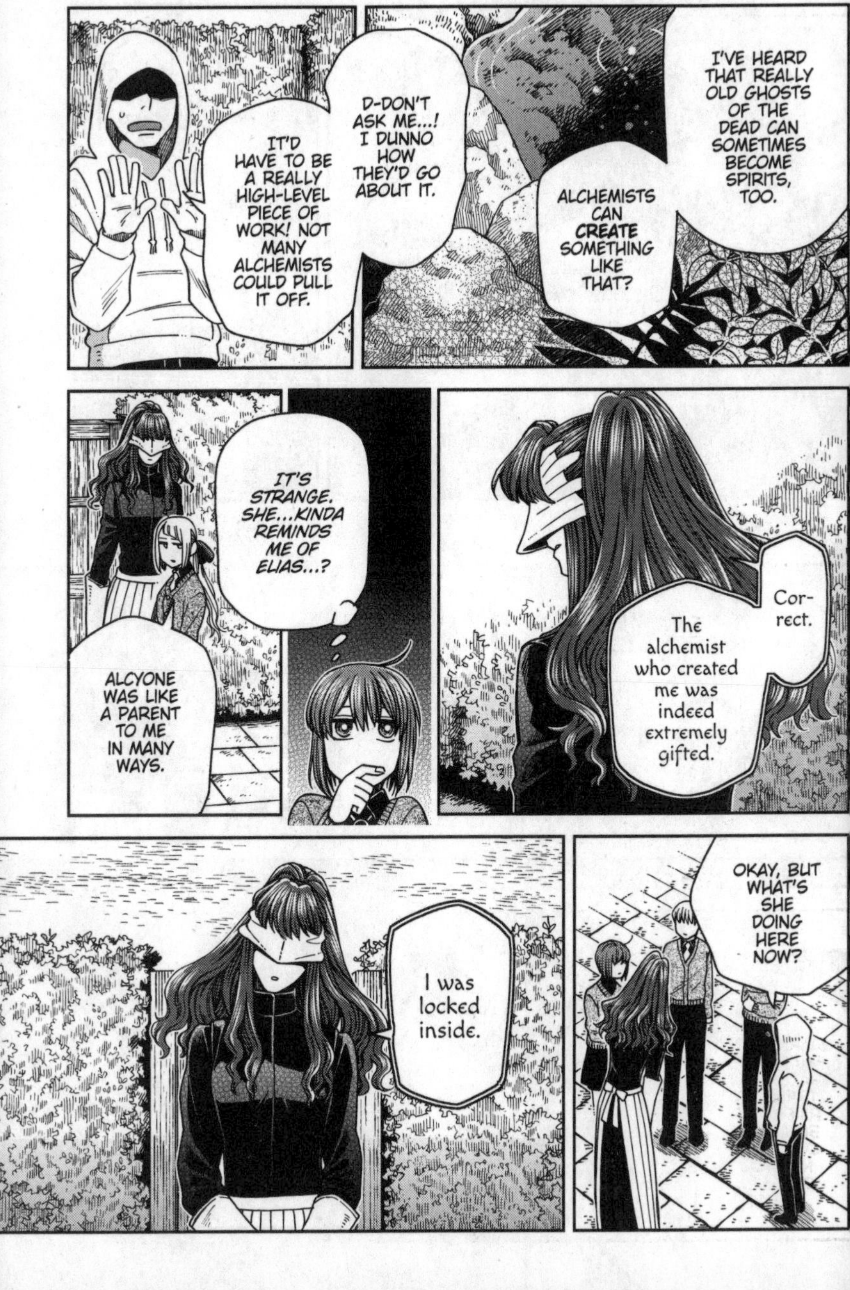
I'VE HEARD THAT REALLY OLD GHOSTS OF THE DEAD CAN SOMETIMES BECOME SPIRITS, TOO.
ALCHEMISTS CAN **CREATE** SOMETHING LIKE THAT?
D-DON'T ASK ME...! I DUNNO HOW THEY'D GO ABOUT IT.
IT'D HAVE TO BE A REALLY HIGH-LEVEL PIECE OF WORK! NOT MANY ALCHEMISTS COULD PULL IT OFF.
Correct.
The alchemist who created me was indeed extremely gifted.
IT'S STRANGE. SHE...KINDA REMINDS ME OF ELIAS...?
ALCYONE WAS LIKE A PARENT TO ME IN MANY WAYS.
OKAY, BUT WHAT'S SHE DOING HERE NOW?
I was locked inside.

I'm currently in a temporary fluid body to enable completion of a minor errand, so I'm unable to leave.

The College has been shut off from the outside world, both physically and magically.

LOCKED ...?

Inside.

HUH ...?

Please pardon the intrusion, but it appears I'll be here until Christmas.

BOW

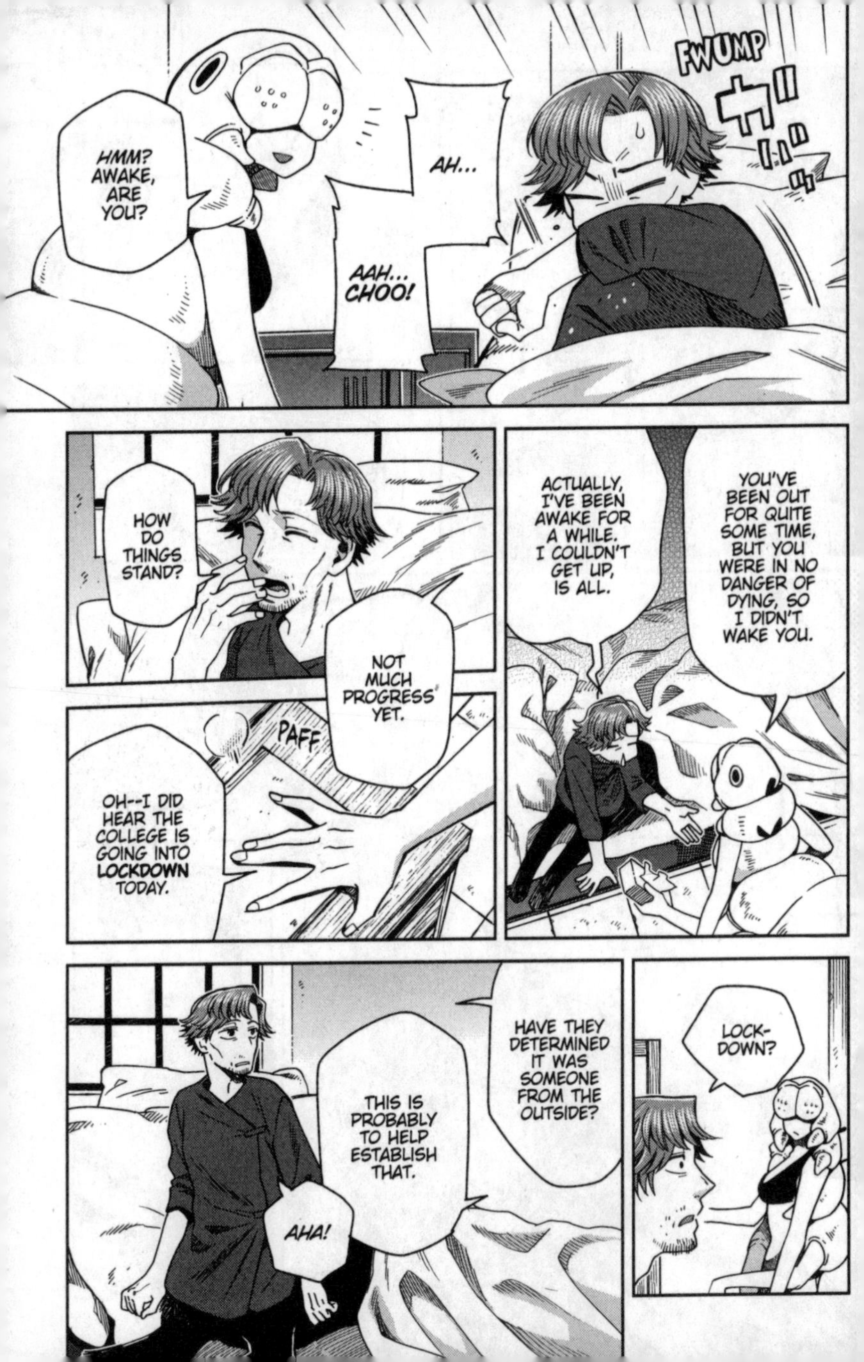
FWUMP
AH...
AAH... CHOO!
HMM? AWAKE, ARE YOU?
YOU'VE BEEN OUT FOR QUITE SOME TIME, BUT YOU WERE IN NO DANGER OF DYING, SO I DIDN'T WAKE YOU.
ACTUALLY, I'VE BEEN AWAKE FOR A WHILE. I COULDN'T GET UP, IS ALL.
HOW DO THINGS STAND?
NOT MUCH PROGRESS YET.
PAFF
OH--I DID HEAR THE COLLEGE IS GOING INTO LOCKDOWN TODAY.
LOCK-DOWN?
HAVE THEY DETERMINED IT WAS SOMEONE FROM THE OUTSIDE?
THIS IS PROBABLY TO HELP ESTABLISH THAT.
AHA!

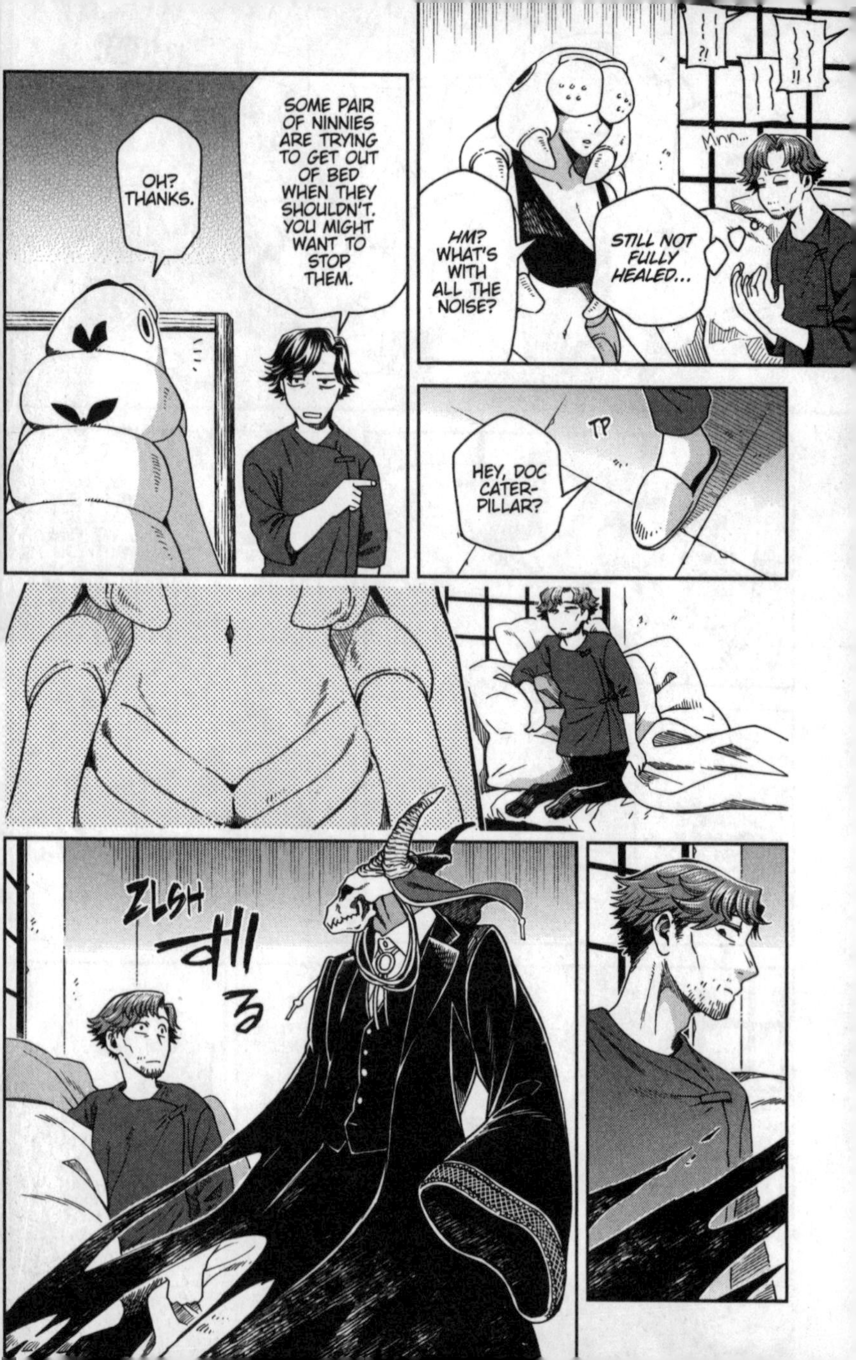
!!
!
?!
Mnn...
STILL NOT FULLY HEALED...
HM? WHAT'S WITH ALL THE NOISE?
TP
HEY, DOC CATER-PILLAR?
SOME PAIR OF NINNIES ARE TRYING TO GET OUT OF BED WHEN THEY SHOULDN'T. YOU MIGHT WANT TO STOP THEM.
OH? THANKS.
ZLSH
する

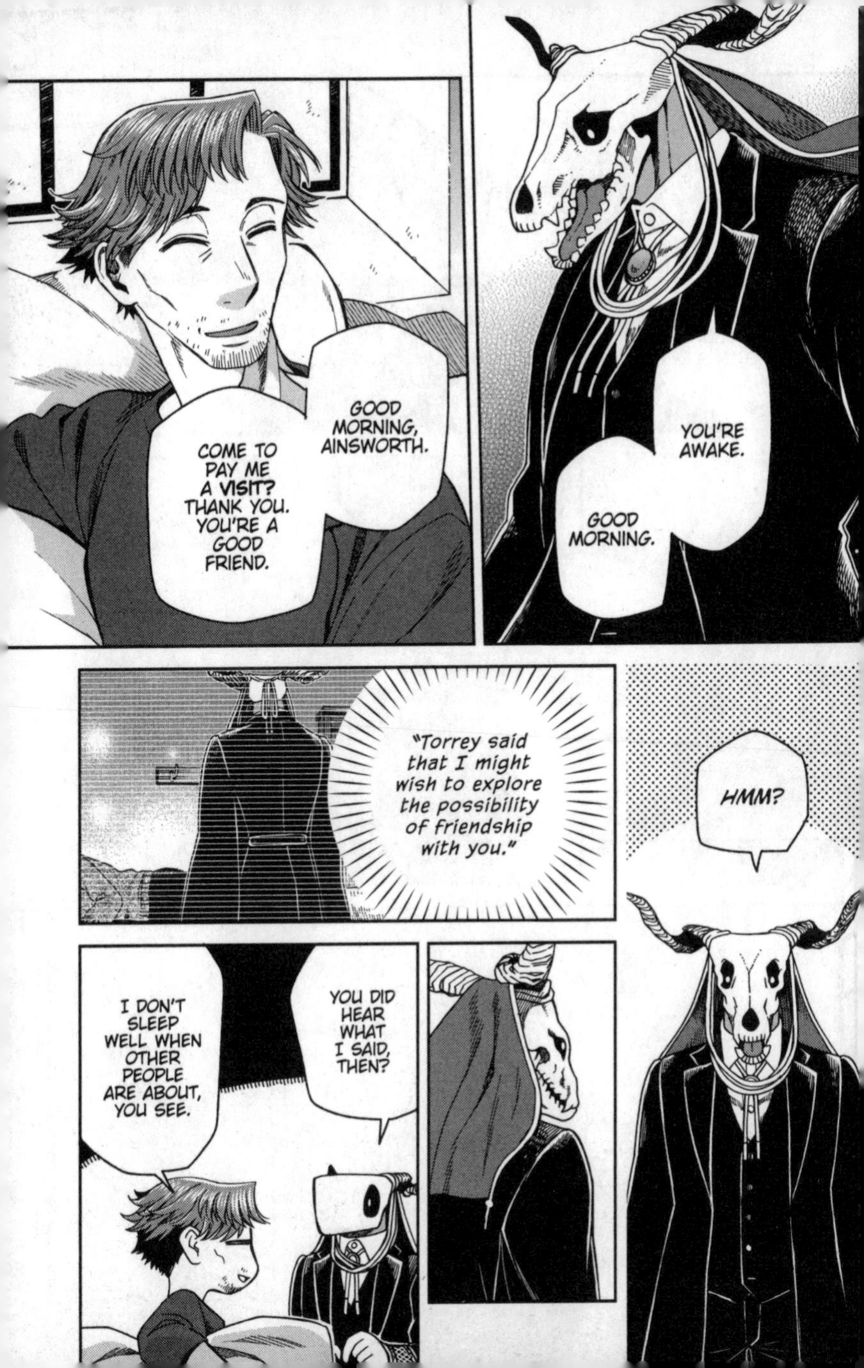

YOU'RE AWAKE.
GOOD MORNING.
GOOD MORNING, AINSWORTH.
COME TO PAY ME A VISIT? THANK YOU. YOU'RE A GOOD FRIEND.
HMM?
"Torrey said that I might wish to explore the possibility of friendship with you."
YOU DID HEAR WHAT I SAID, THEN?
I DON'T SLEEP WELL WHEN OTHER PEOPLE ARE ABOUT, YOU SEE.

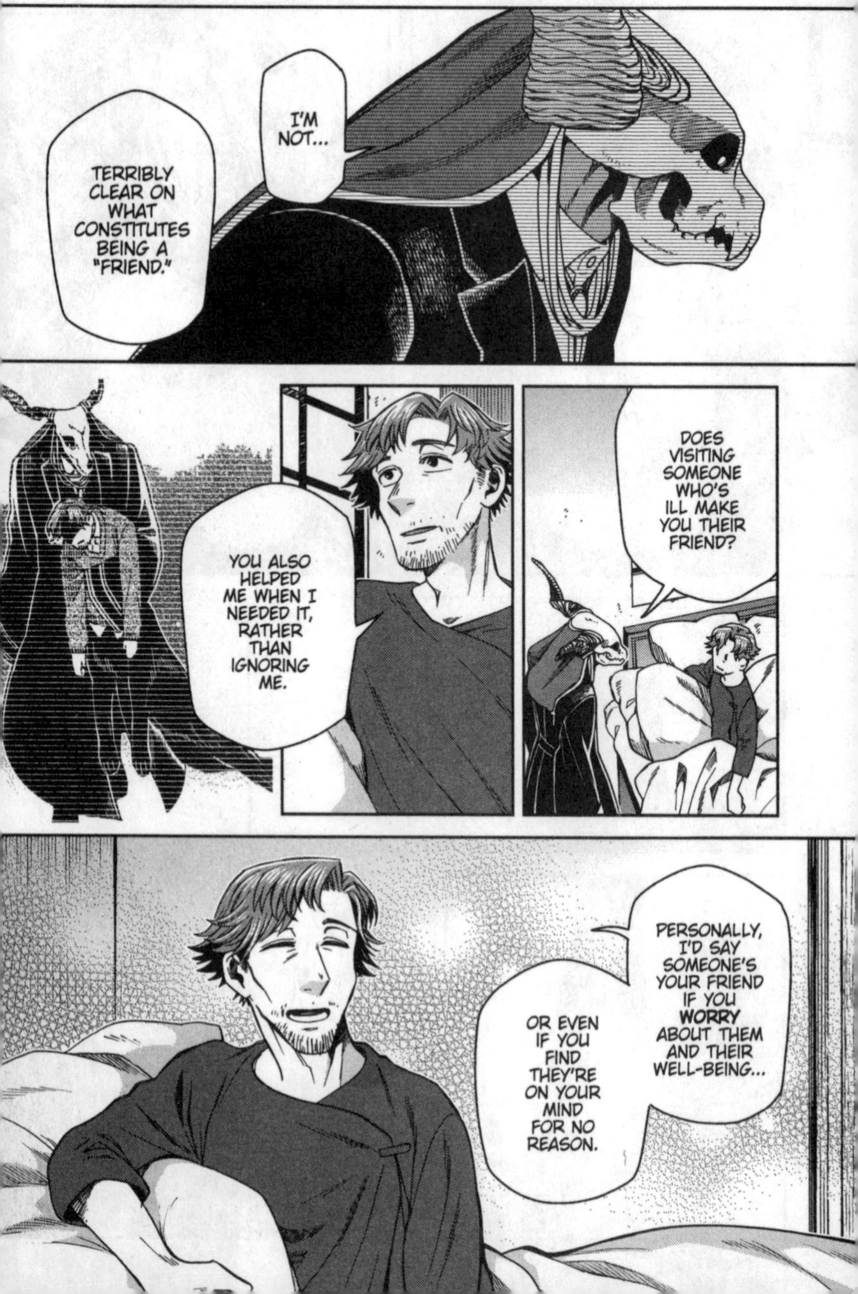
I'M NOT...
TERRIBLY CLEAR ON WHAT CONSTITUTES BEING A "FRIEND."
DOES VISITING SOMEONE WHO'S ILL MAKE YOU THEIR FRIEND?
YOU ALSO HELPED ME WHEN I NEEDED IT, RATHER THAN IGNORING ME.
PERSONALLY, I'D SAY SOMEONE'S YOUR FRIEND IF YOU **WORRY** ABOUT THEM AND THEIR WELL-BEING...
OR EVEN IF YOU FIND THEY'RE ON YOUR MIND FOR NO REASON.

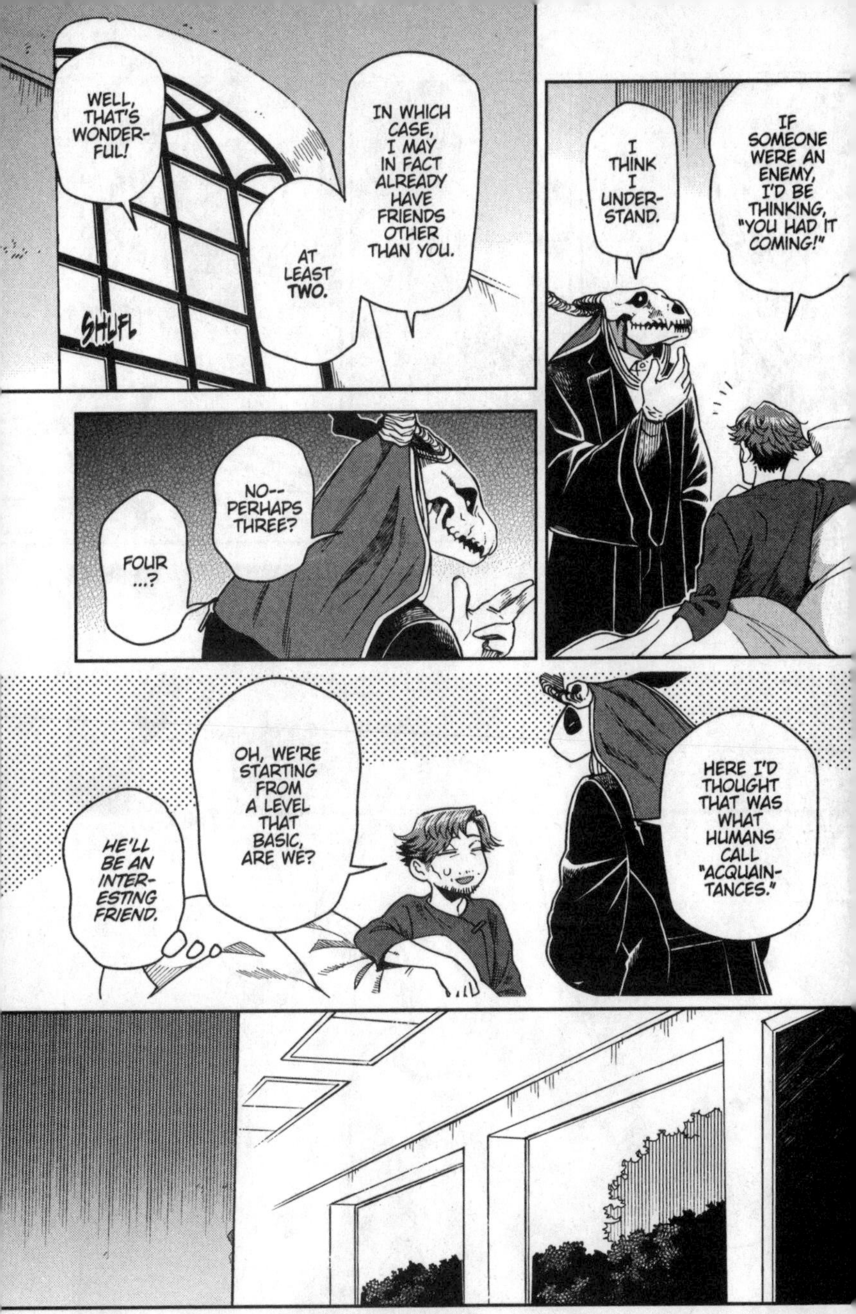
IF SOMEONE WERE AN ENEMY, I'D BE THINKING, "YOU HAD IT COMING!"
I THINK I UNDERSTAND.
WELL, THAT'S WONDERFUL!
IN WHICH CASE, I MAY IN FACT ALREADY HAVE FRIENDS OTHER THAN YOU.
AT LEAST TWO.
SHUFL
NO--PERHAPS THREE?
FOUR...?
HERE I'D THOUGHT THAT WAS WHAT HUMANS CALL "ACQUAINTANCES."
OH, WE'RE STARTING FROM A LEVEL THAT BASIC, ARE WE?
HE'LL BE AN INTERESTING FRIEND.

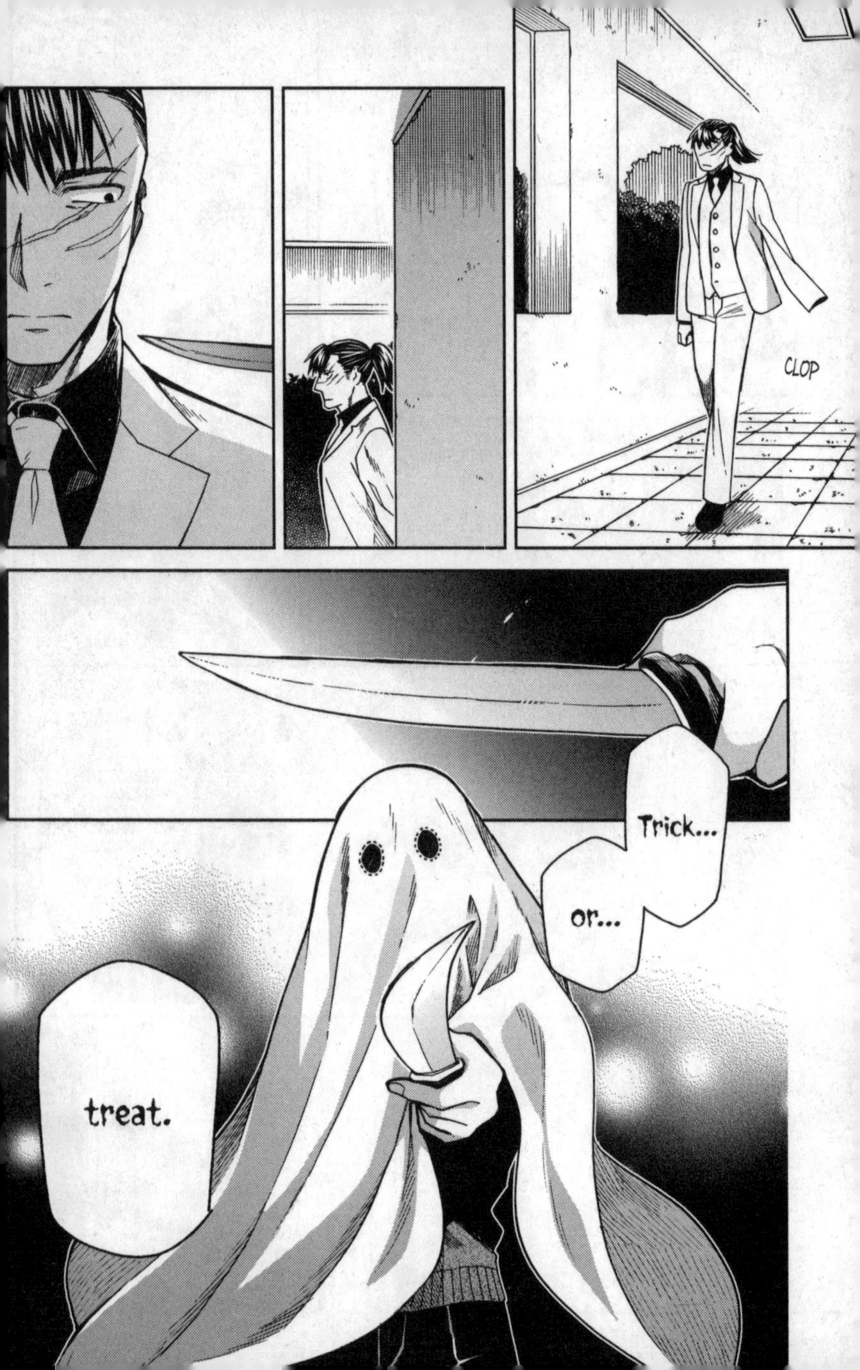
CLOP
Trick...
or...
treat.

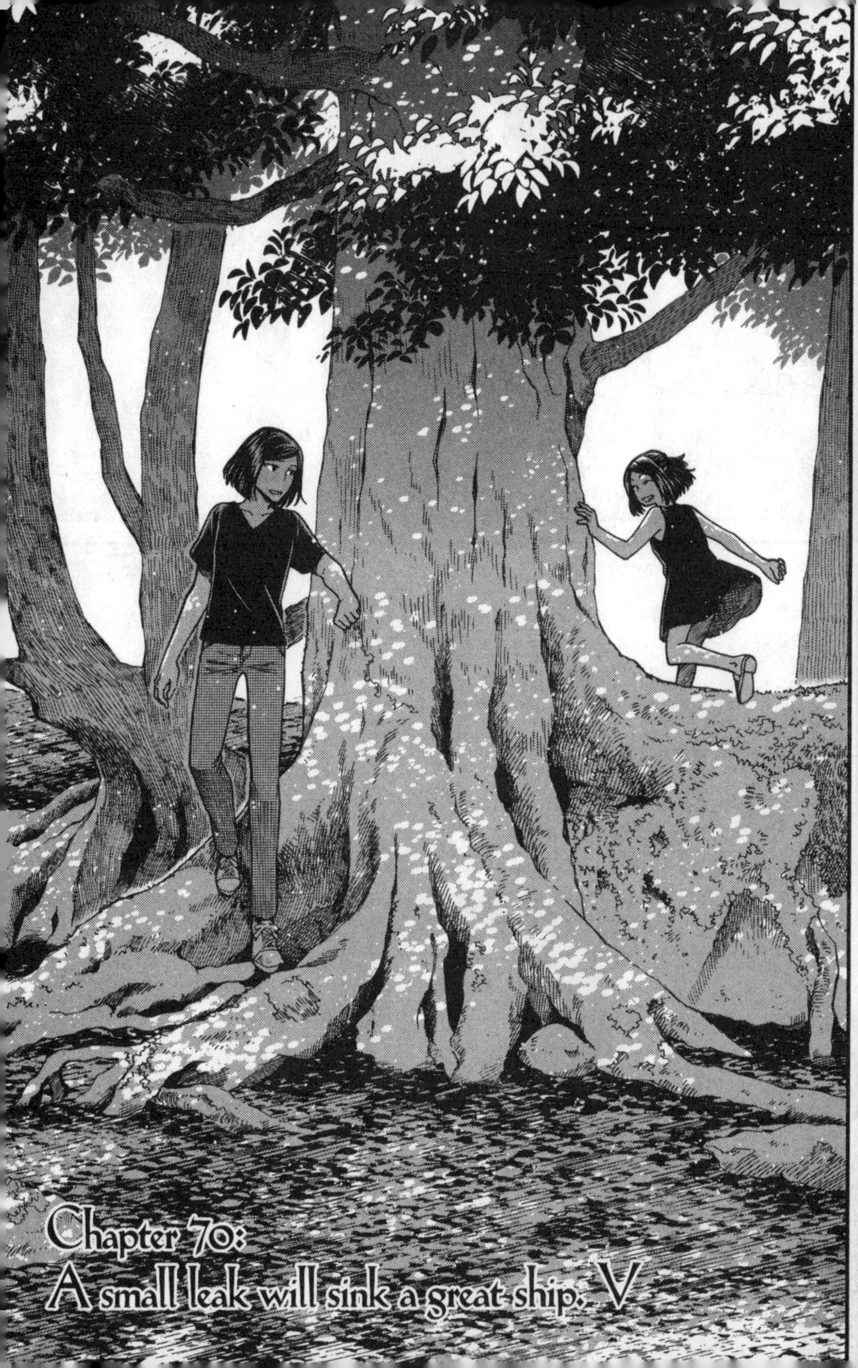
Chapter 70:
A small leak will sink a great ship. V

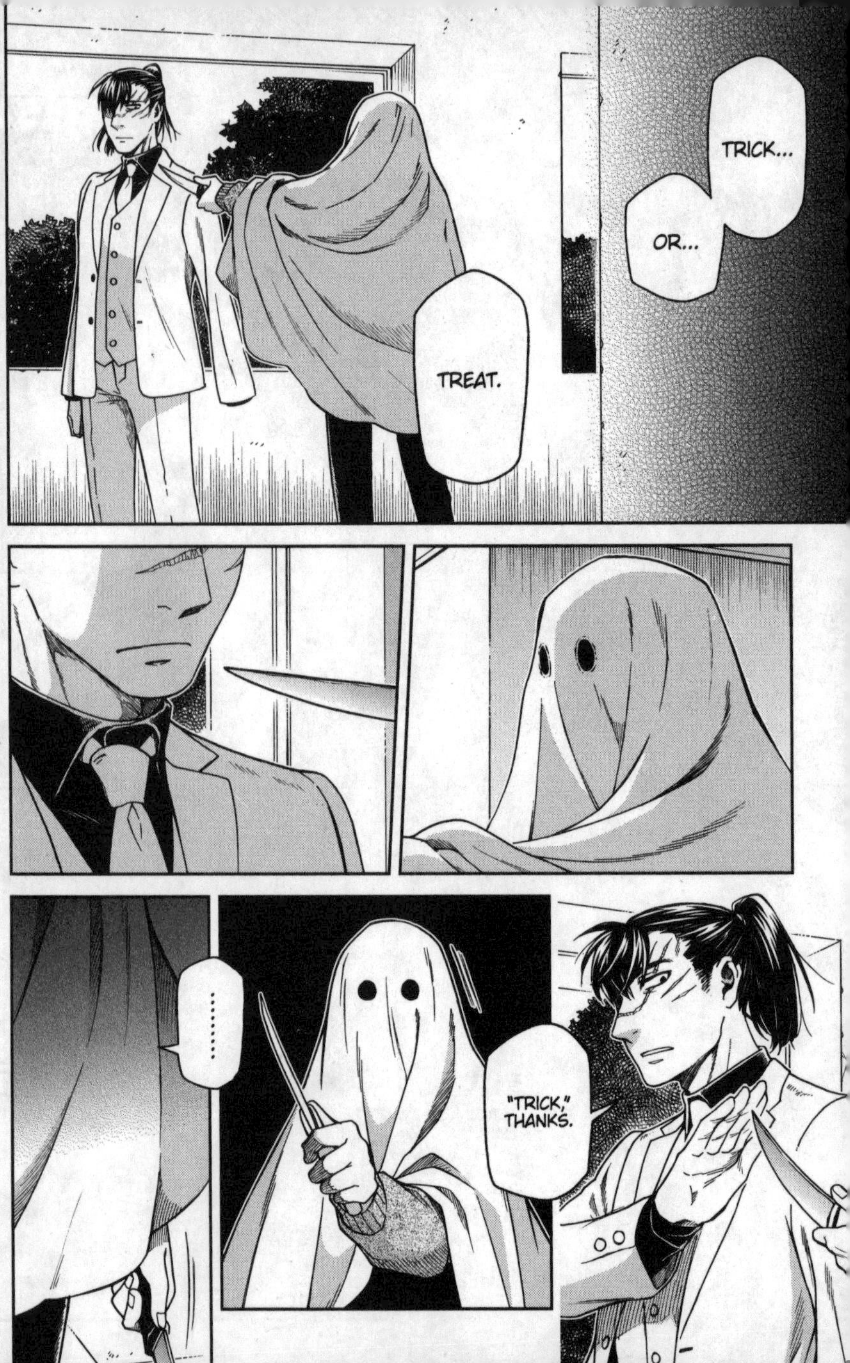
TRICK...
OR...
TREAT.
"TRICK," THANKS.
....

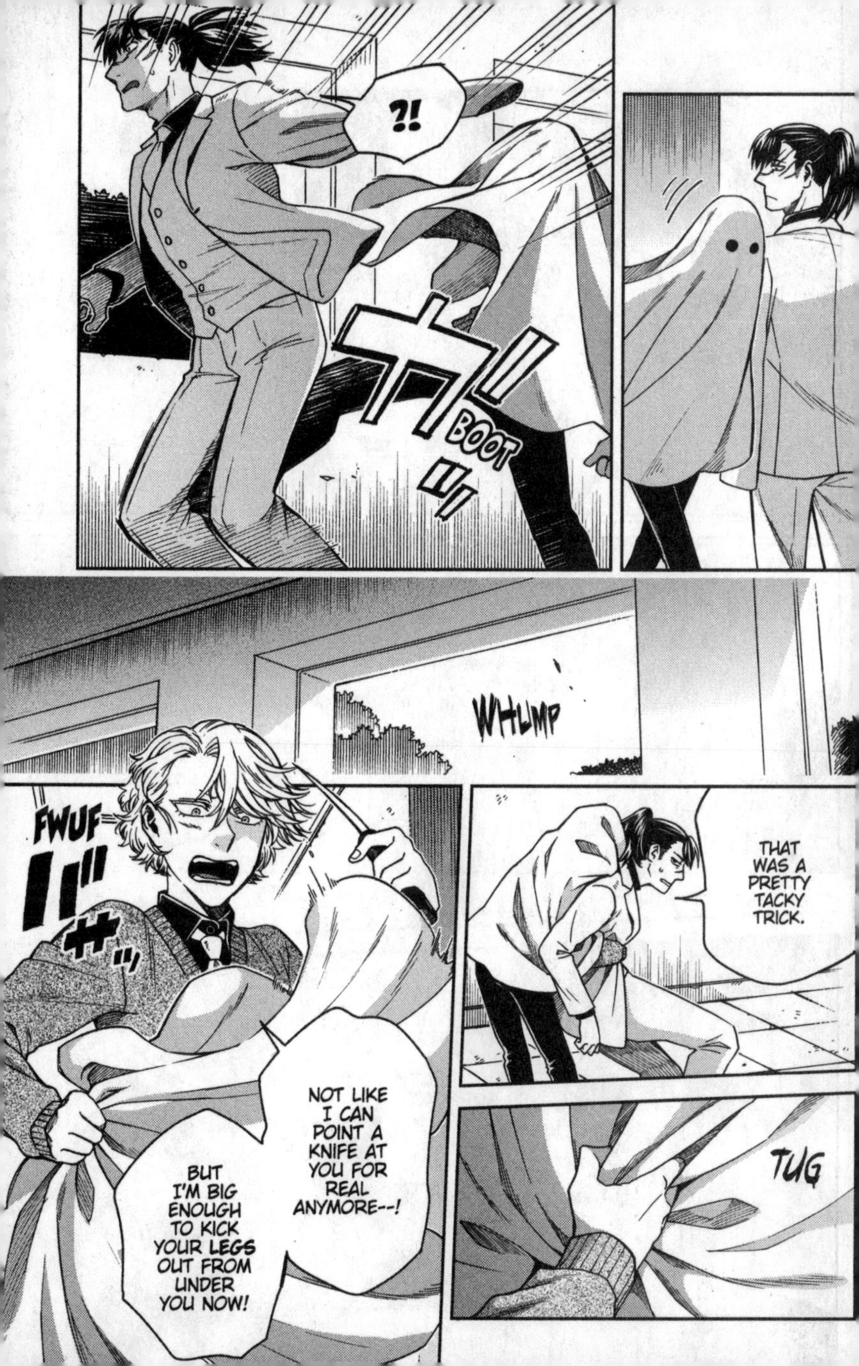
?!
BOOT
WHUMP
THAT WAS A PRETTY TACKY TRICK.
TUG
FWUF
NOT LIKE I CAN POINT A KNIFE AT YOU FOR REAL ANYMORE--!
BUT I'M BIG ENOUGH TO KICK YOUR LEGS OUT FROM UNDER YOU NOW!

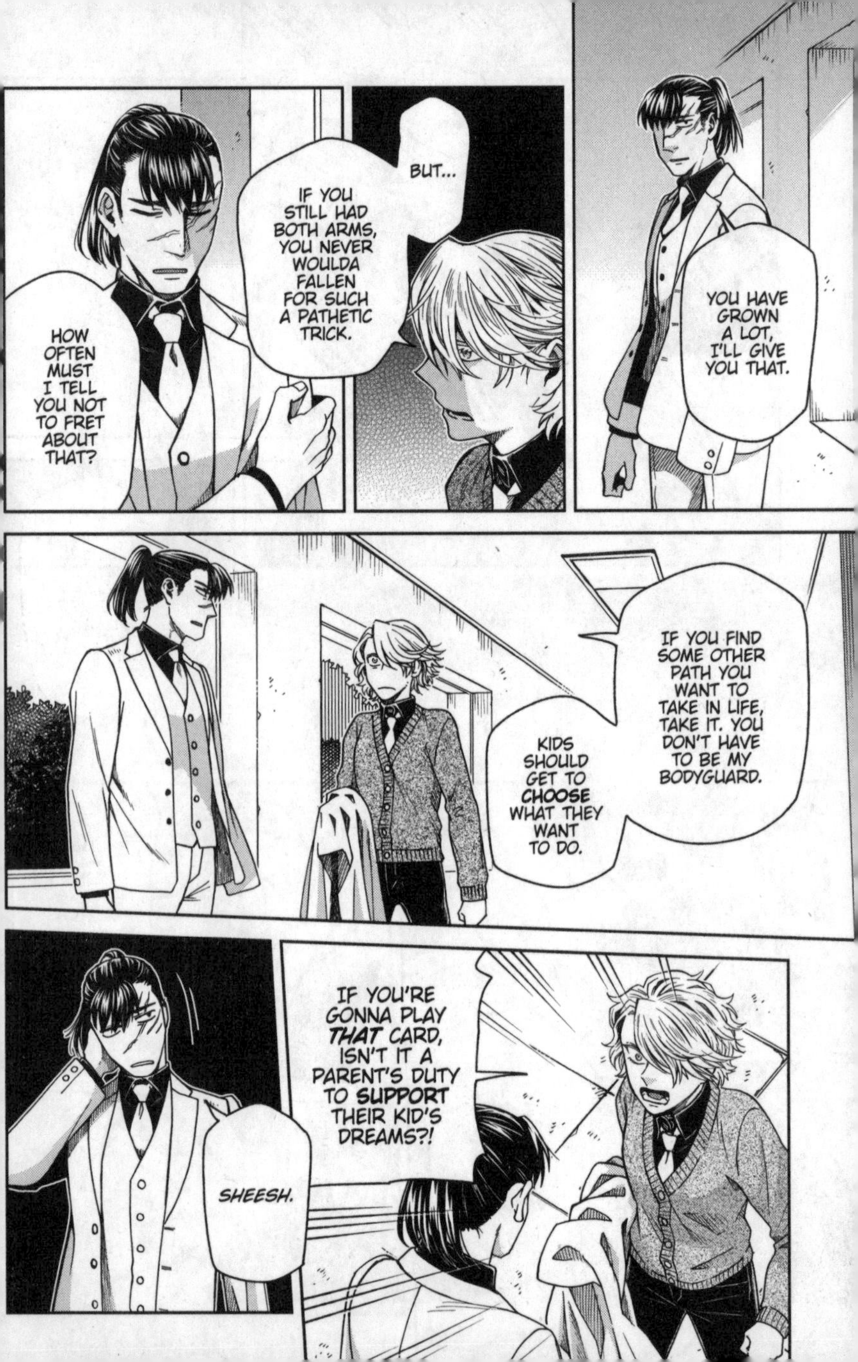
YOU HAVE GROWN A LOT, I'LL GIVE YOU THAT.
BUT...
IF YOU STILL HAD BOTH ARMS, YOU NEVER WOULDA FALLEN FOR SUCH A PATHETIC TRICK.
HOW OFTEN MUST I TELL YOU NOT TO FRET ABOUT THAT?
IF YOU FIND SOME OTHER PATH YOU WANT TO TAKE IN LIFE, TAKE IT. YOU DON'T HAVE TO BE MY BODYGUARD.
KIDS SHOULD GET TO **CHOOSE** WHAT THEY WANT TO DO.
IF YOU'RE GONNA PLAY ***THAT*** CARD, ISN'T IT A PARENT'S DUTY TO **SUPPORT** THEIR KID'S DREAMS?!
SHEESH.

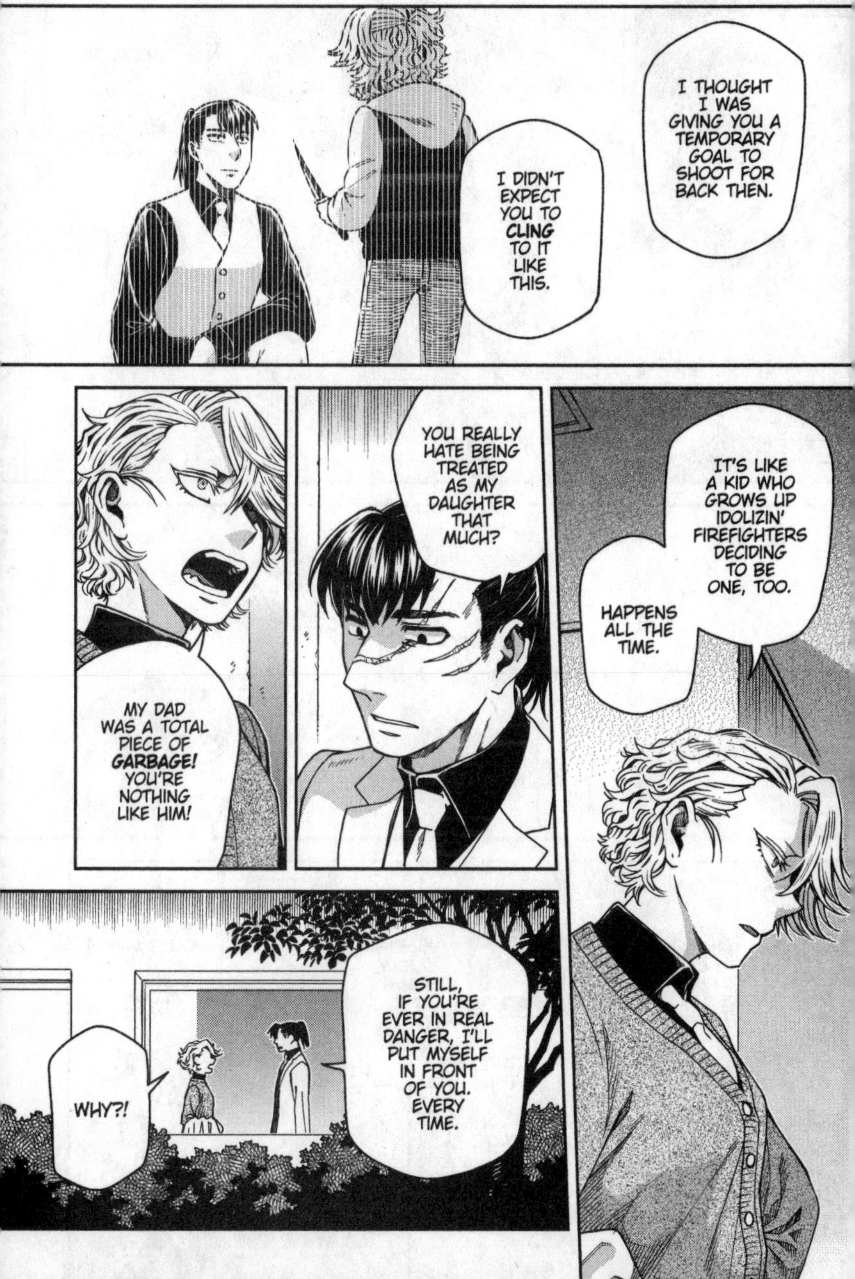
I THOUGHT I WAS GIVING YOU A TEMPORARY GOAL TO SHOOT FOR BACK THEN.
I DIDN'T EXPECT YOU TO CLING TO IT LIKE THIS.
IT'S LIKE A KID WHO GROWS UP IDOLIZIN' FIREFIGHTERS DECIDING TO BE ONE, TOO.
HAPPENS ALL THE TIME.
YOU REALLY HATE BEING TREATED AS MY DAUGHTER THAT MUCH?
MY DAD WAS A TOTAL PIECE OF GARBAGE! YOU'RE NOTHING LIKE HIM!
STILL, IF YOU'RE EVER IN REAL DANGER, I'LL PUT MYSELF IN FRONT OF YOU. EVERY TIME.
WHY?!

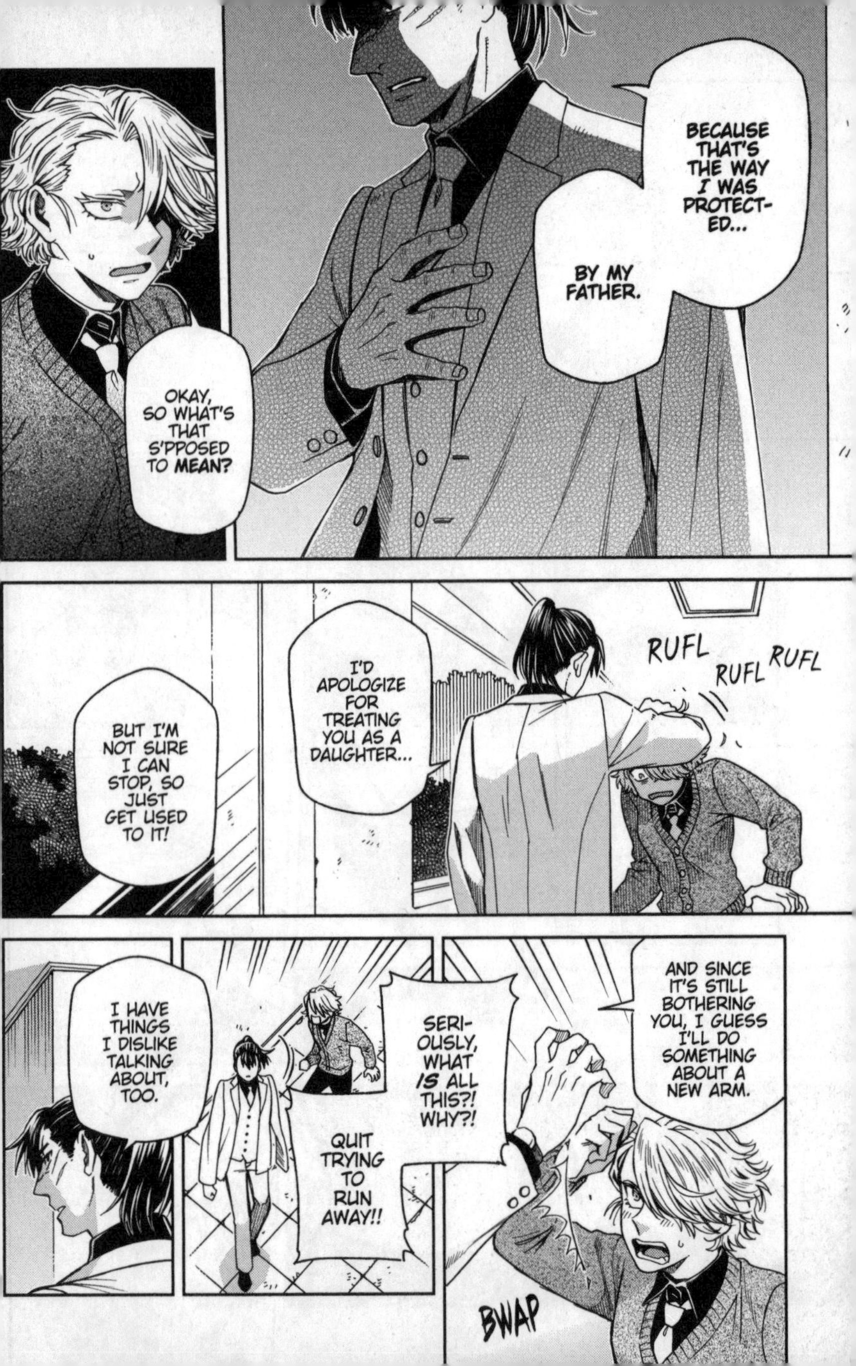
BECAUSE THAT'S THE WAY *I* WAS PROTECTED...
BY MY FATHER.
OKAY, SO WHAT'S THAT S'PPOSED TO MEAN?
RUFL RUFL RUFL
I'D APOLOGIZE FOR TREATING YOU AS A DAUGHTER...
BUT I'M NOT SURE I CAN STOP, SO JUST GET USED TO IT!
AND SINCE IT'S STILL BOTHERING YOU, I GUESS I'LL DO SOMETHING ABOUT A NEW ARM.
BWAP
SERIOUSLY, WHAT *IS* ALL THIS?! WHY?!
QUIT TRYING TO RUN AWAY!!
I HAVE THINGS I DISLIKE TALKING ABOUT, TOO.

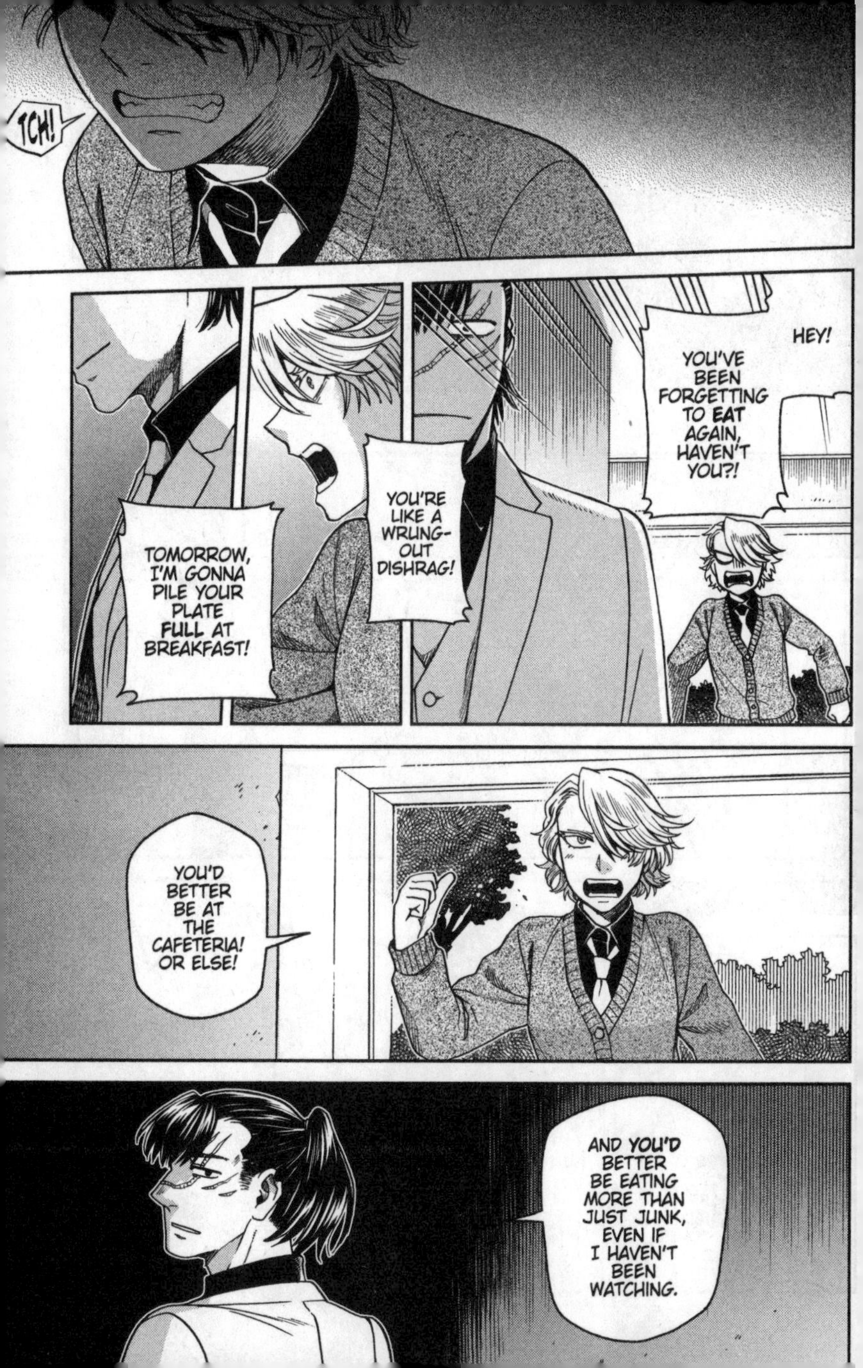
TCH!
HEY!
YOU'VE BEEN FORGETTING TO EAT AGAIN, HAVEN'T YOU?!
YOU'RE LIKE A WRUNG-OUT DISHRAG!
TOMORROW, I'M GONNA PILE YOUR PLATE FULL AT BREAKFAST!
YOU'D BETTER BE AT THE CAFETERIA! OR ELSE!
AND YOU'D BETTER BE EATING MORE THAN JUST JUNK, EVEN IF I HAVEN'T BEEN WATCHING.

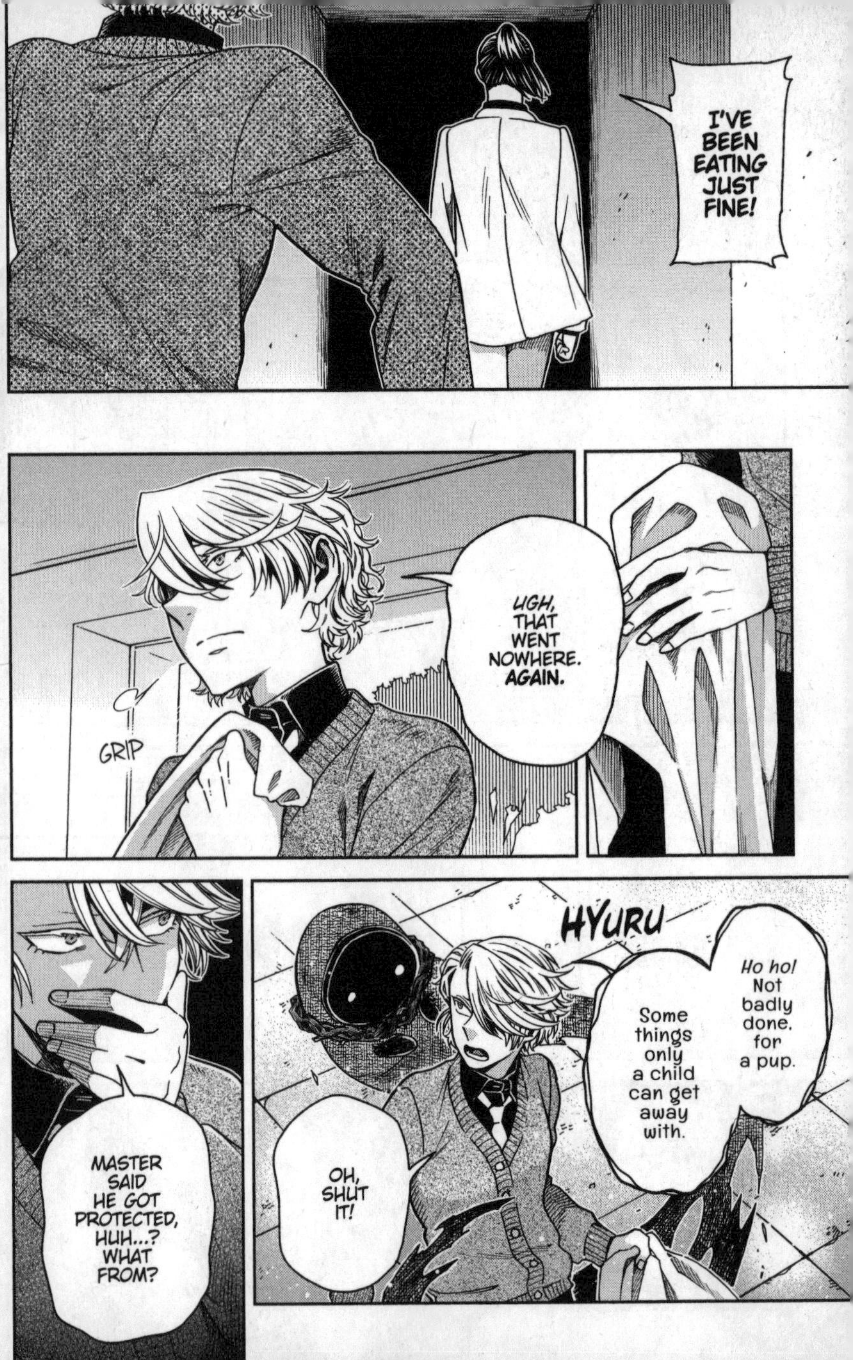
I'VE BEEN EATING JUST FINE!
UGH, THAT WENT NOWHERE. AGAIN.
GRIP
HYURU
Ho ho! Not badly done, for a pup.
Some things only a child can get away with.
OH, SHUT IT!
MASTER SAID HE GOT PROTECTED, HUH...? WHAT FROM?

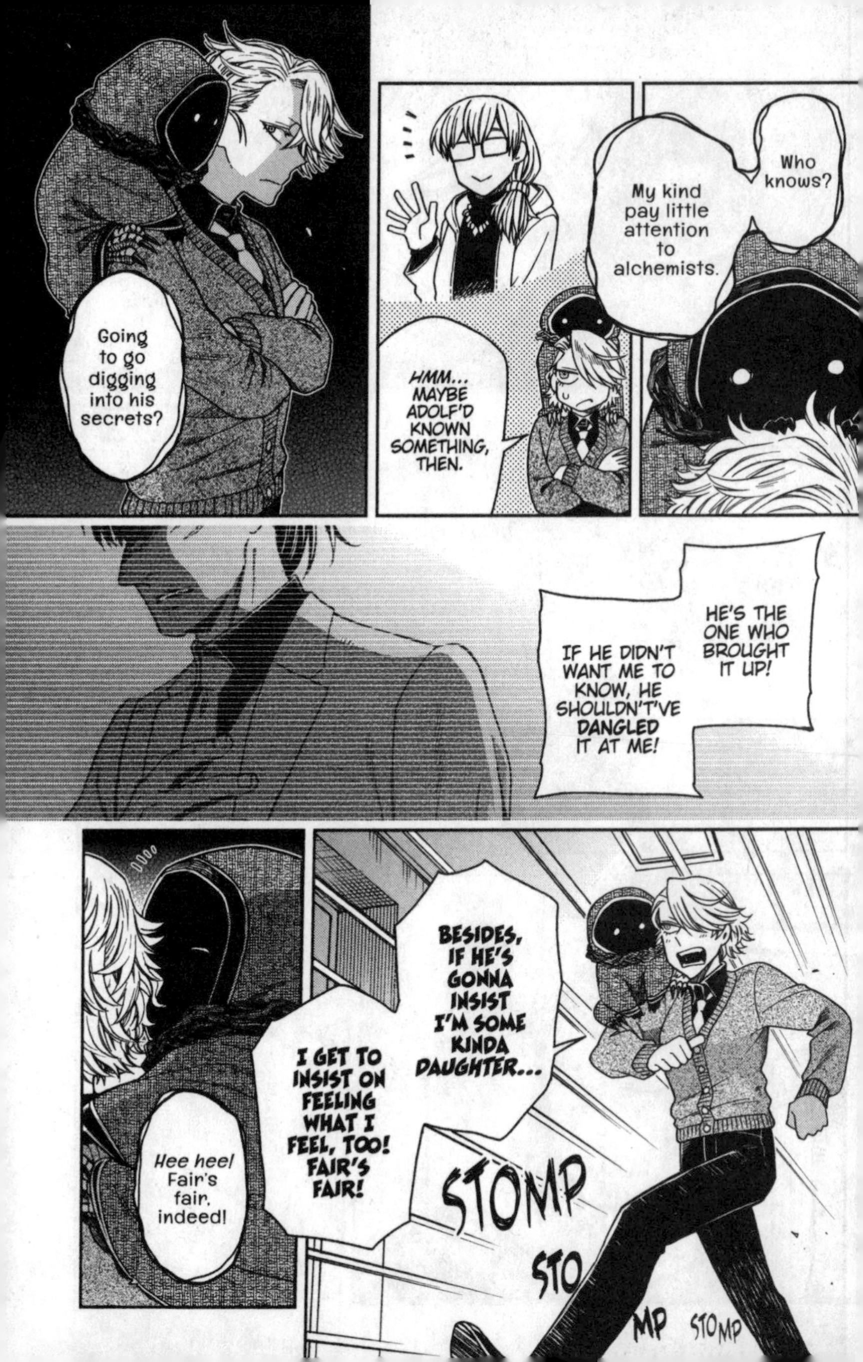
Who knows?
My kind pay little attention to alchemists.
HMM... MAYBE ADOLF'D KNOWN SOMETHING, THEN.
Going to go digging into his secrets?
HE'S THE ONE WHO BROUGHT IT UP!
IF HE DIDN'T WANT ME TO KNOW, HE SHOULDN'T'VE DANGLED IT AT ME!
BESIDES, IF HE'S GONNA INSIST I'M SOME KINDA DAUGHTER...
I GET TO INSIST ON FEELING WHAT I FEEL, TOO! FAIR'S FAIR!
STOMP
STOMP
STOMP
Hee hee! Fair's fair, indeed!

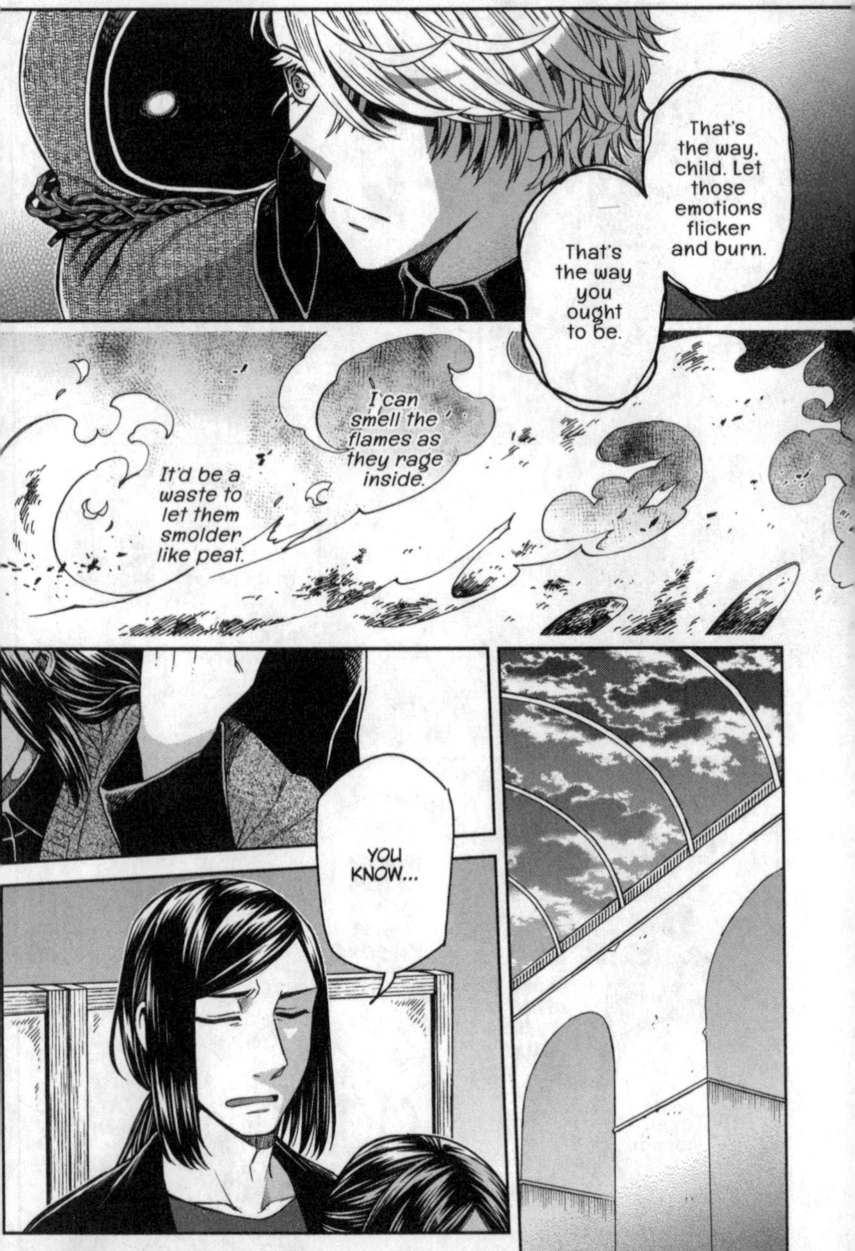
That's the way, child. Let those emotions flicker and burn.
That's the way you ought to be.
I can smell the flames as they rage inside.
It'd be a waste to let them smolder like peat.
YOU KNOW...

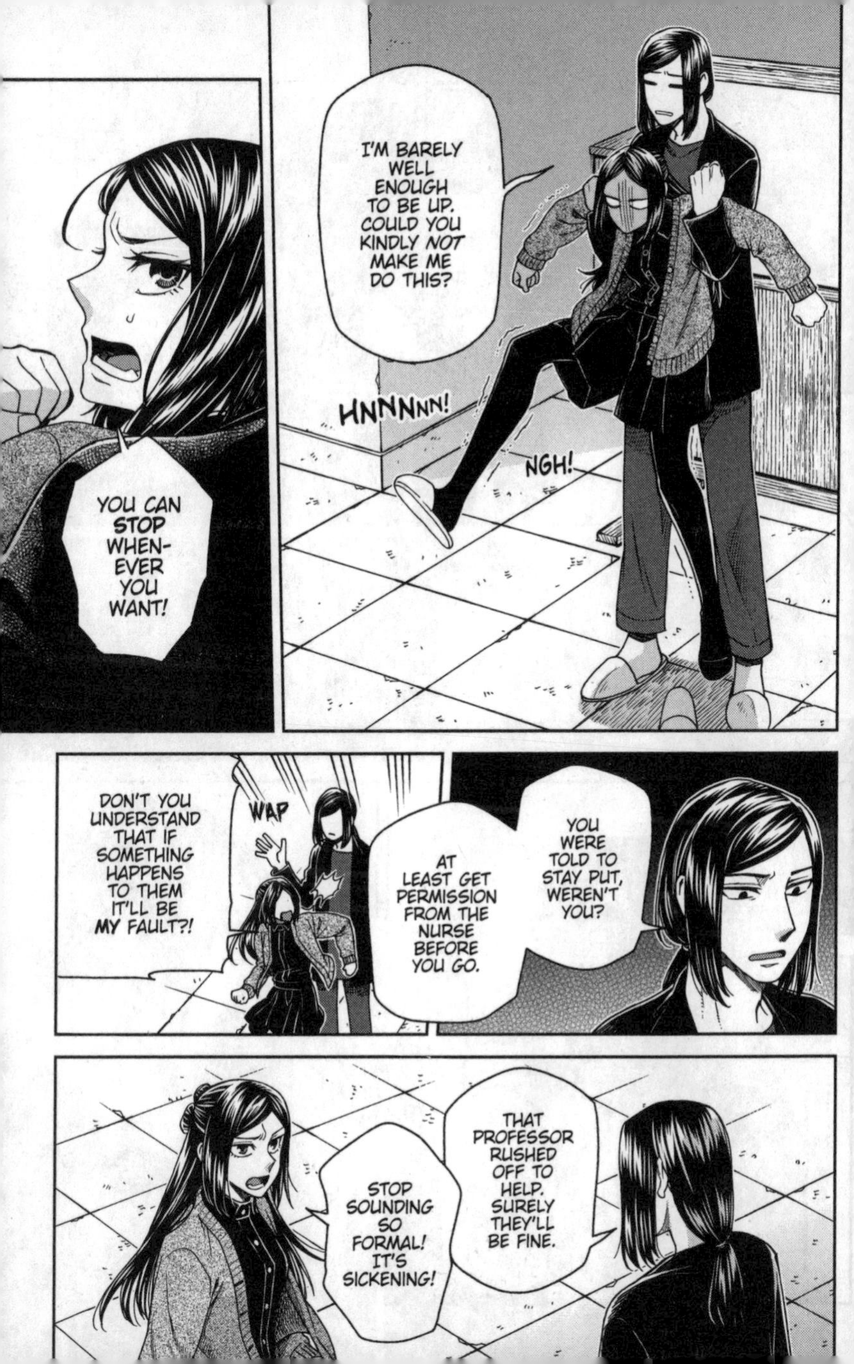
I'M BARELY WELL ENOUGH TO BE UP. COULD YOU KINDLY *NOT* MAKE ME DO THIS?
HNNNNN!
NGH!
YOU CAN STOP WHEN-EVER YOU WANT!
YOU WERE TOLD TO STAY PUT, WEREN'T YOU?
AT LEAST GET PERMISSION FROM THE NURSE BEFORE YOU GO.
WAP
DON'T YOU UNDERSTAND THAT IF SOMETHING HAPPENS TO THEM IT'LL BE **MY FAULT**?!
THAT PROFESSOR RUSHED OFF TO HELP. SURELY THEY'LL BE FINE.
STOP SOUNDING SO FORMAL! IT'S SICKENING!

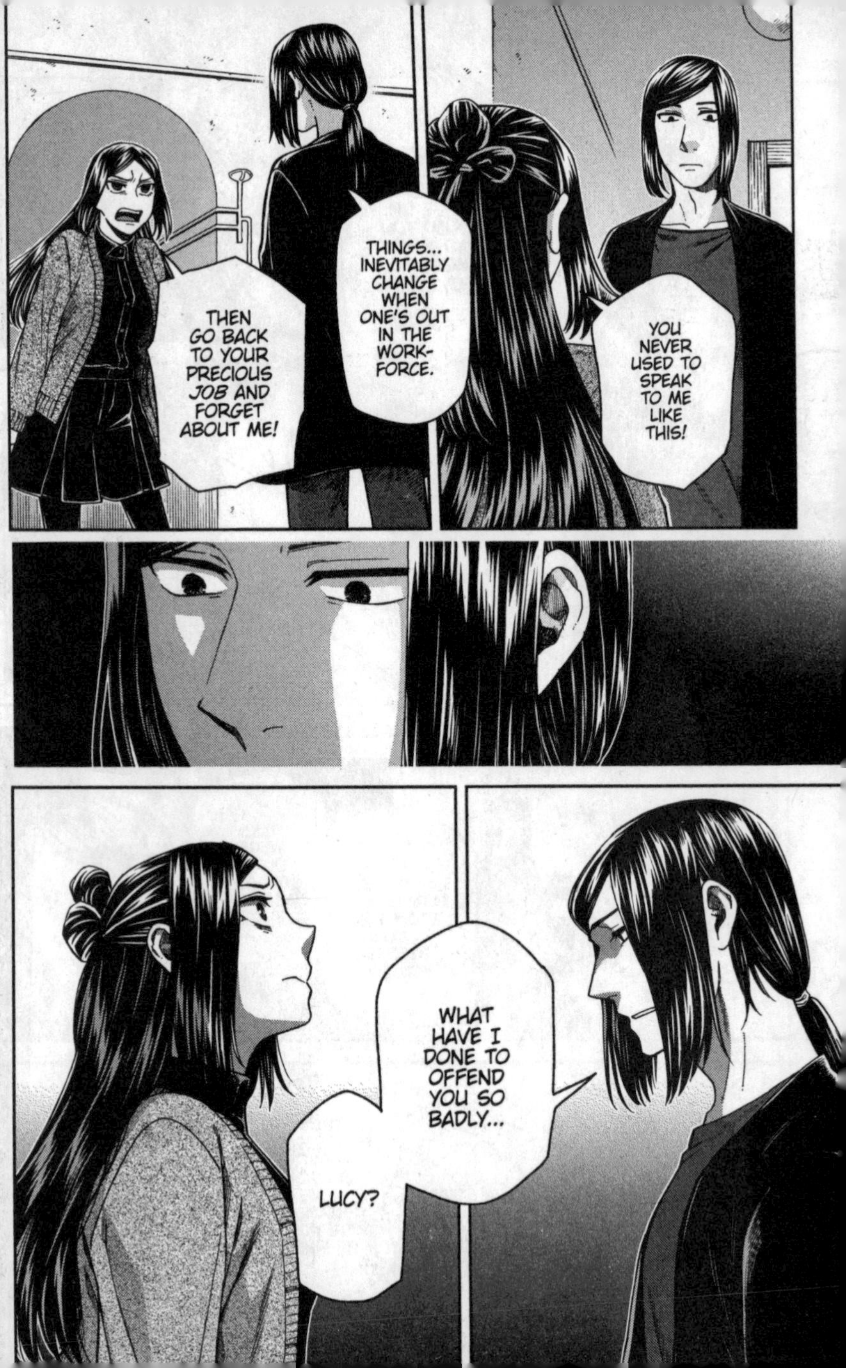
YOU NEVER USED TO SPEAK TO ME LIKE THIS!
THINGS... INEVITABLY CHANGE WHEN ONE'S OUT IN THE WORK-FORCE.
THEN GO BACK TO YOUR PRECIOUS *JOB* AND FORGET ABOUT ME!
WHAT HAVE I DONE TO OFFEND YOU SO BADLY...
LUCY?

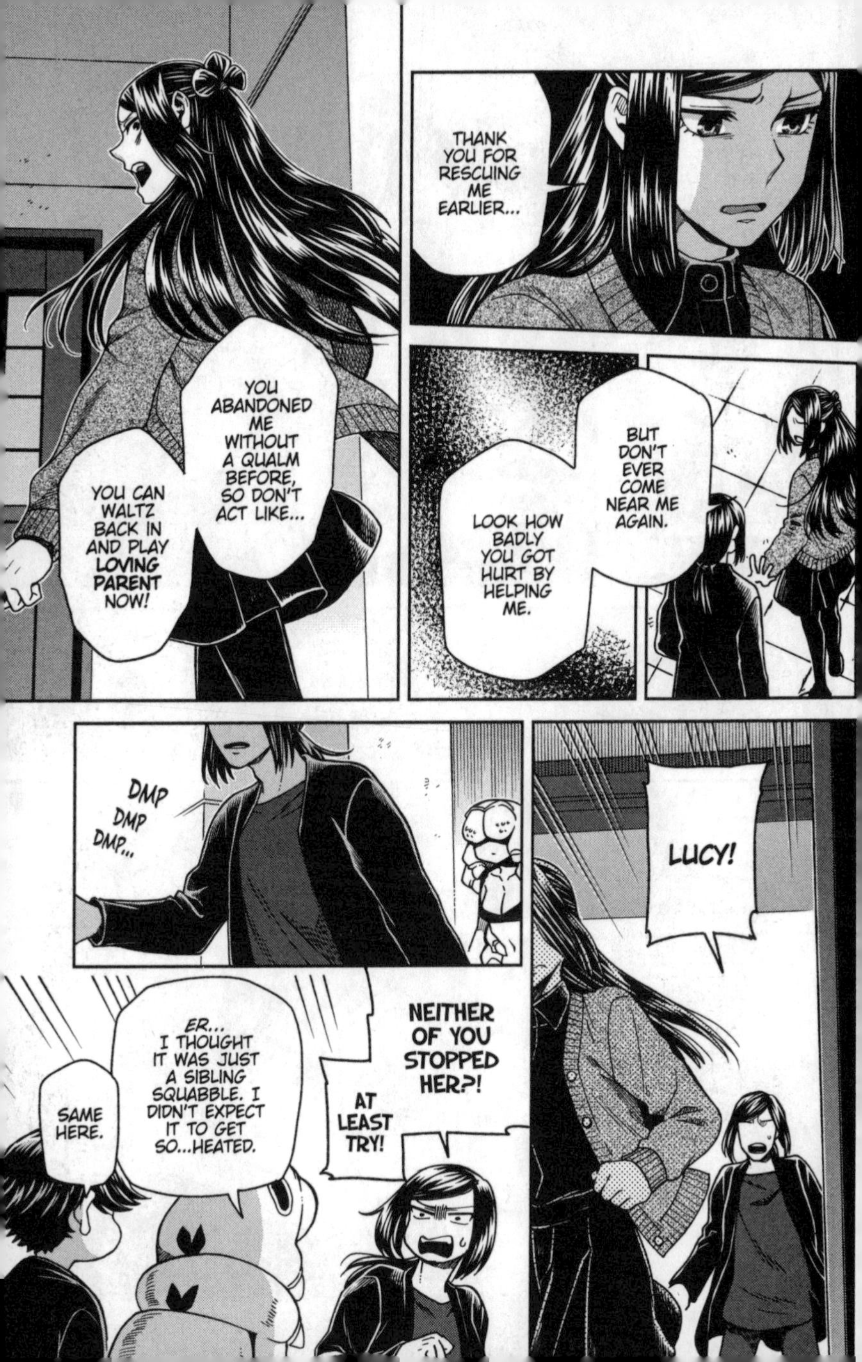
THANK YOU FOR RESCUING ME EARLIER...
LOOK HOW BADLY YOU GOT HURT BY HELPING ME.
BUT DON'T EVER COME NEAR ME AGAIN.
YOU ABANDONED ME WITHOUT A QUALM BEFORE, SO DON'T ACT LIKE...
YOU CAN WALTZ BACK IN AND PLAY LOVING PARENT NOW!
LUCY!
DMP DMP DMP...
NEITHER OF YOU STOPPED HER?!
AT LEAST TRY!
ER... I THOUGHT IT WAS JUST A SIBLING SQUABBLE. I DIDN'T EXPECT IT TO GET SO...HEATED.
SAME HERE.

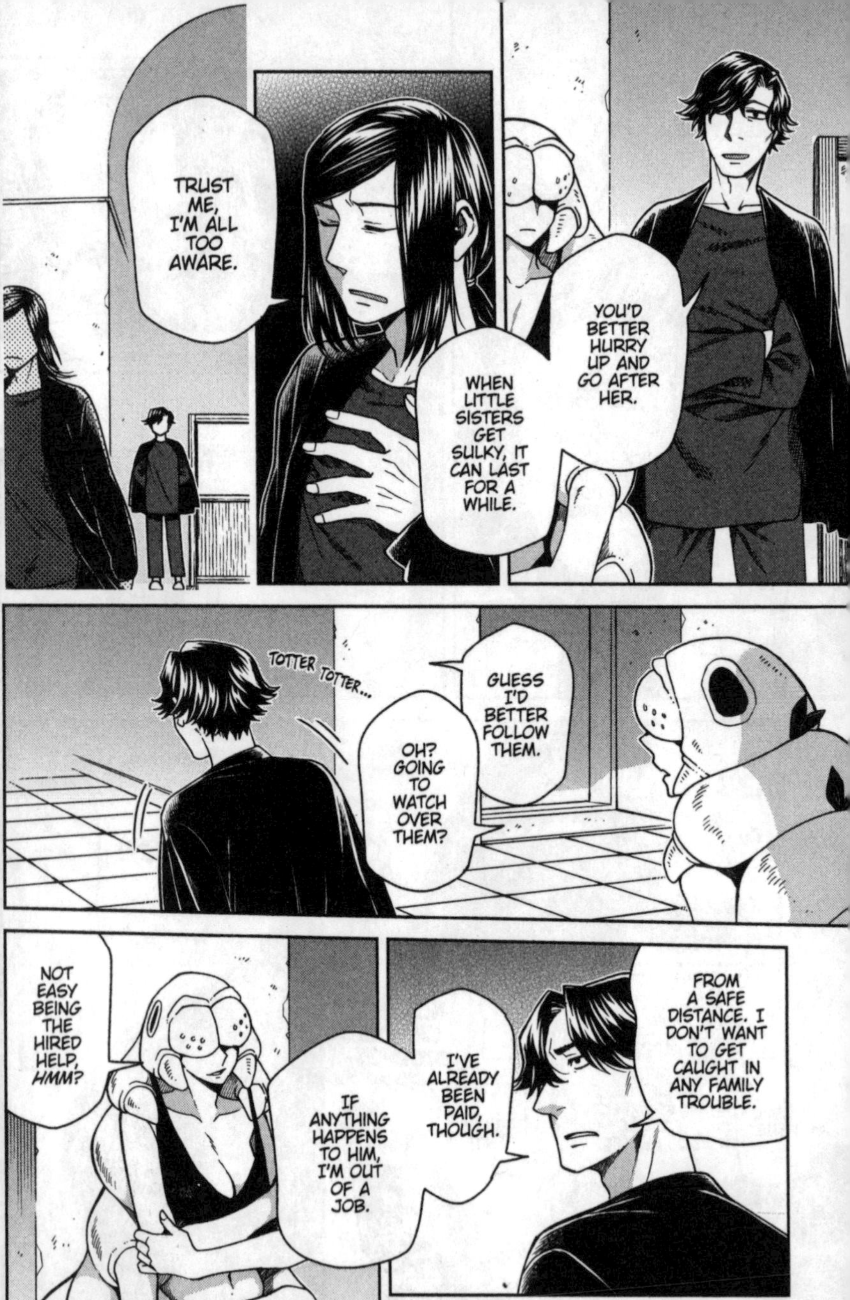
YOU'D BETTER HURRY UP AND GO AFTER HER.
WHEN LITTLE SISTERS GET SULKY, IT CAN LAST FOR A WHILE.
TRUST ME, I'M ALL TOO AWARE.
GUESS I'D BETTER FOLLOW THEM.
TOTTER TOTTER...
OH? GOING TO WATCH OVER THEM?
FROM A SAFE DISTANCE. I DON'T WANT TO GET CAUGHT IN ANY FAMILY TROUBLE.
I'VE ALREADY BEEN PAID, THOUGH.
IF ANYTHING HAPPENS TO HIM, I'M OUT OF A JOB.
NOT EASY BEING THE HIRED HELP, *HMM?*

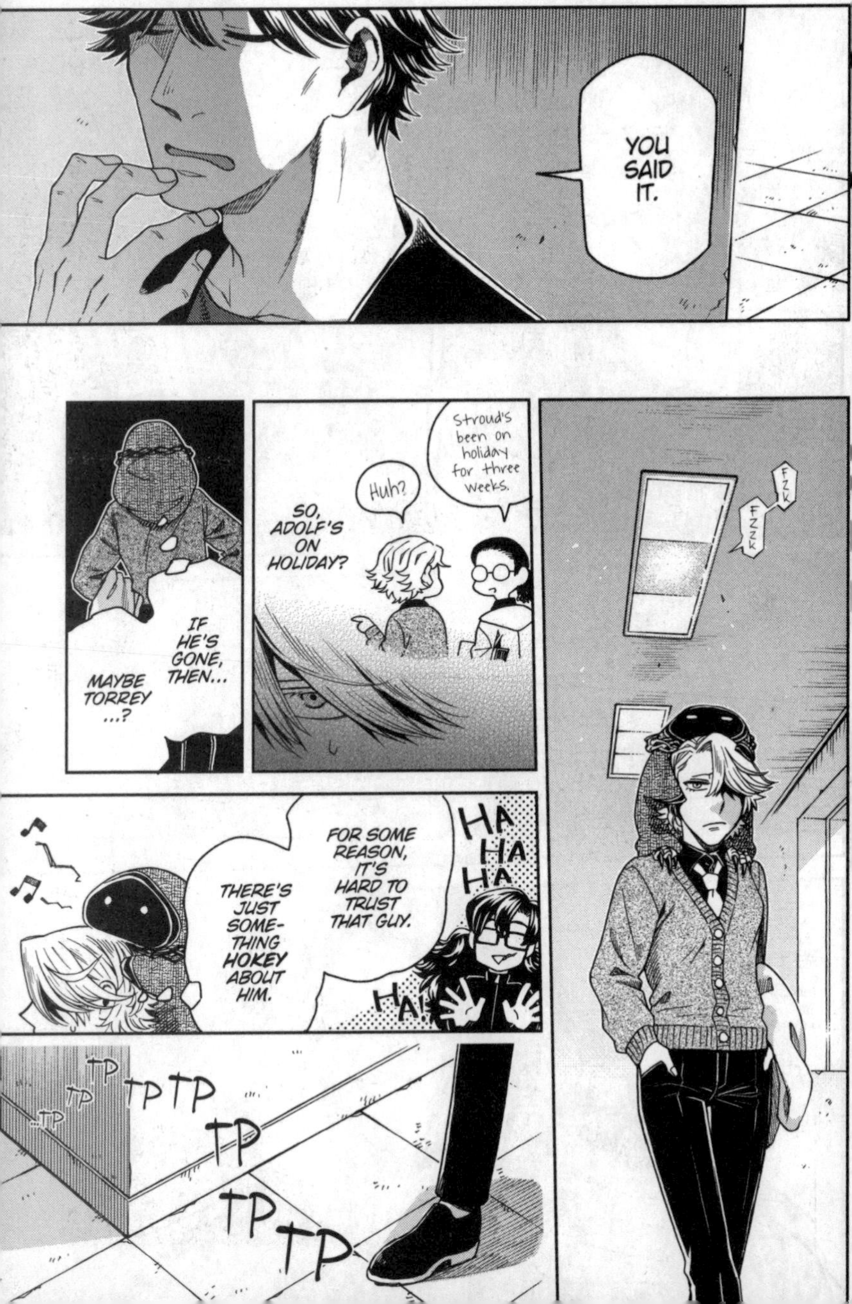

YOU SAID IT.
FZK
FZZK
Stroud's been on holiday for three weeks.
Huh?
SO, ADOLF'S ON HOLIDAY?
IF HE'S GONE, THEN...
MAYBE TORREY ...?
FOR SOME REASON, IT'S HARD TO TRUST THAT GUY.
THERE'S JUST SOME-THING HOKEY ABOUT HIM.
HA HA HA HA HA!
TP TP TP TP TP TP
TP TP
...TP

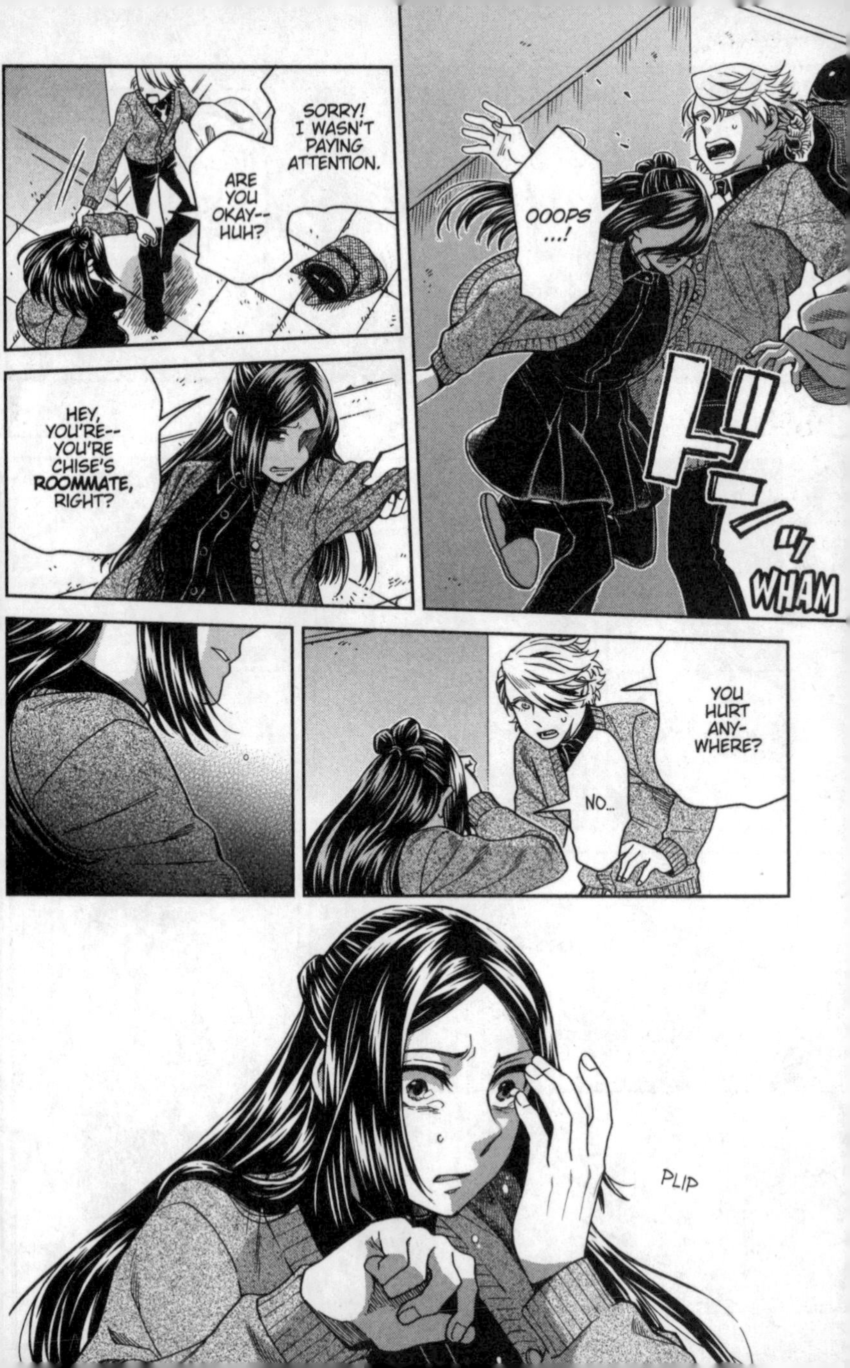
OOOPS ...!
WHAM
SORRY! I WASN'T PAYING ATTENTION.
ARE YOU OKAY-- HUH?
HEY, YOU'RE-- YOU'RE CHISE'S **ROOMMATE**, RIGHT?
YOU HURT ANY-WHERE?
NO...
PLIP

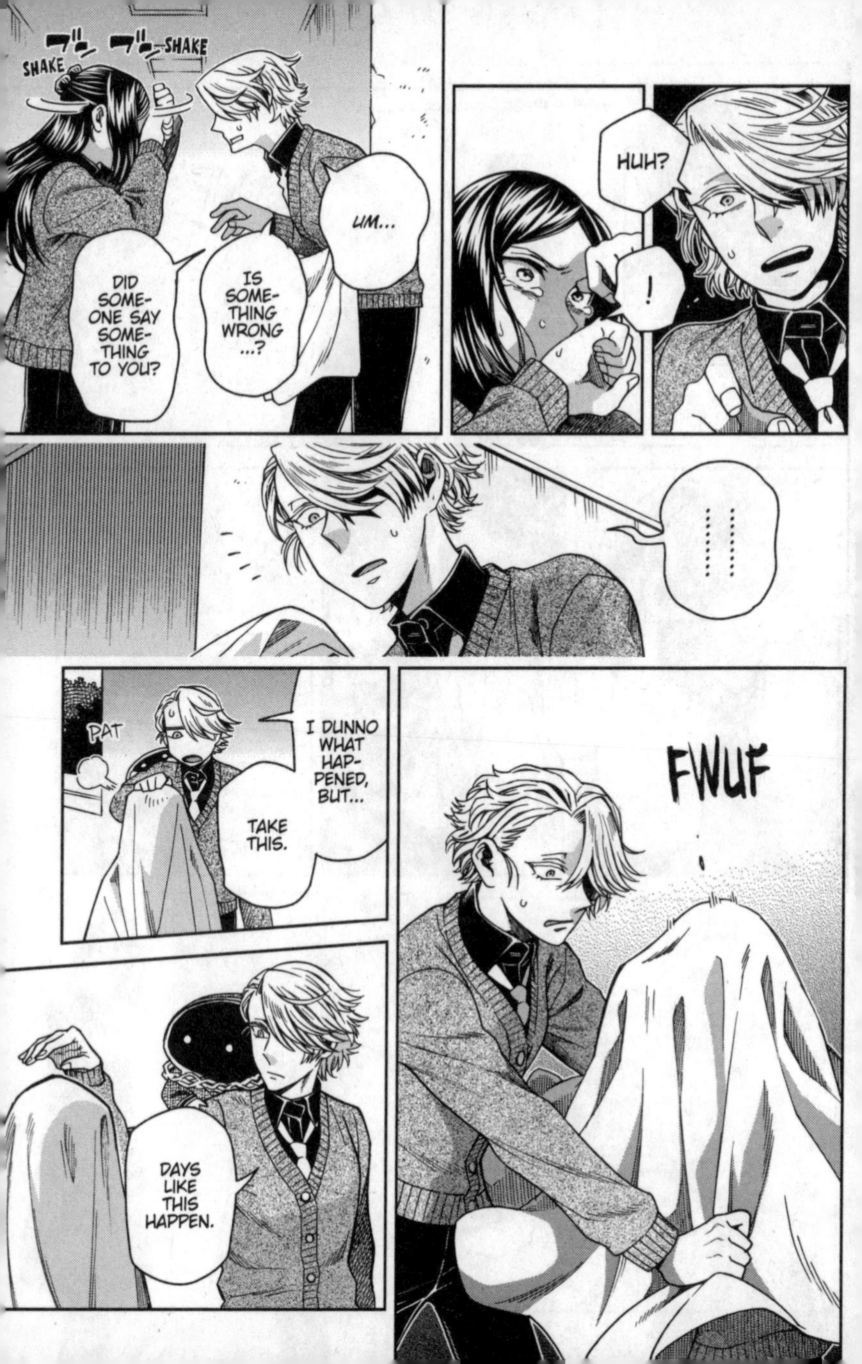
HUH?
!
SHAKE
SHAKE
UM...
IS SOMETHING WRONG...?
DID SOMEONE SAY SOMETHING TO YOU?
......
FWUF
I DUNNO WHAT HAPPENED, BUT...
TAKE THIS.
PAT
DAYS LIKE THIS HAPPEN.

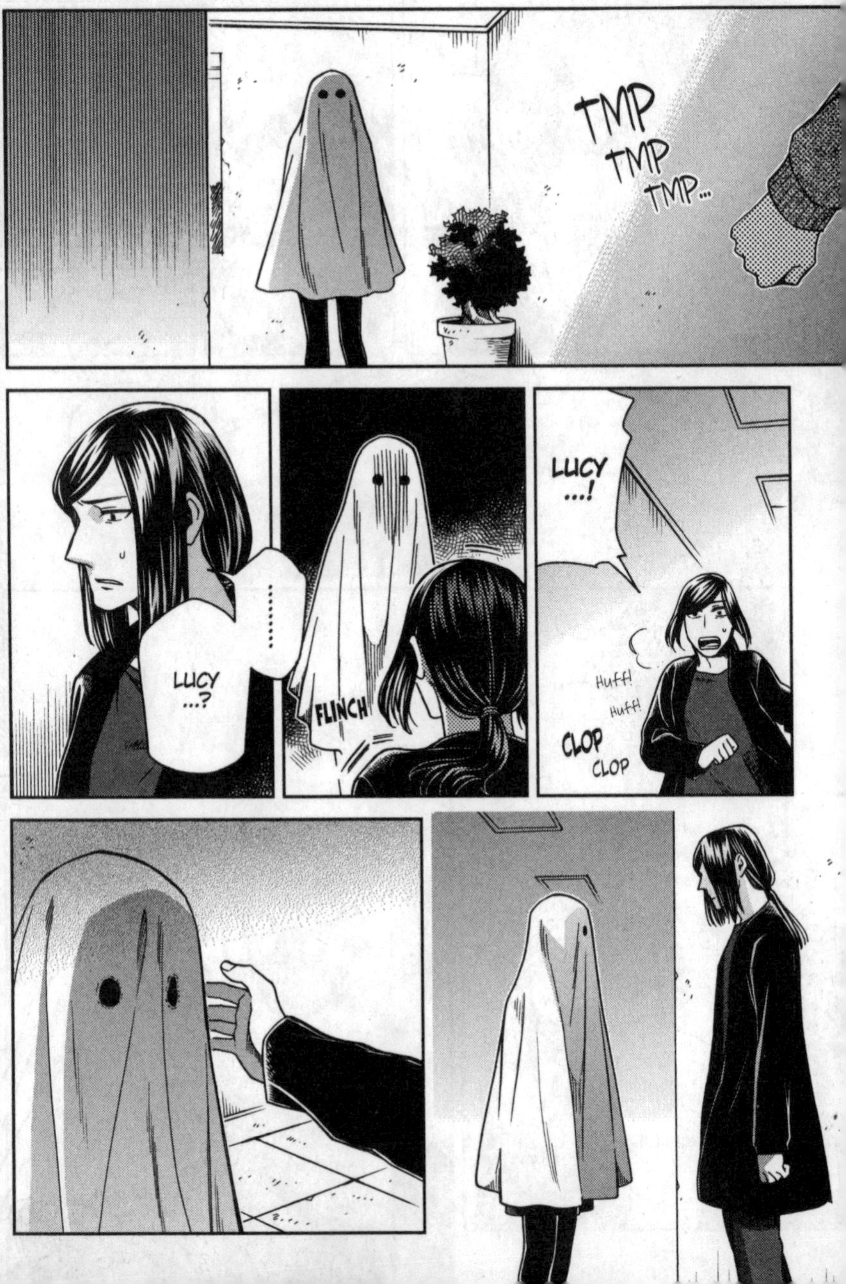
TMP
TMP
TMP...
LUCY ...!
Huff!
Huff!
CLOP
CLOP
FLINCH
......
LUCY ...?

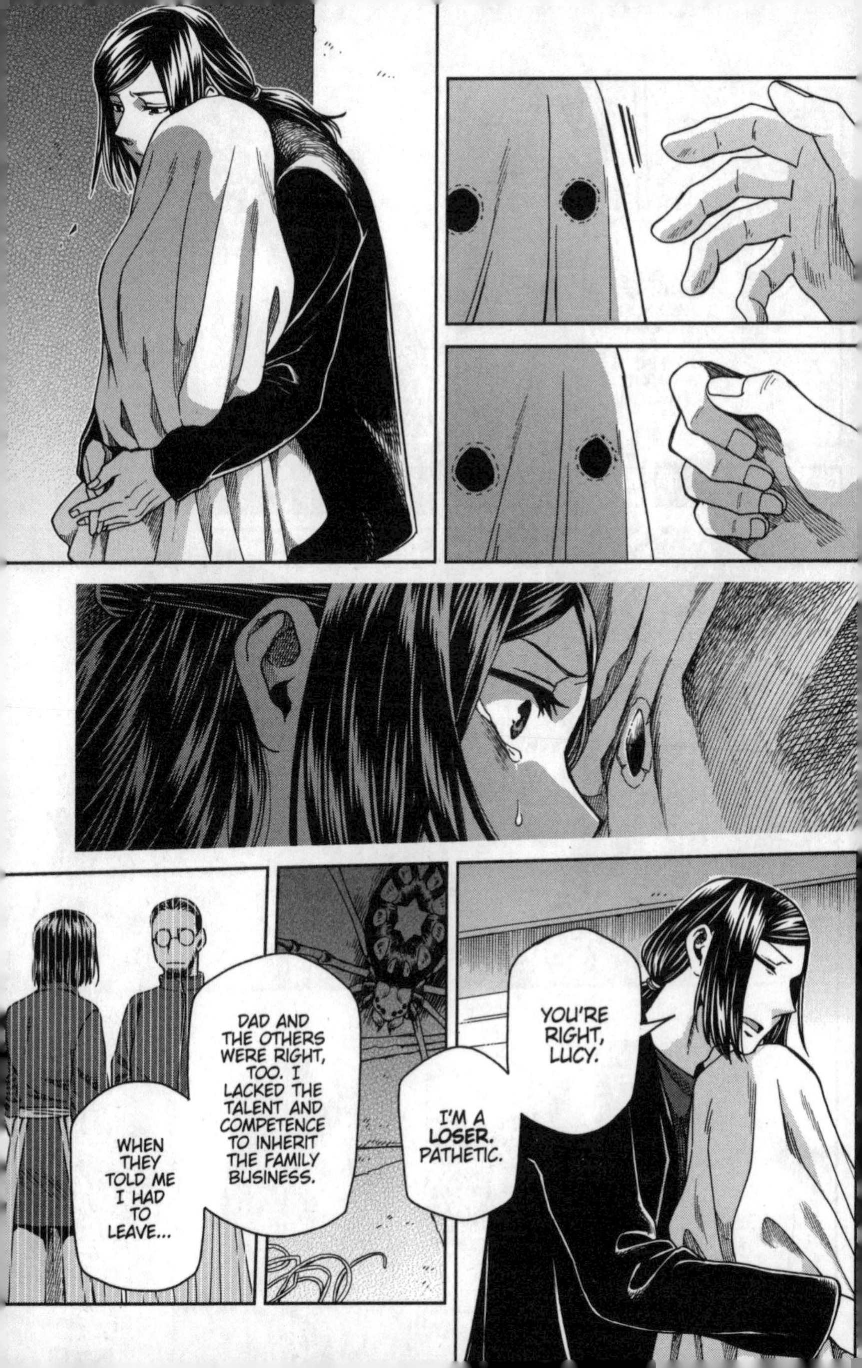
YOU'RE RIGHT, LUCY.
I'M A LOSER. PATHETIC.
DAD AND THE OTHERS WERE RIGHT, TOO. I LACKED THE TALENT AND COMPETENCE TO INHERIT THE FAMILY BUSINESS.
WHEN THEY TOLD ME I HAD TO LEAVE...

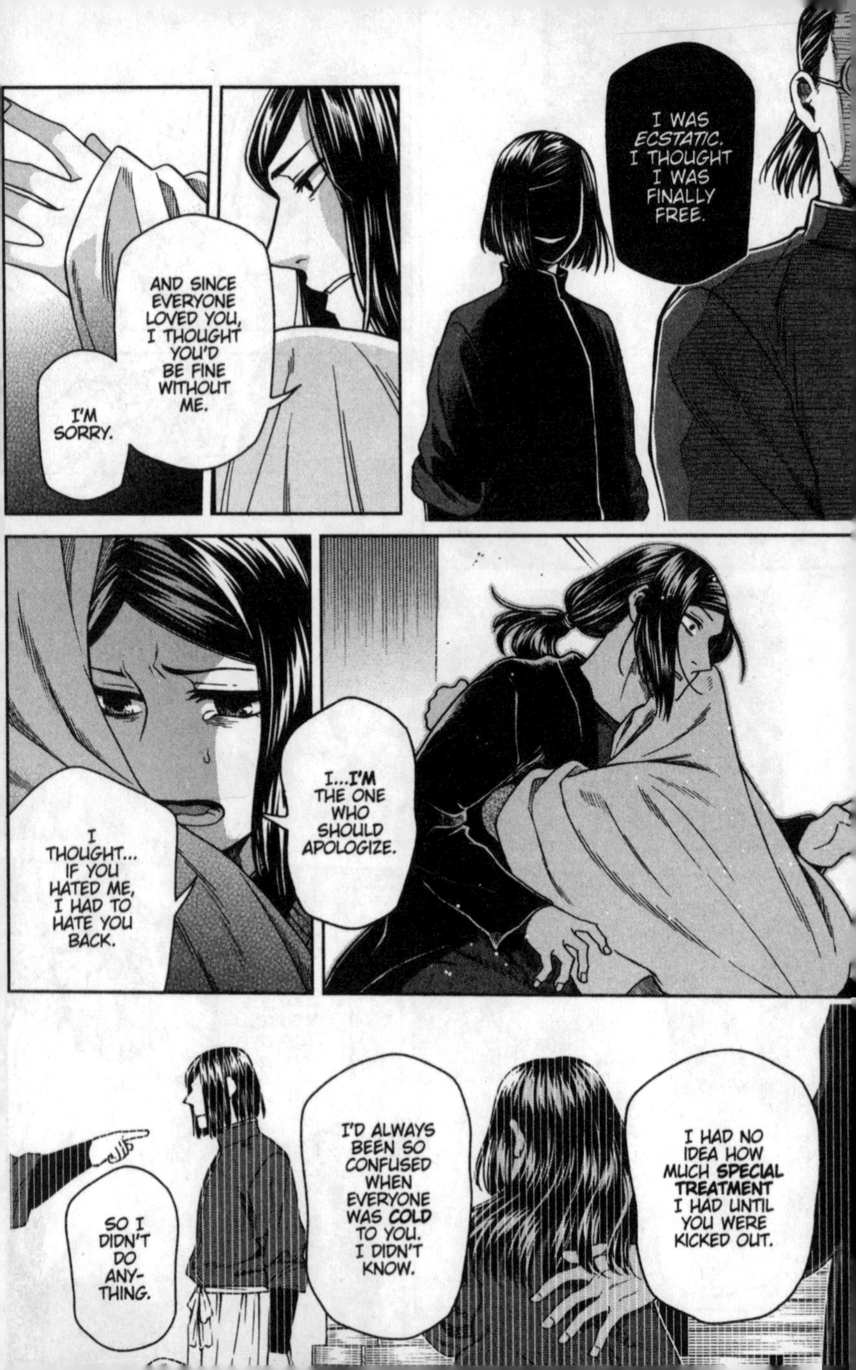
I WAS *ECSTATIC.* I THOUGHT I WAS FINALLY FREE.
AND SINCE EVERYONE LOVED YOU, I THOUGHT YOU'D BE FINE WITHOUT ME.
I'M SORRY.
I...I'M THE ONE WHO SHOULD APOLOGIZE.
I THOUGHT... IF YOU HATED ME, I HAD TO HATE YOU BACK.
I HAD NO IDEA HOW MUCH **SPECIAL TREATMENT** I HAD UNTIL YOU WERE KICKED OUT.
I'D ALWAYS BEEN SO CONFUSED WHEN EVERYONE WAS **COLD** TO YOU. I DIDN'T KNOW.
SO I DIDN'T DO ANYTHING.

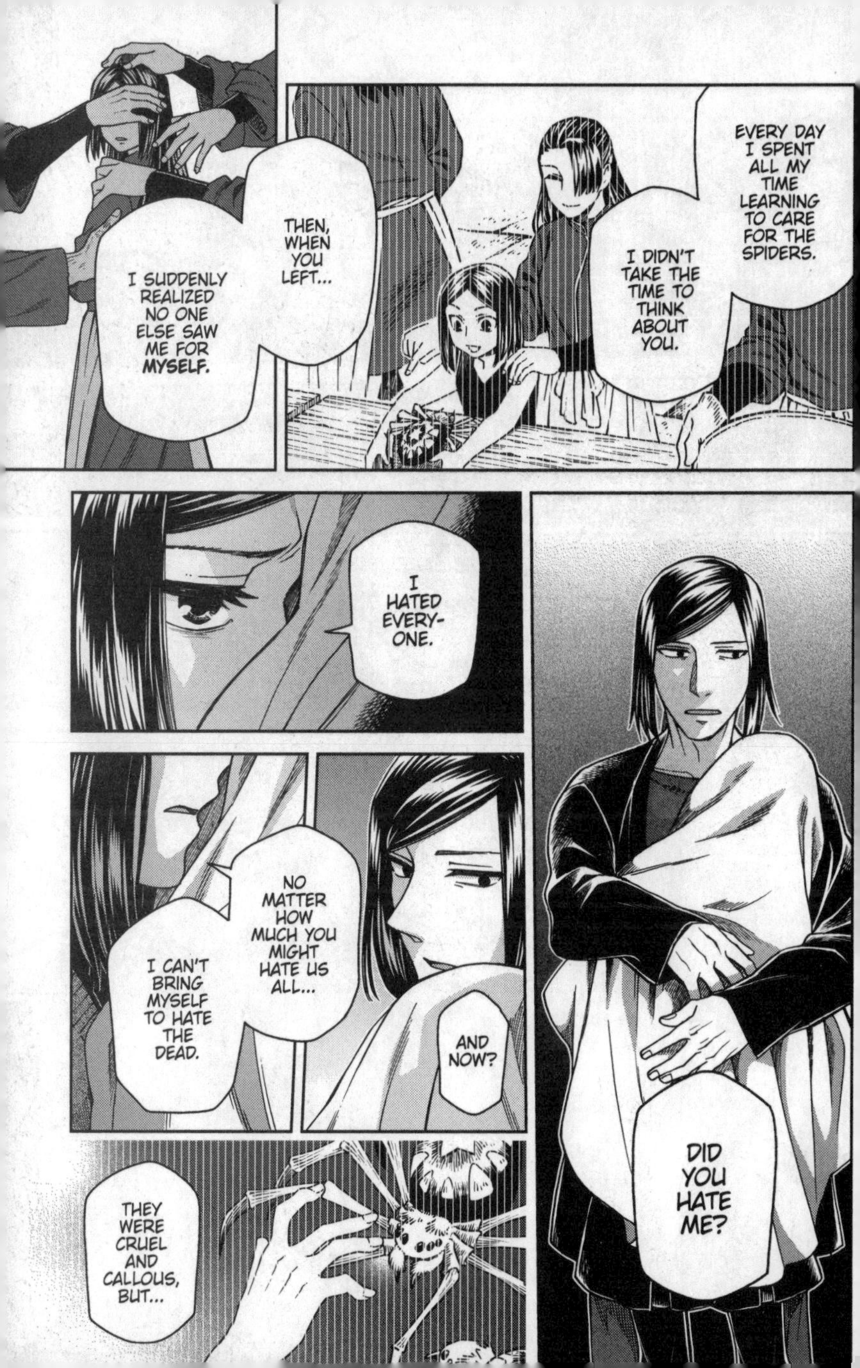
EVERY DAY I SPENT ALL MY TIME LEARNING TO CARE FOR THE SPIDERS.
I DIDN'T TAKE THE TIME TO THINK ABOUT YOU.
THEN, WHEN YOU LEFT...
I SUDDENLY REALIZED NO ONE ELSE SAW ME FOR **MYSELF**.
DID YOU HATE ME?
I HATED EVERY-ONE.
AND NOW?
NO MATTER HOW MUCH YOU MIGHT HATE US ALL...
I CAN'T BRING MYSELF TO HATE THE DEAD.
THEY WERE CRUEL AND CALLOUS, BUT...

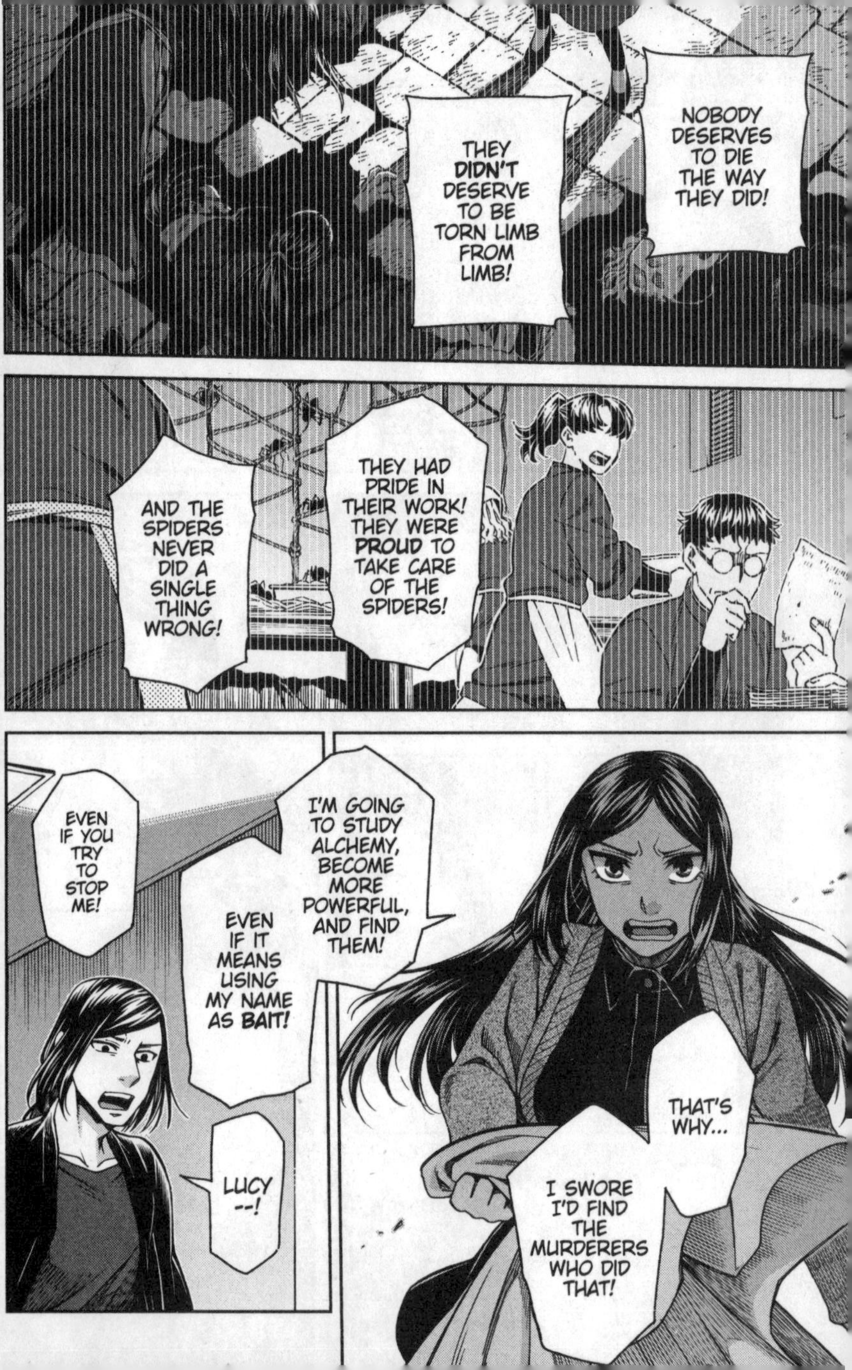
NOBODY DESERVES TO DIE THE WAY THEY DID!
THEY DIDN'T DESERVE TO BE TORN LIMB FROM LIMB!
THEY HAD PRIDE IN THEIR WORK! THEY WERE PROUD TO TAKE CARE OF THE SPIDERS!
AND THE SPIDERS NEVER DID A SINGLE THING WRONG!
THAT'S WHY...
I SWORE I'D FIND THE MURDERERS WHO DID THAT!
I'M GOING TO STUDY ALCHEMY, BECOME MORE POWERFUL, AND FIND THEM!
EVEN IF IT MEANS USING MY NAME AS BAIT!
EVEN IF YOU TRY TO STOP ME!
LUCY --!

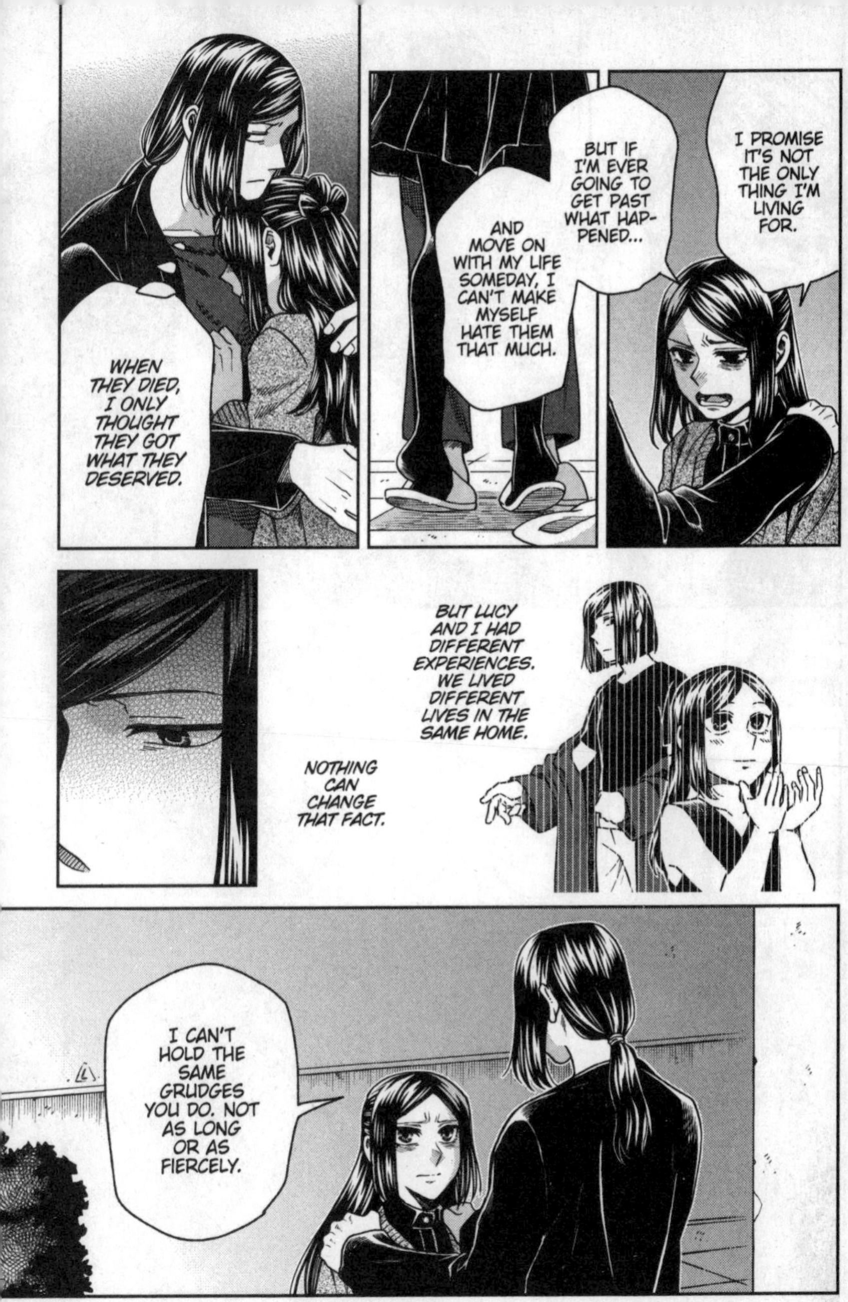
I PROMISE IT'S NOT THE ONLY THING I'M LIVING FOR.
BUT IF I'M EVER GOING TO GET PAST WHAT HAP-PENED...
AND MOVE ON WITH MY LIFE SOMEDAY, I CAN'T MAKE MYSELF HATE THEM THAT MUCH.
WHEN THEY DIED, I ONLY THOUGHT THEY GOT WHAT THEY DESERVED.
BUT LUCY AND I HAD DIFFERENT EXPERIENCES. WE LIVED DIFFERENT LIVES IN THE SAME HOME.
NOTHING CAN CHANGE THAT FACT.
I CAN'T HOLD THE SAME GRUDGES YOU DO. NOT AS LONG OR AS FIERCELY.

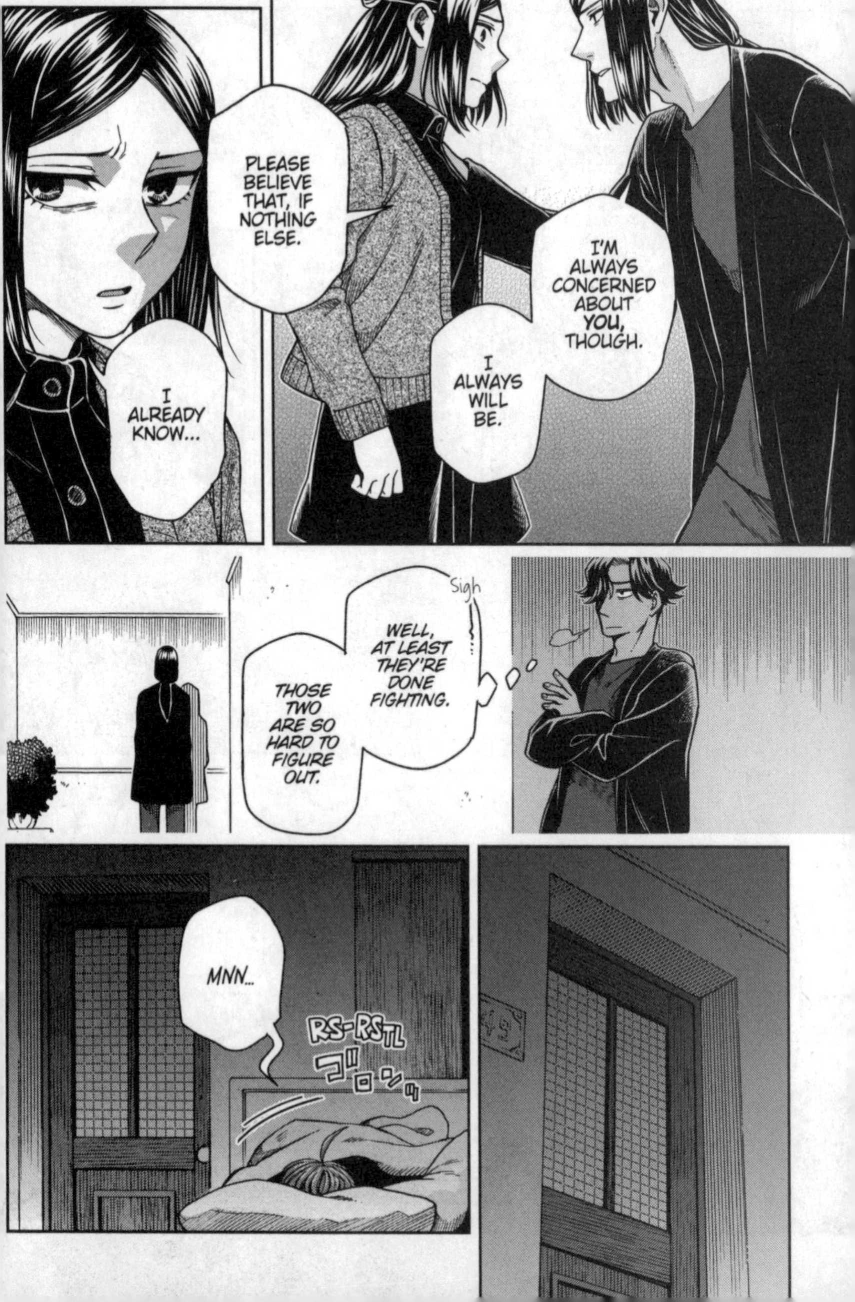
I'M ALWAYS CONCERNED ABOUT YOU, THOUGH.
I ALWAYS WILL BE.
PLEASE BELIEVE THAT, IF NOTHING ELSE.
I ALREADY KNOW...
Sigh
WELL, AT LEAST THEY'RE DONE FIGHTING.
THOSE TWO ARE SO HARD TO FIGURE OUT.
MNN...
RS-RSTL
ゴロンッ

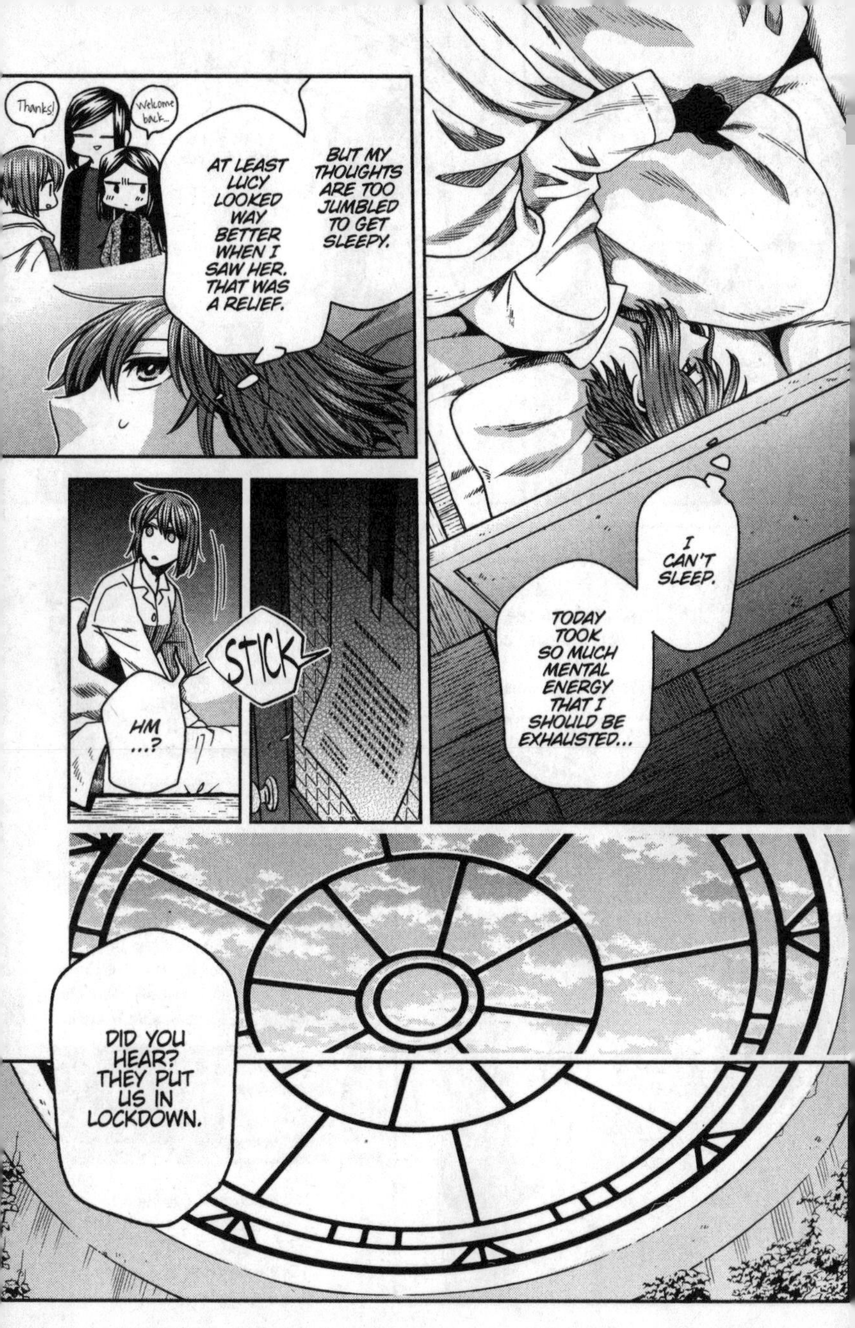
I CAN'T SLEEP.
TODAY TOOK SO MUCH MENTAL ENERGY THAT I SHOULD BE EXHAUSTED...
BUT MY THOUGHTS ARE TOO JUMBLED TO GET SLEEPY.
AT LEAST LUCY LOOKED WAY BETTER WHEN I SAW HER. THAT WAS A RELIEF.
Welcome back...
Thanks!
STICK
HM ...?
DID YOU HEAR? THEY PUT US IN LOCKDOWN.

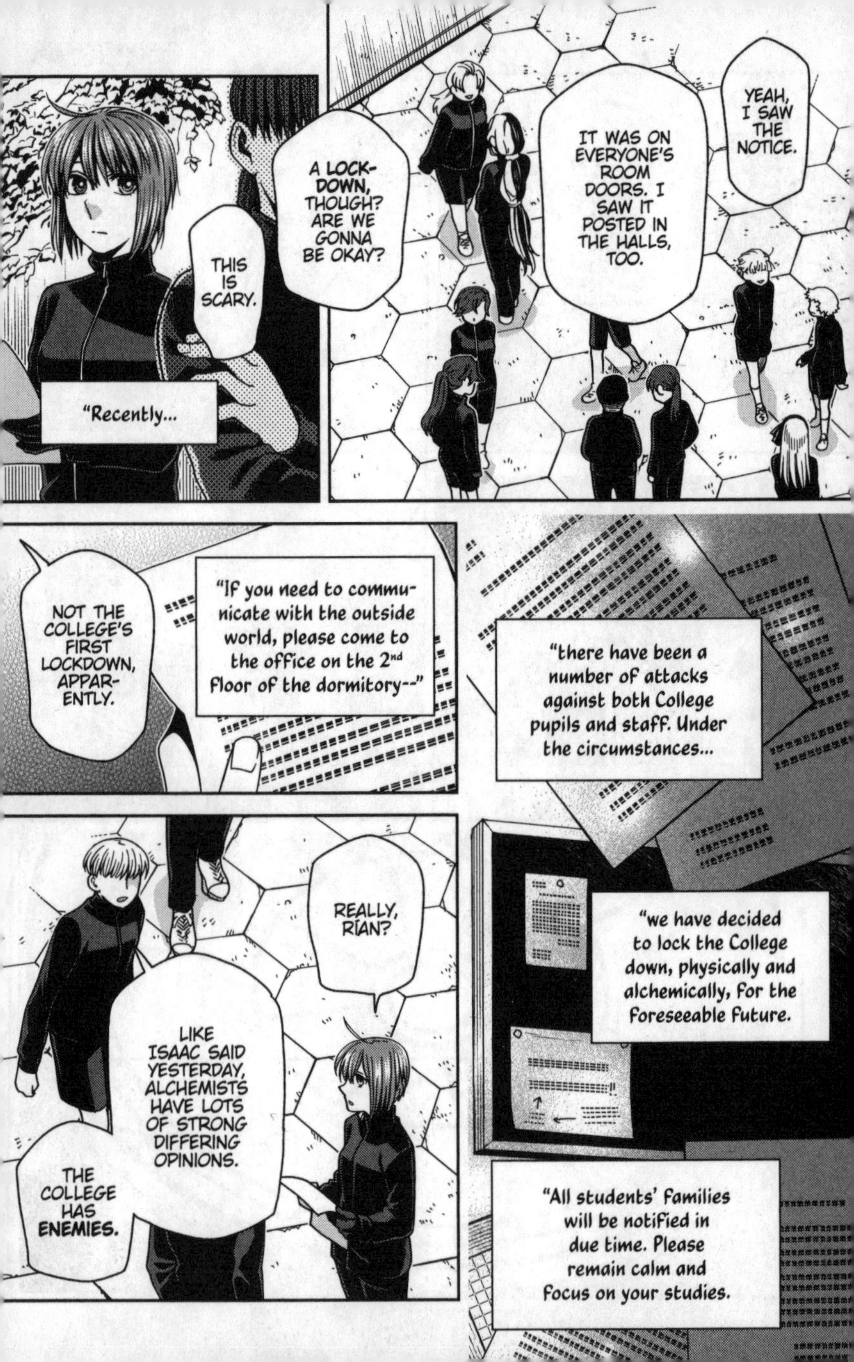
YEAH, I SAW THE NOTICE.
IT WAS ON EVERYONE'S ROOM DOORS. I SAW IT POSTED IN THE HALLS, TOO.
A LOCK-DOWN, THOUGH? ARE WE GONNA BE OKAY?
THIS IS SCARY.
“Recently...
“there have been a number of attacks against both College pupils and staff. Under the circumstances...
“If you need to communicate with the outside world, please come to the office on the 2nd floor of the dormitory--”
NOT THE COLLEGE'S FIRST LOCKDOWN, APPARENTLY.
“we have decided to lock the College down, physically and alchemically, for the foreseeable future.
“All students' families will be notified in due time. Please remain calm and focus on your studies.
REALLY, RÍAN?
LIKE ISAAC SAID YESTERDAY, ALCHEMISTS HAVE LOTS OF STRONG DIFFERING OPINIONS.
THE COLLEGE HAS ENEMIES.

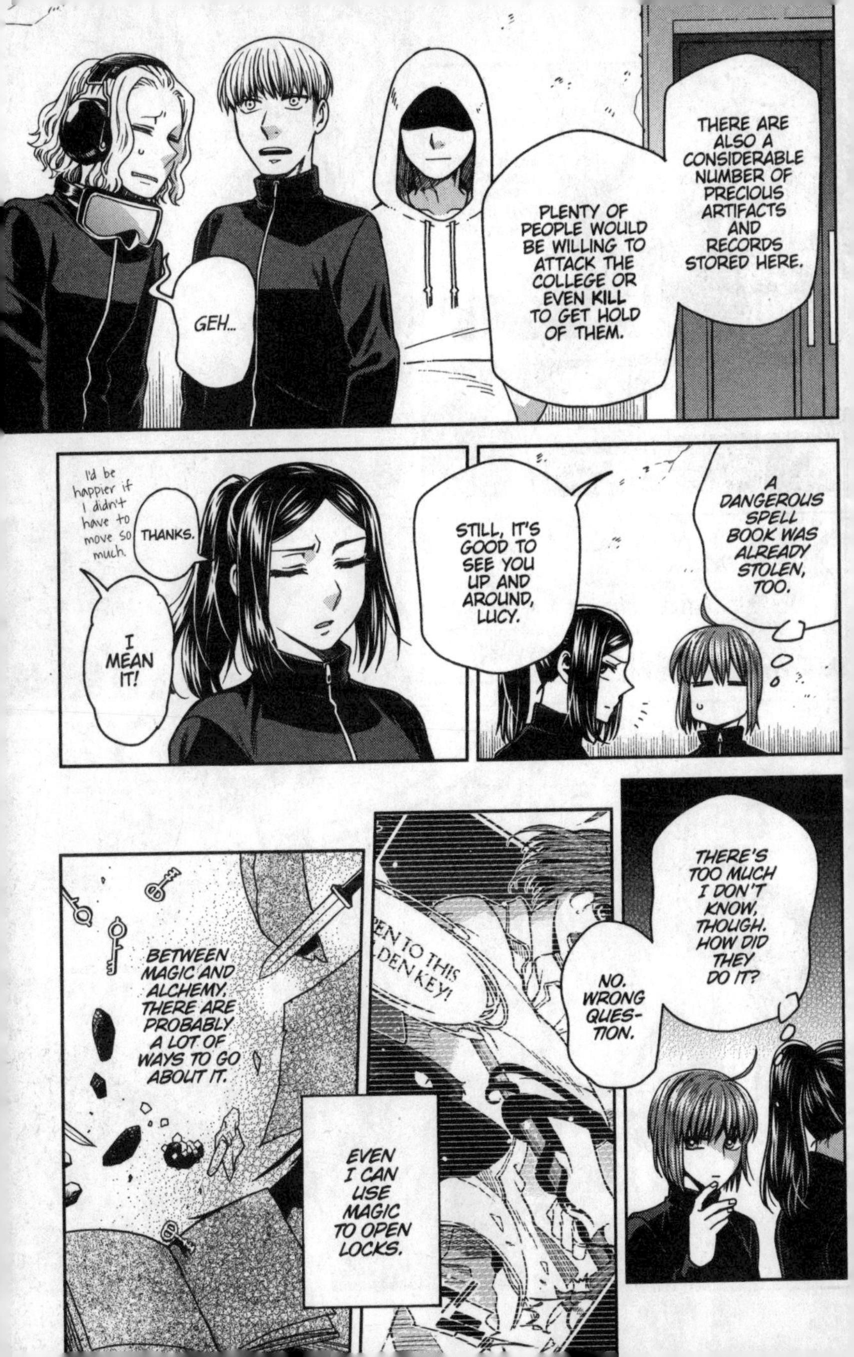

THERE ARE ALSO A CONSIDERABLE NUMBER OF PRECIOUS ARTIFACTS AND RECORDS STORED HERE.
PLENTY OF PEOPLE WOULD BE WILLING TO ATTACK THE COLLEGE OR EVEN KILL TO GET HOLD OF THEM.
GEH...
A DANGEROUS SPELL BOOK WAS ALREADY STOLEN, TOO.
STILL, IT'S GOOD TO SEE YOU UP AND AROUND, LUCY.
THANKS.
I'd be happier if I didn't have to move so much.
I MEAN IT!
THERE'S TOO MUCH I DON'T KNOW, THOUGH. HOW DID THEY DO IT?
NO. WRONG QUES-TION.
EVEN I CAN USE MAGIC TO OPEN LOCKS.
BETWEEN MAGIC AND ALCHEMY, THERE ARE PROBABLY A LOT OF WAYS TO GO ABOUT IT.

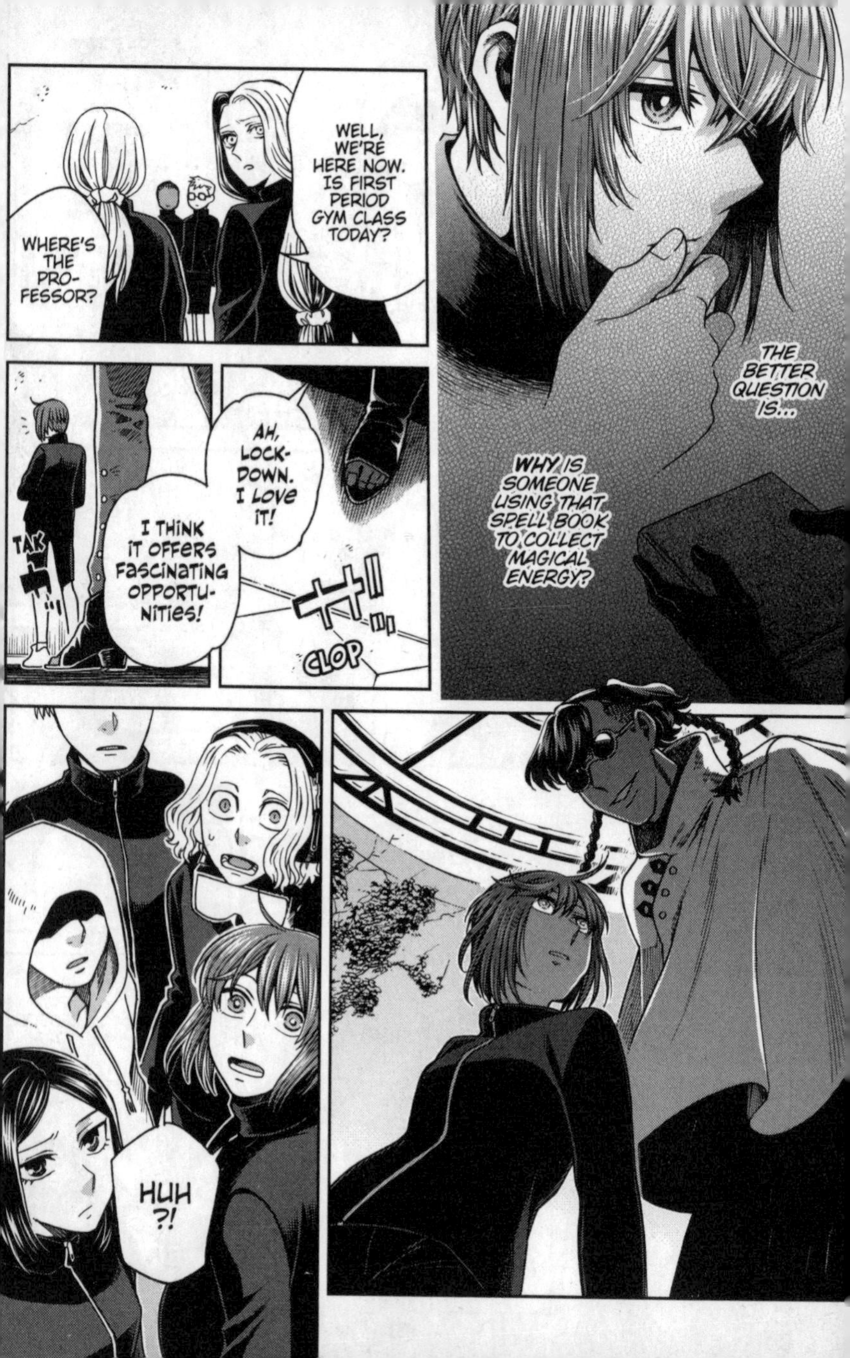
THE BETTER QUESTION IS...
WHY IS SOMEONE USING THAT SPELL BOOK TO COLLECT MAGICAL ENERGY?
WELL, WE'RE HERE NOW. IS FIRST PERIOD GYM CLASS TODAY?
WHERE'S THE PRO-FESSOR?
AH, LOCK-DOWN. I LOVE IT!
I THINK IT OFFERS FASCINATING OPPORTU-NITIES!
CLOP
TAK
HUH ?!

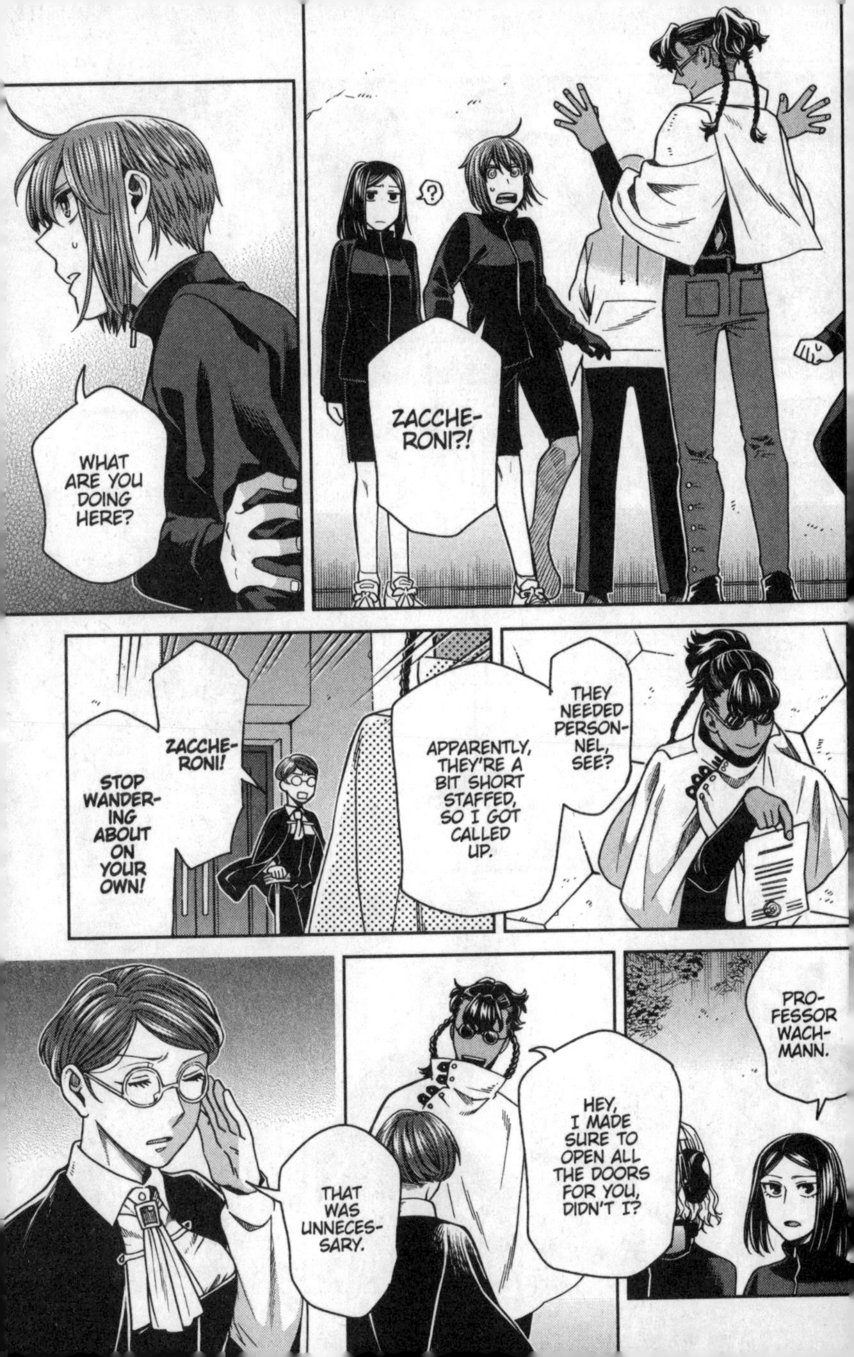
?
ZACCHERONI?!
WHAT ARE YOU DOING HERE?
THEY NEEDED PERSONNEL, SEE?
APPARENTLY, THEY'RE A BIT SHORT STAFFED, SO I GOT CALLED UP.
ZACCHERONI!
STOP WANDERING ABOUT ON YOUR OWN!
PROFESSOR WACHMANN.
HEY, I MADE SURE TO OPEN ALL THE DOORS FOR YOU, DIDN'T I?
THAT WAS UNNECESSARY.

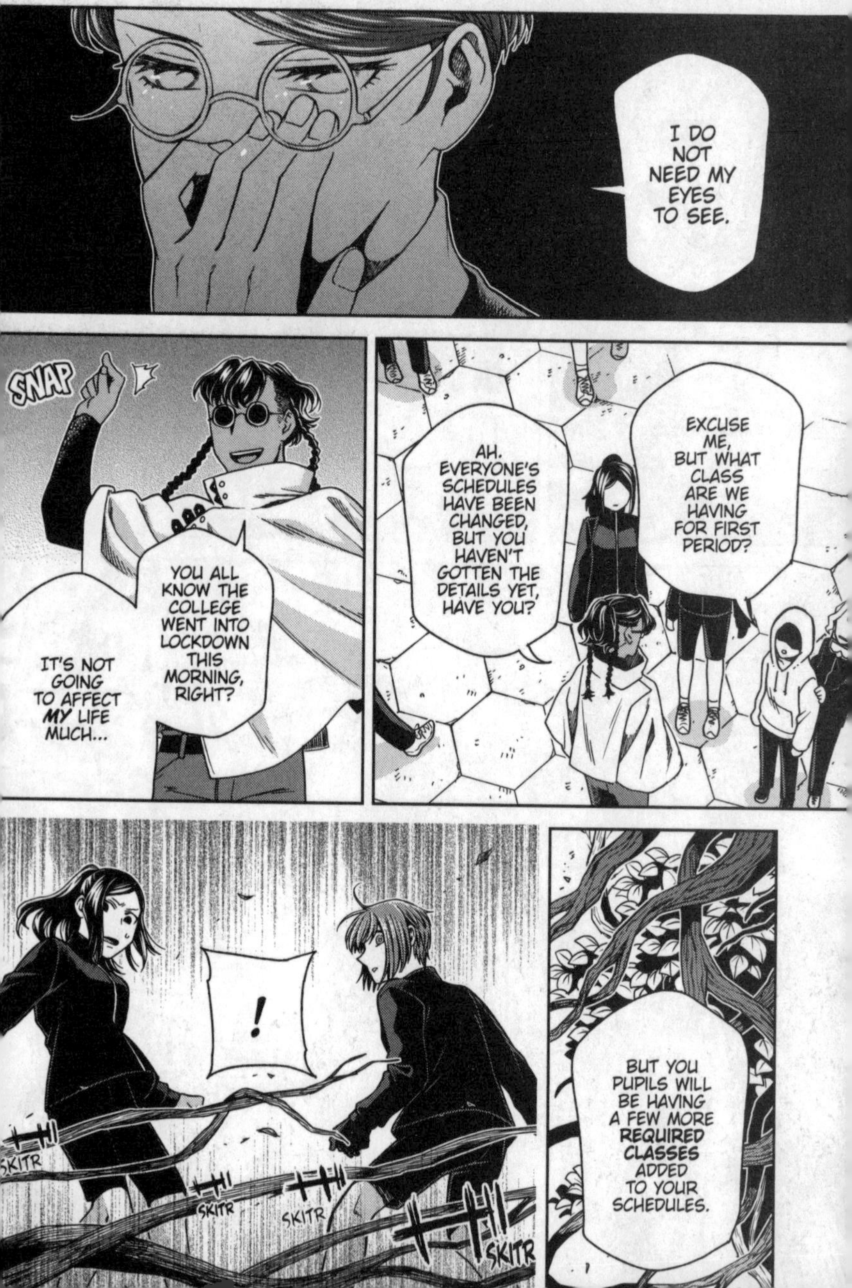
I DO NOT NEED MY EYES TO SEE.
EXCUSE ME, BUT WHAT CLASS ARE WE HAVING FOR FIRST PERIOD?
AH. EVERYONE'S SCHEDULES HAVE BEEN CHANGED, BUT YOU HAVEN'T GOTTEN THE DETAILS YET, HAVE YOU?
SNAP
YOU ALL KNOW THE COLLEGE WENT INTO LOCKDOWN THIS MORNING, RIGHT?
IT'S NOT GOING TO AFFECT *MY* LIFE MUCH...
BUT YOU PUPILS WILL BE HAVING A FEW MORE **REQUIRED CLASSES** ADDED TO YOUR SCHEDULES.
!
SKITR
SKITR
SKITR
SKITR

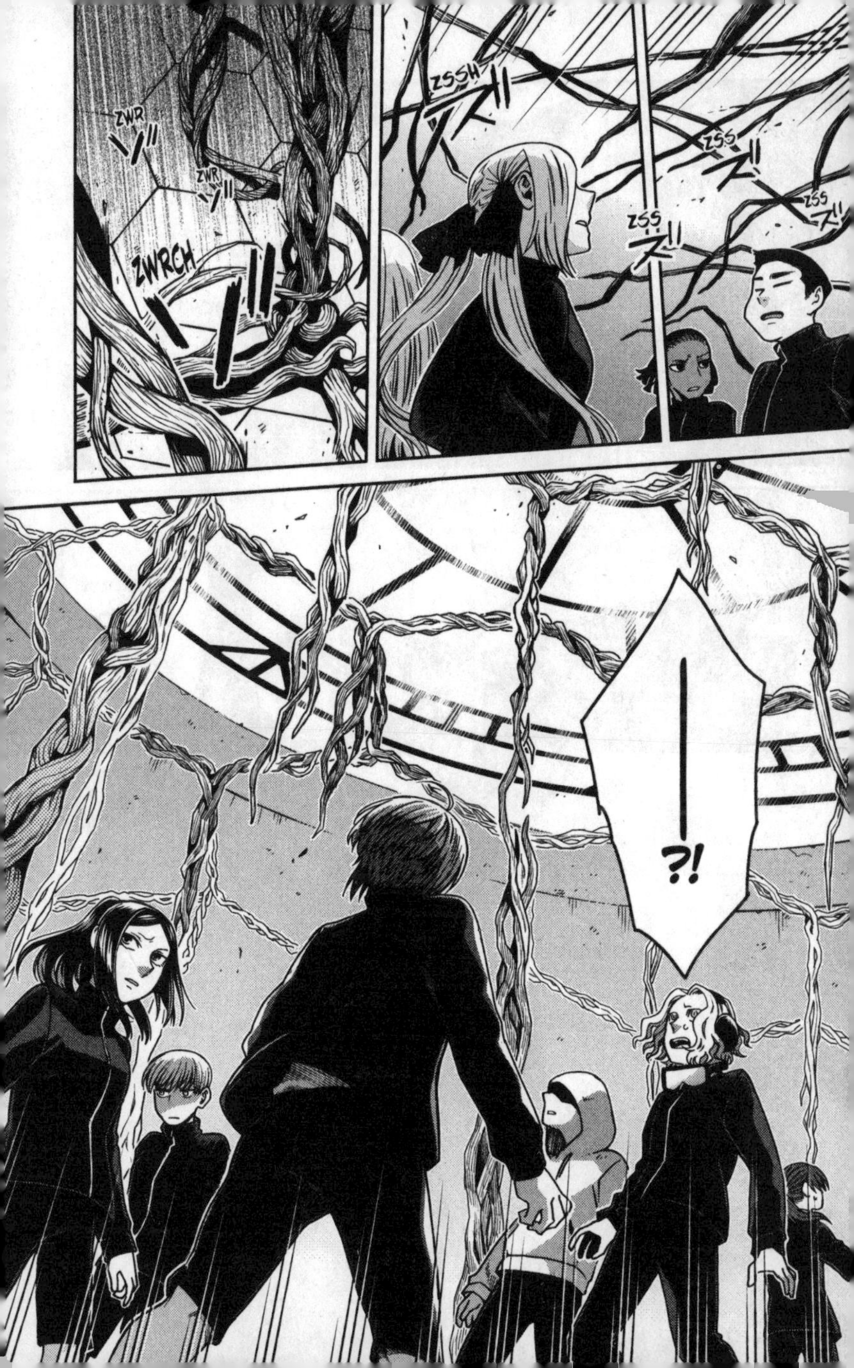
ZSS
ZSS
ZSSH
ZSS
ZWR
ZWR
ZWRCH
—?!

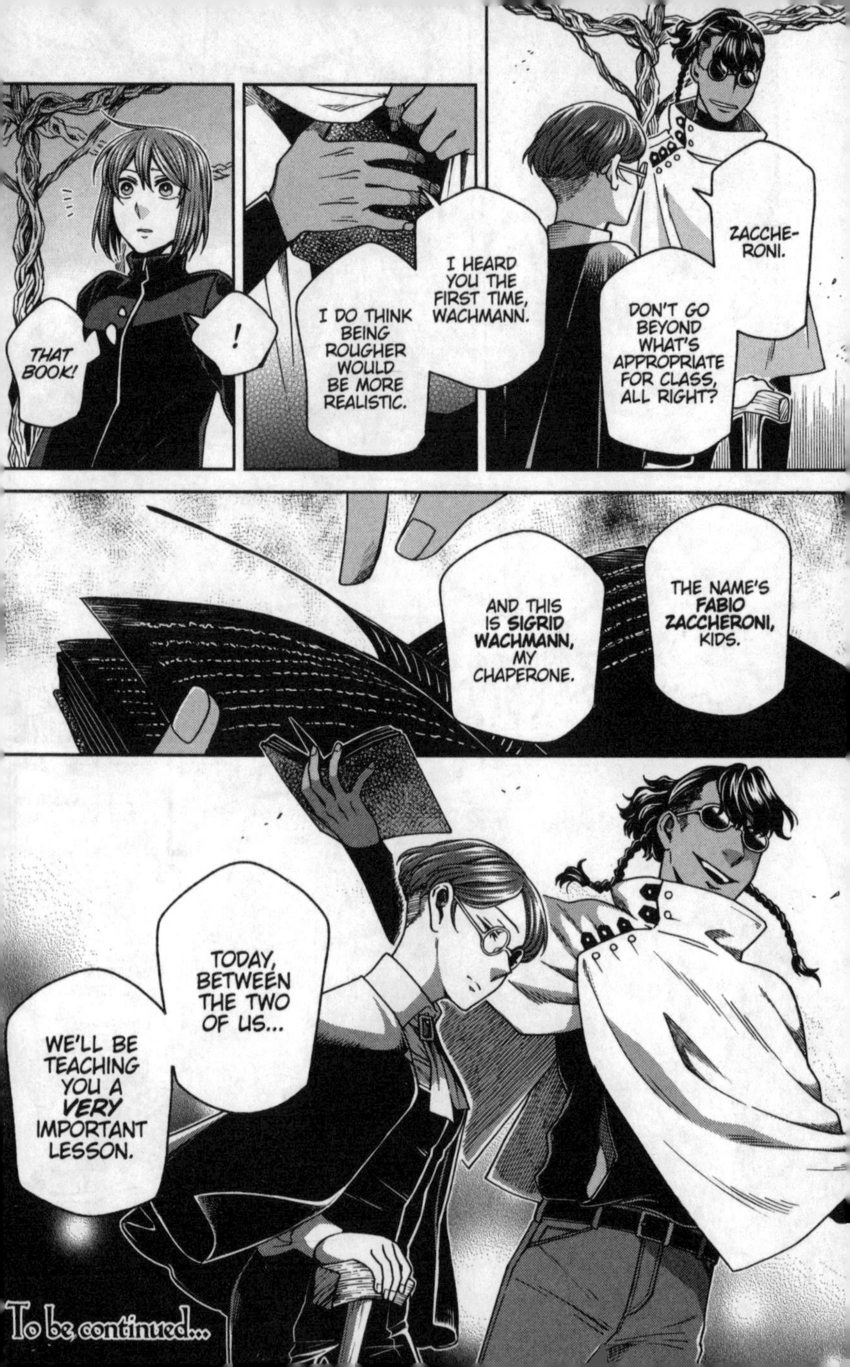
ZACCHE-RONI.
DON'T GO BEYOND WHAT'S APPROPRIATE FOR CLASS, ALL RIGHT?
I HEARD YOU THE FIRST TIME, WACHMANN.
I DO THINK BEING ROUGHER WOULD BE MORE REALISTIC.
!
THAT BOOK!
THE NAME'S **FABIO ZACCHERONI**, KIDS.
AND THIS IS **SIGRID WACHMANN**, MY CHAPERONE.
TODAY, BETWEEN THE TWO OF US...
WE'LL BE TEACHING YOU A *VERY* IMPORTANT LESSON.
To be continued...

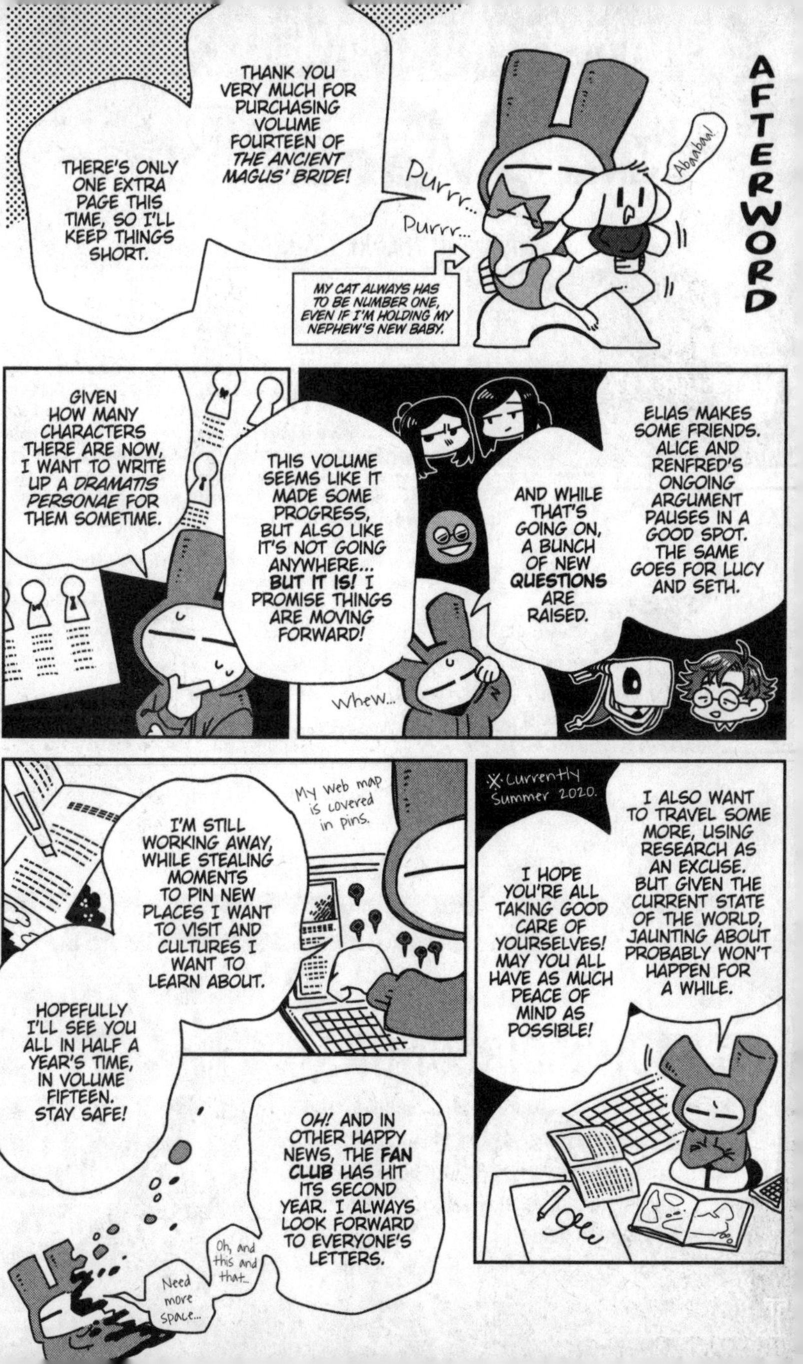
AFTERWORD
Abaabaa!
Purrr...
Purrr...
MY CAT ALWAYS HAS TO BE NUMBER ONE, EVEN IF I'M HOLDING MY NEPHEW'S NEW BABY.
THANK YOU VERY MUCH FOR PURCHASING VOLUME FOURTEEN OF *THE ANCIENT MAGUS' BRIDE!*
THERE'S ONLY ONE EXTRA PAGE THIS TIME, SO I'LL KEEP THINGS SHORT.
ELIAS MAKES SOME FRIENDS. ALICE AND RENFRED'S ONGOING ARGUMENT PAUSES IN A GOOD SPOT. THE SAME GOES FOR LUCY AND SETH.
AND WHILE THAT'S GOING ON, A BUNCH OF NEW **QUESTIONS** ARE RAISED.
THIS VOLUME SEEMS LIKE IT MADE SOME PROGRESS, BUT ALSO LIKE IT'S NOT GOING ANYWHERE... **BUT IT IS!** I PROMISE THINGS ARE MOVING FORWARD!
Whew...
GIVEN HOW MANY CHARACTERS THERE ARE NOW, I WANT TO WRITE UP A *DRAMATIS PERSONAE* FOR THEM SOMETIME.
※Currently Summer 2020.
I ALSO WANT TO TRAVEL SOME MORE, USING RESEARCH AS AN EXCUSE. BUT GIVEN THE CURRENT STATE OF THE WORLD, JAUNTING ABOUT PROBABLY WON'T HAPPEN FOR A WHILE.
I HOPE YOU'RE ALL TAKING GOOD CARE OF YOURSELVES! MAY YOU ALL HAVE AS MUCH PEACE OF MIND AS POSSIBLE!
My web map is covered in pins.
I'M STILL WORKING AWAY, WHILE STEALING MOMENTS TO PIN NEW PLACES I WANT TO VISIT AND CULTURES I WANT TO LEARN ABOUT.
HOPEFULLY I'LL SEE YOU ALL IN HALF A YEAR'S TIME, IN VOLUME FIFTEEN. STAY SAFE!
OH! AND IN OTHER HAPPY NEWS, THE **FAN CLUB** HAS HIT ITS SECOND YEAR. I ALWAYS LOOK FORWARD TO EVERYONE'S LETTERS.
Oh, and this and that...
Need more space...

SEVEN SEAS ENTERTAINMENT PRESENTS

The Ancient Magus' Bride

VOLUME 14

story and art by KORE YAMAZAKI

TRANSLATION
Adrienne Beck

ADAPTATION
Ysabet Reinhardt MacFarlane

LETTERING AND RETOUCH
Lys Blakeslee

COVER DESIGN
Nicky Lim

PROOFREADER
Dawn Davis

EDITOR
Alexis Roberts

PREPRESS TECHNICIAN
Rhiannon Rasmussen-Silverstein

PRODUCTION MANAGER
Lissa Pattillo

MANAGING EDITOR
Julie Davis

ASSOCIATE PUBLISHER
Adam Arnold

PUBLISHER
Jason DeAngelis

THE ANCIENT MAGUS' BRIDE VOL. 14

Originally published in Japan in 2020 by MAG Garden Corporation, Tokyo.
English translation rights arranged through TOHAN CORPORATION, Tokyo.

Seven Seas press and purchase enquiries can be sent to Marketing Manager Lianne Sentar at press@gomanga.com. Information regarding the distribution and purchase of digital editions is available from Digital Manager CK Russell at digital@gomanga.com.

ISBN: 978-1-64505-805-2

Printed in Canada

First Printing: April 2021

10 9 8 7 6 5 4 3 2 1

FOLLOW US ONLINE: ***www.sevenseasentertainment.com***

READING DIRECTIONS

This book reads from ***right to left***, Japanese style. If this is your first time reading manga, you start reading from the top right panel on each page and take it from there. If you get lost, just follow the numbered diagram here. It may seem backwards at first, but you'll get the hang of it! Have fun!!

1
2
3
4
5
6
7
8
9

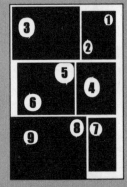